Opera in Italy Today

OPERA IN ITALY TODAY

A GUIDE

by

NICK ROSSI

AMADEUS PRESS
Reinhard G. Pauly, General Editor
Portland, Oregon

On the cover: Teatro Dante Alighieri, the intimate setting for the Ravenna Festival's opera productions, was built in 1852. On stage is the set for the 1991 production of Cherubini's Lodoïska. *Photograph courtesy of the Ravenna Festival.*

ISBN 0-931340-77-2

Printed in Hong Kong

AMADEUS PRESS
The Haseltine Building
133 S.W. Second Ave., Suite 450
Portland, Oregon 97204, U.S.A.
phone 1-800-327-5680 (U.S.A. & Canada only)

Library of Congress Cataloging-in-Publication Data

Rossi, Nick, writer on music.
    Opera in Italy today : a guide / by Nick Rossi.
        p.   cm.
    Includes bibliographical references (p.   ) and index.
    ISBN 0-931340-77-2
    1. Opera—Italy—Guidebooks. 2. Music festivals—Italy—
Guidebooks. 3. Italy—Guidebooks. I. Title
ML1733.R8   1995
782.1'0945'09049—dc20   94-17468
                                                              CIP
                                                               MN

CONTENTS

For
Talmage Fauntleroy,
who first introduced me to opera in Italy

PREFACE

Because the Italian political and economic situation is going through its most troublesome, turbulent days since World War II, season lengths and the numbers of titles in opera seasons change from year to year, mostly to shorter seasons and fewer titles. The seasons as indicated in this book reflect the current status of opera.

Similarly, because the unit of currency, the Italian lira, fluctuates daily, I have chosen not to give exact ticket prices, but rather to reflect whether, by current international standards, they are very expensive, expensive, moderate, or inexpensive.

The titles of operas are given throughout the text in the language of performance. Thus *Don Carlo* refers to the Italian translation of Verdi's *Don Carlos* and to a performance of the Italian rather than the original French version. (During the short-lived Verdi Festival, the two versions were given back-to-back.)

ACKNOWLEDGMENTS

There are countless individuals who have assisted me in preparing this book, and I can only attempt to recall some of the more important persons.

First and foremost, I am deeply indebted to Talmage Fauntleroy, director of opera at the University of South Carolina and Studio Lirico in Cortona, Italy, for introducing me to opera *in* Italy, a richly rewarding and enlightening experience.

To those many individuals associated with various opera houses and festivals, I would like to express a word of profound thanks: Adam Pollock, founder and artistic director of Musica nel Chiostro; Signora Francesca Pini of Teatro Gaetano Donizetti; Signora Luciana Fusi of Teatro Comunale di Bologna; Dr. Renzo Caramaschi, Assessore di Cultura for the Comune di Bolzano; Signora Anna Bergonzellio of Teatro Grande in Brescia; Pietro Maenza of Teatro Bellini in Catania; Assessorato alla Cultura Dott. Emanuele Racchini and Alfredo Gnerucci of Cortona; Alfeo Garini, mayor of Cremona; Aldo Cerboneschi of Teatro Comunale di Firenze; Corrado Bonini of Teatro Carlo Felice in Genoa; Davide Annacchini of Teatro Pergolesi in Jesi; Antonio Veronesi of Teatro del Giglio in Lucca; Aldo Tarabella of Teatro dei Rassicurati in Montecarlo di Lucca; Antonio Taglioni, artistic director, and Alberto Spano of Teatro Rossini in Lugo; Dott. Alberto Panciroli and Dott. Alberto Girolami of Macerata Opera; Sig.ra Luciana Coppini of Mantua; Herbert Handt of the Marlia Festival; Egidio Saracino and Rodolfo Celletti of the Festival della Valle d'Itria in Martina Franca; Renato Garavaglia of Teatro alla Scala; Oreste Zurlini, Assessore alla Cultura in Modena; Sig.ra Susanna Crocigni and Giacomo d'Iasio of the Cantiere Internazionale d'Arte in Montepulciano; Lia De Stefani and artistic director Salvatore Accardo of Teatro di San Carlo of Naples; Sovrintendente Ubaldo Mirabelli, artistic director Girolamo Arrigo, and Giovanni Mazola of Teatro Massimo di Palermo; Claudio Del Monte and Vincenzo Raffaele Segreto of Teatro Regio in Parma; Simona Barbesi and Dino Trappetti for assistance with the Rossini Opera Festival in Pesaro, the Ravenna Festival, and Taormina Arte; Antonella Perciffo of Teatro Municipale di Piacenza; Eros Carloppi, president of Teatro Verdi di Pisa; Annalisa Masselli of I Teatri in Reggio Emilia; Simonetta Scafi and Romolo Baldoni of Teatro dell'Opera in Rome; Aldo Pinasco and Sig.ra Sandra De Natale of Teatro dell'Opera Giocosa in Savona; Donatella Ferrario Ortona and Francis Menotti of the Festival dei Due Mondi in Spoleto; Piero Robba of Teatro Regio in Turin; Dr. Vivian A. Hewitt of the Festival Pucciniano at Torre del Lago Puccini; Nicoletta Cavalieri of Teatro Comunale "Giuseppe Verdi" of Trieste; Cristiano Chiarot of Teatro La Fenice in Venice and Lucio Alfarà, Assessorato alla Cultura of Venice; Dott. Antonio Fanna of the Fondazione Giorgio Cini in Venice; and Maurizio Pugnaletto of the Arena di Verona.

I would also like to extend gratitude to the several distinguished composers and conductors who have given of their time in the development of this book: Luciano Berio, Gian Carlo Menotti, Sylvano Bussotti, Simonetta Puccini (granddaughter of Giacomo Puccini), Riccardo Chailly, Zubin Mehta, Giuseppe Sinopoli, and Giacomo Zani.

My gratitude also to the several individuals who have assisted in providing recordings for evaluation: Giancarlo Bongiovanni of Dischi Bongiovanni; Mario Giampietro of Butterfly Music; Daniele Colombo of Philips; Ornella Farioli of Deutsche Grammophon; Giorgio Cuppini of EMI-Italiana; Eroldo DeVita of Fonit Cetra; Salvatore Caruselli of Frequenz; Giulio Cesare Ricci of Fonè; Mirko Gratton of Decca; Gian Andrea Lodovici of Koch International; Sig.ra Mimma Guastoni of Ricordi; Luciano Rebeggiana and Angelo Curtolo of Nuova Era; and Paolo Rossi of RCA-BMG-Ariola.

Gratitude is also extended for the assistance of editors from Amadeus Press: Reinhard G. Pauly, general editor; Karen Kirtley, managing editor; Frances Farrell, editor; and Margaret Broucek, line editor.

Nick Rossi
Cortona (Arezzo)
15 July 1994

Chapter *1*

THE OPERA SCENE IN ITALY TODAY

Opera in Italy is not only its most important and popular art form, it is a hobby; a sport; a social occasion; a political activity; a source of fun, amusement, and pleasure; and a cause for endless discussion and argument. Italians are not ones to sit quietly in the opera house and let the performance evolve on stage without an attempt to comment on the tenor, the old soprano, the controversial staging, the conductor's tempos. If it is a traditional opera, they will attempt with husky voices that are occasionally off pitch to sing "Celeste Aida" sotto voce along with Radames, or struggle with Violetta's "Ah, fors'è lui" from *La traviata*.

One simply has to admit that Italians love their opera with a passion and reward the artists they like with lengthy applause and cries of "bis" (encore) and "bravi." The less fortunate souls must, likewise, bear the boos and hisses, while the mediocre ones are forced to endure an audience that sits on its hands: Italians give no token applause.

Opera is a pervasive part of life in Italy. For years Giuseppe Verdi's portrait appeared on the 1000-lira note, and pictures of more than a dozen opera composers have appeared on the nation's postage stamps. (Rossini alone has been on more than two dozen different stamps.) Almost every town and city has its group of streets named after the musicians of the lyric theater. Florence has Via Gianbattista Lulli, Via Vincenzo Bellini, Via Gaspare Luigi Spontini, and Via Alfredo Catalani, all centered around Piazza

Since 1985, the engraving of Vincenzo Bellini by Schiaboni has appeared on the front of the 5000-lira note, with the statue of Norma from the Bellini monument in Catania on the reverse. Author's collection.

Giacomo Puccini. Even Italian towns and cities have been named after composers. The tiny hamlet of Le Roncole (four houses, a church, and the *osteria* [country inn] in which Giuseppe Verdi was born) has been renamed Le Roncole Verdi in tribute to Italy's most popular maestro, while the lakeside summer resort that has grown up around Torre del Lago, the name Puccini gave the home he built there in 1900 to replace the original tower beside the lake, is now officially known as the village of Torre del Lago Puccini.

A stop at a newsstand on the streets of a major city will reveal a half-dozen operas on sale on CDs, or two or three available on videocassettes. True, they are not products of the major labels, but they are performances by Callas, Tebaldi, Di Stefano, Corelli, or Pavarotti, offered at (for Italians) bargain prices. Because of Italy's copyright law, radio and television performances as well as in-theater reference tapes—both audio and video—are public domain (copyright-free) after 20 years. This makes it possible to buy for about $20 a complete *La Bohème* on CD at the corner newsstand with Mirella Freni, Gianni Raimondi, and Rolando Panerai, conducted by Herbert von Karajan.

Though visitors to Italy are usually acquainted with only a few theaters—La Scala, San Carlo, La Fenice, and Teatro dell'Opera being the best known—the country boasts over 50 houses that regularly produce opera, to which must be added another 50 that mount an opera every now and then. Though no accurate record has been kept, there must be—conservatively speaking—over 2000 opera houses in Italy. (The official government *Annuario* for 1989 lists 36 major opera houses in addition to 1312 "theaters and musical halls"[1] where operas and concerts are presented; this account lists 62 theaters and musical halls in Milan alone.)

For the visitor to Italy, it is a delight to find that even the smallest towns and villages have their own lyric theater. Campiglia, a little hilltop village of only 2000 inhabitants that dates back to the Middle Ages, is a case in point. It has a charming theater built in 1860, a horseshoe-shaped house of baroque decor that seats 80 in the velvet-cushioned chairs of the *platea* (main floor), and another 90 or so in its three tiers of boxes.

Opera is also a vital part of both radio and television in Italy. In addition to regular broadcasts of opera (both live and from recordings) over radio and television, RAI-Due (one of the three state networks that telecast opera) frequently offers both live and taped performances of outstanding productions. A recent season included *Il trovatore* with Luciano Pavarotti, Mirella Freni, and Placido Domingo; *Mefistofele* with Samuel Ramey from the Maggio Musicale Fiorentino; *La sonnambula* from Rome's Teatro dell'Opera; *Salome* from Spoleto's Festival dei Due Mondi; and from Milan's Teatro alla Scala, *La Bohème*, *Cavalleria rusticana*, and *Adriana Lecouvreur*. During the Mozart Year 1991–92, RAI-Due telecast on consecutive Monday nights the complete cycle of Mozart operas, including both the youthful and incomplete works.

Opera is not only an apt topic for discussion around the dinner table and at the neighborhood bar (in essence a coffeehouse by Anglo-American standards), but wherever Italians may gather. Katia Ricciarelli's bout a few seasons ago with the boos and cat-calls at Milan's Teatro alla Scala was the subject of many articles in Italy's leading newspapers and magazines. Her husband, Pipo Baudo—one of the country's most popular television variety/talk-show hosts—apparently led a soccer-style kicking match in the gallery of the house against the booers while his wife hurled ob-scenities at them from the stage. After several bitter accounts of this appeared in the major newspapers, Baudo's reply, which ap-peared—alongside a picture of his bawling wife in costume—in Rome's *La Repubblica*, was headlined with his words, "*Quei calci? Legittima difesa* [Why soccer? A legitimate defense]."[2]

Similarly, it became front-page news in almost every major Ital-ian newspaper when Luciano Pavarotti's voice cracked on a high note during an appearance at a gala in New York's Lincoln Center. A day later *La Nazione*, published in Florence, devoted its lead editorial on that page to the question of why voices crack.

In order to understand the musical and operatic way of life in Italy and to discuss its most important houses and major festivals, it is helpful to understand the physical and political structure— the infrastructure—of the operatic scene.

State Support of Opera

Though some financial support was provided in the field of opera by the national government as early as 1921, and though the Fascist regime attempted to regulate musical life in Italy dur-ing the 1930s and early '40s (including the remodeling of the opera house in the capital city), it was not until the end of World War II that the present organizational structure in Italy was es-tablished. Law 800, passed on 14 August 1967, governs state sup-port of opera. It decrees that since opera and other forms of mu-sical activity are contributions to the cultural and social progress of the nation, it is in the public interest for the government to as-sure the protection and development of these activities. To this end a central music commission (Comitato Nazionale Italiano Musica) was created within the Ministry of Tourism and Enter-tainment (Ministero del Turismo e dello Spettacolo) to deal specif-ically with the problems of musical subsidies. In typical Italian fashion, the legal structure mandated under Law 800 has been slightly modified almost every year since 1967, a major revision having been effected in 1983. In May of 1993, the Ministry of Tourism and Entertainment was eliminated by referendum; later that year (on 24 December 1993) Law 537 was passed, augmenting and correcting imbalances in Law 800.

Law 800 designated 13 *enti lirici* or opera corporations. ("Opera" in Italian simply means "work" as in the work of a painter, so to refer to what English-speaking people would designate "opera," the Italians, to be clear and quite specific, use the expression *opera lirica*, frequently shortened to *la lirica*.) Because the *enti lirici* are supposed to be autonomous, they are also officially termed *enti autonomi* (the singular forms of these two interchangeable expressions are *ente lirico* and *ente autonomo*). This group of 13 includes 10 opera houses: Teatro Comunale of Bologna, Teatro Comunale of Florence, Teatro Carlo Felice of Genoa, Teatro alla Scala of Milan, Teatro San Carlo of Naples, Teatro Massimo of Palermo, Teatro dell'Opera of Rome, Teatro Comunale "G. Verdi" of Trieste, Teatro Regio of Turin, and Teatro La Fenice of Venice.

To this group, Law 800 added the *spettacoli lirici* of the Arena di Verona, as well as two academic institutions: the Istituto Concerti dell'Accademia di S. Cecilia in Rome (which only produces opera in concert form), and the Istituto del Conservatorio "P. da Palestrina" on the island of Sardinia, a combination conservatory and producer of both symphonic concerts and operas.

This group of 13 is subsidized by the national government on a yearly basis, with the budget—which sometimes approaches up to 85 percent of the total—approved (in theory, at least) about a year in advance. I say "in theory" since many an opera season has begun while the legislature in Rome is still in the midst of argument and debate about the budget and subsidies for the season. In the most recent year for which accurate figures are available, Italy appropriated $430 million of public money for opera, 1/100th of 1 percent of the total state budget.

Though these *enti* are self-governing, it is a highly political governance. The mayor of the city is automatically president of the board, with its members appointed by the city council and approved in Rome. Thus, in order to balance political power in this highly volatile climate, if a *sovrintendente* (the general administrator of an opera house) is a member of the Christian Democratic party, the artistic director must be a member of the Socialist party, and so on, to satisfy all parties (of which there are five major ones). It also means that each time there is a new election (which could be as often as every two years), there will be new *sovrintendenti* and artistic directors if there has been a change in the strength of the parties at the ballot box. The music director is not included on the governing board. Riccardo Muti, music director at La Scala, speaks heatedly of this when he says,

> I believe the Italian system is defective in every field. The surgeon is not admitted to the governing board of the hospital, just as the conductor is not admitted to that of a theater. The laws exclude the expert from the control room! It is a serious mistake, because you should hear the opinion of the person who is to carry out the operation, be it clinical or musical. Under the present system, results are achieved by miracle rather than by normal or rational program.[3]

With regard to finances, Milan's Teatro alla Scala—one of the world's greatest opera houses—received during a recent fiscal year, for example, approximately $61 million from the state, to which were added contributions of $5.8 million from the regional government, $272,000 from donors and private sources, and $14 million from ticket sales. With interest, bequests, and money from record, radio, and television rights, Teatro alla Scala's total budget amounted to $101 million.[4] For this La Scala offered 103 evenings of opera; 16 evenings of ballet with orchestra; 19 of ballet with tape; 23 symphony concerts; three symphony concerts with solo artists; and two concerts with soloists, chorus, and orchestra. Thus, according to figures submitted by La Scala to the government, it accommodated 233,000 spectators.

By way of contrast, Teatro Lirico "P. da Palestrina" in Cagliari, a city of a little over 200,000 inhabitants on the island of Sardinia, received the smallest *ente* subsidy from the state government. For a total of 19 evenings of opera in its 942-seat theater, it received $13 million from the national government toward its total budget of $20 million.

The average ticket price among the *enti* has been around $40; the median at La Scala is closer to $100 (top prices here are usually around $125 to $150 depending on the exchange rate). This has meant that, nationwide, each ticketholder thus receives a personal state subsidy of approximately $110 for his or her trip to the opera! According to official government records, there were during that same calendar year a total of 4019 evenings of opera presented by the *enti lirici*, with a total of 3.4 million tickets sold. (It must be remembered that Italian houses are quite small compared to the auditoriums found in the United States: Teatro alla Scala seats 2015; Teatro La Fenice, 1000; and Teatro San Carlo, 1450, for example.)

The *Teatri di Tradizione*

In 1975 a new and extremely comprehensive law was passed that created *teatri di tradizione* (literally "theaters of tradition," in essence, the important regional houses). Governed by a national commission and their own local government (the theaters, in this instance, are not state owned), the *teatri di tradizione* receive some financial support from the state. Today there are 24 *teatri di tradizione*, theaters of historical and artistic merit that provide opera for the provincial cities in which they are located: Teatro Petruzzelli of Bari, Teatro Donizetti of Bergamo, Teatro Grande of Brescia, Teatro Massimo Bellini of Catania, Teatro Sociale of Como, Teatro Comunale "Alfonso Rendano" of Cosenza, Teatro Comunale "Amilcare Ponchielli" of Cremona, Teatro Comunale of Ferrara, Teatro Comunale "G. B. Pergolesi" of Jesi, Teatro Politeama Greco of Lecce, the Comitato Estate Livornese of Livorno, Teatro Comunale del Giglio of Lucca, Teatro Arena Sferisterio of Macerata, Teatro Sociale of Mantua, Teatro Comunale of Modena, Teatro Coccia of Novara, Teatro Regio of Parma, Teatro Municipale of Piacenza, Teatro Comunale "G. Verdi" of Pisa, Teatro Alighieri of Ravenna, Teatro Municipale "Romolo Valli" of Reggio Emilia, Teatro Sociale of Rovigo, Teatro ente concerti "Marialuisa De Carolis" of Sassari, and Teatro Comunale of Treviso.

There are approximately another 50 theaters that are neither *enti lirici* nor *teatri di tradizione* but that offer, from time to time, performances of opera. Teatro Rossini in Lugo and Teatro Chiabrera in Savona, for example, offer unusual works each season in excellent productions by almost-forgotten composers: Ferdinando Paër, Leonardo Vinci, Baldassare Galuppi, and Giovanni Paisiello, for example.

Originally the opera season in Italy coincided with Carnival, that liturgical period beginning on 26 December and extending

19

through Shrove Tuesday to Ash Wednesday and the beginning of Lent. As the church's influence on secular life lessened, theaters started their seasons earlier and frequently extended them into and beyond Lent. As demonstrated in the season chart at the end of this chapter, Teatro Comunale of Bologna usually opens first with one or two "pre-season" operas in September; Teatro Regio in Parma still abides by tradition and opens on 26 December; while Milan's Teatro alla Scala has established the saint's day of Milan (St. Ambrose)—7 December—as its annual opening date.

With few exceptions, Italian houses follow the *stagione* system (*stagione* literally means "season") rather than the repertory system prevalent in the United States. In the *stagione* system, only one opera is mounted at a time, a production that may be repeated at an *ente lirico* anywhere from three or four to a dozen times before it closes and another work is produced. Unless there are four or more performances of a work, there are usually no changes in the cast; for works with performances in excess of five or six, usually two casts are listed.

The length of a season and the number of different operas presented varies from house to house, determined in large measure by the amount of money Rome decides to offer each theater, be it an *ente lirico* or *teatro di tradizione*. Most *enti lirici* offer six to 10 different operas a season; the *teatri di tradizione*, one or two to five or six. The Italians use the word *cartellone* to refer to the fare for the season, with a *cartellone* for the year announcing the titles of the operas, their composers, and the artists, conductor (*maestro concertatore e direttore*), stage director (*regista*), and chorus master (*maestro del coro*) associated with each production. The *cartellone* also announces the dates and hours of performances.

Originally each theater, particularly the *enti lirici*, produced their own operas, but with state financial support being greatly curtailed year after year and inflation raising the cost season after season for everything from stage sets to singers, the Italian houses are beginning to share productions with each other and with foreign theaters; the Royal Opera, Covent Garden, the Bastille Opéra, and the National Theater of Munich come immediately to mind.

While all opera was originally performed in Italy in Italian, the scene has changed since World War II. Most houses now offer opera in its language of origin: Strauss and Wagner in German, Britten and Gershwin in English, Debussy and Gounod in French. More and more Russian literature—especially operas by Tchai-

The *cartellone* for the 1908–09 season in Rome lists the titles of 11 operas as well as the names of singers, conductors, and choreographers, among other information. Courtesy Teatro dell'Opera.

kovsky and Mussorgsky—is produced in Russian in the major houses. Although La Scala has so far avoided the issue, supertitles are making their appearances in the major houses for operas sung in English, German, French, and Russian.

The opera buff who visits Italy will, of course, have a rare opportunity to enjoy unusual, seldom-heard, and esoteric operas of the past as well as 20th-century works, but he or she will discover that the "tried and true" in Italy, as elsewhere, usually means *Aida*, *La traviata*, *Madama Butterfly*, and *La Bohème*.

As you will discover in the following chapters, Italian opera houses tend to be small in size, intimate in feeling, and excellent in acoustical quality. Most major houses seat from 1000 to 1500 patrons between the main floor (*platea*) and the tiers of boxes found in almost all houses. The regional theaters average about 600 seats, ranging in size from as few as 400 to as many as 2000. For an *Aida* or *Bohème*, the house is usually sold out, no matter its size or location. For other works, attendance generally averages around 85 percent of the house.

Because the *enti lirici* offer evenings of ballet as well as opera and present their orchestras in symphonic concerts in addition to sponsoring chamber music, the theaters are in operation for most of the period between October or November and May or June. The smaller regional theaters that have shorter opera and concert seasons are also used as venues for dramatic theater for the community, with most offering 10 to 14 different plays per season, sometimes—but not always—in multiple performances. Such productions are by touring companies, and almost always you will find on a season's *cartellone* plays by Shakespeare, Goethe, Rostand, Ionesco, Pirandello, Goldoni, Ayckbourn, Cocteau, and Molière—all in Italian, of course. Though opera houses have occasionally doubled as movie theaters in the past—particularly in the 1930s and again in the '40s and '50s—most have now reverted to what we might term legitimate theaters.

Following a disastrous theater fire in Turin, the Italian state legislature passed stringent new laws governing the electrical wiring of theaters and the number and location of emergency exits. The insistence of the state government finally led most Italian opera houses in the late 1970s and early '80s to completely refurbish their theaters by installing new wiring and adding fire doors. (Pisa wins the prize for the most architecturally attractive new fire escape; Florence the prize for the most garishly ugly one.) For the-

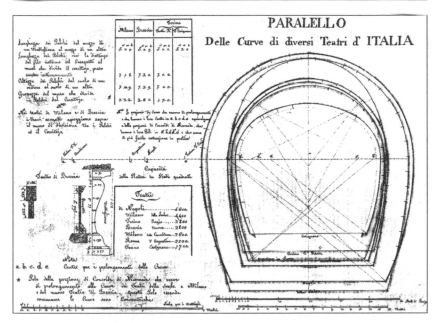

Superimposed are the horseshoe curves of various Italian houses. From the bottom (where the houses meet the stage) these curves represent Milan's La Scala, Naples's San Carlo, Brescia's Grande, Rome's Argentina, and Turin's Regio and Carignano theaters. Courtesy Biblioteca dell'Accademia Albertina, Turin.

aters still procrastinating, the law finally clamped down. The 1986 summer run of *Tosca* in Florence, for example, was halted by state inspectors until stairs made out of hastily erected scaffolding were placed in the already-ugly foyer to provide additional escape routes from the balcony.

Unfortunately this safety edict has kept many little gems of Italian theaters closed, their owners too strapped for funds to bring the buildings up to code. Livorno's Teatro Goldoni, an acoustically marvelous house according to the "old timers," is a case in point. Built in 1847, it is a traditional theater that used to accommodate some 1286 patrons.

Practical Information for the Opera Buff

There is no such thing in Italy as a ticket agency; all concert and opera tickets are available only from the box office (*biglietteria*) of the theater sponsoring the performance. Similarly, there is no single source of information as to what is playing and where. For the visitor in Italy, the best source is the excellent magazine *L'Opera*, which gives a full listing each month for the theaters in Italy. (It does not provide advance information, unfortunately.) I would refer those who want advance information to the listings in Britain's *Opera* magazine or suggest they write to theaters in cities they will visit. Addresses and telephone numbers appear in the following pages for each opera house. Please be aware that the telephone system in Italy is very antiquated, overburdened, and frequently out of order (especially during heavy rain and thunder and lightning storms). The state system, SIP, has awarded an enormous contract to a foreign firm to completely redo the entire Italian phone system, but that will not take place for another five to 10 years. In the meantime you will see several numbers listed for many hotels and theaters. This is because there is no automatic switching from a busy line to a non-busy one. If the first number you call is busy, you must try the second or third. The international code for Italy is 39; the local codes within Italy are prefaced by a 0, which it is not necessary to employ when calling from the outside. There is no fixed number of digits in Italian phone numbers; they vary from five to seven digits in most cases. Usually the telephone at an opera house is answered by the *portiere*, the doorkeeper or porter at the stage door, who in most cases is unable to answer even the simplest question. Since they rarely speak English, be prepared to ask for the office or department you want, and they will transfer you. While the *portiere* is almost always on duty (though the telephone may remain unanswered during coffee breaks), remember that all Italian opera houses are closed on Mondays, and most opera offices close on workdays from about 1:00 to 3:00, 3:30, or even 4:00 P.M. for lunch. These offices, including the *biglietteria*, then remain open until about 7:00 or 7:30 P.M. Curtain time is generally 8:00 or 8:30 P.M., although for Strauss, Wagner, and other longer operas, the time may be advanced to 7:30 P.M. Programs (which include cast lists; the full libretto in Italian; sometimes a synopsis in English, German, and/or French; and articles about the opera of the evening) are sold in the lobby and vary in price from Lit. 6000 or 7000 (approximately $5.50 to $6.40) to Lit. 10.000 ($9.00). Handsome in appearance, sturdily bound, and full of interesting information and usually excellent photographs and illustrations, they make worthy souvenirs. If you choose not to purchase one, write the cast list down before you enter the house as there are no free programs. Unlike the custom in English houses, it is not customary to tip the usher for showing you to your seat, nor are the ushers prepared to sell you a program should you have failed to purchase one in the lobby.

All traditional Italian opera houses have a bar, generally located in the large foyer on the first floor (the second floor, using the American floor-numbering system). As with all Italian bars, it is necessary to go to the cashier (the *cassa*) first and obtain a receipt (a *scontrino*), which will indicate exactly how much you have paid and the items purchased. Generally at intermissions, but seldom before the opera, there will be a line at the cash register. To save time and patience, decide on what you and your friends will want to eat or drink before you arrive at the cash register. Then take the *scontrino* to one of the bartenders and place your order. The most popular items include *caffè* (espresso only); aperitifs, in particular the "specialty of the house," a spumante (a sparkling light Italian wine); sandwiches (usually dry and not very filling); and pastries (usually quite good if one likes Italian pastries). Prices are generally moderate at the theater bar in comparison to similar situations in American and British opera houses.

Summer Festivals

During the summer months almost every Italian town, city, or village has a music festival of some sort, many devoted to or including the performance of opera. (The government *Annuario* lists 248 music festivals;[5] this figure probably represents about 50 percent of the actual total.) Among the most notable festivals are those devoted to the works of a specific composer: Bergamo's Donizetti e il suo tempo (Donizetti and His Time), Pesaro's Rossini Opera Festival, Catania's Bellini Festival, and Torre del Lago Puccini's Puccini Festival. There is also the well-known Festival dei Due Mondi of Gian Carlo Menotti in Spoleto as well as Hans Werner Henze's Cantiere Internazionale d'Arte located in Montepulciano. Unusual programs of infrequently heard operas are offered at many of the festivals: Festival della Valle d'Itria in Martina Franca, Operaincanto in Terni, and Settembre Musica in Turin. For beauty of location there are Taormina Arte on the island of Sicily and the Ravenna Festival in the north. There are also instances in which the summer offerings could better be described

25

as "spectacles" rather than "festivals": the Arena di Verona with its capacity of 16,000, for one.

To this lengthy list of professional opera houses and festivals must be added the training programs that sponsor opera productions. Several privately operated apprenticeship programs offer interesting and sometimes unusual fare when it comes to mounting operas. The Scuola di Musica di Fiesole outside Florence has offered a number of Mozart and Monteverdi operas directed by Claudio Desderi; Studio Lirico in Cortona, midway between Florence and Rome, has staged Italian *primas* (the first Italian performances) of works by such diverse composers as George Frideric Handel and Mario Castelnuovo-Tedesco and is now engaged in Rinascita Cimarosiana (Cimarosa Reborn), presenting an unknown Cimarosa opera each summer at Teatro Signorelli in Cortona. As.li.co.—the acronym for the Laboratorio Lirico di Alessandria located in Milan—frequently presents works of importance by non-Italian composers.

It must be noted that Italy's 57 national conservatories and 16 *istituti pareggiati* ("equalized institutes" considered on the same level as the state conservatories but located in more provincial cities) do not ordinarily offer staged performances as part of their training programs. Incipient artists, usually around age 25, expect to go directly from conservatory classrooms onto the professional stage.

Unlike England and the United States, there are neither amateur nor community opera companies in Italy. Almost every city, however, has at least one Amici della Musica (Friends of Music) organization, many of which sponsor lectures about opera or present *concerti lirici* (opera recitals); once in a while, one will offer a concert-reading of an opera with piano accompaniment. In addition, there are a number of admiration societies throughout the country, including L'Associazione Amici della Lirica Tito Schipa in Lecce, the Club Katia Ricciarelli in Florence, the Circolo del Bel Canto Beniamino Gigli in Monfalcone, and the 700-member Club Luciano Pavarotti, which was founded in Carpi in 1979.

Opportunities for Young Artists

Many young singers inquire about career opportunities in Italy in the belief that the country's more than 100 active opera companies and festivals offer excellent entry-level opportunities for those who wish to establish careers in the lyric theater. Unfortunately Italian law and culture mitigate against this.

The *teatri di tradizione*—the smaller houses ideal for young, developing voices of potential—are limited by state law and may hire only Italian citizens or members of the European community, thus ruling out for young Americans the chance to enter the field in one of the smaller provincial houses. There are rare, rare exceptions, of course, cases in which it can be legally proved that no Italian artist has the right credentials for a particular part. For example, a young American countertenor—one who has been an Italian resident for 10 years and has near-perfect Italian diction—auditioned before the artistic director of one of the important *teatri di tradizione* for the *prima* of an opera commissioned for the reopening of this newly renovated theater. Both the artistic director and the composer himself were pleased with the American's voice and wished to offer him the role, so the determined artistic director studied the books until he found the loophole: a clause about foreign instrumentalists being eligible if they played rare or unusual instruments. On opening night, the non-Italian countertenor was on stage in the part for which he had auditioned, though he had to carry—and on occasion play—a small pair of finger cymbals, the rare and unusual instrumental part the composer had gladly added to his score so as to have the voice he wanted.

The *enti* can, of course, hire whomever they please, but for La Scala or La Fenice, for example, to employ a foreign singer suggests that the person is already a soloist of international acclaim. And even then, the subconscious Italian national pride comes to the fore. Non-Italian artists must be notably better than their native counterparts to be considered for casting, for Italian critics consider any foreign artist fair prey for heavy criticism. Cheryl Studer and Chris Merritt, for example, were highly censured in the Italian press when they opened the season at La Scala recently in Verdi's *I vespri siciliani*, taken to task essentially for their non-Italian, non-Verdian voices.

Granted, several American artists have established major reputations in Italy. One thinks immediately of Marilyn Horne, Samuel Ramey, and June Anderson. Without exception, however, each had well-established (even if somewhat limited) reputations before he or she came to Italy, and they all had to make many outstanding appearances on stage there before the Italian public hailed them as the superb artists they are.

One of the enticements generating interest among non-Italian singers for roles in Italy is the pay scale, rumored to be the highest of any country in the world. (The Italians have the highest taxes of any country in Europe, which necessitates this high scale.) Since singers' fees account for about 20 percent of the total budget today as compared with 7 percent a few years ago, the *sovrintendenti* collectively drew up a price-fixing list recently in order to "keep the lid on." They established that the maximum any artist could be paid was $26,000 per performance. It has been reported by the Italian press that this high-scale group includes José Carreras, Placido Domingo, Mirella Freni, Alfredo Kraus, Luciano Pavarotti, Ruggero Raimondi, Samuel Ramey, and a few others. Eva Marton set the all-time record, however, by obtaining $48,000 for one performance of *Manon Lescaut* during the 1988 summer festival at Macerata's open-air Arena Sferisterio.

The Italian tradition of recommendations also inflates prices: singers (in all the major cities, but especially in Rome) are often "recommended" by politicians, and the veteran music critic Giorgio Gualerzi speculates that while artistic directors may be above corruption, other influential opera house administration members probably are not.[6] Raina Kabaivanska, one of Italy's favorite sopranos, is outspoken on the subject: "It's who you know that counts. I recently sang Tosca for $13,000 with an inexperienced baritone, unsuited to his part, who got $24,000. Several times I've been told openly, 'We give you less because you don't have to pay anyone.'"[7]

Soloists are hired on a "per-performance" basis. Thus, should a strike occur before the first performance, the soloists will have spent their rehearsal time in vain: no pay. I recall several years ago when the orchestra of Teatro Comunale in Florence went on strike the day of the first scheduled performance of *Il trovatore*. Luciano Pavarotti, an astute businessman as well as a good tenor, had negotiated a contract for the entire period he was required to be in Florence. What resulted was that Pavarotti received every Italian lira indicated in his contract for sitting it out in his hotel room, while most of the other soloists went without a single lira.

As to artists' agents and representatives in Italy, it is a rather murky picture. When the first laws were passed after the war with reference to opera houses and other musical entities, it was tacitly decided that the state government would establish its own clearinghouse or agency for musicians, thus representing all artists—

domestic and foreign—for the entire country. That such an organization never came into existence is typical of the many things
that are supposed to happen by state mandate and never do.

This has meant that until quite recently, private artists' agents
were illegal in Italy, and the few that had been in existence operated outside the law, with little legal protection afforded either
the agent or artist. Slightly over a decade ago the legislature ac-
knowledged that it was impractical and not very democratic to
consider a single government clearinghouse for all artists. It was
then agreed that individual agents were an acceptable solution to
the need for artists' representation. The quirk in the law that followed, however, was the stipulation that no agent could be an ex-
clusive agent. Thus, with singers and musicians able to be represented by several competing agencies, the effectiveness of the few
that exist becomes limited. It has also meant that when an artist so
represented by multiple agents receives a contract, the singer must
often pay each of the agents the standard fee regardless of which
agent was actually responsible for the contract in question. Unlike
Germany, where they virtually control the market, Italy consid-
ers agents of limited value.

For those interested in working in Italy in a non-soloist capacity, it should be noted that *enti* do hire foreigners on the basis of
auditions for their permanent choruses, corps de ballet, and orchestras. In such cases, contracts are extended for only a single
season at a time and do not provide the typical Italian fringe benefits of sick leave and retirement. In contrast, Italians are hired
for the chorus, corps de ballet, and orchestra by means of *concorsi*
(examinations) and with the offer of a lifetime contract. Carlo
Maria Badini, the president of AGIS—the acronym for the Italian
General Association for Entertainment—laments that when he
was *sovrintendente* of La Scala, "I could fire no one! The arthritic
violinist, the toothless trumpeter, the chorister who sang out of
tune, the ballerina who twisted her ankle every time she danced,
they all had permanent employment, a job for life!"[8]

The Contemporary Lyric Scene

So just what is the state of opera in Italy today? Like everything
else in the country, opinions differ even among leading authorities.
Carlo Fontana, the former *sovrintendente* of Teatro Comunale in
Bologna and now *sovrintendente* of La Scala in Milan, paints an

optimistic picture: "The average standard of opera performance in Italy is possibly the highest in the world. I have seen performances in Vienna and London that would not be considered passable even in one of our provincial theaters."[9]

By contrast, Luciano Berio—Italy's most famous living composer—uses almost nothing but black paint to complete his picture:

> As far as music is concerned, the Italian state is utterly indifferent, frequently dishonest, and nearly always incompetent. But it sticks its nose in and is ruining the country's musical life, just as it already has ruined the postal service, the hospitals and the railways. . . . Many opera houses have been reduced to semipolitical, semi-mafioso garbage.[10]

What then should a visitor expect? Which authority is correct? There is truth in both statements, and reality lies somewhere in between. In a land in which opera is so much a part of life, the picture cannot be all that dark! One has only to attend an *Aida*, a *Bohème*, or a *Nabucco* to realize that people all around you in the audience are humming (usually quite noticeably but enthusiastically off-key) the arias with the stars on stage. They know the plots; they know the lyrics; and when it is a new work, even though the singing is in their own language, they follow along with libretto in hand during the performance.

I recall the year I moved to Italy having a discussion with the artistic director of Studio Lirico. We were debating whether Tosca's first name was Flora or Floria. We were walking down Via Garibaldi in Milan at the time, and he suggested that all we had to do to settle the argument was to stop the first person we met on the street and ask the question. It was true: the response "Floria" came back immediately.

Short of heaven, life is not ideal anywhere. Those of us who choose to live in Italy enjoy its cultural life, its natural beauty, the warmth and friendliness of its people, and the innumerable opportunities it provides to enjoy the lyric theater and operas of nearly every type and sort, most of them wonderfully performed. We realize, of course, we have a price to pay: trains that almost never run on time, a postal system that manages to delay letters or lose them regularly. What we receive in return for our patience and forbearance is briefly sketched in the following chapters: magnificent opera houses, ambitious opera programming, the world's greatest artists on stage, and exciting festivals of unusual, almost forgotten operatic fare.

Buon viaggio! (Have a good journey!)

Operatic Seasons

For cities with both regular and summer seasons, the summer season is shown in black.

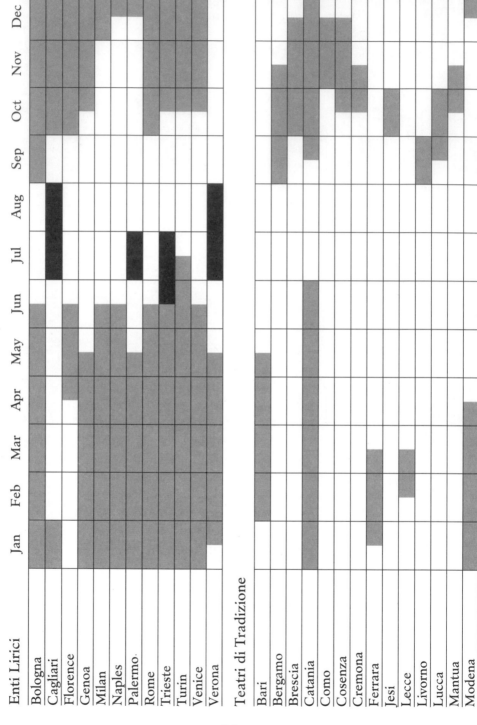

	Jan	Feb	Mar	Apr	May	Jun	Jul	Aug	Sep	Oct	Nov	Dec
Novara						■						
Parma	■	■	■	■								■
Piacenza				■						■	■	■
Pisa										■	■	
Reggio Emilia	■			■						■	■	
Rovigo										■	■	■
Treviso									■	■	■	■

Festivals with Opera Performances

	Jan	Feb	Mar	Apr	May	Jun	Jul	Aug	Sep	Oct	Nov	Dec
Barga								■				
Batignano								■				
Benevento							■	■				
Bolzano								■				
Fano								■				
Fermo								■				
Macerata							■	■				
Martina Franca							■					
Montepulciano								■				
Pamparto							■					
Perugia									■				
Pesaro							■	■				
Ravenna							■					
San Gimignano												
Sassari												■
Savona											■	
Siena								■				
Spoleto							■					
Tagliacozzo							■					
Taormina								■	■			
Terni									■			
Torre del Lago							■	■				
Trapani							■					

33

Chapter 2

THE MAJOR ITALIAN
OPERA HOUSES

Since the world's first public opera house opened in Venice in 1637, neither fires nor bombardments, kings nor dictators have been able to impede opera's progress, prominence, and importance in Italy. Though Luciano Berio may lament that "opera is dead" and complain that for two centuries it "ate up" the nation's musical resources, talent, and money, opera is still the preeminent musical attraction for both Italians and visitors throughout the land.

Opera houses in Italy have been categorized with reference to their location and importance. The major ones are in large cities, with each designated officially as an *ente autonomo* (literally an "autonomous corporation"). In order to understand the political and financial structure of these *enti*, we need to look briefly at the opera situation in Italy when self-governing houses came into existence during the early 1920s.

Until then, two types of administrations could be found in Italian opera houses: the impresario system and the general managership. The first, the impresario system, was by far the more common throughout the 19th century. Under this form, each city or town owned its most important theater as a public entity, while members of aristocratic and noble families owned their own individual boxes (a situation not unlike a modern condominium). Each year the town council, along with a committee of boxholders, met and decided upon an impresario whom they licensed to organize the opera season; this bipartite committee guaranteed to make up any losses the season might incur.

The impresario's responsibility was to schedule repertory and select casts, conductors, and sets that would attract the largest audience possible. Seasons usually opened on 26 December, the beginning of Carnival (for which many new operas were commissioned), and concluded on Shrove Tuesday, the day before Ash Wednesday and the beginning of Lent. The *cartellone* was ordinarily made up of two to four different operas in succession, each given multiple performances. For the most part the orchestra and chorus comprised local musicians and singers; in smaller towns, extras were brought in to fill vacancies. Under this system, the more tickets the impresario sold, the more money he earned.

While the public in the 19th century had clamored for the latest operas—works by Rossini, Donizetti, and Bellini during the first half of the century and Verdi and Puccini in the second half—the scene began to change by the early 20th century. The public no longer craved new operas, but rather wanted the older masterpieces. Theaters emptied for contemporary operas in the 1920s and '30s. This meant that the works of Verdi and Puccini, and, with the bel canto revival, the operas of Rossini, Donizetti, and Bellini were the lyric pieces that filled the houses. All this posed serious problems for the impresario who could not adjust to this major change in public taste.

As for singers, the best of the Italians, starting with Enrico Caruso, learned that they could make much more money in opera houses in the United States and Argentina than they could in their native land. In addition, as Harvey Sachs judiciously points out,

> The effect of Wagner's half-century-old ideas concerning the unity of voice, action, scenography, and orchestra, and Verdi's less overtly polemical efforts in the same direction, had begun to make themselves felt in some of the major Italian houses. The realization of these reforms, however, required major mechanical overhauling of the old theaters: construction or deepening of orchestra pits, updating of lighting systems, and improvement of facilities for creating and installing sets. Performers needed longer rehearsal periods to prepare each aspect of a production and put the parts together. Faced with the diminishing availability of star singers,

how could an impresario also confront the mounting costs resulting from the demand for more refined productions?[1]

Milan's Teatro alla Scala, then as now Italy's most famous and most prestigious opera house, began to have troubles as early as 1897, when an entire season had to be canceled for lack of funds. When it was reopened the following year, it no longer functioned with an impresario. Rather its fortunes were entrusted to a principal conductor who served in the capacity we now call artistic director; that person was assisted by a general manager. Both were the employees of an administrative council: a group of leading figures from the city's artistic, financial, and artistic circles, presided over by a nobleman-boxholder. This board was responsible for guiding and advising the conductor and manager, and for raising funds from three principal sources: the boxholders' society, a new association of shareholders, and the City of Milan. Under this reorganization, the impresario's duties were reduced to those of an agent who leased singers from his roster and took a percentage of their earnings.

According to reliable reports of the time, the system seemed to work reasonably well in the few larger houses that adopted it, but most houses were uninterested in this reorganizational plan. By the end of World War I it was obvious that some kind of reform was necessary if the Italian houses were going to function. Two principal factors affected and effected the major change that followed, both factors being men of iron will and determination: Arturo Toscanini and Benito Mussolini, Il Duce.

Arturo Toscanini, installed as principal conductor at Milan's Teatro alla Scala, had some very specific ideas about music and artistic enterprises and their funding. With the assistance of the liberal senator Luigi Albertini (editor of Milan's nationally important newspaper, *Corriere della Sera*) and Emilio Caldara (Milan's socialist mayor), Toscanini formulated a new concept, that of an *ente autonomo*, a self-governing, nonprofit society. As this concept was implemented, the old societies of boxholders and shareholders were dissolved. Gradually, the boxes were made available to the general public. Similarly, the city gave up its titular ownership of the theater, although the mayor continued (and continues to this day) to assume the presidency of the administrative council.

Financing was established in several ways: the city made an annual contribution; the public subscribed a certain amount; there were private donations; and a surtax of 2 percent was levied on the admission tickets of all other theaters, movie houses, and public places of entertainment in Milan and its province. Thus, as Sachs relates,

> La Scala, which had been forced for economic reasons to shut its doors in 1917, was able to reopen them at the end of 1921 as a result of the new administrative system—a model of combined public and private responsibility in a city whose strong theatrical tradition touched every echelon of society.[2]

With the *ente autonomo* in Milan as a guide, other struggling opera houses changed their administrative organizations within the following two years to the *ente* structure: Bologna's Teatro Comunale, Florence's Teatro Comunale, Genoa's Teatro Carlo Felice, and Turin's Teatro Regio. At a meeting of the directors of these theaters in 1926 (a meeting Toscanini markedly did not attend), a national plan for the administration of all Italian theaters began to develop. Naples's Teatro San Carlo soon joined in, and talk began of federal subsidization via a 5 percent surtax on the gross box-office earnings of all performances of "operatic, dramatic and mime works, Italian or foreign, given in theaters, institutions, recreation circles, associations, etc."[3] Thus, between government subsidies and the inherent restrictions and regulations for *enti autonomi*, their "autonomy" was born dead.

As Harvey Sachs notes, part of Toscanini's opposition to the newly established *ente* structure "stemmed from mistrust of union participation in executive decisions."[4] But that is exactly what the state government attempted to control, for they felt "artists should be kept off the executive councils of artistic organizations in order to avoid corruption in the allotment of work."[5] The corruption thus feared from choices and appointments made by artists was replaced by a corruption par excellence effected by the politicians who then appointed the members of the executive councils, the *sovrintendenti*, and the artistic directors. These same public servants even encouraged the hiring of certain artists who were their personal friends or the friends of fellow politicians to whom they owed favors.

Though the end of the Fascist regime concluded such meddling with the opera scene, the new republic quickly spawned its own brand of control. Up until the major referendum of 22 May 1993, the chief office concerned with opera and the distribution of funds for opera production was the Ministero del Turismo e dello Spettacolo (Ministry of Tourism and Entertainment), under whose guidance and funding such other artistic endeavors as cinema, dramatic theater, reviews, "varied art," symphony concerts, bands, competitions, popular music, and cinematography fell. Because this national office had wielded tremendous power in the distribution of enormous funds, the Italian people indicated at the ballot box a desire for a more honest, equitable system. Unfortunately, in eliminating the Ministry of Tourism and Entertainment by referendum in 1993, no substitute was immediately provided.

Finally, in March 1994, the president of Italy declared—by Law 537—that opera in Italy would be governed and administered by a Department of Spectacle and Entertainment under the direct supervision of the president. (A minister had been the administrator under Law 800.) The new department is to be headed by a chief (*capo*) who is appointed by the president (Gianni Letta, undersecretary to the president, was the first appointee to this position). Only time will tell whether this change is an improvement or simply a different form of political domination and control of Italy's world of opera.

When I asked Gian Carlo Menotti, who was appointed artistic director of Rome's Teatro dell'Opera in the fall of 1992, how opera survives in Italy under these conditions, he shrugged his shoulders and replied, "Well, we have this huge deficit and a season to plan. We have no idea how or when the money will be distributed, but somehow we get a *cartellone* together, cast our operas, call in the scene designers and directors, and get opera on stage."[6]

The Structure of the *Enti Autonomi*

The *enti autonomi lirici* today include Teatro Comunale in Bologna, Teatro Comunale in Florence, Teatro Carlo Felice in Genoa, Teatro alla Scala in Milan, Teatro San Carlo in Naples, Teatro Massimo in Palermo, Teatro dell'Opera in Rome, Teatro Comunale "Giuseppe Verdi" in Trieste, Teatro La Fenice in Venice, and the Arena di Verona in the city of that name. The other two state *enti* are not specifically "lyric" theaters: the Istituzione dei Concerti del Conservatorio Musicale di Stato "Giovanni Pierluigi da Palestrina" in Cagliari on the island of Sardinia, which is both a conservatory of music and the sponsor of symphony concerts and opera, and the Accademia Nazionale di Santa Cecilia in Rome, which is the nation's leading conservatory and sponsor of the only nationally endowed symphony orchestra.

The mayor is always *presidente* of the city's *ente autonomo*. In addition there is a *sovrintendente*, who used to be nominated by decree by the state minister of tourism and entertainment and approved by the local city council; a *direttore artistico* (artistic director), nominated by the administrative council of the theater; and a *consiglio di amministrazione* (governing board of directors) made up of three representatives from the local community (one of which must be from a minority political party), a representative from the province, a representative from the region, a representative from the provincial tourist office, a representative from the community tourist office, the director of the local conservatory of music, a representative from the tourist industry, three representatives from the theater workers' union, two representatives from the musicians' union, and the artistic director. With the exception of special positions (the mayor, the director of the conservatory, etc.) the representatives are nominated by the local city council or the various unions, with all choices dictated by political affiliations. This means that in a city such as Rome where the party in power changes frequently, the *sovrintendente* and the artistic director change just as often. Between 1989 and 1991 Teatro dell' Opera had three different sets of *sovrintendenti* and artistic directors, all men of caliber, but also men of differing political parties! Ordinarily, to keep everyone happy, if the *sovrintendente* is of the principal party in power, the artistic director is from the chief minority party. Cities without great fluctuation in civic administration—Palermo and Trieste, for example—have administrative staffs that have rarely changed in the last decade, and their *sovrintendenti* and artistic directors have been able to develop programs of importance and excellence for their cities.

Each of the *enti* receives the major part of its income from the state, up to 85 percent. Individual contributions are now becoming a force in the funding of these institutions, out of necessity, while contributions by commercial enterprises are of minor importance at the moment. Fortunately or unfortunately, as the case may be, the faltering Italian economy necessitated a drastic change in state contributions in 1989, when the Fondo Unico per lo Spettacolo (United Fund for Entertainment), which had been supporting opera, movie theaters, and concerts to the tune of about $680 million, cut $76 million in 1989, the same amount in 1990, and $194 million in 1991. True, the Chamber of Deputies decided to offset some of the reductions by transferring between 1988 and 1990 some $200 million from unspent funds originally marked for theater repairs, but the big cut still stands. "Now we are very worried," says Paolo Manca, a vice-secretary-general of the Associazione Generale Italiano dello Spettacolo, a member-supported national association of entertainment-industry entrepreneurs. "Only three years after the law establishing the Fondo Unico per lo Spettacolo was passed, everything is again at stake."[7]

This budget-slashing stems from a constantly swelling government deficit, an estimated $89 billion in 1988–89. To combat it, Rome cut $11 billion in arts funding in 1990 alone. Such fiscal realism, however, does not necessarily mean a lesser commitment to art. Franco Carraro, a former minister of tourism and entertainment, proposed the introduction of tax shelters (a completely new concept in Italy) to encourage private funding. "Companies and individuals would be allowed to invest up to half their earnings, tax free, in artistic productions and up to 20 percent as donations to nonprofit organizations."[8]

Whether this scheme will work is another question. "We don't have the habit of private financing," notes Manca. "Italian industry is not used to investing in culture." Giorgio Strehler, co-founder of Teatro Piccolo in Milan, agrees: "I think institutions should live with public money. Just at a time when we find ourselves under the brutal assault of so many products of an advertising subculture, the state funds should be directed to an art theater." Bruno Cagli, a former *sovrintendente* of Rome's Teatro dell' Opera and one of the guiding spirits of the Rossini Opera Festival in Pesaro, is more optimistic. "I think this system can be reformed and the theaters made more responsible for their operating expenses. But this does not mean that you can suddenly use an ax and make cuts indiscriminately."[9]

For those interested in such things, the total budgets of three principal *enti* in 1990, using the exchange rate of Lit. 1100=$1.00 U.S., were as follows: Rome's Teatro dell'Opera, $102,000,000; Milan's Teatro alla Scala, $92,020,000; and for the Teatro San Carlo in Naples, $37,609,000.[10] The figures were compiled from information voluntarily submitted by each *ente* to the *Annuario EDT dell'Opera Lirica in Italia* (EDT Annual of Opera in Italy), published by EDT Edizioni di Torino, Silvana Ottolenghi, editor-in-chief.

The *Cartellone*

Because state subsidies are decreasing at an alarming rate, the various *cartelloni* seem to lose a title every other year or so. And whereas in former times each theater mounted its own production of every title, "shared" and "borrowed" productions are becoming an economic necessity. As Elda Tessore, *sovrintendente* of Turin's Teatro Regio, confides,

> I think we must learn to share productions among the *enti*, for it is obvious that there have to be some drastic reductions. It is foolish, for example, for Teatro alla Scala and Teatro Regio to both mount new productions of Puccini's *La fanciulla del West* as we did in 1991, since the two theaters are only 153 kilometers [95 miles] apart.[11]

What this means for the tourist, however, is that he or she will find the same production being offered in several different cities. A case in point is the Pier Luigi Pizzi production of Handel's *Rinaldo*, which was first produced by Parma's Teatro Regio in 1985 and was remounted during the 1991–92 season (with cast changes) at Teatro Municipale "Romolo Valli" in Reggio Emilia and Teatro Verdi in Pisa.

Perhaps the greatest frustration for people trying to plan opera-going as part of a trip to Italy is trying to find out what opera is playing where and when. There is no such thing in Italy as a central listing (just as there are no ticket agencies). The excellent Italian magazine of the lyric theater, *L'Opera*, publishes a fairly comprehensive list of operas scheduled for performance throughout Italy, including a list of casts, conductors, and directors, but the list is monthly. In other words, the October issue will list only performances during October. And, true to Italian custom, the October issue does not appear on the newsstands until around the 5th to the 10th of the month. (For those who subscribe, it is even worse as the Italian postal system takes an additional five to 10 days in delivering it!)

For a person trying to make an inquiry outside of Italy, the approaches to this challenge are limited. The British magazine *Opera* publishes season announcements (including casts, conductors, and directors) as they are received in London. Thus, although they almost always carry full details of the *cartelloni* of Bologna, Genoa, Milan, Palermo, and frequently the other *enti*, there is no pattern to the appearance of such announcements. *Opera News* in the United States and *Opera Canada* carry some listings, but again, expect no uniformity as to which companies are included or when a listing might be published.

You can always write individual opera houses for their season brochures, but this is a time-consuming exercise since the turn-around time for a response—airmail both directions—is between four and six weeks. You should also figure that not every responding house will send the brochure by airmail (surface mail takes roughly three months). The drop-out rate will be about 35 percent; by this I mean opera houses that simply will not respond. At this moment Genoa is the only place that charges (Lit. 10.000) for sending a brochure. I wish I could be more optimistic and helpful, but these are the frustrating facts.

Timely Matters

Because Italy, like the rest of Europe, is on a 24-hour clock, curtain times are announced in papers, magazines, and brochures as 20.00, 20.30, or 21.00. (Simply subtract 12 and add a P.M. to obtain the time you recognize). Except in the provinces and in cases of emergency, performances generally begin within five to seven minutes of the posted time. Doors of theaters ordinarily open 30 minutes before curtain.

The starting hour poses a bit of a challenge for eating dinner, as Italian restaurants simply do not open before 19.30 (7:30 P.M.), and it is difficult, if not impossible, to be served a dinner in an Italian restaurant in an hour or less. For those attending performances at *enti* this should be no problem as the major cities in which they are located all have excellent restaurants that serve a full dinner until at least midnight, so one can eat stylishly after the performance. In the provinces, however—at the *teatri di tradizione*, for example, described in Chapter 5—dinner is a problem because in most instances everything in town is closed by the end of a performance. Possible solutions include eating a few sandwiches at a local bar or a pizza at a pizzeria before curtain time.

Visitors to Italy should stand warned that starting times and even the operas scheduled are sometimes changed at the last minute. I recall missing the Prologue to Rimsky-Korsakov's *The Legend of Czar Saltan* because the starting time had been advanced a half-hour from that announced on brochures and tickets. It had been discovered that the performance would last past midnight if the originally scheduled 8:00 P.M. starting time had been observed—and for the orchestra to play even one minute past midnight would have doubled their salaries and added a staggering sum to the theater's budget. From what I observed, most patrons had been apprised of the change of hour, possibly alerted by an announcement in the local paper that I had not seen, having come some distance by train just for the performance.

Similarly I recall traveling to Reggio Emilia to enjoy a performance of Britten's *Albert Herring*, a production announced for 8:00 P.M. After I had arrived and checked into a hotel, I wandered over to the opera house to pick up my tickets only to learn that because it was Sunday, the performance had been changed to a matinée at 2:00 P.M. All I found at the theater were other music critics from out of town and ignorant of any time change.

The most ludicrous situation I encountered involved Naples's Teatro San Carlo. *Musical America* had commissioned me to write a story, "Opening Nights at Important Italian Opera Houses," so, among other houses, I had written Teatro San Carlo requesting a pair of seats for *Macbeth*. Fortunately, my companion, a colleague from Florence, knew Italian opera houses and their customs and suggested we phone to confirm everything in Naples before boarding the train—a most fortuitous suggestion, for the opening night had been postponed three weeks. When the new date arrived, I telephoned again from Florence, this time before leaving the house for the train station, and was informed that indeed they held a pair of tickets for us for that evening's performance of *The Nutcracker*. "That's a ballet, not an opera!" I protested, and thinking he had some musical imbecile on the line, the man at the press office replied, "Of course it's a ballet." After calming down a bit I discovered that yet a third date had been selected for the performance of Verdi's *Macbeth*, which was indeed to open the opera season. (I did eventually make the trip to Naples and write the story.)

I mention these events not because they are common, but because they do occur; I can't think of another country where you might encounter, even on rare occasions, similar situations. To be forewarned is to be somewhat forearmed.

Dressing for the Opera

Dressing for the opera is much the same in Italy today as it must be throughout the world of music: only as formal as one chooses. Opening nights for the season are the most elegant. While Milan's Teatro alla Scala announces in print that black tie and formal gowns are *de rigueur*, Teatro Regio in Turin (truly, from what I have seen, the most naturally elegant and formal of all) simply assumes that everyone knows and observes the custom of formal attire for opening night. At Rome's Teatro dell'Opera, it is an entirely different scene, since Rome is the nation's capital city and at least half the audience on opening night are, to use the colloquial expression, "freebies"—senators and their wives, officers of the government and their families, or members of the diplomatic corps (both to Rome and to Vatican City). The show, in this case, is in the house rather than on stage, with each matron trying to look more stylish and *à la mode* than the other. With the exception of individual opening nights for each new production of the season, typical evening wear seems to be the norm: for the boxes and in the orchestra (stalls/parterre), suits for the men, attractive dresses of daytime length for the ladies (rather than cocktail-length dresses or evening gowns). As one goes up in seating to the balconies and galleries, the attire becomes less formal.

Making Reservations and Buying Tickets

Because ticket prices seem to become more expensive each season and because the exchange rate at the time of purchase greatly affects the cost to a foreign patron, no specific figures are given in the following sections. Rather I indicate very expensive (usually a top from Lit. 200.000 to Lit. 250.000), expensive (a top from Lit. 100.000 to Lit. 150.000), and average (a top around Lit. 50.000). Most theaters have balcony tickets (basically there is no such thing as "standing room" in Italy) available at the box office just before the performance. Some of these can be as inexpensive as Lit. 10.000.

When it comes to selecting a location and purchasing a ticket, one should command several Italian expressions:

ticket	*biglietto*	(bee-LYET-toh)
box office	*biglietteria*	(bee-lyet-teh-REE-ah)

main floor	*platea*	(plah-TEH-ah)
main floor seat	*poltrona platea*	(pohl-TROH-nah plah-TEH-ah)
box	*palco*	(PAHL-co)
center box	*palco centrale*	(PAHL-co chen-TRAH-leh)
side box	*palco laterale*	(PAHL-co lah-teh-RAH-leh)
row	*ordine*	(OR-dee-neh)

Names for the upper reaches of a theater sometimes differ. If you are at the box office or have a season brochure (*depliant*, after the French word), there is usually a sketch of the house that names the component sections. Generally speaking, the space immediately above the tiers of boxes is called a *galleria* (gahl-leh-REE-ah), an area similar to the balcony in the United States. (Sometimes there are two, one above another.) Ordinarily seats in the *galleria* are numbered (meaning "reserved seats"), and in some theaters, a patron must purchase a reserved-seat ticket, which represents only a seat, and an admission ticket for passage into that section of the theater.

In most theaters, the least expensive seats, those farthest from the stage and at the top of the house, are unreserved and sold at bargain prices, usually (but not always) just during the hour before curtain. This section is generally called the *loggione* (loh-gee-OH-neh), literally the "loge" in the sense of a seat in the *loggia* (LOH-gee-ah), or open-fronted gallery. This is what we would call a gallery seat, and these chairs are generally unnumbered and available only on a first-come, first-seated basis.

Though most theaters use the same expressions, you occasionally encounter an unusual one, such as *barcaccia* (bar-CAH-chee-ah) at Teatro Politeama Garibaldi in Palermo. This simply means "stage box," a box that is actually a part of the depth of the proscenium arch. Several theaters, including the Garibaldi, use the expression *anfiteatro*, which literally means amphitheater and refers to the first section of seats in the balcony.

Because most Italian opera houses are laid out in the shape of a horseshoe (Florence, Genoa, and Turin are the principal exceptions), patrons should be aware of limitations in boxes. In most theaters boxes accommodate four people; some of the larger boxes accommodate six. This means that the two or three people in the front of the box have a fairly good view of the stage, depending on the location of the box. The two or three people at the back of the box, who generally occupy elevated chairs the height of bar stools (but with backs!), have a more limited view in center boxes. There is little or almost no view of the stage from the extreme side boxes.

In most theaters, box seats are not numbered, the rule again being—if you have not rented the entire box—first come, first seated. In several theaters, when an entire box is purchased, individual admission tickets must be purchased as well.

Most ticket offices are open during the opera season every day except Monday. (All theaters as well as all museums in Italy are closed on Mondays: no rehearsals, no performances, no visitors, no box office!) As with most everything in Italy, there are morning and afternoon hours. Though they vary a bit from town to town and theater to theater, in general, hours are from 10:00 A.M. to noon, and from 4:00 to 6:00 P.M. Almost no one at any box office speaks English, but they are very kind and accommodating and try to understand what a patron wants. For those who speak no Italian, I would suggest handing the box office attendant a slip of paper indicating the essential information: date and hour of performance, opera title, number of *biglietti*, seat location (using the appropriate Italian word), and price (in lire).

Unfortunately, for those who would like to make ticket reservations before leaving home, there is no simple solution. Since there are no ticket agencies in Italy, all opera tickets must be purchased directly from the opera house involved, unless one is on a guided tour in which case the tour agency takes care of this matter. As of this writing, Venice's Teatro La Fenice is the only theater that will accept charge card payment; thus, prepayments must be made in Italian lire via either an international postal money order or an international bank draft. And to further frustrate the would-be traveler, the Italian postal system is abominable, as I've said. I would urge you to send all important letters by registered mail with return receipt.

In the following sections I indicate ticket-purchasing procedures as outlined by the individual *enti*. Though generally the same in each case, there are some slight variations. The best procedure, if it is feasible, is to encourage a good friend (I say "good" advisedly because it means waiting in line) who lives in the city you plan to visit to purchase tickets for you, and repay this friend in Italian lire when you arrive.

For the tourist who personally goes to the box office, be aware of the date tickets go on sale for a specific production, and also be

47

aware that there is no such thing in Italy as a line to stand in, a queue. If you see people in line, they are bound to be foreigners. Rather, there is always a crowd around the ticket window, and in order to keep your self-designated "place in line," you must elbow and shove and endure some scowls—and even some nasty Italian phrases. (Note that they do it to each other, too!) If you are brave and perhaps a bit ruthless, use just a little more of the elbow, wear an aura of nonchalance, and thus manage to reach the box office several patrons ahead of your expectation. (You must remember, to the Italians, this—like driving a car—is both a custom and a sport).

Buona fortuna!

Teatro Comunale
BOLOGNA

The evening of 14 May 1931 was to have been an auspicious occasion for Bologna's Teatro Comunale, for on the theater's 168th anniversary, Arturo Toscanini, the most revered maestro of his time, was engaged to conduct a program of music by his friend and mentor, Giuseppe Martucci (1856–1909). An early champion of the youthful Toscanini as a conductor, Martucci was a former director of the conservatory in Bologna, and had conducted the Italian *prima* of Wagner's *Tristan und Isolde* at Bologna's Teatro Comunale. Unfortunately what was planned as a stellar evening became the blackest page in the history of Italian music.

Toscanini had made it known that not only would he not conduct the "Marcia Reale" (the Italian national anthem) or the Fascist hymn "Giovinezza" before the concert as requested by the governor of Bologna, he would not allow his concertmaster to direct them either. As the maestro approached the theater for the scheduled concert he found his pathway blocked by a large group of Fascists headed by His Excellency Leandro Arpinati, the undersecretary of the interior, representing the government in Rome. As Toscanini tried to enter through the stage door, he was slapped in the face. His chauffeur quickly came to his aid, forced a path back to their waiting Cadillac, and drove the maestro back to the Hotel Brun.

When word reached the angry crowd that the concert had been canceled, a large group of young Fascists gathered under Toscanini's hotel window to sing "Giovinezza" in raucous voices.

Toscanini in his Cadillac with chauffeur Emilio Monier, a few days before the driver had to come to his rescue on the night of 14 May 1931, when Fascists blocked the maestro's entrance to the opera house. Author's collection.

Through Ottorino Respighi, who acted as a courier for Arpinati, word was passed to Toscanini that he must leave town before 6:00 A.M. the following day or his safety could not be guaranteed. Toscanini thereupon vowed he would never conduct in Italy again until liberty had been restored, a promise faithfully kept.

To the credit of the Bolognese, let it be said that the concert of Martucci's music was given 60 years later to the day, on 14 May 1991, with music director Riccardo Chailly on the podium. This was part of a celebration/convention entitled "Bologna for Toscanini," with speeches given in the opera house's Foyer Rossini by Walfredo Toscanini, the maestro's grandson; Gottfried Wagner, the composer's great-grandson; and Harvey Sachs, author of the most recent Toscanini biography.

Bologna in Historical Perspective

Because of its strategic location at the geographical center of Italy, Bologna has been known over the centuries not only as an important trade center and gateway to the north and all of Europe but also as a seat of learning (its university is the oldest in Europe). Founded as Felisina in Etruscan times, the city became a Roman colony in 189 B.C. under the name Bononia, and one can still see in the center of town the traces of an old Roman camp. In addition to its two tall brick towers that lean at strange angles, the city today is most characterized by its arcaded streets, altogether some 32 kilometers (20 miles) of pillared porticos that arch across sidewalks within the city's 13th- and 14th-century walls.

The founding of the University of Bologna in the 11th century led many scholars—including Dante and Petrarch—to this center of learning. The chair of music at the university was first sanctioned by a papal bull of 1450, and in the intervening years many musicians and composers have studied at the Bologna Conservatory—now quite properly named after its most famous teacher and the founder of its enormous and tremendously important library, Giovanni Battista Martini, more affectionately known as Padre Martini. Gioachino Rossini was the director of the conservatory in 1850, a school whose former students included both the young Mozart and a youthful Gaetano Donizetti.

During the middle of the 18th century, Bologna desired an opera house, so Antonio Galli Bibiena was engaged to design a theater, jointly financed by the papacy and the senate, that would

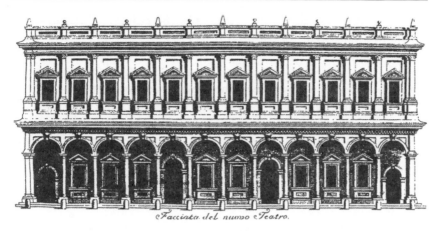

Facciata del nuovo Teatro.

The facade of Bologna's Teatro Comunale, designed by Bibiena, in an engraving of 1771 inscribed by Lorenzo Capponi and printed in Bologna. Courtesy Teatro Comunale di Bologna.

seat no more than 1000 patrons. Antonio was a third-generation Bibiena, the family of architects who became known throughout the baroque era for their refinements in the art of building theaters and scenic decorations both in Austria and Italy.

Today in the Foyer Rossini one can still see the wooden model Antonio Bibiena built, complete with the complicated baroque mechanisms used to change scenery and achieve special effects. Designed in the famous horseshoe shape so popular in the 18th century, Bologna's Teatro Comunale has four tiers of boxes (100 boxes altogether, with four chairs each); it seats 482 in the *platea* (orchestra/stalls). Altogether Bibiena's theater for Bologna is one of the brightest gems in the Italian collection of opera houses: refined and elegant, with its décor in subtle ivory and gold, its main auditorium at once imposing and majestic with the frescoed ceiling and ornate chandelier. Its shape and size lend a sense of intimacy, and the house offers near-ideal acoustics and excellent sightlines. And in keeping with a city famous for its pillared arcades, the front of the house (which faces Piazza Respighi) is made up of a dozen rounded arches, each supported by pairs of pillars of classical design.

For the opening of the house on 14 May 1763, Christoph Willibald Gluck—who had triumphed with his impressive *Orfeo ed Euridice* the year before in Vienna—was commissioned to compose a work for the occasion. With a libretto by Pietro Metastasio based on the ancient warfare of the Etruscans and Romans, Gluck wrote *Il trionfo di Clelia* and invited young Carl Ditters von Dittersdorf to accompany him on the long journey from Vienna to Bologna to see the work properly staged. Though young Dittersdorf complained he did not have the money to make the trip ("Ah, in that case, of course, nothing can come of the matter,"[12] Gluck answered in stark, cold words), friends contributed funds and the two set off for Italy. Gluck, who loved money, food, and good parties, enjoyed himself immensely in Bologna, for the opera singers gave a benefit concert to raise money for him, and the citizens gave frequent parties for the composer during the opera's 17 days of rehearsals.

Unfortunately the opera was not a success, and its 28 performances did not cover the costs of the production, which had been underwritten by 56 public-minded guarantors. Gluck blamed the opera's shortcomings on the "imprecise Italian orchestra," while the Bolognese signaled their displeasure with a ditty in their own dialect, penned and printed in the local paper on the occasion of Gluck's departure:

> *Dman el Part el Cluch,*
> *El va per Triest;*
> *Ch'al faga ben prest,*
> *Perchè el è un gran Mamaluch.*

> Tomorrow Gluck departs,
> He goes by way of Trieste;
> Let him be quick about it,
> For he is a great Mameluke.[13]

According to printed records, *Il trionfo di Clelia* has not been heard since, anywhere.

This less than glorious opening of the house did not in any manner thwart its artistic and social success. In 1805 Napoleon attended a reception held at the theater in his honor, and in 1809 Gioachino Rossini, then 17, was appointed harpsichordist for the theater.

As Italian music critic Davide Annacchini astutely observes,

> To place the role of the Comunale of Bologna in its rightful spot in opera history, it is useful to recall the part the city it-

IN BOLOGNA
NEL NUOVO PUBLICO TEATRO

Inventato dal celebre Sig. Cavaliero Antonio Galli Bibiena Bolognese, primo
Architetto, ed Ingegnere Teatrale delle LL. MM. II. RR.

LA PRIMAVERA DELL' ANNO 1763.

SI RAPPRESENTA IL DRAMMA INTITOLATO

IL TRIONFO DI CLELIA

Del celebre Signor Abbate Pietro Metastasio Poeta Cesareo

LA MUSICA SARA'

Del Signor Cavaliero Criftofaro Gluk al fervizio delle MM. LL. II. RR.

GLI ATTORI SARANNO

Signora Antonia Girelli Aguillar.	*Signor Giovanni Manzoli.*
Signora Cecilia Graffi.	*Signor Giuseppe Tibaldi.*
Signor Giovanni Tofchi.	*Signor Gaetano Ravanni.*

Inventore, e Direttore de' Balli Monfieur Augufto Hus Maftro della Reale Corte
di S. M. il Re di Sardegna, efeguiti dalli feguenti.

Madame Mimi Gambucci Favier, Virtuofa di Ballo di S.A.R. l'Infante di Spagna Duca di Parma ec.ec.ec.	Monfieur Augufto Hus fuddetto.
Signora Maria Efter Boccherini Viganò.	Signor Onorato Viganò al fervizio delle MM. LL. II. RR.
Mademoifelle Ippolita Prin.	Signor Antonio Porri Fiorentino.

E FUORI DE' CONCERTI

Signora Coftanza Tinti Salamon.　　Sig. Francefco Salamon detto di Vienna.

Tutte le Scene fono invenzione del fuddetto Signor Cavaliero Antonio Galli Bibiena.
Il Veftiario farà tutto nuovo di ricca, e vaga invenzione del Signor Pietro Antonio Biagi Bolognefe.
Il Mecanifmo Teatrale è Opera del Signor Petronio Nanni Machinifta Bolognefe.
Le Recite, che fi rapprefenteranno nelli giorni del Mefe di Maggio faranno li 14. 15. 17. 18. 22. 23. 24. 28. 29. 31.
Nelli giorni del Mefe di Giugno faranno li 2. 4. 5. 6. 7. 8. 9. 11. 12. 14. 15. 18. 19. 21. 22. 25. 26., e 29.

In BOLOGNA per il Saffi Succeffore del Benacci.　　Con licenza de' Superiori.

The *manifesto* or poster announcing performances of Gluck's *Il trionfo di Clelia*, commissioned for the opening of the "new public theater" in Bologna, 1763. Courtesy Teatro Comunale di Bologna.

self has had in the development of Italian opera. For the entire 18th century and for a good part of the 19th century, Bologna was the heart of the production center. Most of the impresarios, theatrical agents, singers, dancers, set and costume designers of Italy, and often of the rest of Europe, were based in Bologna.[14]

Opera in Bologna

Though Teatro Comunale in Bologna has presented inaugural performances of a number of operas over the years, few of them have enjoyed more success than Gluck's venture. On the other hand, because Bologna is such an intellectual center and so cosmopolitan in its outlook, the Comunale has been instrumental in introducing both French and German operas to Italy, including Gluck's *Orfeo ed Euridice* in 1771 and his *Alceste* in 1778; Daniel Auber's *La muette de Portici* in 1847; Otto Nicolai's *Der Templer* in 1849; the Irish composer Michael Balfe's *The Bohemian Girl* in 1854; and Jacques Halévy's *La Juive* in 1868. Verdi enjoyed a particular success at Bologna in 1867 with his opera *Don Carlo*. Written originally for the Paris Exhibition of 1867, where it was unsuccessfully staged in March of that year, an Italian translation was made for its production at Teatro Comunale on 26 October of the same year, when it was welcomed with enthusiasm. The conductor was Angelo Mariani, the Elisabetta his mistress, Teresa Stolz, shortly to become an object of Verdi's interest and attention. The profitable relationship between conductor and composer was soon to end in a bitter feud, one exacerbated by Mariani's rejection of Verdi's invitation of 1868 to join him in Bologna for a project honoring Gioachino Rossini with a jointly composed requiem. Mariani did earn further national honor, however, by championing the music of Richard Wagner: he directed the first production in Italy of *Lohengrin* at Bologna, where it was an immense success in contrast to its later fiasco in Milan, and obtained for Wagner the honorary citizenship of Bologna.

Though Verdi and Wagner were exact contemporaries, both born in 1813, their music seemed worlds apart to the 19th-century Italians, and it was difficult to introduce the works of the German composer in a land that honored and revered Verdi. The latter's name had not only been an acronym during the Risorgimento for Vittorio Emanuele, Re d'Italia, but the composer was elected a

54

representative in 1861 to the country's first democratic Senate. Ironic that it was Angelo Mariani, a great friend of Verdi's, a champion of Verdi's music, and the first truly great conductor at Bologna's Teatro Comunale, who successfully introduced Wagner's music to Italy.

Chorley—the 19th-century English writer on musical subjects—frankly admitted that Mariani gave "the only good orchestral performance I have encountered in Italy,"[15] and a more recent writer summed up his qualifications thus:

> Mariani exercised an extraordinary personal fascination on all those who were under his direction. For him, no matter the name of the composer, the music he conducted at the moment was always the most beautiful, and he threw himself into it with all his soul. . . . At rehearsal nothing escaped him in the orchestra or on stage.[16]

About Mariani's introduction of *Lohengrin* at Teatro Comunale on 1 November 1871, the German stage director who assisted with the production, Ernst Frank, noted the collaborative efforts of all the artists involved:

> At the end of rehearsals in the small hours of the morning, when the orchestra would rehearse the prelude to the first or third act, it never occurred to anybody to leave—even the stagehands stayed to listen! And the chorus who were paid just for the production, not the season, studied the music for two months with extraordinary enthusiasm though they received no extra pay.[17]

The Season at Teatro Comunale

The opera season in Bologna today usually extends from November until June and includes about seven or eight different operas, each offered seven or eight times. While the majority of works come from the Italian repertory, the season usually includes at least one or two German operas (Richard Strauss and Richard Wagner are the most frequently represented) and an occasional Russian title, such as Mussorgsky's *Boris Godunov* or Tchaikovsky's *Evgenij Onegin*. (Supertitles in Italian are now employed at the Comunale for operas performed in the original German or

Russian languages.) The theater has also been active in presenting contemporary music. The first performance in Italy of Hans Werner Henze's *The English Cat* was given during the season of 1985–86, and a production (from La Scala) of Henze's opera for children, *Pollicino*, was offered during the 1990–91 season. An opera especially commissioned by Bologna's Teatro Comunale, Adriano Guarnieri's *Trionfo della notte* (an "*azione liriche* in one act, four pictures" based on Pier Paolo Pasolini's cryptic, existentialist collection of poems, "Religion of My Time"), was given six performances in the Comunale's Teatro delle Celebrazione during the season of 1986–87, and for the 1989–90 season, the Comunale presented the world *prima* of Fabio Vacchai's *Il viaggio*, based on a poem in Romagnolo dialect by Tonino Guerra.

In addition to those titles already mentioned, a summation of the most recent seasons indicates a preponderance of operas by Verdi, a number of works by Puccini, and a fair sampling of lyric pieces by other composers: Bellini's *I Capuleti e i Montecchi* and *I puritani*; Busoni's *Doktor Faust*; Cilea's *Adriana Lecouvreur*; Donizetti's *La figlia del reggimento*; Mascagni's *Le maschere*; Massenet's *Manon*; Mozart's *La clemenza di Tito, Don Giovanni*, and *Die Zauberflöte*; Paër's *Achille*; Puccini's *La Bohème, La fanciulla del West, Madama Butterfly*, and *La rondine*; Rossini's *Mosè* and *Il Signor Bruschino*; R. Strauss's *Capriccio* and *Intermezzo*; Verdi's *Un ballo in maschera, Don Carlo, Giovanna d'Arco, Falstaff*, and *Rigoletto*; and Wagner's *Das Rheingold, Die Walküre*, and *Siegfried*.

Luigi Ferrari, Bologna's artistic director during the 1980s, outlined the philosophy behind the theater's choice of repertory and artists:

We in Bologna believe that opera begins and ends with the voice. Our repertory is based, however, on a concept of interpretation in its fullest sense: the interpreter as singer, conductor, director. We try to offer new readings of classic works structured around powerful vocal pillars.

We make our musical choices first and then begin to work on the staging. We have always tried to avoid certain directorial excesses: the meaningless updating of works, for example—*The Merry Widow* set in Berlin besieged by the Russians, or *I vespri siciliani* with American troops disembarking on the beaches. We have always tried to offer a modern reading, but never one at variance with the libretto.

56

An opera season has the life of a cicada: it is short and lasts for seven or eight (at the maximum, 10) performances. Normally each production is repeated once; then it disappears— at least from the Bologna stage. We avoid the exploitation that is characteristic of the repertory system. Our *stagione* system may appear more costly, but this is misleading. The real cost is the permanent staff; they eat up the money, and with reason: they are genuinely productive and on show. Guest artists account for 9 to 10 percent of the costs, the production 5 to 6 percent. Allowing for some 15 or so performances—plus the possibility of reviving the show in another theater—such costs are amply justified.[18]

Riccardo Chailly, director of the Amsterdam Concertgebouw Orchestra and the music director in Bologna, has done much to enhance the quality of the instrumental ensemble. "Bit by bit we are retiring the older players and attracting the extremely gifted young people who are around today. With more rehearsals and better discipline, too, we are improving the sounds that come from our orchestra pit."[19]

The list of conductors who have appeared in the Bologna theater the last few seasons is an impressive one that includes—in addition to Chailly—Claudio Abbado, Sergiu Celibidache, Myung-Whun Chung, Peter Maag, Lorin Maazel, Zubin Mehta, Zoltan Pesko, Simon Rattle, Esa-Pekka Salonen, Giuseppe Sinopoli, and Hubert Soudant.

The theater's roster of vocal artists is equally impressive with such leading sopranos as June Anderson, Montserrat Caballé, Ileana Cotrubas, Mariella Devia, Mirella Freni, Cecilia Gasdia, Raina Kabaivanska, Johanna Meier, Aprile Millo, Edda Moser, Carol Neblett, Elena Obraztsova, Margaret Price, Luciana Serra, and Katia Ricciarelli. Featured mezzos include Martine Dupuy, Brigitte Fassbaender, Christa Ludwig, and Margarita Zimmermann. The list of tenors includes Giacomo Aragall, José Carreras, Siegfried Jerusalem, Luis Lima, William Matteuzzi, Chris Merritt, Luciano Pavarotti, and Gösta Winbergh. Among the baritones are Renato Bruson, Paolo Coni, Claudio Desderi, Leo Nucci, Juan Pons, Gino Quilico; bass-baritones Nicolai Ghiaurov, Ruggero Raimondi, Samuel Ramey; basses Paata Burchuladze, Giorgio Surjan; and *basso buffo* Enzo Dara.

Practical Matters

Tickets in Bologna are expensive, but the quality of the productions is excellent. The box office is located at the front left of the house, Largo Respighi 1, I-40126 Bologna (telephone 051/529.999), and is open Monday through Friday from 3:30 to 7:00 P.M. and on Saturday from 9:30 A.M. to noon and again from 3:30 to 7:00 P.M. The box office is closed on Sundays and holidays. On a day of performance, the box office opens two hours before the performance and closes one hour after the opening curtain. The box office is closed on Saturdays from 11 June through 31 July. The sale of gallery tickets (usually at less than $10) takes place two hours before curtain time, and sales are limited to three tickets per person.

Seats can be booked by mail; telephone orders are not accepted. Up to four tickets per opera may be requested, and two choices each of dates and seat locations should be indicated. Upon receipt of confirmation, payment must reach the box office within 15 days or the reservation will be canceled. Payment—in Italian lire—should be sent by postal money order, made payable to Ente Autonomo Teatro Comunale di Bologna. Ticket orders are filled in the order they are received, based on the postal cancelation. Orders should arrive not more than 10 days before the first date of sale. The *depliant* indicates the first date of sale for each opera.

For the Armchair Fan

There are no books in English about Bologna's Teatro Comunale, but the following two books in Italian are excellent. The magazine article in Italian is also quite good, the one in English quite superficial.

Trezzini, Lamberto. 1987. *Due secoli di vita musicale: Storia del Teatro Comunale di Bologna*. 3 vols. Bologna: Nuova Alfa Editoriale. The most complete story of the theater, in three volumes. The first is devoted to a complete history of the house, and the second to a "critical listing of repertory and performers from 1763 to 1966," while the third volume carries the list from 1966 to 1986. There are a number of excellent black-and-white illustrations, including several views of Galli Bibiena's wooden model of the house designed for Bologna, along with pictures of the composers and artists prominent in the history of the theater.

Guadagnola, Pasquale. 1989. *Un'idea dell'Opera*. Bologna: Grafis Edizione. An oversized, beautifully printed collection of color photographs and black-and-white illustrations of productions at Bologna's Teatro Comunale from 1984 to 1989, with special chapters dealing with Chailly's work at the theater, the stage directors represented during this period, and a chronology of performers and repertory.

Annacchini, Davide. 1987. "Il Teatro Comunale di Bologna." *L'Opera* (June): 47–53. A brief account of the theater and its history with excellent color illustrations, printed in Italy's leading opera magazine.

Hirst, David. 1989. "Teatro Comunale di Bologna." *Opera Now* (September): 8–10. An extremely superficial and not-too-informative story "about" the Comunale in Bologna. (There are more anecdotes than informative facts in the text.) At this date this is the only article printed in English about the theater.

The following albums recorded in Bologna's Teatro Comunale with its chorus and orchestra and with Riccardo Chailly on the podium provide an aural view of the house.

Puccini, Giacomo. *Manon Lescaut*. Decca 421 426-2; with Kiri Te Kanawa, José Carreras, Paolo Coni, Italo Tajo, William Matteuzzi, and Margarita Zimmermann.

Verdi, Giuseppe. *Macbeth*. Decca 417 525-2; with Leo Nucci, Shirley Verrett, Samuel Ramey, and Veriano Luchetti.

Verdi, Giuseppe. *Rigoletto*. Decca 425 864-2; with Luciano Pavarotti, Leo Nucci, June Anderson, Shirley Verrett, and Nicolai Ghiaurov.

The following two albums were also recorded at Teatro Comunale with its chorus and orchestra, this time with Gianluigi Gelmetti on the podium.

Mascagni, Pietro. *Le maschere*. Ricordi/Fonit Cetra RFCD 2004; with Amelia Felle, Maria José Gallego, Vincenzo La Scola, Giuseppe Sabbatini, and Enzo Dara.

Puccini, Giacomo. *La Bohème*. EMI/Angel 7 54124-2; with Daniela Dessì, Giuseppe Sabbatini, Paolo Gavanelli, Alfonso Antoniozzi, Carlo Colombara, and Adelina Scarabelli.

Teatro Comunale
FLORENCE

Florence is where it all began. And though the guidebooks say nothing about them, the monuments of that important development known as opera are still here, all within easy walking distance of the Palazzo Vecchio and the Uffizi: the *palazzo* of Count Giovanni Bardi di Vernio where the Camerata met and formulated the "rules" for the new art form that came to be called opera; the *palazzo* of Count Jacopo Corsi, in which the very first work in this new style—the *stile rappresentativo*—was presented, Jacopo Peri's *Dafne* to a text by Ottavio Rinuccini; and the Sala Bianca of Don Antonio dei Medici's Pitti Palace, where, for the celebration of the marriage of Henri IV of France to Maria de' Medici, Giulio Caccini's *Euridice*—the first opera for which the score survives— was performed.

The Bardi Palace, a block-square monolith of gray stone located at Via dei Benci 5—midway between the Uffizi and the church of Santa Croce—is austere but imposing when seen from the street. Recently used as an office building with its central courtyard given over to antique dealers, it is today owned by the government and employed as a school, the Liceo Statale "Niccolò Rodolico." While the building itself is not open to the public, you can glance through the main entranceway into the quiet central courtyard and imagine yourself there 400 years ago when such Florentine noblemen as Vincenzo Galileo, the father of the astronomer and himself a composer of lute music and madrigals, as well as the composers Jacopo Peri and Giulio Caccini (surnamed Romano), the poet Ottavio Rinuccini, and the aristocratic amateur musicians Pietro Strozzi and Jacopo Corsi—the Camerata Fiorentina—met here to discuss the revival of Greek classical music. On the assumption (which was correct) that Greek tragedies were originally sung rather than merely spoken, these noblemen came to the conclusion (which was faulty) that music should always be subservient to words. In the process they formulated three rules for their new music: 1) the text must always be clearly understood, a condition achieved by using a solo voice with the simplest possible accompaniment (no contrapuntal writing here!); 2) the words must be sung with correct and natural declamation, as they would be spoken (thus barring the regular dance meters of such popular songs as the "villanella"); and 3) such melodic music must not depict merely the graphic details in the text, but should interpret the feeling of the whole passage.

It is interesting to note that although history books clearly state that opera was "born" at the palace of Count Bardi, the plaque to the right of the main entrance praises the military effort of the count before suggesting that he had something to do with the birth of opera:

> In this building lived Giovanni Count of Vernio whose military valor at the sieges of Siena and Malta, joined with his study of science and love of letters and the cultivation of poetry and music, helped foster the interest of the celebrated Camerata . . . who returned the art of music, barbarized by the foreign Flemings [a somewhat biased claim!] to the sublimity of Greek melopoeia, and opened the way for the reform of melodrama through sung recitative and melody that gave way to modern art at the close of the century.
>
> 1532–1612[20]

A half-dozen blocks away—on the extremely busy and traffic-laden Via Strozzi (at its intersection with Via de' Tornabuoni)—stands the somewhat more ornate and impressive palace of Jacopo Corsi. Although the interior has been completely remodeled to serve the purposes of the Banca Commerciale Italiana, you can, with a bit of fantasizing, imagine what it was like on the night of 6 October 1597 (not 1594 as some books have it), when the world's first opera was presented in the presence of Don Giovanni Medici *e d'alcuni de principali gentiluomini de la città* (and other principal gentlemen of the city). Pietro de' Bardi, Giovanni's son, vividly recalled that experience in a letter written some 40 years later:

> The first poem to be sung on stage in *stile rappresentativo* was the story of *Dafne*, by Signor Ottavio Rinuccini, set to music by Peri in a few numbers and short scenes and recited and sung privately in a small room of the Palazzo Corsi. I was speechless with amazement. It was sung to a consort of instruments.[21]

Giulio Caccini's *Euridice* was performed at the Palazzo Pitti on the night of 5 October 1600 as part of the festivities celebrating the wedding of Maria de' Medici and Henri IV of France in the Sala di Don Antonio, a salon known today as the Sala Bianca, or White Salon. Since the Pitti Palace is open to the public (9:00 A.M. to 2:00 P.M. daily, except Monday), a stroll through the Galleria Palatina and Monumental Apartments will bring the days of the Bardis and Corsis and Peris alive again for the imaginative visitor. And if you are lucky, you might even find a concert or recital scheduled in the evening or on a Sunday afternoon in the Sala Bianca. During the summer of 1994, *Euridice* was mounted in the *cortile* of the Pitti Palace.

Though opera was born in Florence, its growth and development were centered elsewhere, and, ironically, relatively little opera is heard in the city today, perhaps three or four operas during the fall/winter season of Teatro Comunale, and another two or three in the spring during the Maggio Musicale Fiorentino, a festival that, in the main, is presented neither by nor for the Florentines.

The Theaters of Florence

There are three principal theaters in Florence in which opera may be heard: Teatro della Pergola (the oldest of the three), Teatro Verdi, and Teatro Comunale, the latter the principal venue in Florence today for opera, concerts, and ballet.

Although Teatro della Pergola has undergone several alterations, it appears today essentially as it did in 1656, the architectural creation of Ferdinando Tecco. Commissioned by a private club, the Accademia degli Immobili, Tecco transformed a warehouse of the Florentine wool workers into one of the most charming and elegant opera houses in the world. While during the Renaissance theaters influenced by Palladio and Roman architects tended to be circular in design, Tecco changed the style with his oval-shaped Teatro della Pergola.

Still in use (it is located at Via della Pergola 18), its record of *primas* is formidable and includes world premieres of operas by Paisiello, Salieri, Gluck, Donizetti, Verdi, and Mascagni. Cherubini's father, Bartolomeo, was the harpsichordist there in the latter part of the 18th century, and major operas of both Meyerbeer and Mozart were first heard in Italy at the Pergola. *Robert le Diable*, *Les Huguenots*, *Le Prophète*, and *Dinorah* all reached the stage here within a decade of their Parisian premieres, while Mozart's *Le nozze di Figaro* traveled intact from Vienna to Florence in two

An 18th-century engraving of the Medici's Pitti Palace in Florence, where the first performance of Caccini's *Euridice* was given on 5 October 1600; Peri's opera of the same title was performed the following evening. Author's collection.

years and *Don Giovanni* made it from Prague in five. (No other theater in Italy mounted either of these two operas until the season of 1811!) Naturally enough, the first Italian performance of the Viennese master's *Die Entführung aus dem Serail* also took place at Teatro della Pergola—153 years after it was written, in 1935!

Teatro Verdi opened on 10 September 1854, built on the site of the ancient Stinche prison. For this reason, it was first called Teatro delle Antiche Stinche. In 1901, after a period of being known as Teatro Cherubini, it was renamed the Verdi. Over the years the theater has gone through a number of restorations and has served a variety of purposes. Following the renovation of 1950 it presented such international personalities as Josephine Baker, Frank Sinatra, Ava Gardner, Louis Armstrong, Ella Fitzgerald, Yma Sumac, Carmen Miranda, and Jane Russell. After the disastrous flood of 1966, it was refurbished and served as a movie theater; then, during the early 1980s, Zubin Mehta started to schedule concerts by his Teatro Comunale Orchestra here. On 30 January

1985, the theater was closed by the state government pending the implementation of certain safety features (additional emergency exits, electrical wiring, etc.). Following its reopening in 1987, Teatro Verdi has been used both for operas during the Maggio Musicale and for opera recording purposes.

Teatro Verdi (a baroque, horseshoe-type theater with 19th-century décor) seats some 1538 patrons in its six tiers of boxes and orchestra (stalls/parterre). While Teatro Verdi certainly provides a more typical and pleasant ambiance for opera than Teatro Comunale, the principal theater in use today, the Verdi's lack of backstage and rehearsal space and technical equipment makes it of limited use when planning a season.

Teatro Comunale is both the name of the *ente autonomo* (the state-supported entity) that sponsors concerts and operas in Florence and the name of the building at Corso Italia 12 that serves as the venue for the presentation of those concerts and operas and contains the rehearsal halls and offices of the *ente*. It is a strange building to say the very least.

Built originally in 1862 and known then as the Politeama Fiorentino (and subsequently as the Arena Nazionale in 1868 and the Anfiteatro Umberto in 1869, among other names), it was, in the words of the community magazine of the time, *Firenze*, "a grandiose amphitheater created for equestrian or dramatic shows of every kind appropriate for festivals and public shows."[22] The facade consisted of seven stone arches, three of which framed doors and the other four, windows. Past a "spacious vestibule" one entered the unroofed amphitheater, which consisted of the orchestra (stalls/parterre), a tier of boxes, and a large U-shaped balcony that, at the back center, was topped at a level higher by a huge covered gallery. Altogether the arena seated 6000. Though it could hardly have been a very sympathetic setting for opera—either visually or aurally—from 1871 to 1876 such works were mounted as *Poliuto*, *Macbeth*, *L'africana*, *L'italiana in Algeri*, *I vespri siciliani*, and *Semiramide*.

In 1881 the Politeama became an academy and in 1882 produced Verdi's *I lombardi* as its inaugural event. During 1896 alone the Politeama presented 69 performances, a season consisting of such works as *Cavalleria rusticana*, *Zanetto*, *I pagliacci*, *La traviata*, *Il trovatore*, *I pescatori di perle*, and two ballets, *Excelsior* and *P. Micca*.

Around the turn of the century standards dropped tremen-

An old photograph, probably from the 1880s, of Florence's Teatro Comunale when it seated some 6000 spectators. Operas such as *Traviata, Trovatore, Pagliacci,* and *Cavalleria rusticana* were presented in this outdoor amphitheater. Courtesy Teatro Comunale di Firenze.

dously, and vaudeville, operettas, and other forms of theater—including horse shows—occupied the amphitheater. In 1911 the newly formed Società Italiana Anonima Teatrale reactivated full seasons of operas; its inaugural season included *Saffo, La Bohème, Madama Butterfly, Sansone e Dalila,* and *Don Pasquale,* each with a cast of well-known artists. All went well until 1917 when the Politeama was commandeered to stage wartime benefits for the soldiers. Though opera performances began again after the armistice, they were hardly distinguished productions.

In 1928 a permanent orchestra was established—the Stabile Orchestra Fiorentina—under the baton of Vittorio Gui. While Gui remained its permanent conductor until 1936, the list of guest conductors during the early years includes all the great names of the era: Arturo Toscanini, Victor De Sabata, Wilhelm Furtwängler, Pierre Monteux, and Otto Klemperer. In addition, a notable group of composers conducted their own music: Riccardo Zan-

The facade of Teatro Comunale (now minus the clock on top), designed by architect Telemarco Buonaiuti in 1862. Courtesy Teatro
Comunale di Firenze.

donai, Pietro Mascagni, Igor Stravinsky, Richard Strauss, Ildebrando Pizzetti, and Alfredo Casella.

In early 1933 the spring festival known as the Maggio Musicale
Fiorentino was announced in the hope of reviving both national
and international interest in the music of this city where opera
was born. Although originally intended as a triennial affair, it
immediately became biennial, and then eventually an annual
celebration.

In 1938 the amphitheater was enclosed with a roof, although
the covering still had an opening in the very center, an "eye" as it
was called, that served for both ventilation and light. On 1 May
1944, the stage was partially destroyed by bombs; repair work was
implemented and the theater reopened for use during the 1945–46
season.

It was not until 1958 that the amphitheater was completely renovated and turned into a true indoor theater with a full roof and
cushioned chairs instead of stone benches. At the same time new
lighting and mechanical systems were installed on stage and air-
conditioning added for the house. Tragedy then struck. On 4 November 1966, the entire ground floor of the theater was inundated
for 23 days by the waters of that year's disastrous flood. This com-

Though Florence's Teatro Comunale was enclosed during a major renovation in 1938, there was still an opening in the center of the roof (visible in this old photograph), what the Florentine's called the "eye" of the theater. Courtesy Teatro Comunale di Firenze.

pletely destroyed the chairs of the orchestra and first tier as well as musical instruments, stage sets, costumes, and lighting units. Once again refurbished, the theater reopened with Monteverdi's *L'incoronazione di Poppea*. Additional work was then begun: new office space was developed by acquiring the building next door, an area that now contains the added orchestra and chorus rehearsal rooms. A new chamber theater with 600 seats—Teatrino del Comunale (later renamed Teatro Ridotto and then Piccolo Teatro, as it is known today)—was added for concerts, conventions, debates, shows, and cultural activities.

In the late 1980s Zubin Mehta, as music director, initiated the electronic enhancement of sound for the theater, whose acoustics were never particularly good. Then, during the season of 1989–90 it was discovered by the city health department that a great quantity of asbestos had been used for insulation in the air-conditioning system. The house was subsequently condemned and closed for three years while the situation was remedied. During this three-year period the number of operas offered in each half of the season was somewhat curtailed, with concert performances at Cinema Puccini substituted in at least one instance for a staged production.

Since the establishment in 1933 of the Maggio Musicale Fiorentino, Florence has had, in essence, two seasons: the fall/winter, which begins around 1 October and ends in late February, and spring, the Maggio Musicale Fiorentino. Administratively and artistically they are two parts of the same entity and share the same staff, including the *sovrintendente* (Massimo Bogianckino, former mayor of Florence and former director of L'Opéra in Paris), artistic director, and principal conductor (Zubin Mehta, also music director of the Israeli Philharmonic).

Except for the numbering of the festival (the one in 1998, for example, will be the 60° Maggio Musicale Fiorentino), there is little that makes this a true "festival" in either theme or spirit. Both fall/winter and spring seasons are built around the production of three or four operas plus a half-dozen or so symphonic concerts (with one or two of the latter featuring the chorus and guest soloists in major choral works such as Verdi's *Requiem* and Stravinsky's *Symphony of Psalms*). The spring "Maggio" (as the Florentines refer to it) generally offers symphony concerts, chamber recitals, and frequently an adventuresome foray into contemporary music in addition to opera productions.

The Fall/Winter Opera Season

The fall/winter season of opera in Florence is quite traditional and conservative today, with a large part given over to the standard works of Bellini, Donizetti, Rossini, Verdi, and Puccini, though there have been in the past some singular moments and productions: Mascagni's *Iris* conducted by the composer and Bellini's *Norma* with Claudia Muzio in 1929; Beethoven's *Fidelio* with Eva Turner in 1930; Bellini's *La sonnambula* with Toti Dal Monte in 1932; Zandonai's *Francesca da Rimini* with Gina Cigna in 1934; Verdi's *Rigoletto* with Ferruccio Tagliavini, Gino Becchi, and Giulietta Simionato (Maddalena) in 1939; Ermanno Wolf-Ferrari's *I quattro rusteghi* with Iris Adami Corradetti and Fedora Barbieri in 1941; Donizetti's *L'elisir d'amore* with Tito Schipa in 1942; Maria Callas and Cesare Siepi in *Norma* (1948); Mussorgsky's *Boris Godunov* with Nicola Rossi-Lemeni in the title role conducted by Artur Rodzinski in 1950; Tito Gobbi as Falstaff in Verdi's masterpiece of the same name; Rossini's *Mosè* with Boris Christoff and Rosanna Carteri in 1951; Verdi's *Nabucco* with Tito Gobbi (Nabucco), Boris Christoff, and Paolo Washington, conducted by Tullio Serafin in 1954; Gershwin's *Porgy and Bess*, Menotti's *The Medium*—both firsts for Florence—and Mussorgsky's *The Fair at Sorochinsky* with Rossi-Lemeni and Giuseppe Valdengo in 1955; Stravinsky's *The Nightingale* with Mattiwilda Dobbs in the title role coupled with Ravel's *L'heure espagnole* with Hugues Cuenod as Torquemada in 1961; and, in 1966, *Rigoletto* with Luciano Pavarotti and Renata Scotto, conducted by Carlo Maria Giulini.

A typical fall season, that of 1990 opened on 18 November with Menotti's *The Telephone* coupled with Negri's *Pubblicità, ninfa gentile* for 14 performances, followed by Bellini's *La sonnambula*, which opened on 3 February for six performances with Cecilia Casdia as Amina, and the ever-popular *Cavalleria rusticana* by Mascagni, which opened on 2 March for eight performances with Ghena Dimitrova as Santuzza.

The Maggio Musicale Fiorentino

With the exception of a few years in the early 1980s, when Italy's best-known contemporary composer, Luciano Berio, served as guest artistic director of the Maggio, the spring festival has had little to characterize it from the fall season. Berio was the exception. For example, he exploited the Orpheus legend by presenting variations of it in both traditional and unusual locations. These "reincarnations" ranged all the way from the production of Monteverdi's masterpiece in the Salone dei Cinquecento (Hall of the 1500s) of Palazzo Vecchio, to a contemporary pop/rock version offered in the *cortile* (courtyard) of a palace on Via Scala.

The early years of the Maggio did offer some unusual and—at least for the Florentines—unknown works. The first Maggio, for example, offered in addition to Verdi's *Nabucco* directed by Carl Ebert, Donizetti's *Lucrezia Borgia* with Beniamino Gigli; Spontini's *La vestale* with Rosa Ponselle; Shakespeare's *A Midsummer Night's Dream* presented in the Boboli Gardens of the Pitti Palace with Mendelssohn's instrumental music; and in the cloister of Santa Croce, Ildebrando Pizzetti's setting of the 16th-century *La rappresentazione di Santa Ulvia*. Other early Maggios included Rossini's *Mosè*, conducted by Vittorio Gui and directed by Carl Ebert, and Rameau's *Castor et Pollux*, directed by Pierre Chereau (1935); Ottorino Respighi's *Maria Egiziaca* with Maria Caniglia in the title role (1937); and the world premiere of Riccardo Malipiero's *Antonio e Cleopatra* and the Florentine premiere of *La fiamma* (1938). Following the war, Maggio highlights included the world premieres of Ildebrando Pizzetti's *Vanna Lupa* in 1949 and *Ifigenia* in 1951, Luigi Dallapiccola's *Il prigionero* in 1950, Mario Castelnuovo-Tedesco's *Aucassin et Nicolette* in 1952 and prize-winning *Il mercante di Venezia* in 1961, and Gian Francesco Malipiero's *Il figliuolo prodigo* and *Venere prigioniera* in 1957. There were also Italian premieres of Lully's *Armida* in 1950, Haydn's *Orfeo ed Euridice* with Maria Callas in 1951, Menotti's *Amahl and the Night Visitors* and Prokofiev's *War and Peace* in 1953, Britten's *The Turn of the Screw* in 1955 and *Billy Budd* in 1965, Cherubini's *Gli abenceragi* in 1957, Janáček's *Jenůfa* in 1960 and *Věc Makropulos* in 1966, Krenek's *Jonny spielt auf* in 1963, and Shostakovich's *The Nose* in 1964.

Recent seasons of the Maggio have offered the following: in 1988, Britten's *Peter Grimes*, Sylvano Bussotti's *L'ispirazione*, and Puccini's *Il trittico*; in 1989, Debussy's *Pelléas et Mélisande*, Mozart's *Idomeneo*, Bellini's *I puritani*, and Strauss's *Der Rosenkavalier*; and in 1990, Rimsky-Korsakov's *The Legend of the Invisible City of Kitezh* sung in Russian (with supertitles), Donizetti's *Parisina*, Verdi's *Il trovatore* with Luciano Pavarotti, and Kurt Weill's *The Rise and Fall of the City of Mahagonny*, conducted by Jan Latham Koenig and directed by Graham Vick.

The 56th Edition of the Maggio (1993) included on its *cartellone* many programs in addition to the production of four operas. It opened on 27 April with a production of *Jenůfa* conducted by Semyon Bychkov with Katarina Ikonomu in the title role. Then followed Richard Strauss's "recitation with piano," *Enoch Arden*, coupled with Poulenc's one-act, one-person opera, *La voix humaine* (with Renata Scotto as the protagonist); Bizet's *Carmen*; and Mozart's *Die Zauberflöte*, the latter two operas conducted by Zubin Mehta. Orchestral concerts included the Vienna Philhar-

70

monic with Zubin Mehta, the London Symphony Orchestra with Sir Georg Solti, and the Maggio Orchestra directed by Bychkov, who also conducted a concert by the Orchestre de Paris. In addition to the Diaghilev Ballet, there were solo recitals by Andras Schiff (piano), Krystian Zimerman (piano), and Yo-Yo Ma (cello), and a two-piano recital by Katia and Marielle Labèque. The contemporary composers encountered included Vinko Globokar, Luciano Berio, and Karlheinz Stockhausen. The Maggio concluded on 27 June with the final performance of *Die Zauberflöte*.

Practical Matters

From among the 46 different evenings and matinées of operas, concerts, and recitals that made up the 56th Maggio, for example, four different types of season tickets were available, varying both in the number of events and titles.

For those who wish to order in advance, requests for four or fewer season tickets—which are expensive—will be honored beginning the first week of April by the box office at the theater. There is a 10 percent surcharge for those ordering by mail. (Preference is given to senior citizens over 65. These persons should place their requests a week earlier.) All orders should be accompanied by a postal money order in lire payable to account number 26880500, Ente Autonomo del Teatro Comunale, Servizio Abbonamenti, Via Solferino 15, I-50123 Florence. No telephone requests will be accepted, and "orders will be filled in the sequence in which they are received."

Individual tickets may be purchased at the box office after the first week of April. The box office is located at Teatro Comunale, Corso Italia 16 (telephone 055/277.9236), and is open Tuesdays to Saturdays from 9:00 A.M. to 1:00 P.M.

For the Armchair Fan

Unfortunately no publication in English gives the story of Teatro Comunale and the history of its operatic productions, but there are two excellent books in Italian, one on the history of the theater itself (with some excellent black-and-white illustrations), the other, a definitive record (of some 505 pages!) of the musical seasons from 1929, when the permanent orchestra was established, to the flood of 1966. Though the latter is written in Italian, the

71

chronology—which makes up half the book—can be understood by most people unfamiliar with Italian, and, as a bonus, the book also contains 109 excellent black-and-white photographs

Roselli, Piero, Giuseppina Carla Romby, and Osanna Fantozzi Micali. 1978. *I Teatri di Firenze*. Florence: Casa Editrice Bonechi, s.r.l. (società a reponsabilità limitata).

Pinzauti, Leonardo. 1967. *Il Maggio Musicale Fiorentino: Dalla prima all trentesima edizione*. Florence: Vallecchi Editore Firenze.

There are two excellent albums representative of the Maggio productions: Verdi's *Il trovatore*, recorded in Teatro Comunale in 1990 with essentially the same cast that had just performed it as part of the Maggio Musicale Fiorentino; and Donizetti's *L'elisir d'amore*, recorded in Teatro Verdi in 1986 with the chorus and orchestra of the Maggio Musicale Fiorentino.

Donizetti, Gaetano. *L'elisir d'amore*. Deutsche Grammophon 423 076-2; with Barbara Bonney, Gösta Winbergh, Bernd Weikl, Rolando Panerai, and Antonella Bandelli; Orchestra e Coro del Maggio Musicale Fiorentino; conducted by Gabriele Ferro.

Verdi, Giuseppe. *Il trovatore*. Decca 430 694-2; with Luciano Pavarotti, Antonella Banaudi, and Shirley Verrett; Orchestra e Coro del Maggio Musicale Fiorentino; conducted by Zubin Mehta.

Teatro Carlo Felice
GENOA

Most Italian lyric theaters mount outstanding productions of both comic operas and tragic masterpieces. Genoa's Teatro Carlo Felice has the distinction of having mounted, a few seasons ago, a production that was at the same time a comic farce and a dramatic catastrophe. Unfortunately, the most moving moments of this production took place not on stage, but behind the scenes.

This tale begins in the fall of 1985 when the board of directors of Teatro Comunale dell'Opera di Genova (the *ente*'s official name) decided under the guidance of President Cesare Campart (who was also the mayor of Genoa) that their lyric enterprise in Genoa needed to do something to attract more attention. The board felt that over the years—since the days in the 18th and 19th centuries when there were more than 40 theaters in Genoa and along the coasts of the adjoining Rivieras—the general Italian public and foreign visitors in particular were losing sight of this Ligurian city as a center of opera and were instead focusing their attention on the more prominent opera centers of Milan, Venice, and Rome. Franco Ragazzi, the *sovrintendente*, made a suggestion, an idea that had the blessing of Luciano Alberti, the artistic director of the theater: engage one of the very controversial *registi* (stage directors) to present some scandalous production for the forthcoming season that would engender attention in the international press. With the agreement of the board, Ken Russell was hired to direct Arigo Boito's *Mefistofele*.

That is the Prelude to our story. In Act I (of *our* story, not Boito's), Russell decided to modernize the Faustian legend, making the title character (to be sung by Paata Burchuladze) a superhuman type in a Superman costume; Margherita (sung by Adriana Morelli) was to be housewifely, with her "prison" in Act III her kitchen. (As she sang "L'altra notte in fondo" she continuously ironed one of Faust's shirts; later, accused of having drowned her child and murdered her mother, she retrieved the baby's cadaver from the washing machine and opened the refrigerator door to reveal her dismembered mother.)

Act II of our story now begins. Vladimir Delman, the conductor, was so disgusted with the tastelessness of the whole thing that he walked out on the production between the *sitzprobe* (the last musical run-through) and the dress rehearsal. Edoardo Müller was brought in at the last possible moment to conduct, and the curtains parted on time for the opening night of the 1987 season on 23 January. The public booed and whistled, stamped their feet and hissed. The music critics damned *Mefistofele* all over again. (I wrote, in my review for the International Edition of the *Christian Science Monitor*, that the production was "not shocking, not scandalous; it was simply ridiculous.")

The public was so incensed that the board, with the approval of the ministry in Rome, fired Luciano Alberti as artistic director. But that was not enough to pacify the Genovese who continued to grumble. Within weeks, in disgust, Franco Ragazzi resigned as *sovrintendente*.

Thus, this comic tragedy, having played itself out with a conductor who walked out, an artistic director who was fired, and a *sovrintendente* who resigned, did draw attention to Genoa and its opera company, but for all the wrong reasons.

The Story of Teatro Carlo Felice

The *Mefistofele* anecdote is really only a "teaser," a curtain-warmer as it were, for the comedy of errors enacted in the reconstruction of Teatro Carlo Felice. Designed by Carlo Barabino, Teatro Carlo Felice (named after the Savoyard who was king of Piedmont and Sardinia from 1821 to 1831) opened in 1828. During World War II the theater was bombed in October 1942 and then hit again during an aerial attack in August 1943. A direct strike in September 1944 put the theater completely out of commission. In spite of attempts as late as 1962 to make space in the remnants of the edifice for orchestral rehearsals (with other theaters and halls being used for public performances), the administration finally vacated the premises and moved lyric productions to Teatro Margherita, a movie house that was dressed up to serve as best it could. (It was at the Margherita that the *Mefistofele* story took place.)

It is necessary to go back a bit in time for the beginning of our "comedy of errors" to 1946, the year after World War II ended and Italy became a republic. During this year, in their anxiety to have their opera house rebuilt, the Genovese announced the first design competition for the rebuilding of Teatro Carlo Felice. When the personnel on the administrative board changed the following year because of elections (a new political party was then in the majority), the new board aborted the plans for the design competition. Then, in 1949, with another political change, the original contest was reinstated. Thirteen designs were presented, out of which five were selected. In 1950 the plans by well-known Italian theater architect Pasquale Chessa were selected as the winner.

In 1951 the administrative board presented Chessa's design to the examining committee of the City of Genoa, a "busy" group that did not get around to looking at the drawings for two years. Finally, after three years of deliberation, the Consiglio Superiore dei Lavori Pubblici (Superior Board of Public Works) asked for certain modifications in the drawings. Two years later, in 1958, Chessa, in association with an architect named Vittoria, submitted revised plans. No action followed, so in 1959 Chessa took the City of Genoa to court, demanding that construction begin within 60 days. A year later the case came up in court and Chessa lost. The city council thereupon put his drawings in a drawer and hired the-

The facade of Genoa's Teatro Carlo Felice as seen in a 19th-century engraving. Courtesy L'Ufficio Stampa, Teatro Carlo Felice.

ater-designer Carlos Scarpa to begin all over again with a new set of plans for rebuilding the bombed-out theater. Later that same year, Scarpa submitted his designs.

It took the City of Genoa eight years to look over these new plans and suggest certain modifications. The following year—1970—the commission approved the then-modified drawings, but everything came to a complete halt three years later. The citizens of Genoa blocked the project in 1973, demanding that Teatro Carlo Felice include within its walls a theater for spoken drama as well as the originally planned lyric theater.

Scarpa went back to the drawing board (to use a cliché quite appropriate in this case), and in 1977 presented a revised set of plans. By 1979 the commission had approved them and it looked, at long last—some 31 years after the initial decision to rebuild—as though Teatro Carlo Felice was going to be rebuilt. But time, the grim reaper, inexorably took its toll: Scarpa died. Tragically—in this ongoing comedy of errors—Scarpa's assistants (including Zavellani Rossi) refused to sign off on the project even though both Scarpa, the director of the project, and his chief engineer, Bertolini, had died.

Thus we arrive at February 1981, a point in time at which "this shameful history of common administration is as yet unfinished!"

A photograph of Genoa's Teatro Carlo Felice taken shortly after the bombardment of August 1943. Courtesy L'Ufficio Stampa, Teatro Carlo Felice.

(to quote a local music critic).[23] The administration then announced still another (the third) competition. By 1984 a design had been selected; the goal was now to complete the renovations by 1992 in time for the 500th anniversary celebration of Columbus's historic voyage. In September of 1984, the plans by architect Ignazio Gardelli and his associates were let out for contract.

Incredibly, as Daniele Rubboli points out,

> No one, it seems, had added up the public expenditures on this project between its inception in 1946 and the awarding of the contract in 1984 with reference to contests, meetings of committees, courses and recourses, legal adventures and misadventures, time wasted, paper—both legal and other types—expended, hours of useless work, materials used or thrown away, assignments made and cancelled.[24]

This long scenario starts to draw to a close when, on 11 October 1985, the official sign was posted in front of Teatro Carlo Felice announcing the renovations, naming the contractors, listing the names of the board of administration, and announcing the fact (as required by law) that from this point on, the project would cost an

The interior of Teatro Carlo Felice following the bombing attacks of August 1943. Courtesy L'Ufficio Stampa, Teatro Carlo Felice.

estimated $105 million. (It ended up costing more than 120 billion lire, roughly $200 million.)

On 7 April 1987, the first stone of the new Teatro Carlo Felice was laid with pomp and ceremony, and the curtain closed on our "comedy of errors" on the night of 20 October 1991—some 45 years after it had begun—with a performance of Verdi's *Il trovatore* in the newly rebuilt Teatro Carlo Felice.

Opera in Genoa

Lest anyone think that opera in Genoa has always been the target of jokes, let me quickly refute that idea, for there have been many glorious nights of opera in that city by the Ligurean Sea. The two stories I have related—the *Mefistofele* comic tragedy, and the rebuilding "comedy of errors"—should be regarded as intermezzi, humorous moments meant for laughs between the serious acts of music-making that are the tradition in Genoa. During the 18th and 19th centuries, for example, the city of Genoa was one of the important opera centers of Europe, certainly one of Italy's

77

greatest. The picture at that time, however, was of a greatly different Genoa, for it was then a major seaport, the city itself an elegant tourist center. During the 18th century there were more than 40 theaters producing opera on the Riviera, which stretches along the Gulf of Genoa from Marseilles to La Spezia, with the city of Genoa dividing it into the Riviera Levante (to the east) and the Riviera di Ponente (to the west). By the 19th century this area boasted important theaters in such towns and cities as Pietra Ligure, Chiavari, Albenga, Finalborgo, Bordighera, Sarzana, La Spezia, Albaro, Oneglia, Sampierdarena, Sestri Ponente, Savona (the only opera theater still functioning today out of all of these), Porto Maurizio, Ventimiglia, Cairo Montenotte, Altare, Rapallo, Sestri Levante, Alassio, and Loano. A visitor in those days would have found *cartelloni* listing such lyric works as Rossini's *L'italiana in Algeri*, Gazzaniga's *Il convitato di pietra*, Mayr's *La rosa bianca e la rosa rossa*, Zingarelli's *Giulietta e Romeo*, Cimarosa's *Il matrimonio segreto*, and Meyerbeer's *Il crociato in Egitto*.

By the beginning of the 19th century, the city of Genoa itself had 13 active theaters: Teatro dei Dilettanti di San Lorenzo, Il Festone dei Giustiniani, Teatro dell'Oratorio del Rosario, Teatro del Campetto, Teatro Diurno dell'Acquaverde, Teatro Colombo, Teatro Apollo, Teatro Sant'Agostino, Teatro Paganini, Teatro Andrea Doria (later known as Politeama Genovese, a theater used after World War II up until the reopening of Teatro Carlo Felice for symphony concerts), Teatro Andrea Podestà (later known as Teatro del Popolo, then Teatro Edmondo Rossoni), Teatro delle Mura di Santa Chiara, and Anfiteatro delle Peschiere.

The clamor on the part of the busy theatergoing Genovese for a grander house for lyric opera resulted in an initiative to build a new theater. In order to assure the success of this project, the would-be theater was named the Carlo Felice after the reigning king. The design was entrusted to Carlo Barabino, who realized a classic structure of pillars and porticos. There are two faces to the theater: the principal facade with Corinthian columns facing Piazza San Domenico (today Piazza De Ferrari) with a statue of the "Genius of Harmony" in front (the work of sculptor Giuseppe Gaggini); and a bolder, more massive facade made up of solidly square pillars on Via Carlo Felice (today Via XXV Aprile) with the windows of the theater's famous *ridotto* (foyer) looking across the balcony above the porticoed entrance.

Inside, in the *sala* or main hall, there are five tiers of boxes arranged in a horseshoe configuration, the house accommodating altogether some 2500 patrons (the main hall was 47 meters/155 feet from the back wall to the stage). The ornate ceiling that towers some 17 meters (56 feet) off the floor was designed by Nicola Cianfanelli and Michele Canzio. With these details and its spacious *ridotto*, Teatro Carlo Felice was judged the finest salon in Genoa.

The theater opened on 7 April 1828 with a performance of Vincenzo Bellini's *Bianca e Fernando*. Of the performance with artists Adelaide Tosi, Giovanni David, and Giuseppe Rossi, the local music critic wrote, "The artists surpassed themselves: great voices, a variety of tastes in movement, all with singable [cantabile] expression, variety and vivacity of action. These excellent singers demonstrated that they fully understood this excellent opera."[25]

Between the first and second performances of the Bellini opera, the theater offered a highly successful performance of the ballet *Gli adoratori del fuoco*, composed for the occasion by Galzerani. Then followed Rossini's *Il barbiere di Siviglia* (given at Teatro Carlo Felice on 6 April and the following night at Teatro Vigne) and his *L'assedio di Corinto*, mounted on 31 May. Appropriately for the city of Genoa, birthplace of Christopher Columbus, *Cristoforo Colombo*, by Francesco Morlacchi, was presented on 21 June.

Over the years since its inauguration, Teatro Carlo Felice has not only welcomed to its podium a young Arturo Toscanini, Pietro Mascagni, Ottorino Respighi, Richard Strauss, and Tullio Serafin among others, its *cartelloni* have listed many well-remembered artists: Rosina Storchio, Beniamino Gigli, Titta Ruffo, Mattia Battistini, Claudia Muzio, Gilda Dalla Rizza, Conchita Supervia, Toti Dal Monte, and Aureliano Pertile.

The transfer of performances to Teatro Margherita occasioned by the bomb damage of World War II in no way affected the quality of the *cartelloni*, for the company opened at Teatro Margherita in 1960 with a Franco Zeffirelli production of *Lucia di Lammermoor* starring Joan Sutherland, a huge success soon followed by others featuring artists such as Maria Callas and Luciano Pavarotti. The caliber of productions was such that Teatro Comunale dell'Opera di Genoa made tours in 1969 to Poland, Bulgaria, East Germany, Israel, France, and China, with Luciano Pavarotti appearing as Rodolfo in Puccini's *La Bohème*.

Teatro Carlo Felice Today

The newly rebuilt Teatro Carlo Felice in Genoa boasts the most modern and advanced stage facilities in Italy: in addition to a movable turntable some 15 meters (50 feet) in diameter that is surrounded by a supplemental movable ring some 19 meters (63 feet) across, it has six movable bridges; three trap doors in the floor; electronically operated house and fire curtains; three movable cranes for mounting spotlights; two power cranes on bridges on either side of the stage and two at the back of the stage; and a stage floor with some 30 separate lifts at the front (each 2.5 by 4 meters/8 by 13 feet) and 15 upstage (4 by 5 meters/13 by 17 feet). The stage lighting system is completely computerized, and the stage provided with electronic "sound enhancement" capabilities as well as complete television facilities, both in-house and for public telecasts. The main hall, now rectangular in shape (and reduced to a depth of 44 meters/145 feet between the back wall and the stage) seats 1399 on the main floor (*platea*) and 504 in the balcony (*galleria*). At the back of the main floor and along the side walls at the same level is one rather ordinary-looking (I'm tempted to say "ugly") row of boxes; another row of boxes is located at the back of the balcony and along the side walls at that same height. Altogether there are 76 box seats, with space in a mini-gallery for 21 people.

In addition to this main hall, the newly reopened Teatro Carlo Felice features an auditorium of 200 seats that is completely independent of the main auditorium and can be used for lectures and meetings. Teatro Carlo Felice also has a principal ticket office, four bars (including one that opens off the *piazza*), an entrance atrium, a special hall for exhibits, a principal foyer (660 square meters/8085 square feet in size), another foyer for the ground floor, another for the balcony, six cloak rooms, an infirmary, and, in the main hall, seating facilities for the physically handicapped. Backstage there are a large orchestra rehearsal room as well as six adjacent practice rooms; two chorus rehearsal rooms, one for 130 singers, the other for 50; and three vocal study rooms. There are two ballet rehearsal halls and a staging room. In addition there are 25 dressing rooms, eight shops for scenic construction, and office space at that same height.

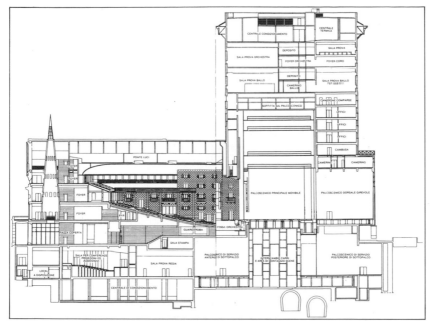

A longitudinal section of the "new" Teatro Carlo Felice, opened in 1992. The *piazza coperta* is a covered atrium; the *guardaroba*, a cloak room; the *sala stampa*, a press room; the *fossa orchestra*, the orchestra pit; the *palcoscenico principale movibile*, the principal moveable stage; the *palcoscenico dorsale girevole*, the rotating rear stage; the *sala prova*, a rehearsal room; the *uffici*, offices; and the *camerino*, a dressing room. Courtesy L'Ufficio Stampa, Teatro Carlo Felice.

The Season at Teatro Carlo Felice

The opera season in Genoa ordinarily opens in mid-October and lasts until early January with around four titles on the *cartellone*, each presented about eight times. The inaugural season in the new theater offered a selection of four titles: two operas (*Il trovatore* and *Un ballo in maschera*) and two ballets (Béjart's *Death in Venice* and the Maryinsky Theater from St. Petersburg's *Oration for the Age of Aquarius*). The season of 1992–93, celebrating the 500th Anniversary of Christopher Columbus, was more ambitious:

Puccini's *La Bohème*
with Mirella Freni, Peter Dvorsky, and Daniela Mazzuccato;
conducted by Roberto Abbado
(8 performances)

81

Netherlands Ballet
(6 performances)

Aterballetto
(5 performances)

Rossini's *Il barbiere di Siviglia*
with Bruno Pola, Gloria Scalchi, Rockwell Blake, and Simone
Alaimo; conducted by Evelino Pidò
(8 performances)

Bizet's *Carmen*
with Martha Senn, Giorgio Merighi, and Giorgio Zancanaro;
conducted by Rafael Frühbeck de Burgos
(8 performances)

Ballet Nieves Ongay
(3 performances)

Verdi's *Don Carlo*
a production from the Maryinsky Theater of St. Petersburg
(8 performances)

Rossini's *Le siège de Corinthe*
with Luciana Serra; conducted by Paolo Olmi
(6 performances)

Waite's *The Black Rider*
direction by Robert Wilson; a production of the Thalia Theater
(5 performances)

Lehár's *La vedova allegra*
conducted by Daniel Oren
(14 performances)

Rossini's *Il barbiere di Siviglia*
with Rockwell Blake, Bruno Praticò, Armando Ariostini, and
Sonia Ganassi; conducted by Evelino Pidò
(4 additional performances in July)

Practical Matters

As in most major houses, tickets in Genoa are expensive, but
unlike most major houses, they are easy to book.

Ticket reservations may be made at the box office (*biglietteria*) at the Galleria Cardinal Siri, off Galleria Mazzini, next to the theater. Ticket sales are now completely computerized, and the box office is open Monday through Saturday from 12:30 to 7:30 P.M. On performance days, the box office is open an hour and a half before curtain time.

For mail orders, the coupon in the theater's brochure must be used, specifying the opera's title, three optional dates, the seating location, and the number of tickets desired; include complete mailing information (name, address, and telephone number) in the space provided. Patrons will be notified of confirmations. Payment may then be made by credit card (American Express/MasterCard/Visa/Carta Sì). When ordering by mail, requests and payments should be sent to E. A. Teatro Comunale dell'Opera, Passo al Teatro 4, I-16121 Genoa.

Reserved tickets are to be picked up no less than an hour before curtain; the order is canceled without reimbursement otherwise. (The theater accepts no telephone orders.) The box office opens around 10 January for the sale of opera tickets for the entire season.

Those interested in receiving Teatro Carlo Felice information by mail—including the season brochure—should enclose Lit. 10.000 as a postal contribution either in paper currency or an international money order payable to Servizio Relazoni Esterne, Passo al Teatro 4, I-16121 Genoa.

For the Armchair Fan

While there is nothing published in English about Genoa's Teatro Carlo Felice, there is an excellent paperback booklet of 63 pages in Italian. In addition to a history of the theater (accompanied by period black-and-white photographs), there is a thorough description of the new house including both public and backstage areas, intriguing schematics, and 31 superb color photographs.

Iovino, Roberto. 1991. *Il Carlo Felice: Due volti di un teatro*. Genoa: Sagep Editrice.

For those interested in hearing a production by this company, the following performance was recorded there live in January 1989.

Puccini, Giacomo. *Turandot*. Nuova Era 6786/87; with Ghena Dimitrova, Nicola Martinucci, Cecilia Gasdia, and Roberto Scandiuzzi; Orchestra e Coro del Teatro Comunale dell' Opera di Genova; conducted by Daniel Oren.

Another interesting disc (actually two CDs remastered from 78-rpm original recordings) is made up of operatic excerpts, not necessarily performed at Teatro Carlo Felice, but sung by artists who have at one time or another appeared at the theater.

Un secolo di voci al Teatro Carlo Felice di Genova [A Century of Voices at Teatro Carlo Felice of Genoa]. Nuova Era HR 4408/09.

Teatro alla Scala
MILAN

Though opera houses look imposing—structures of marble and stone, wood and stucco—there is a spirit within each house that is the heritage of the artists who have trod its boards, the conductors who have raised their batons, the composers who have pored over page after page of manuscript paper, putting down the thousands of notes whose sound, when brought to life, is the very essence of opera.

The spirit of Teatro alla Scala is nowhere better represented than in the story of Giuseppe Verdi and the rugged path he traveled from the gravest of heart-rending tragedies to the greatest triumphs the Italian world of opera has ever known. This tale begins in 1840, on a cold, dark, snowy night in Milan. The young composer paced the streets near the theater—with a commission for a comic opera in his pocket. Neither of the two operas he had so far written had enjoyed much success, and the last two years for him had been filled with great personal loss. First his infant daughter, Virginia, and then his infant son, Icilio, had died; within months, his wife followed their two children to the grave. Depressed and overwhelmed, the composer vowed never to write another note of music.

As he was leaving the Galleria—that wonderful glass-enclosed arcade that stretches from Piazza del Duomo to Piazza La Scala in front of the theater—the 28-year-old composer bumped into Bartolomeo Merelli, the director of Teatro alla Scala.

It was snowing hard, and he took my arm, [Giuseppe Verdi later wrote of this evening] and persuaded me to accompany him as far as his office at La Scala. On the way we chatted about this and that, and he told me he did not know where he was going to turn for a new opera; he had engaged [Otto] Nicolai who hadn't begun to work yet because he was unhappy with the libretto.

"Just imagine," cried Merelli, "here is a libretto by Solera, superb! magnificent! absolutely extraordinary! Tense, grandiose, dramatic situations, beautiful verses! Take it, just take it and read it over."

"What on earth shall I do with it? I am in no humor to read librettos."

"It won't kill you; read it, and then bring it back to me again." And he gives me the manuscript. It was written on large sheets in big letters, as was the custom in those days. I rolled it up and went away.

While walking home I was seized with a sort of vague anxiety, a profound sadness, an anguish that gripped my heart. I got to my room, and throwing the manuscript on the writing table, I stood for a moment motionless before it. The book, as I threw it down, opened; my eyes fell on the page and I read the line: "*Va, pensiero, sull'ali dorate.* [Go, thought, on golden wings.]"

I read on, and was touched by the stanzas inasmuch as they were almost a paraphrase of the Bible, the reading of which always delighted me.

I read one page, then another; then determined, as I was, to keep my promise not to write any more, I did violence to my feelings, shut up the book, and went to bed. But *Nabucco* was running furiously through my brain, and sleep would not come. I got up and read the libretto again—not once, but two or three times, so that in the morning I had it by heart. Yet my resolution was not shaken, and in the afternoon I went to the theater to return the manuscript to Merelli.

"Isn't it beautiful?" says he.

"Very beautiful."

"Well, set it to music."

So saying, he took the libretto, thrust it into my overcoat pocket, pushed me out of the room and locked the door in my face.

What was I to do? I went home with *Nabucco* in my pocket. One day a verse, the next day another; one time a note, another a phrase . . . and little by little the opera was written.[26]

Today the melody of that chorus, "Va, pensiero"—the nostalgic chorus of the Jews in *Nabucco* that laid the foundation of Verdi's fame and was struck up spontaneously by the crowd at Verdi's funeral—is probably the best-known melody in all of Italy. School students, soccer fans, Italians of every ilk and type, can not only sing "Va, pensiero," they can sing it in the four-part harmony in which Verdi composed it.

And though Teatro alla Scala may abide by their rule and custom of no encores—"Va, pensiero" is the exception. Every production of *Nabucco* at La Scala within recorded memory has had this famous chorus applauded and greeted with cries of "bis" and "encore" until it is repeated.

As for the 28-year-old composer, he went on to a lifetime of composition as all opera fans know, introducing for the first time at Teatro alla Scala such works as *I lombardi* (1843), *Giovanna d'Arco* (1845), *Simon Boccanegra* (1881), and *Don Carlo* (1884), completing his last two—and just possibly his two finest, *Otello* and *Falstaff*—when he was 73 and 79. And what of La Scala? Verdi's name is everywhere inscribed, his masterpieces still the heart of its repertory.

The Story of Teatro alla Scala

Teatro alla Scala—"born of fire"[27] and still standing foursquare in spite of the ravages of the bombing raid in August 1943 that nearly destroyed the building—is unquestionably the most important opera house in Italy, and for much of its 200-year history has probably been the most famous opera house in the world.

The first "ancestor" of La Scala dates from 1594 when Juan Fernandez de Lelasco, governor of Milan, wanted—for the festivities that were to accompany his son's forthcoming marriage—"a space or stage in which to present spoken comedies." The *cortile* (courtyard) of the Ducal Palace (today Milan's city hall) was found to be ideal and was inaugurated as a theater with *La caduta di Fetonte*, the mythological story of the downfall of Phaeton, whom Zeus struck down for borrowing the chariot of the sun and riding it so close to the earth that he could have set the whole Earth on fire. The myth was enacted by dancers "to the accompaniment of music."[28]

Four years later, festivities were occasioned by Margherite of Austria's marriage to Philip III of Spain, with the courtyard space this time enhanced to serve as a site worthy of the name, the Court Theater. A vast, rectangular salon with 24 pillars was erected, with spaces for spectators both on the ground floor and in a specially constructed balcony. Permanently established in 1613, this theatrical space dedicated to music was thrice destroyed by fire, built, as it was, essentially of wood and illuminated during performances by candles and flaming torches. Each time it was rebuilt in a more grandiose and elegant manner. After all, fires were the order of the day, and theaters the most likely things to burn. Thus—as with singers who, when in bad voice, are replaced by others—theaters, when burned, were succeeded by a new structure.

Following the second fire there was a debate as to whether or not the reconstructed edifice should be called a *teatrino* (little theater) and devoted to comedies, a "Teatro della Commedia" as it were. Music, however, won out, and Gian Domenico Barbieri of Parma—a student of Bibiena, the most renowned theater architect of the day—was selected for the project. Work began on 26 April 1717 under the supervision of Francesco Corio-Visconti and was completed within a year. In this most elegant of all theaters, the long season stretched from November of one year to August of the next, with the *cartelloni* offering opera seria, opera buffa, bal-

Teatro Ducale in Milan in an engraving dating from around 1750. The theater opened in 1717 in the palace of the Archduke of Milan; it burned to the ground on 26 February 1776. Author's collection.

87

let, acrobats, jugglers, and festival balls. The scenery was grandiose in design, the costumes gorgeous.

This was a period when the theater provided a full evening's pleasure. Patrons arrived an hour or so before curtain time to enjoy a coffee and a flavorful sorbet, a custom that gave rise to today's expression in Italian theaters—*parti da sorbetto*—for the commencement of the show. There were conversations and visits between patrons of various boxes, and games of *faraone* (literally "guinea hens") led to many a wealthy patron's downfall for the evening.

Such games and conversations were interrupted by the arias and dances on stage, with differing opinions of these, in turn, cause for still further conversation. (More than one singer "lectured" the noisy audience from the stage!) Conduct at Teatro Ducale and eventually at La Scala up to the 19th century was incredible. Such visitors as French magistrate and scholar Charles de Brosses were appalled at what they found. He noted,

> Not even in the market do they make so much noise! It's not enough that each one talks, greets his friends and screams when the singers appear on stage without listening to them, the people in the orchestra express their admiration for the music by beating their canes against the benches [military personnel and servants of the boxholders sat on moveable benches]; at this signal the spectators in the boxes then throw myriad printed sheets containing sonnets lauding the performers' virtuosity streaming down onto the stage.[29]

Teatro Ducale (which stood beside the site of today's Palazzo Reale, or Royal Palace) was, in spite of this nefarious conduct, already establishing a tradition of greatness. Mozart—but a lad of 14—presented his *Mitridate, re di Ponto* there on opening night (26 December) in 1770 and four years later, for the marriage of Ferdinand, archduke of Austria, to Beatrice d'Este, staged his *Ascanio in Alba*. By popular demand he returned for "opening night" the following year with *Lucio Silla*.

Less than a month later, during a run of Tommaso Traetta's *Merope*, the Ducale was destroyed by fire. The boxholders, who at that time actually owned the theater (an arrangement much like a condominium today), had just drawn up a new agreement, and the poor impresario watched helplessly as not only the theater but all his costumes and scenery were totally ruined.

Fortunately for the music-loving Milanese, an architect named Giuseppe Piermarini from Foligno appeared on the scene. He had not only designed the Palazzo Reale but also the Royal Villa in Monza and the house of Count Bigli on Via San'Antonio. Piermarini convinced Count Bigli to let him use one of his properties—a structure that had once been the kennel of Barbarò Visconti—as a temporary theater that was then named Teatro Interinale or Interim Theater.

While there were many suggestions as to where the new permanent theater should be located, attention focused on an old church situated at the beginning of a street named Contrada del Giardino (known today as Via Manzoni), the most important residential thoroughfare in the Milan of that day, the site of palaces of important families such as the Trivulzos and Borromeos. The church itself was dilapidated and in serious need of repair. The site of this church of Santa Maria alla Scala (named after its founder, Beatrice della Scala of Verona) seemed to be the spot.

The large piazza one finds today in front of Teatro alla Scala did not exist at that time. Rather the street (where the streetcar stop is today) was lined with houses, so that Piermarini designed a facade for the theater that was meant to be viewed from across the street, not from across a great open square.

(Halfway through the 19th century the houses were pulled down, thus opening the huge piazza we find today, a square backed by the old Marino palace, once the property of a wealthy merchant from Genoa. That palace now belongs to the city and is used for municipal offices; a decision was made by the city after the piazza was opened up to redo the back of this palace—which faces Teatro alla Scala—so that it looks identical to the front, facing Piazza San Fedele.)

Appropriately for a theater arising phoenix-like out of the ashes of a fire, a bas-relief for the front gable of Teatro alla Scala was designed by Giocondo Albertalli that depicts Phaeton—the offspring of the Sun and Merope—madly driving his father's chariot of fire across the sky. (This same mythological legend had been depicted on the ceiling of the ducal theater.)

Several columns from the crypt of the church of Santa Maria alla Scala have been preserved and may be seen in the basement of Teatro alla Scala; its painting of the Madonna now hangs in the church in Piazza San Fedele.

Although proffered to Gluck, who declined because he was at

An etching of Teatro alla Scala dating from the late 18th century. Though the theater looks the same today, it now faces a piazza rather than a street. Author's collection.

work on *Iphigénie en Tauride* and *Echo et Narcisse*, the commission for the new theater's inaugural production went to Antonio Salieri, Kapellmeister of the court in Vienna (Milan was under Austrian rule at the time). The work *Europa riconosciuta* made its first appearance on 3 August 1778. It was a festive piece made up of 38 vignettes, including a tempest at sea, an earthquake, battles, cavalcades, and the like, that demonstrated the mechanical marvels of the new stage.

Teatro alla Scala became almost immediately one of the marvels of the music world, seating some 2500 (in a city that could count only 130,000 inhabitants) and with orchestra space that could accommodate 70 players, an extremely large area for that day. This spot was on a level with the orchestra (stalls/parterre), for the pit at La Scala was not to be built until 1906 at the request of Arturo Toscanini, who had been inspired by Wagner's "mystical gulf." The sets for Salieri's *Europa riconosciuta* were created by the Galiari brothers, who were among the most celebrated artists of the day.

EUROPA RICONOSCIUTA

DRAMMA PER MUSICA

DA RAPPRESENTARSI

NEL NUOVO REGIO DUCAL TEATRO
DI MILANO

Nella folenne occafione del fuo primo aprimento
nel mefe d' Agofto dell' anno 1778.

DEDICATO

Alle LL. AA. RR.

IL SERENISSIMO ARCIDUCA

FERDINANDO

Principe Reale d'Ungheria, e Boemia, Arciduca d'Auftria,
Duca di Borgogna, e di Lorena ec., Cefareo Reale
Luogo Tenente, Governatore, e Capitano
Generale nella Lombardia Auftriaca,

E LA

SERENISSIMA ARCIDUCHESSA

MARIA RICCIARDA
BEATRICE D'ESTE

PRINCIPESSA DI MODENA.

IN MILANO,

Appreffo Gio. Batifta Bianchi Regio Stampatore
Colla Permiffione .

The libretto printed for opening night, 3 August 1778, at Teatro alla Scala. As was the custom of the time, the composer's name (Antonio Salieri) does not appear on the cover. Courtesy Istituto storico germanico, sezione storia della musica, Rome.

Count Pietro Verri—who shared a box with the Marchese Cesare Beccaria—described his impressions in a letter written to his brother two days later.

The music and the voices have marvelous resonance since the orchestra, the boxes and many other elements of the theater are made of wood; the rest of it is made up of masonry—

the walls, the passage-ways, dressing rooms and boxes—which gives one a tranquil feeling after the fires [of the earlier theaters].

The orchestra had 30 violins, 13 bowed basses [*basso da arco*], two bassoons, eight violas, four trumpets, four horns, six oboes, two flutes, timpani, harpsichord; in all, more than 70 players.[30]

Because Teatro alla Scala—like its predecessor, Teatro Ducale—was at this time a private theater, the boxes were the property of their respective subscribers/owners, with each boxholder's family coat of arms prominently displayed on the front of the box. And, as can still be noticed today, each box was decorated in an individual and slightly different manner. Boxes also had large anterooms where servants could prepare a hot meal for those gathered in the boxes. This "kitchen" had a small window from which leftovers could be tossed out, a practice provoking storms of protest from the unfortunate pedestrians below who were excluded from the elegant ritual of the theater, so the police finally ordered grates placed over each such window.

Altogether the theater has four tiers of boxes, numbering 18 on each side of the royal box, with one more box in the fourth tier, which is uninterrupted. At first there were five tiers of boxes and a gallery, but at the end of the 18th century the fifth tier was turned into the first gallery in order to accommodate more patrons. The orchestra—which, as previously mentioned, contained movable benches—waited for almost a century to have fixed chairs installed.

The royal box was reserved for the viceroy. In 1799 work to demolish it began on orders from the directorate of the republic of Milan, but on 29 April the Austrians returned to Milan, and with them the old order. The royal box remains.

Unfortunately, today the original design by Piermarini is only represented in the better part of the facade and in a small part of the interior, including the wonderful sweeping curve of the boxes. From 22 to 26 December 1830, the theater was closed for renovations. The smoke from the thousands of candles that had burned over the years had completely blackened all the decorations, which were then repainted by the famous scenographer Alessandro Sanquina. His restoration can still be seen today, although not in the right side and ceiling of the theater, which were reconstructed after the bombings of August 1943.

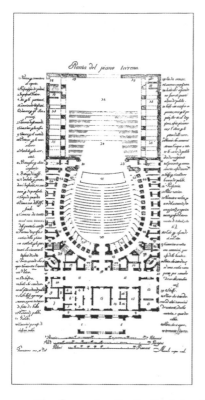 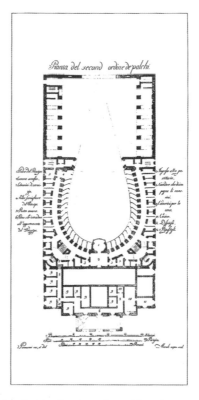

The floor plan for La Scala's *platea* (orchestra/parterre) and for the second *ordine* (row) of boxes. Chairs were arranged freely in the orchestra and standing room until 1891, when the orchestra was fitted with rows of fixed chairs, 772 seats in all. The original plan called for three tiers of 36 boxes each; two tiers of 39 boxes each; and, at the very top, a balcony. Courtesy Istituto storico germanico, sezione storia della musica, Rome.

In 1881 the Edison Electric Company was founded, and two years later the lighting system at La Scala, which had first used candles and then illuminating gas, was transformed with electric lighting.

The original foyer no longer exists. The one on the upper level was rebuilt in 1933, and the larger, more elegant lounge that opened off the main auditorium was destroyed in 1955 in order to enlarge the theater.

The stage over the years became a kind of proving ground for new technology. Conceived with the idea of scenes painted on canvas curtains that could be lifted and lowered between acts, the stage area is very narrow. Because the theater is today surrounded on all sides by streets, there is no possibility of widening that stage area. Nicola Benois and the engineer Luigi Lorenzo Sacchi divided the stage floor into panels with elevators, forming independent planes that can be raised and lowered to create a great variety of three-dimensional designs.

Teatro alla Scala's fame as a lyric theater really began in 1788 when a regular *cartellone* was instituted. Mozart's music filled the then-new house for the first time on 19 September 1807 with *Così fan tutte*, and Gioachino Rossini, barely 20 years of age, presented his *La pietra del paragone* on 26 September 1812. The public was so enthusiastic about the work that it had to be repeated no less than 53 times, including a command performance for the viceroy of Italy.

The house's *primas* began with Saverio Mercadante's *Elisa e Claudio* in 1821, which was a great hit; it was followed by his *Il giuramento* in 1837. Gaetano Donizetti had less success with his early efforts. *Chiara e Serafina, ossia I pirati* was a fiasco in October 1822; his reputation hardly improved with his next works for La Scala: *Lucrezia Borgia*, *Gianni di Parigi*, and *Maria Padilla*.

Vincenzo Bellini had his introduction to La Scala in 1831 with *Norma*, an opera given 34 times altogether, although its reception on opening night was rather cold. Its cast included Giuditta Pasta, Giulia Grisi, and Domenico Donzelli.

From 1830 to 1840 La Scala became the most important theater in the world. It presented more than 40 *primas*, which earned for this period the sobriquet the "Golden Era." On the evening of 17 November 1839, La Scala produced the first performance of an opera by the 26-year-old Giuseppe Verdi, whose name was to become synonymous with opera: *Oberto, conte di San Bonifacio*. A year later La Scala produced his opera buffa, *Il finto Stanislao, ossia Un giorno di regno*, but it was really on 9 March 1842 that Verdi truly triumphed at Milan's Teatro alla Scala with his *Nabucco*.

The story of La Scala is actually many stories: that of a building, of politics, of singers, of composers, of bel canto and romanticism and *verismo*. It is the story of new compositions: Arrigo Boito's *Mefistofele* in 1868, Amilcare Ponchielli's *La Gioconda* in 1876, and Alfredo Catalani's *La Wally* in 1892. Not many years later, other creators entered the La Scala scene: Giacomo Puccini, Pietro Mascagni, Umberto Giordano, Francesco Cilea, Franco Alfano, Ildebrando Pizzetti, Ottorino Respighi, and Riccardo Zandonai. And we must not forget the "foreigners" either: the warm reception given Gounod's *Faust*, the boos and catcalls against the *Lohengrin* of Wagner, a composer who finally succeeded at La Scala with *Die Meistersinger* in 1889.

Jules Massenet was immediately successful with his *Hérodiade* in 1882, as were the works of Bizet, Thomas, Tchaikovsky, and Richard Strauss. (Any good history of La Scala will also relate the storm of protest that was aroused when Toscanini proposed the world premiere of the latter's *Salome* for La Scala.)

It was not until the season of 1858 that announcements started to carry the names of the music directors. Each was first titled a *maestro concertatore* (the term we use today for concertmaster), for they either directed the music from the harpsichord, or later as principal violinists from their first chair desks. During Verdi's time, the conductors began to stand and conduct with their hands and arms and even with a baton. Franco Faccio was the first European to conduct *Aida* (in 1872) and *Otello* (the world premiere in 1887). Arturo Toscanini's monumental contributions to La Scala were followed by such illustrious conductors as Edoardo Vitale, Tullio Serafin, Gino Marinuzzi, Antonio Guarnieri, and Victor De Sabata. These maestros were succeeded by Gianandrea Gavazzeni, Antonio Votto, Herbert von Karajan, Leonard Bernstein, Wolfgang Sawallisch, and later by Claudio Abbado, Carlos Kleiber, and Riccardo Muti.

Along with these names go those of the great vocal artists: Giuseppina Grassini, Andrea Nozzari, Henriette Meric-Lalande, Carolina Ungher, Maria Malibran, and Giuseppina Strepponi (who was to become Verdi's second wife). The list would also include Teresa Stolz, the Viennese Maria Waldmann, Adelina Patti, and Francesco Tamagno; Mattia Battistini, the Wagnerian Giuseppe Borgatti, Enrico Caruso, and Chaliapin; and Toti Dal Monte, Lina Pagliughi, Ebe Stignani, Beniamino Gigli, Tito Schipa, and Aureliano Pertile. They were followed by Giulietta Simionato, Maria Callas, Ettore Bastianini, Renata Tebaldi, Mario Del Monaco, Giuseppe Di Stefano, Franco Corelli, Montserrat Caballé, Joan Sutherland, Placido Domingo, and many others.

It was with Toscanini that Wagner entered the repertory at La Scala, with the maestro's suggesting "pairings": *Die Meistersinger* and *Falstaff* (1898–99), *Siegfried* and *Otello* (1899–1900), for example. Toscanini also instigated other policies and customs: a better musical "grooming" of the chorus, a punctual downbeat for the start of a performance, and no encores. He was able to implement these reforms—most of which still remain in effect—but the theater declined to renew his contract after his first three-year period.

Toscanini, however, returned in 1907, and with his return the quality of playing in the orchestra improved tremendously according to critics of the time. He then directed three novelties: Claude Debussy's *Pelléas et Mélisande*, Gustave Charpentier's *Louise*, and, at last, Richard Strauss's *Salome*. It was in this period of time (1918–20) that Teatro alla Scala became a public institution, an *ente autonomo* (the first such public corporation in Italy), largely through the efforts of Toscanini who was assisted in this endeavor by Emilio Caldara and Senator Albertini.

Many years later there was a musical/political battle at La Scala between Arturo Toscanini and Il Duce, Benito Mussolini, with the latter demanding that the official national anthem, "Marcia Reale," and the Fascist hymn, "Giovinezza," be played before every performance. Fresh from his experience described in the section on Teatro Comunale di Bologna, Toscanini refused and did not return to La Scala until that triumphant concert marking the reopening of the theater after the war.

Although Teatro alla Scala was partially destroyed during the bombing of August 1943, the Milanese—desperately short of food and housing, and in grave financial straits because of the war—rebuilt the house in record time. La Scala reopened on 11 May 1946, with a gala concert conducted by Arturo Toscanini. Five thousand people stood in the piazza in front of the theater to hear it over loudspeakers.

Following the war La Scala did not abandon its commitment to contemporary operas and soon scheduled works by the "new" generation: Petrassi, Pizzetti, Honegger, Ghedini, Britten, Berg, Prokofiev, Bartók, Dallapiccola, and Stravinsky. In 1951 opening nights were changed from the beginning of Carnival (26 December) to the feast day of St. Ambrose, patron saint of Milan, 7 December. One of the startling events of contemporary opera was the evening of 15 March 1981, when for the first time the music of Karlheinz Stockhausen appeared on the *cartellone*: *Donnerstag aus Licht*—a spectacle of music both live and electronic lasting some five hours that was greeted simultaneously with boos and applause. The *prima* of his second opera in this *Licht* series—*Samstag aus Licht*—also a Teatro alla Scala production, was presented in Milan's Palazzo dello Sport on 25 May 1984.

In 1983 La Scala's seating capacity was reduced by the police in the interest of safety, so that today it accommodates precisely 2015 spectators: 500 in the balconies, 800 in the boxes, 676 in the orchestra (stalls/parterre), and 39 in standing room.

There are a number of workshops within the theater itself: dressmaking, shoemaking, woodworking, and prop and wig design, but the main work of set construction takes place in the La Scala studios on Via Baldinucci alla Bovisa. Similarly, rehearsals occur at the old movie theater–turned–rehearsal hall, the Sala Abanella.

There are also schools within the La Scala "family." The School of Dance was founded in 1813, and after World War II, the Center for the Perfection of Operatic Artists (usually translated more idiomatically as "Master Classes for Vocal Artists") was established. One of the most important innovations, La Scala per i bambini (La Scala for Children), was implemented in 1987; for details see Chapter 7.

La Scala's fame lives on in the works of new composers and in the music-making of new voices. Recent seasons have included such *primas* as Franco Mannino's *Il principe felice* and Flavio Testi's *Riccardo III* in 1987; and Lorenzo Ferrero's "opera for marionettes" *Le bleu-blanc-rouge et le noir*, Hans Werner Henze's "musical fable" *Pollicino*, Azio Corghi's *Blimunda*, and Henze's *Lo sdegno del mare* in 1990. In 1992 La Scala introduced minimalist Salvatore Sciarrino's "electronic" work, *Perseo e Andromeda*.

The newer voices include those of Gary Lakes, Warren Ellsworth, Giuseppe Sabbatini, Luca Canonici, Luciana Serra, Sumi Jo, Bruce Ford, Gösta Winbergh, Rockwell Blake, Chris Merritt, Gregory Kunde, Vinson Cole, Tiziana Fabbricini, Giusy Devinu, Mariella Devia, Ruth Ziesack, Cecilia Bartoli, and Gloria Banditelli among a host of others.

The Season at La Scala

The opera season always opens on the evening of 7 December; it extends until mid-July and consists of opera, concerts, and ballet, altogether about 150 nights of music-making, of which approximately 80 are devoted to opera.

La Scala follows the *stagione* system (one opera at a time in multiple performances), though there is almost always a brief overlapping between the opera disappearing from the *cartellone* and the opening one. Thus, with careful planning, the short-term visitor to Milan may take in two different operas during a brief stay. In addition, of course, there are recitals by the major vocal artists of the world.

The 1991–92 season, for example, began on 7 December with Wagner's *Parsifal*, conducted by La Scala's music director, Riccardo Muti. The opening-night cast included Placido Domingo, Wolfgang Brendel, Waltraud Meier, Robert Lloyd, Hartmut Welker, and Kurt Rydl. During the run of nine performances, the title role alternated between Domingo, Gary Lakes, and Warren Ellsworth.

Then followed nine performances of Auber's *Fra Diavolo* with Giuseppe Sabbatini/Luca Canonici and Luciana Serra/Sumi Jo. Eight performances of Richard Strauss's *Arabella*—a production that came from the Bavarian State Opera in Munich—were conducted by Wolfgang Sawallisch. Eleven performances of Puccini's *Manon Lescaut* with Lorin Maazel on the podium alternating with Armando Gatto followed. The seven performances of Gluck's *Iphigénie en Tauride* were conducted by Riccardo Muti and Eric Hull, with the principal roles sung by Carol Vaness/Sylvie Brunet, Thomas Allen, and Gösta Winbergh/Vinson Cole. Then followed 8 performances of *La traviata*, with Muti and Gatto alternating again and with Tiziana Fabbricini and Giusy Devinu sharing the honors as Violetta Valery. *Lucia di Lammermoor* was a Pier'Alli production conducted by Gianandrea Gavazzeni, who alternated with Armando Gatto on the podium; Mariella Devia, Tiziana Fabbricini, and Denia Mazzola alternated in the 13 performances of it. Myung-Whun Chung conducted all six performances of Shostakovich's *Lady Macbeth of Minsk*, a coproduction with the Bastille Opéra of Paris, and Riccardo Muti and Alberto Zedda shared the podium for the seven performances of Rossini's *La donna del lago*, a Werner Herzog production with Rockwell Blake/Bruce Ford, Chris Merritt/Gregory Kunde, June Anderson/Cecilia Gasdia, and Martine Dupuy/Jennifer Larmore. The season closed with five performances of *Cristoforo Colombo*, a ballet to music of Gaetano Donizetti featuring Carla Fracci, to honor the 500th anniversary of Columbus's discoveries in the New World.

In addition to the season's operas, La Scala offered two *Manifestazioni straordinarie*: two performances of Mozart's *Die Zauberflöte* conducted by Sir Georg Solti and a single performance of Mozart's *Requiem* conducted by Riccardo Muti to mark the occasion of the Mozart bicentennial. Then, on 29 February 1992—the 200th anniversary of the birth of Rossini—Riccardo Muti conducted that composer's *Stabat Mater*. Later in the season there was a special concert conducted by Lorin Maazel in memory of Victor De Sabata.

Teatro alla Scala—in addition to operas, ballets, and concerts (the latter conducted by Krzysztof Penderecki, Luciano Berio, Carlo Maria Giulini, Georges Prêtre, and other distinguished maestros)—offered some distinguished artists in recital: Renato Bruson, Editha Gruberova, Bernd Weikl, José van Dam, Felicity Lott and Ann Murray (a joint recital), Peter Schreier, Cheryl Studer, and Kathleen Battle.

Practical Matters

Tickets for performances at Teatro alla Scala are not only very expensive but also very difficult to come by since the house is Italy's most famous, most prestigious, and most frequented. Single tickets purchased at the box office are available 15 days before an opera opens and may be purchased at the box office located on Via Filodrammatici, on the left side of the theater, where the old Piccolo Scala was located. This box office is now completely computerized.

Ticket orders may be placed by registered mail with a return receipt card or by fax. A patron may purchase a maximum of two seats at a time. The order must include the following: 1) a photocopy of a bank draft (in Italian lire) marked "account payee only" made payable to Ente Autonomo Teatro alla Scala Ufficio Biglietteria for the price of the requested seats plus a 10 percent booking fee (the actual bank draft is to be presented at the ticket office when you collect your tickets); 2) the name of one opera only, indicating a maximum of three dates, listed in order of preference; 3) a precise indication of desired seats (orchestra, box, etc.) as well as the type and number of the seats according to the chart accompanying the La Scala season booklet; and 4) a contact telephone number and address.

This information should be sent via fax to 02/88.79.297; seat allocation will be based on the date of the fax. A reservation may also be made by mail, addressing your request to the Biglietteria, Teatro alla Scala, Via Filodrammatici 2, Milan. According to Teatro alla Scala,

Seat allocation will be determined on the basis of the date of the post mark on the envelope, provided that the booking application arrives no more than three months and no less than one month prior to the performance and that there are still seats allocated for postal bookings available for that performance (these amount to 20 percent of the total seats for subscription performances and 30 percent in the case of non-subscription performances). The La Scala management will accept no responsibility for the incorrect or late delivery of booking applications due to negligence, or any cause whatsoever, attributed to postal services.

The La Scala ticket office will inform applicants of the seats allocated and how the tickets may be collected. If reserved tickets are not collected within two hours of the scheduled starting time of the performance, the booking "shall be canceled" according to the management.

I would remind visitors that the chairs in each box are not numbered. It is a first-come, first-served affair, although it is customary to reserve an entire box and then wrangle with one's friends over who gets which seat. Would-be box guests at La Scala should know that some of the box seats have a limited view of the stage. Official policy states: "The management regrets that it cannot give refunds to patrons who, having reserved a single seat in a box, find themselves in a position with limited or no view of the stage."

For those who wish to purchase tickets after their arrival in Milan, the *biglietteria* is open every day from noon to 7:00 P.M., excluding the following Italian national holidays: 1 November, 8 December, 25 and 26 December, 1 and 6 January, Easter Sunday and Monday, and 1 May. On days when evening performances are scheduled, the ticket office remains open until 8:15 P.M. or until 15 minutes after the start of the performance.

Tickets for standing room, at approximately $10 each, go on sale 45 minutes before the scheduled starting time at the Piazza della Scala ticket office, the "Museo" entrance (on the left side of the theater).

For those with physical disabilities, La Scala's management reserves an area in the orchestra for use by those confined to wheelchairs, as well as any accompanying persons. The price for such tickets is the same as a numbered seat in the second gallery.

It is obligatory to leave all umbrellas, hats, bags, cameras, and any video recording equipment in the cloakroom. The management also requests that gentlemen check overcoats and top coats. This service is free of charge. The management "advises that formal dress is recommended on opening nights. Gentlemen are kindly requested to wear a tie and jacket for all performances."

Brochures for and announcements of Teatro alla Scala performances can be mailed to your home for a Lit. 10.000 fee. Payments must be made via bank draft marked "account payee only" in Italian lire made payable to Ente Autonomo Teatro alla Scala, and addressed to Ufficio Spedizioni Teatro alla Scala, Via Filodrammatici 2, Milan. This fee also includes the La Scala season calendar.

Reservations may be made directly from the United States, Canada, and Great Britain, though the time frame imposed by the theater makes it rather impractical except in special cases. According to the bulletin published by La Scala,

> Foreign citizens may reserve tickets for all non-subscription performances . . . throughout the opera and ballet season directly from their country of residence either at any of the following offices of the Compagnia Italiana Turismo (CIT) or at all CIT travel agencies abroad. All foreign reservations must be made no more than 10 days prior to a specific performance.

> Great Britain—CIT England Ltd.
> London—50/51 Conduit Street, tel. 434.3844
> Croydon—Marco Polo House, 3–5 Lansdowne Road,
> tel. 686.0677

> U.S.A.—CIT Travel Service Inc.
> New York—666 Fifth Avenue, tel. (212) 396-1987
> Chicago—333 North Michigan Ave., tel. (313) 332-5334
> Chicago-Bensenville—765 Route 83, Suite 105,
> tel. (708) 644-6651

> Canada—CIT Travel Service Inc.
> Montreal—2055 Peel St., Suite 102, tel. (514) 845-9101
> Toronto—111 Richmond St. West, tel. (416) 364-4724

For the Armchair Fan

There is an extremely interesting, well-illustrated book in English on the history of Milan's Teatro alla Scala.

Arruga, Lorenzo. 1976. *La Scala*. Trans. Raymond Rosenthal. New York: Praeger Publishers.

Two new books, both in Italian, chronicle the history of Teatro alla Scala and its artists. The first comes with six CDs; the second is complemented by 800 photographs.

Celletti, Rodolfo, and Marco Contini. 1992. *Grandi Voci alla Scala: Da Tamagno alla Callas*. 2 vols. Milan: Teatro alla Scala.

Aniasi, Aldo, et al. 1992. *La Scala, 1967–91: La cronologia completa degli spettacoli degli ultimi 25 anni con tutti gli interpreti*. 2 vols. Milan: Teatro alla Scala.

While there are countless recordings of opera on LPs, cassette tapes, and CDs of La Scala productions, almost all were actually recorded at Sala Abanella, the old movie theater on the outskirts of town used by La Scala as a rehearsal hall. Sony was the first company to actually record in Teatro alla Scala. The following performances were recorded live during their respective runs.

Cherubini, Luigi. *Lodoïska*. Sony Classical RSCD 2450 S2K 47290; with Mariella Devia, Bernard Lombardo, Thomas Moser, Alessandro Corbelli, William Shimell, and Mario Luperi; Orchestra e Coro del Teatro alla Scala; conducted by Riccardo Muti. Recorded live in February 1991.

Pergolesi, Giovanni Battista. *Lo frate 'nnamorato*. Ricordi/EMI CDS 754240-2; with Nicoletta Curiel, Amelia Felle, Nuccia Focile, Alessandro Corbelli, Bruno Di Simone, Bernadette Manca di Nissa, Elizabeth Norberg-Schulz, Luciana d'Intino, and Ezo Di Cesare; Orchestra del Teatro alla Scala; conducted by Riccardo Muti. Recorded live in December 1989.

There are recordings made under different circumstances that give an aural view of the La Scala of an earlier generation.

Verdi, Giuseppe. *Un ballo in maschera*. EMI 7 47498 8; with Maria Callas, Giuseppe Di Stefano, Tito Gobbi, and Fedora Barbieri; Orchestra e Coro del Teatro alla Scala; conducted by Antonio Votto. Originally recorded in 1957 (location not specified, but probably Sala Abanella).

Puccini, Giacomo. *Tosca*. GDS 2CD 101; with Giuseppe Di Stefano, Renata Tebaldi, Tito Gobbi; Orchestra e Coro del

Teatro alla Scala; conducted by Gianandrea Gavazzeni. Recorded live on stage, 12 December 1959.

Mascagni, Pietro. *Cavalleria rusticana/L'amico Fritz*. Fonit Cetra DOC 58 (LP only); with Giulietta Simionato, Franco Corelli [Cavalleria], Mirella Freni, Gianni Raimondi, and Rolando Panerai [*L'amico Fritz*]; Orchestra e Coro del Teatro alla Scala; conducted by Gianandrea Gavazzeni. Recorded live on 7 December 1963; the LP is probably derived from the tape made for the opening night broadcast over RAI radio.

Teatro San Carlo
NAPLES

Once upon a time there was a king named Carlo. The year was 1737, and the kingdom of Spain and Naples had been united for four years under the rule of his father who had usurped the Neapolitan throne. Carlo was small in stature, awkward in movement, and inelegant in gesture. He had a long, thin nose and a horrible set of ugly teeth that could be seen whenever he smiled or laughed (which was not too often!). Though he was the king, he hated the pomp and ceremony of the royal court. Not too learned, and scarcely a lover of art, he seemed the least likely to instigate a major Neapolitan renaissance. But that is the paradox of our story. By carefully choosing his councilors and advisors—particularly the outstanding, ever-present, and severely feared Bernardo Tonucci —our king was able to bring about reforms that brought his kingdom into the modern age. (Good advice and accident together accomplish some remarkable feats!)

When Carlo ordered that a royal hunting lodge be built, the preparations for the foundation accidentally uncovered Herculaneum and eventually Pompeii. In his quest for display pieces for his Neapolitan palace, Carlo established one of the most famous porcelain factories in the world at Capodimonte. And at Caserta, he built one of the largest and most glorious royal palaces in all of Europe. But most important to our story was his desire for a regal theater to be part of the royal palace in Naples, one that would be much larger and more beautiful than the Court Theater, already a part of the Palazzo Reale.

Though no lover of opera, Carlo realized that it was an essential part of Neapolitan life. Because Teatro San Bartolomeo, Naples's

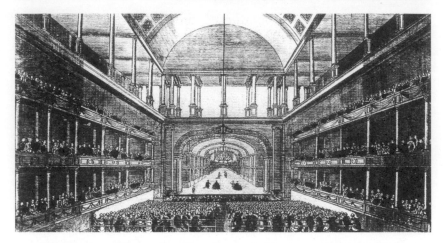

The interior of Teatro San Bartolomeo in Naples as seen in an 18th-century engraving. Courtesy L'Ufficio Stampa, Teatro S. Carlo di Napoli.

principal theater, had become rather dilapidated under Austrian rule, and because it was located inconveniently on a narrow street, Carlo decided to have it pulled down. On the initiative of Prince Charles of Bourbon, king of the Two Sicilies and Naples, and later to be King Carlos III of Spain—the oldest still-functioning opera house in the world was born. Built in 270 days, the theater is physically part of the Palazzo Reale, with the stage area attached by corridors to the palace itself.

The doors of this magnificent theater opened for the first time on 4 November—the saint's (Carlo's) name day—in the year 1737, some 41 years before Teatro alla Scala began, some 51 years before Venice's Teatro La Fenice first saw the light of day. The royal curtain parted on a mythical melodrama by Pietro Metastasio—*Achille in Sciro*, set to music by Domenico Sarro. (It was truly a royal theater. Only the king could lead the applause or request an encore.)

The decoration of Real Teatro di San Carlo (Royal Theater of San Carlo) was exquisite, sporting, as it did, the king's coat of arms joined together with the shield of the Bourbons—three silver lilies in a field of azure blue—enhanced with 21 other heraldic emblems and symbols associated with the royal family. To Carlo, whose name has graced the theater since its opening, not only the Neapolitans, but the entire lyrical world owes a debt of gratitude.

The day after the Carlo opened, the *Gazzetta di Napoli* dedicated the major part of the chronicle to this event. It read in part:

We have seen an incredible number of people at the new theater, the boxes filled with ladies who were richly gowned and wearing precious jewels. The men, the *cavaliers*, were likewise dressed for a sumptuous gala. Altogether it was a joyous occasion, the evening full of geniality and high spirits.[31]

The munificence of the new Bourbon monarch was everywhere in evidence. He was, according to the paper, "absolutely marvelous [*meravigliosamente*] in establishing this theater with its ample size and perfect architecture, not only the finest to be found in Italy, but in all of Europe. And, in its beauty and balance, it recalls the power and glory of the structures of ancient Rome."[32]

In his treatise of 1776 describing the theater, Francesco Milizia wrote:

The San Carlo is horseshoe-shaped, like a semi-circle whose extremities are prolongated in line with each other and extend to the stage. There are six tiers of boxes with a superb Royal Box in the middle of the second tier. The construction is all of stone; the scale is magnificent, the access passages spacious as are the corridors.[33]

In his textbook on architecture written in 1782, Pierre Patte wrote:

This edifice is greatly superior to all other modern theaters in Italy. The entrance rises three steps from the piazza and divides the patrons into two columns, the guests then passing through a long vestibule which leads them to the orchestra or the corridors to the boxes. Its total size is 270 by 180 feet [82 by 54.5 meters], more or less. The orchestra [stalls/parterre]—or, in other words, the size of the *sala*—extends 66 feet [20 meters] and is almost as wide. It has the shape of a racket or bellows. It has six orders of boxes in perpendicular lines of which 70 belong to the principal families of Naples. The ceiling is concave and rises to a height of 66 feet [20 meters]. The proscenium opening of the stage is around 50 feet [15 meters] both in width and height. The stage itself is 114 feet [34.5 meters] deep, and at its back a room with a ramp has been designed especially for use by horses, military processions, triumphal parades and the like.[34]

The nobility, which seemed to prefer the second tier of boxes (perhaps because the royal box was on that level), purchased them at a cost of 700 ducats (about $2000 in today's currency), and paid a yearly fee of between $500 and $600. Seats for a single performance in the orchestra (stalls/parterre) cost but 3 carlini (about $1), including admission to the theater. Smoking was permitted in the corridors, encores were encouraged (once indicated by His Royal Highness), and liveried attendants stood by to serve the needs of both patrons and artists. Pastries and sorbets were available in the vestibules, all for the delight of the audience. One visitor, in a letter, remarked on this "Neapolitan atmosphere": "At San Carlo you go mostly to see and be seen."[35]

"If you want good music," Jean Jacques Rousseau wrote in his Encyclopédie, "you have to go to Naples."[36]

Altogether the city not only provided composers for its own theater, but for the entire continent, from London to Lisbon and from Paris to St. Petersburg. When Alessandro Scarlatti settled in Naples in 1707, he established a dynasty of locally trained composers. Among them were Leonardo Vinci and Leonardo Leo, two of the earliest composers of comic operas in the Neapolitan dialect. Nicola Porpora, who eventually became Haydn's first teacher, also worked in Naples. Perhaps today's best-known composer from this era is Giovanni Battista Pergolesi, who, in addition to his comic operas, produced one of the finest *opere serie* of the early 18th century, *Olimpiade*. Other important composers of this post-Scarlatti Neapolitan group include two who were responsible for developing richer and more idiomatic orchestral accompaniments: Niccolò Jommelli and Tommaso Traetta. Three composers who excelled in comic opera (opera buffa) followed: Niccolò Piccinni, Giovanni Paisiello, and Pasquale Anfossi. The comic opera in Naples at the end of the century is best represented by Domenico Cimarosa, a prolific composer who left more than 65 operas to his credit.

Let it be said that this was an era with a voracious appetite for new operas. According to opera historian Donald Jay Grout, "A tabulation of 40 leading composers of that period shows nearly 2000 works, or an average of about 50 operas each."[37]

All this made Naples, along with Venice, the preeminent center of music. Joseph Jérôme Lalande, in his *Voyage d'un François en Italie* of 1769, noted:

Music is the special glory and triumph of the Neapolitans. It seems as if there the ear-drums are more taut, more in tune to harmony and more musical than elsewhere in Europe. The whole nation sings; gestures, timbre, rhythm of syllables, the very substance of everyday conversation—all breathe music and harmony. Thus Naples is the principal source of Italian music, of great composers and excellent operas; it is there that Corelli, Vinci, Rinaldo [di Capua], Jommelli, . . . Leo, Pergolesi, Galuppi, Perez, Terradeglias, and so many other famous composers have produced their masterpieces.[38]

Known for both opera buffa and opera seria, it was in this latter category that Naples and its theater made a major contribution. Opera seria was formal and complex, with elaborate display arias, its subject matter drawn from ancient history or classical mythology. Its carefully constructed librettos of high literary standard struck a balance between dramatic continuity and emotional expression through the coupling of recitative and aria. As the century progressed, vocal display gave way to exhibitionism, and it was against this abuse in particular that Gluck and Calzabigi instigated their operatic reforms in *Orfeo ed Euridice*.

Opera buffa, in turn, arose from the comic scenes and subplots of the late baroque era and out of the intermezzi played between acts of an opera seria, and it offered freshness and spontaneity in its frivolous subject matter, its everyday language in the colorful Neapolitan dialect, and its imaginative vocal and orchestral treatment. From humble beginnings the genre rose to eminence, culminating in Mozart's *Così fan tutte* toward the end of the century.

With the fire of 12 February 1816 that destroyed Teatro San Carlo, the first chapter of its story closed. By the time a rebuilt theater opened on 12 January 1817, only eleven months later, a new monarch, Ferdinando I, had ascended to the throne.

The new *sala* measured approximately 23 by 31 meters (76 by 102 feet), with 184 boxes rising in six tiers, plus, of course, the royal box. The acoustics of the theater were greatly improved, largely through the redesign of the stage area, which then measured 35 by 36.5 meters (116 by 121 feet). The stucco decorations were redone by Camillo Guerra and Gennaro Maldarelli, who attempted to duplicate the earlier designs. The concave ceiling was painted with a scene of Apollo being presented to Minerva as the greatest poet in the world. Other changes took place over the following years: the creation of a pit for the orchestra (suggested by Verdi), the installation of electric lighting in 1890, and a new foyer and additional artists' dressing rooms built in 1937.

Today Real Teatro San Carlo looks much as it did when Stendhal visited it on 17 January 1817, for its second inauguration: "There is nothing in all of Europe like Teatro San Carlo; all others pale in comparison. The eyes are dazzled, the soul enraptured."[39]

The theater reopened with *Il sogno di Partenope* by Giovanni Simone Mayr. Then followed the most momentous period for lyric opera in Naples with the appearance of three important figures: Domenico Barbaja, Isabella Colbran, and Gioachino Rossini.

Domenico Barbaja, who was to become the impresario not only at Naple's Teatro San Carlo, but eventually and simultaneously of opera houses in Venice and Vienna, was, according to Stendhal,

> by birth a Milanese, a sometime waiter in a coffee-house who, by gambling, and more especially by holding the bank at faro and by running a gaming-house, had amassed a fortune worth several millions. Signor Barbaja, who had received a thorough early grounding in business methods in Milanese commercial circles, among the host of French army-contractors who were making and losing fortunes every six months in the wake of the battalions, had, and still has, a good eye for the main chance.[40]

Barbaja's first real coup after he arrived in Naples was to engage the beautiful contralto Isabella Colbran, who captivated, in rapid succession, the demanding public, the king, and Rossini, whose first wife she became. She had black hair and sparkling dark eyes, a "Junoesque beauty" (she had come from Spain). A local critic said that "her voice is of exceptional amplitude and splendid timbre in both middle and low registers, and her agility in fioritura [florid and ornamented] passages is secure, clear and agile."[41]

She made her Neapolitan debut as Giulia in Spontini's *La vestale* in 1811, and later triumphed in Mayr's *Medea in Corinto*, and Spontini's *Fernand Cortez*. She also appeared many times in the Mozartian repertory: *Don Giovanni* and *Le nozze di Figaro*.

As for Rossini, he made his first appearance at Teatro San Carlo on 4 October 1815 with his *Elisabetta, regina d'Inghilterra*, which was followed by the world premiere of his comic *La gazzetta* in September of the following year, this in turn followed a little over two months later by *Otello, ossia Il moro di Venezia*. His *Armida* bowed in during the season of 1817, and *Mosè in Egitto* the following year (March 1818), a year that closed in December with his *Ricciardo e Zoraide*. During the year 1819, Rossini presented premieres at Teatro San Carlo of *Ermione*, the pasticcio *Eduardo e Cristina*, and *La donna del lago*. His last two operas for the San Carlo were *Maometto II* in 1820 and *Zelmira* in 1822, an astounding record for either a single composer or a single opera house.

As a talent scout (to use the modern expression), Barbaja was no less astute when it came to enlisting the services of Vincenzo Bellini, a composer who had graduated from the conservatory in Naples. Bellini made his operatic debut in Naples in 1823 with his first opera, *Adelson e Salvini*; then followed *Bianca e Fernando* a year later, the last of Bellini's works to have a *prima* at Teatro San Carlo, but far from the last Bellini work to be presented here.

Barbaja's next acquisition was Gaetano Donizetti, whose original creations for Teatro San Carlo were absolutely overwhelming: two operas in 1822; three in 1823; two in 1824; one in 1826; and two in 1827, including the frequently revived comedy, *Le convenienze ed inconvenienze teatrali* (sometimes played in America as *Viva la mamma*). There were three new operas for Naples in 1828 and three in 1829, two of the latter being the recently revived *Elisabetta al castello di Kenilworth* and *I pazzi per progetto*. The three new works for the San Carlo of 1830 included *Anna Bolena*. Then followed two new operas for Naples in 1831, two in 1832, and one each in 1834 and 1835, the latter being Donizetti's most famous creation, *Lucia di Lammermoor*. The year 1836 saw the birth of the comic works *Il campanello di notte* and *Betly*, as well as the dramatic *L'assedio di Calais*. Donizetti's last major work for Naples was *Roberto Devereux* in 1837.

Another composer whom Barbaja hired for Naples was Severio Mercadante. Barbaja also discovered Salvatore Cammarano, who wrote the librettos of *Lucia di Lammermoor* and *Roberto Devereux* for Donizetti and *Alzira*, *Luisa Miller*, and *Il trovatore* for Verdi, just to mention the most important of his creations for Teatro San Carlo.

Barbaja's death in 1841 marked a turning point in the history of the San Carlo. Verdi's association with Naples early in his career was very much an off-and-on affair, and to all intents and purposes ended when the composer left in 1853 with *Il trovatore* tucked under his arm for production elsewhere. Only the maestro's *Alzira* in 1845 and his *Luisa Miller* in 1849 were given their *prima*s at Teatro San Carlo.

After Italian unification, the San Carlo's prestige was eclipsed by that of the northern houses, so that even Naples's most illustrious native sons—Ruggero Leoncavallo and Enrico Caruso—had relatively little association with their home town's *tempio della lirica* (temple of opera).

Restored most recently in 1984, the theater was closed during the season of 1990 for the implementation of certain required safety features. Naples's 640-seat Teatro Mercadante (which had actually preceded Teatro San Carlo in construction) was used for the interim, a period which was necessarily devoted to smaller productions: Britten's *The Rape of Lucretia*, Fioravanti's *Le cantatrici villane*, and Mannino's *Le notte bianche*. Following its most recent restoration, Teatro San Carlo seats some 1450 patrons.

To this day Neapolitans are not only extremely proud of their opera house, they are true opera fans. Unfortunately because of the political turmoil in which Naples is always involved, the administration of Teatro San Carlo changes frequently, a situation that precludes intelligent long-range planning.

The Season at Teatro San Carlo

The season at Teatro San Carlo generally begins in mid-December and concludes between late May and mid-June. Generally the *cartellone* includes six operas, each presented five or six times. Like most Italian houses, the San Carlo follows the *stagione* system. The *cartellone* for the 1991–92 season is quite typical:

Rossini's *Elisabetta, regina d'Inghilterra*
with Anna Caterina Antonacci, Chris Merritt, and
Rockwell Blake; conducted by Alberto Zedda
(5 performances)

Verdi's *La forza del destino*
with Giuseppe Giacomini, Ghena Dimitrova, and
Piero Cappuccilli; conducted by Daniel Oren
(6 performances)

110

Donizetti's *Don Pasquale*
with Bruno Praticò, Eva Mei, and Luca Canonici;
conducted by Franco Petracchi
(6 performances)

Wagner's *Der fliegende Holländer*
with Michael Burt, Janis Martin, Robert Schunk,
Dieter Schweikart, and Herbert Lippert;
conducted by Zoltàn Pesko
(5 performances)

Puccini's *La Bohème*
with Maria Dragoni and Gösta Winbergh;
conducted by Gustav Kuhn
(7 performances)

Rossini's *Messa di Gloria*
conducted by Gustav Kuhn
(bicentennial celebration; 5 performances)

Cilea's *Adriana Lecouvreur*
with Raina Kabaivanska, Nunzio Todisco, and Dolora Zajick;
conducted by Daniel Oren
(6 performances)

Practical Matters

Information on the *cartellone* may be obtained from the Promocenter, Via Cappella Vecchia 11, I-80132 Naples; telephone 081/764.3900, 764.3976, or 764.4150. This office is open from 9:00 A.M. to noon daily, except Sundays.

Tickets—which are very expensive in Naples—may be purchased at the box office, Biglietteria del Teatro San Carlo, located at the front left of the main entrance to the theater, Via San Carlo 98/F, telephone 081/797.2331 or 797.2332. For information or reservations this office is open from 10:00 A.M. to 1:00 P.M. and from 4:30 to 6:30 P.M. daily, except Mondays and holidays.

Planning a visit to Teatro San Carlo is both frustrating and rewarding. It is frustrating in the sense that the season is poorly organized, and both the dates and titles of operas tend to change frequently at the last moment, without any previous or public notice. In spite of the Promocenter and *biglietteria*, it is extremely difficult to acquire essential information. Representatives never an-

111

swer letters, so either telephone (if you speak Italian) or go in person. (Even then, satisfaction is certainly not guaranteed.)

A visit can be rewarding because Teatro San Carlo is not only one of the most beautiful—and, for its size, the most intimate—opera houses in the world, but it has the finest acoustics I have encountered anywhere, surely the delight of every soloist who has performed there. The repertory at Teatro San Carlo is always interesting, the casting generally of the highest order, the productions good, and an evening spent at the theater a thorough delight.

For the Armchair Fan

There is a little booklet in Italian (16 pages altogether) available for sale on occasion at the house, though they never seem to know where to find copies when someone wants to buy one! It gives the bare facts in a somewhat engaging manner, and, as its centerpiece, provides an architect's cross section of the entire building. The second book—also in Italian—is quite the opposite, chock-full of information.

> Altavilla, Gianni. 1988. *Il Teatro di San Carlo: Duecentocinquanta anni di storia*. Naples: L'Ufficio Stampa e Relazioni Esterne del Teatro di San Carlo.
>
> Marinelli Roscioni, Carlo, ed. 1987. *Il Teatro San Carlo: La cronologia 1737–1987*. Naples: Casa Editrice Napoli.

Teatro San Carlo has not figured too prominently in recent years in the recording field. For those curious about the sound of productions in that theater, the albums listed below provide a fair idea. The original tapes were recorded for in-house reference purposes and never intended for commercial recordings, so (with caution) you might sample the following.

> Donizetti, Gaetano. *Lucia di Lammermoor*. BM/Butterfly Music BMCD 003; with Cristina Deutekom, Luciano Pavarotti, Domenico Trimarchi, and Silvano Pagliuca; Orchestra e Coro del Teatro San Carlo di Napoli; conducted by Carlo Franci. Recorded live on 2 May 1970.
>
> Verdi, Giuseppe. *Il trovatore*. Bongiovanni GAO 101/2; with Mario Filippeschi, Aldo Protti, Antonietta Stella, and Fedora Barbieri; Orchestra e Coro del Teatro San Carlo di Napoli; conducted by Franco Capuana. Recorded live on 7 December 1957.

2 Designed in 1583 by Andrea Palladio, Teatro Olimpico in Vicenza is one of the most important historical theaters in Italy. This is the view patrons originally had upon entering the theater. Courtesy dell'Assessorato alla Cultura del Comune di Vicenza.

3 The canal entrance to Teatro La Fenice in Venice, for patrons arriving by gondola. Photograph by the author.

1 Pesaro's Teatro Rossini. The house curtain *delle muse* (of the muses) represents the fountain of Hippocrene, which springs forth on the summit of Mount Helicon in Greece, a spot sacred to the muses. Photograph by Amati Bacciardi, courtesy Rossini Opera Festival.

4 The *sala* of La Fenice. Altogether this intimate and elegant theater holds 1000 patrons. Photograph by G. Bonannini, courtesy Teatro La Fenice di Venezia.

5 The ornate and delicate details on the front of the boxes at Teatro La Fenice in Venice. Photograph by Arici and Smith, courtesy Teatro La Fenice di Venezia.

6 Closing concerts of the Festival dei Due Mondi are held in the piazza in front of the historic cathedral of Spoleto. Courtesy Festival dei Due Mondi.

7 The original 1740 facade of Turin's Teatro Regio, photographed during the season of 1991. This facade, in keeping with the design of the adjacent Royal Palace, masks an ultramodern opera house. Courtesy Teatro Regio di Torino.

8 The *sala* of Turin's Teatro Regio, which seats 1756 patrons. There is only one tier of boxes, grouped around the elliptical edge of the house. Courtesy Teatro Regio di Torino.

9 The final scene of Teatro Regio's production of Luigi Dallapiccola's *Ulisse* in Turin. Photograph by S. Seroppiana, courtesy Teatro Regio di Torino.

10 Giuseppe Verdi's *Nabucco* at the Baths of Caracalla in the 1991 production directed by Renzo Giacchieri, with sets and costumes by Fiorenzo Giorgi. Nello Santi was the musical director. Photograph by Corrado M. Falsini, courtesy Teatro dell'Opera di Roma.

11 Teatro San Carlo in Naples, with perhaps the best acoustics of any opera house in the world, seats 1450. Courtesy Teatro S. Carlo di Napoli.

12 The *sala* of Rome's Teatro dell'Opera consists of three tiers of boxes, two balconies, and the main floor, altogether accommodating 1600 patrons. Photograph by Corrado M. Falsini, courtesy Teatro dell'Opera di Roma.

13 Taormina's ancient Greco-Roman amphitheater in the fore-
ground, Mount Etna in the background. Courtesy Taormina Arte.

14 The apse of Sant'Apollinare in Classe, built
in the first half of the 6th century, was the setting
for the 1990 Ravenna Festival's presentation
of Beethoven's Ninth Symphony with Carlo
Maria Giulini on the podium. Courtesy Ravenna
Festival.

15 The piazza in front of the church of San Francesco was the setting for a performance of Cherubini's *Messa solenne* in 1991. Riccardo Muti conducted the Orchestra Filarmonico and the Coro Lirico della Scala. Courtesy Ravenna Festival.

16 The facade of Teatro Bellini in Catania bedecked with flags and illuminated for the opening night of the Festival Belliniano 1991. Photograph by Angela di Blasi, courtesy Teatro Massimo Bellini di Catania.

17 The *sala* of Teatro Rossini in Lugo has three tiers of boxes, a balcony, and a level for standees. Altogether it accommodates 448 patrons. Courtesy Teatro Rossini di Lugo.

18 Teatro Massimo in Palermo opened its doors in 1897. Its 35-stair approach is guarded by a pair of bronze lions, and the bust at the front left on the lawn, underneath the palm trees, is of Richard Wagner. Photograph by Federico Allotta, courtesy Teatro Massimo di Palermo.

19 The scene on the house curtain of Teatro "G. B. Pergolesi" in Jesi is a vivid portrayal of "The Arrival of Frederick II at Jesi," painted in 1850 by Luigi Mancini, a local artist. Courtesy Teatro "G. B. Pergolesi."

20 Teatro Regio in Parma opened in 1829; its *sala* is made up of four tiers of boxes and a balcony, altogether accommodating 1440 patrons. Courtesy Teatro Regio di Parma.

21 Reggio Emilia's Teatro Municipale "Romolo Valli." The *sala*, with four tiers of boxes rising above the main floor and a balcony, accommodates 1200 patrons. Photograph by Piero Casadei, courtesy Teatro Municipale "Romolo Valli" di Reggio Emilia.

Teatro Massimo
PALERMO

Beneath the palm trees of Sicily, next to Palermo's monumental opera house—Teatro Massimo—stands a bust, but not of Palermo's most famous native son, Alessandro Scarlatti, composer of over 66 operas. Rather one is faced with the stony visage of that scion of German music, Richard Wagner, who—during the season of 1881–82—lived just down the street from the Massimo at the Hôtel des Palmes (today the Grande Albergo e delle Palme), where he completed the final pages of his last opera, *Parsifal*.

This choice for veneration is only one of the many paradoxes in the musical life of Palermo, for it is one of the oldest cities in Italy, yet has the newest of the major opera houses; it is a theater that prides itself on *primas*, yet did not present a single Mozart opera until the season of 1947. Boasting one of the largest stages in the world for opera, Teatro Massimo has been closed for reconstruction and renovation almost as much as it has been open. Yet, in spite of all the negative aspects, the opera season in Palermo is one of the most interesting, fascinating, and varied to be found in Italy.

Palermo, today a city of about 750,000 people, is Phoenician in origin; Roman in the celebrated mosaics of the Villa Bonnano; Arab in the mosques that serve today as churches; and French, German, and Spanish in its monuments, architecture, and street names. As one recent visitor recalled,

The artistic glamour of Palermo's past is strongly reflected by rare Greek metopes in the Museo Nazionale, sparkling mosaics in the Cappella Palatina, and sumptuous royal tombs in the cathedral. Architectural splendor must have been accompanied by appropriate music, which is less in evidence only because it is not built of stone. The Greek temples and theaters scattered over the island [of Sicily] all resounded with music in antiquity. Pindar dedicated 15 victory odes to the Sicilians, and the names, though not the compositions, of the musicians Empedocles and Theocritus are recorded. The height of medieval Sicilian cultural glamour around 1200, as apparent by the foundation of [the city] of Monreale, coincides with the activities of the troubadours and minnesingers. One usually thinks about them as poets, but one must not overlook the fact that they sang their verses. Although many of the melodies were improvised and are therefore lost to us, others have been preserved and are rewarding to hear. We know that the Norman King William II kept excellent singers at his Palermo court, but the Hohenstaufens themselves were musicians (a common enough quality among rulers if one remembers the Habsburgs, Henry VIII, Frederick the Great, and also Nero).

Henry VI, whose tomb is in the Palermo Cathedral, was an illustrious minnesinger. Of his son Frederick II the chronicle tells that . . . "he could read, write, and sing, and compose secular and religious songs." He also invited musicians from Provence and Germany to Palermo. What did the music sound like? The Italian poet and literature professor, Carducci, has an ear for it: "Princes, barons, judges, attorneys in the retinue of Frederick II sang of the joys and sorrows of love with sometimes so ardent a passion that it continues to burn in the ditties of the Sicilian people even today."[42]

Opera in Palermo

Opera began in Palermo in the year 1658 with a performance of an anonymous *Serse* for the inauguration of the Accademia di Musica in Teatro dello Spasimo, a theater that had been established as early as 1582 in an ancient church where Raphael's so-called "Madonna dello Spasimo" was to be seen. Since that date well over three centuries ago, musical spectacles of one type or another have been regular fare in Palermo, though opera as such did not enter into prominence until the opening of Teatro di Santa Cecilia, built by the Unione dei Musici at the end of the 17th century. That theater opened on 28 October 1693 with *L'innocenza pentita* by the poet Vincenzo Giattino and set to music by the Palermitano composer Ignazio Pollice. During these early years, most of the operas performed were the creations of local composers and librettists, including several operas of Alessandro Scarlatti that were mounted during the seasons of 1690 and 1702.

In 1726 the *Palermitani* decided on a new theater for opera, and, by private subscription, built a house that was to bear several names—Santa Lucia, Santa Caterina, dei Travaglini—and was at first devoted to opera buffa. It soon became a rival of the Santa Cecilia, until in the year 1809 it was reconstructed and endowed with the name Real Teatro Carolino (after that of Queen Maria Carolina, consort of Ferdinand I of Bourbon) and took precedence over the Santa Cecilia.

During the early decades of the 19th century, musical life, if we are to believe music historians, was at its height, a brilliant period in which Teatro Carolino was one of the few theaters in Italy to remain open throughout the year. The *cartelloni* varied between opera seria, opera buffa, and ballet. During the 1825–26 season, Donizetti was commissioned to write and conduct the *prima* of a new opera for Teatro Carolino (*Alahor in Granata*); in 1829–30, Balfe sang there as a baritone and began his brilliant career as an opera composer with *I rivali di se stessi*, a work that earned him honorary membership in the Accademia Filarmonica Palermitana. Other than these rare occasions, the repertory was much the same as at other Italian houses of the time, featuring operas by Cimarosa, Paisiello, Paër, and Fioravanti, and then the major works of Rossini, Bellini, Donizetti, and eventually Verdi.

After the union of Sicily with the kingdom of Italy in 1860, Teatro Carolino changed its name to the Real Teatro Bellini. Because of budget restrictions and rising costs, seasons became shorter, and deficits rolled over from one year to the next. Finally the *Palermitani* elected to build a new house by subscription, and in 1864 launched a campaign for a new theater. Four years later, a design competition for it was initiated by a committee headed by Gottfried Semper, who had, two decades earlier, designed the Royal Opera House for Dresden and went on to design the Festspielhaus in Bayreuth for Richard Wagner. The competition was won by a native son, Giovanbattista Basile. His plan was grandiose, with the stage space designed to be the largest in Europe (though by its completion it was second in size to that of the Salle Garnier, L'Opéra, in Paris). Altogether it took 33 years of political intrigue, polemics, and lawsuits before the structure was finally completed. There is no question about it: the opera house is an imposing building fully worthy of its name, Teatro Massimo (*massimo* is the Italian for "maximum, greatest, largest"). To celebrate the opening in 1897, Verdi's *Falstaff* was scheduled, though no one bothered to invite the composer. As this initial season progressed, Enrico Caruso appeared as Enzo in Ponchielli's *La Gioconda*.

A pair of bronze lions guard the 35-stair approach to Teatro Massimo's porticoed entrance, where six pillars decorated in the

Basile's sketches for his prize-winning design for Teatro Massimo in Palermo. Courtesy Teatro Massimo di Palermo.

then-popular Liberty style dominate its porch. Towering over the whole building (and the square in which it is located) is a copper-covered dome, green with the patina of age. The main *sala* is horseshoe-shaped, made up of 182 boxes in five tiers, plus 460 seats on the main floor. These, together with 288 places in the balcony, accommodate 1316 patrons.

The stage itself is 38.5 by 28.5 meters (127 by 94 feet) and surmounted by a gridiron for flying (lifting sets in and out), which towers 48 meters (158 feet) in height. The proscenium opening measures 12.5 meters (41 feet) in width by 6 meters (20 feet) in height. In addition to the main *sala*, there is a handsomely decorated foyer, the Sala Pompeiana, a circular room decorated in designs and colors associated with Pompeii. On the opposite side of the house, Basile designed the royal salon for the king on the second level, and, on the ground floor, a casino. A spacious coffee shop completes Basile's added social amenities.

In 1936 Teatro Massimo was designated an *ente autonomo*, and in the following years it presented some of Italy's finest vocal artists including Beniamino Gigli, Maria Caniglia, Tito Gobbi, Magda Olivero, and Gino Becchi. During the season of 1949 Maria Callas sang Brünnhilde in *Die Walküre*, and she returned in 1951 to be the protagonist of *Norma*. Renata Tebaldi sang Margherita in the 1953 production of Boito's *Mefistofele*. In 1952 Giuseppe Di Stefano sang Rigoletto, which he followed—together with Clara Petrella—in 1954 with Massenet's *Manon* and *Werther* in 1955. A much-celebrated production of Offenbach's *Les Contes d'Hoffmann* in 1957 introduced Thomas Schippers to the podium. Joan Sutherland first appeared in Palermo in 1960 in *Lucia di Lammermoor*, which the coloratura followed the next year with Bellini's *I puritani*. The *Palermitani* also recall the debut of Alfredo Krauss, who substituted in the second act for an ailing tenor in *Rigoletto*. Luciano Pavarotti first appeared in Palermo with Antonietta Stella in 1964 in *Madama Butterfly*. Other highlights include Franco Zeffirelli's productions of *Norma* (1958), *Falstaff* (1960), and *Lucia* (1960); Nicola Benois's productions of *Aida* (1952), *Mefistofele* (1958), and *Kovantchina* (1963); and Wolfgang Wagner's direction of *Tristan und Isolde* (1960) and *Die Walküre* (1962).

Teatro Massimo's productions did quite a bit of traveling between 1958 and 1972: in 1958 and 1962 it took *Tosca*, *Turandot*, *Fanciulla del West*, and *La Bohème* to the Puccini Festival at Torre

Basile's sketches for the internal decorations and capitals of Teatro Massimo. Courtesy Teatro Massimo di Palermo.

del Lago; in 1963 at Busetto—Verdi's home town—Teatro Massimo presented *Otello* and *Trovatore*; at the Wiesbaden Festival in 1960, *Turandot* and *Falstaff*; and at Stuttgart in 1961, *Puritani* and *Bohème*, and in 1962, *Otello* and *Don Pasquale*. At Paris's Italian Opera Festival at the Théâtre des Champs Elysées in 1962, Teatro Massimo presented *Turandot*, *Otello*, and *Don Pasquale*. The latter work was repeated at Schwetzingen in 1965 along with Cimarosa's *Il matrimonio segreto*. In 1969 the Palermitano theater took *Simon Boccanegra*, *Don Pasquale*, and *Il barbiere di Siviglia* to Dubrovnik, and Teatro Massimo's international travels concluded in 1972 with its presentations at the XXVI Edinburgh Festival of Verdi's *Attila*, Bellini's *La straniera*, and Rossini's *Elisabetta, regina d'Inghilterra*.

Though Teatro Massimo presented 18 world premieres between 1903 and 1972, none survived, with the exception of Nino Rota's *Il cappello di paglia di Firenze* of 1955. Most of the composers, too, of these first presentations have been forgotten today with the possible exceptions of Umberto Giordano, whose *Mese mariano* was presented in 1910, and Gianfrancesco Malipiero, whose *Merlino maestro d'organi* was mounted in 1972.

Teatro Massimo's record of historical revivals is far more impressive: Bellini's *I Capuleti e i Montecchi* (1954), *Il pirata* (1958), *Beatrice di Tenda* (1959), and *La straniera* (1968); Rossini's *Il Conte Ory* (1967) and *Elisabetta, regina d'Inghilterra* (1971); Ottorino Respighi's *Semirama* (1987); Ildebrando Pizzetti's *Fedra* (1988); and Franco Alfano's *Risurrezione* (1990).

Teatro Politeama Garibaldi

In actuality the *ente autonomo* Teatro Massimo of Palermo presents operas at three venues, including Teatro Politeamo Garibaldi and Teatro di Verdura di Villa Castelnuovo, in addition to its own theater designed by Basile.

In 1866 Giuseppe Damiani Almajda won the design competition for a variety-type theater that was to be called Teatro Politeama Garibaldi (*politeama* translates literally as "theater"). Strange and interesting in appearance, it looks from the front to be a circular structure, Pompeiian in style and decoration with a double portico. Its principal entrance greatly resembles the Arc de Triomphe, complete with galloping horses and warriors in bronze high atop the arch.

119

The Garibaldi was inaugurated in 1874 with Bellini's *I Capuleti e i Montecchi*. During the season of 1892–93 Arturo Toscanini conducted performances at this theater of Catalani's *Loreley*, Wagner's *Der fliegende Holländer*, Mascagni's *Cavalleria rusticana*, Ponchielli's *La Gioconda*, Bellini's *Norma*, Verdi's *Rigoletto*, and Rossini's *Il barbiere di Siviglia*. Singers of that early period included Dame Nellie Melba and Francesco Tamagno among many important others. On 24 April 1896 Teatro Garibaldi mounted a highly successful performance of Puccini's recently completed *La Bohème*, an opera that had just failed in Turin for some strange reason.

With the opening of Teatro Massimo in 1897, the Politeama Garibaldi fell into disuse for opera and was employed, instead, for other types of theater attractions. Then, in 1974, when the Massimo was closed for restoration, the entire opera season was moved to the Garibaldi. In 1978, with the appointment of Ubalao Mirabelli as *sovrintendente* and Girolamo Arrigo as artistic director, the seasons took on a fresh, new appearance, and both the Massimo and Garibaldi were pressed into service, with the Garibaldi serving as the venue for contemporary works that have included Britten's *The Turn of the Screw*, *The Beggar's Opera*, and *The Rape of Lucretia*; Prokofiev's *The Angel of Fire* and *War and Peace*; Gershwin's *Porgy and Bess*; Poulenc's *Les Mamelles de Tirésias*; Janáček's *Jenůfa*; Menotti's *The Consul*; Strauss's *Die schweigsame Frau* (in 1988); Krenek's *Jonny spielt auf* (an Italian *prima*); and Wagner's early *Das Liebesverbot* and Gilbert and Sullivan's *The Mikado* (in 1990).

Though Teatro Garibaldi appears to be round, the main *sala* is in the traditional horseshoe shape, with a columned gallery above the proscenium arch. There is a total of 28 boxes (with five seats per box) and 21 double boxes (with 10 seats each); there are 376 chairs in the *anfiteatro* (the front of the balcony) and 572 seats (which cannot be used) in the stage *anfiteatro*. Thus the actual seating capacity is 1298. The stage is much smaller than the Massimo's: only 18 by 15 meters (59 by 50 feet). The proscenium opening is 12.5 meters (41 feet) wide and 7 meters (23 feet) high.

Teatro di Verdura di Villa Castelnuovo

Located on Viale del Fante near the Parco della Favorita in Palermo, Teatro di Verdura di Villa Castelnuovo (Theater of the Villa Newcastle), a *teatro all'aperto* or open-air theater, was inaugurated during the season of 1958. (The first production was *Otello*, starring Mario Del Monaco.)

The house itself consists of outdoor chairs placed on a slightly inclined "main floor"; at its rear a series of bleachers with benches has been erected. Altogether Teatro di Verdura seats some 1450 spectators on the main floor (*platea*) and 200 on the unnumbered benches at the back.

Today, according to the *sovrintendente*, Ubaldo Mirabelli, Teatro di Verdura offers each summer "an opera, an operetta, two ballets, a music-theater work, or an evening of songs."[43] Over the years such interesting works have been heard here as the Ibsen-Grieg *Peer Gynt*, the Byron-Schumann *Manfred*, and the Shakespeare–Duke Ellington *Così dolce tuono*. Musicals have included *West Side Story* and *A Chorus Line* and the Italian operettas *Cin-Ci-là*, *Il paese dei campanelli*, and *Scugnizza*, as well as Kálmán's *Czardas Princess* and Lehár's *The Merry Widow*. Evenings of ballet have included appearances by such world-famous companies as the Alvin Ailey American Dance Theater, Igor Moisseiev, the Dance Theatre of Harlem, Les Grands Ballets Canadiens, the San Francisco Ballet, the Bolshoi, the Kirov, and the London Festival Dancers.

The Season at Teatro Massimo

The *cartellone* at Palermo's Teatro Massimo is anything but routine, and generally exciting in many ways: repertory, casting, conducting, and stage productions. Teatro Massimo seems to be one theater whose season is not dictated by the box-office take alone, but whose administration feels an obligation to present the unusual as well as the traditional. Mirabelli explains:

> It is necessary first of all to specify that for us, repertory is synonymous with our heritage, and we must, among our 10 different titles each season, regularly offer for young people and the working community the most important and best-known works of our heritage.[44]

Even though Teatro Massimo offers such important heritage pieces—*Otello*, *Tosca*, and *Anna Bolena* during the 1990–91 season, for example—the *cartellone* never falls into the traditional pattern (the rut) of the bulk of Italian opera houses. As Mirabelli proudly states,

121

For many years Teatro Massimo has been unique in featuring the works of Italian composers of the 1900s: Rieti, Busoni, Malipiero, Casella, Respighi, Pizzetti, Montemezzi, Alfano. In 1991, from the 22nd of March to the 13th of April we gave the people a chance to hear the work of one of their own composers, a Sicilian, *Dafni* by Tumbarello Lea Mulè [an important composer of the Fascist era largely forgotten by the rest of Italy], with a libretto by Ettore Romagnolli, the great Hellenist who is almost forgotten today.[45]

Though Teatro Massimo was closed for security reasons for seven years while its wiring and emergency systems were completely overhauled, it was certainly not a period of inactivity, as Mirabelli relates:

> Rather than remaining completely inactive the Politeama always responds with a dignified solution. By offering special season tickets for students and workers, we have managed to bring to the theater a vast and unexpected number of citizens. Music is a unique moment of encounter for the community. I am convinced that opera is indispensable to the growth of society, and we all know how much culture Sicily has to offer. Furthermore, as you will read, our seasons are ever more stimulating, offering traditional titles, the unusual and ballet. From Mulè to Wagner, from Rossini to Verdi, we have tripled our productions [during the 1990–91 season] and balanced budgets, thanks to the financial support of the region. Its contributions, in particular, serve to aid the international cultural diffusion of unknown operas that are a part of the great treasure of the opera repertory.
>
> We offer employment to 574 people; we provide work for artisans; and, thanks to our laboratories where we produce everything ourselves, we are the second-largest "producing" agency in Palermo, second only to the naval yard. I believe then that opera is well served.[46]

One of Mirabelli's most inspired decisions was to have his artists and productions travel around Sicily. Since 1980 Teatro Massimo has presented opera throughout western Sicily, in particular at Castellamare del Golfo (Trapani) and at Castello di San Nicola di Trabia, where they have presented their annual Festival dell'Opera Gioiosa (Humorous Opera Festival) each July and August. For it they mount the wonderful *opere buffe* of the 18th century, works that range from Pergolesi's *Livietta e Tracollo* and *La contadina astuta* in 1983 to Cimarosa's *I tre amanti* in 1990 and *Le astuzie femminili* in 1993 and Paisiello's *La molinara* in the same year.

The opera season in Palermo begins between early December and early January and lasts until late May or early June. It consists of eight to 10 events (operas and ballets), each presented eight to 12 times, with some performances scheduled at Teatro Politeama Garibaldi, others at Teatro Massimo.

The 1992 season (which opened on 11 January and closed on 2 June) is typical of the varied repertory presented:

Donizetti's *Lucrezia Borgia*
with Denia Mazzola, Elena Zilio, Salvatore Fisichella,
and Lajos Miller; conducted by Gianandrea Gavazzeni
(8 performances)

Szymanowski's *King Roger*
with Nancy Shade and Igor Piavko; conducted by Karl Martin
(8 performances)

Bellini's *La sonnambula*
with Mariella Devia, Ramon Vargas, and Roberto Scandiuzzi;
conducted by Donato Renzetti
(10 performances)

Leoncavallo's *La reginetta delle rose*
with Alessandra Ruffini, Martha Senn, and Luca Canonici;
conducted by Massimo De Bernart
(8 performances)

Borodin's *Il principe Igor*
with soloists, chorus, and orchestra from the Kirov Opera and
Ballet Theatre of St. Petersburg;
conducted by Valerij Gergiev
(10 performances)

Verdi's *Aida*
with Natalia Troitskaya, Luciana D'Intino, Nicola Martinucci,
and Tom Fox; conducted by Maurizio Arena

Giordano's *Andrea Chenier*
with Katia Ricciarelli, Giuseppe Giacomini, and Tom Fox;
conducted by Maurizio Arena

In addition to these were Honegger's ballet, *Fedra, leggenda e mito*, for 10 performances with Carla Fracci, and an evening of ballet (*Pyramyde-el Nour* and *Mozart Tangos*) in 12 performances by the Ballet Béjart Lausanne.

Practical Matters

While ticket prices are very expensive at Teatro Massimo for the regular patron, there are attractive alternatives as indicated earlier, most, however, for local residents, students, and workers. Teatro Massimo does offer affordable ticket packages for students and senior citizens. A season ticket for nine events runs just under $100 on the main floor, even less in the balcony. A similar four-event ticket runs about half that price for Teatro Massimo's out-of-town performances. There are various other types of packages, too, including a three-event season ticket for elementary school children that costs between $25 and $50 depending upon whether the seats are in the balcony or on the main floor. Requests for season announcements, pertinent information, and ticket orders should be sent to the Biglietteria, Teatro Massimo, Piazza Verdi, I-90138 Palermo. The telephone number there is 091/581.512. For events at Teatro Garibaldi, one should write its ticket offices at Piazza Politeama, I-90139 Palermo; telephone 091/584.334. Teatro di Verdura is located at Viale del Fante 78/b, I-90146 Palermo; telephone 091/518.287 or 516.561. Ticket offices are open every day, except Mondays and holidays, from 10:00 A.M. to 1:00 P.M. and from 4:00 to 7:00 P.M.

For the Armchair Fan

Though the history of opera in Palermo is an interesting and fascinating story for the opera buff, nothing has appeared in print in English. There are in Italian several fragmented accounts, each conveying part of the story.

Rubino, Maria Adele. 1988. *Teatro Massimo di Palermo*. Milan: SL Edizioni. A good account of Teatro Massimo itself from its inception in 1864 to the season of 1988.

Pirrone, Gianni. 1984. *Il Teatro Massimo di G. B. Filippo Basile a Palermo*. Rome: Officinia Edizioni. A detailed account in nine chapters of Basile's design and its execution, including excellent black-and-white illustrations and photographs.

Martinez, Corrado. 1980. *Il Teatro Massimo: 40 anni di attività artistica dalla costituzione dell'ente autonomo 1936–1975*. Palermo: Edizioni Priulla. An illustrated chronology of performances—including the symphony and chamber music seasons—given at Teatro Massimo between 1936 and 1975.

The following three albums provide an excellent aural picture of the diversity of repertory in Palermo: in turn a traditional work, an 18th-century revival, and an opera buffa from the summer Festival dell'Opera Gioiosa.

Cimarosa, Domenico. *I tre amanti*. Bongiovanni GB 2105/6; with Martina Musacchio, Renzo Casellato, and Ernesto Palacio; Orchestra "La camerata di Mosca"; conducted by Domenico Sanfilippo. Recorded live at the Festival dell'Opera Gioiosa in July 1990.

Spontini, Gaspare. *La vestale*. Nuova Era 2379/80; with Leyla Gencer, Renato Bruson, Robleto Merolla, Agostino Ferrin, and Franca Mattiucci; Orchestra e Coro del Teatro Massimo di Palermo; conducted by Fernando Previtali. Recorded live in Teatro Massimo, 4 December 1969.

Verdi, Giuseppe. *Macbeth*. Great Opera Performances GOP 705; with Giuseppe Taddei, Leyla Gencer, Mirto Picchi; Orchestra e Coro del Teatro Massimo di Palermo; conducted by Vittorio Gui. Recorded live at Teatro Massimo, 14 January 1960.

Teatro dell'Opera
ROME

It was the spring of 1708 when George Frideric Handel returned to Rome after presenting his first Italian opera, *Rodrigo*, in Florence for the duke of Tuscany. An exciting new commission awaited him: the creation of a special work for Count Ruspoli (in whose palace Handel was staying), a work that was to be called an oratorio since in his over-religious zeal the pope—Innocent VII—had closed the opera house in Rome.

Count Ruspoli spared neither pains nor money in preparing for the forthcoming Handel piece. A special stage was set up in one of the largest rooms of his elegant palace, Palazzo Bonelli on Piazza SS. Apostoli. The principal decoration was to be an enormous painting of the Resurrection by Ceruti, framed by the Ruspoli coat of arms. The count had an ornate frontispiece made for the stage showing the full title of Handel's new work, *Oratorio per la risurrettione di Nostro Signor Gesu Cristo*, in letters cut out of transparent paper to be lit from the back with 70 lanterns. He had the walls adorned with damask and velvet in brilliant shades of crimson, scarlet, and yellow; and there were to be 16 candelabra so that the large audiences could easily read the text of the work. (More than 1500 libretti were printed, suggesting the count expected the new piece to play to packed houses on the occasions of its Easter Sunday and Easter Monday performances.) Ruspoli had special music stands created for the orchestra, their legs shaped like fluted cornucopiae with his and his wife's coats of arms painted on them. He engaged a mammoth orchestra, to be led from the podium by his regular *maestro di musica*, Arcangelo Corelli. A special platform was built for the 40 string players (23 violins including Corelli, four *violette*, six *violoni*, six *contrabassi*, and one bass viol); in addition, the ensemble was to include two trumpets and a trombone, and four oboes that presumably were to double on flute and recorder.

Though "the first of the sumptuously stage-managed performances (non-dramatic, of course) went off successfully"[47] (as Jonathan Keates suggests in his biography of Handel), the pope got wind of the production and demanded that the young lady singing the role of the Magdalene—Margherita Durasanti, perhaps the most famous soprano of her day and an artist Handel was later to employ on many occasions in London—be immediately replaced. A woman was not to sing in public during Holy Week; the pope actually threatened a public flogging. A castrato called Filippo replaced her, and the Easter Monday performance apparently went off as successfully as the one the day before. A pleased Count Ruspoli thereupon lavishly rewarded his artists with diamond, emerald, and ruby rings.

Resurrezione (as the work is now commonly called) is a glorious, triumphant bit of Handelian writing full of heralding trumpets and flourishing fanfares, of pomp and ceremony, but it might just as easily have been an opera. All that would have been needed was a bit of stylized dramatic movement on stage.

The story of Handel and his oratorio, and the effort to circumvent the pope's ban on operas, suggests the fate of the lyric theater in Rome, an art form ever-popular here but eternally at the mercy of the theologian and politician, of popes and kings and presidents and even of Il Duce himself.

Opera in Rome

The first opera productions in Rome were, like those in Florence in the early 17th century, sumptuous entertainments held in the private palaces of the most powerful Roman families. Particularly lavish productions were given by the Barberini family at their splendid new Palace of the Four Fountains between 1634 and 1656. Other extravagant centers included one inaugurated by the Marchese Capronica in 1678 and an extremely important and popular one fitted up by Cardinal Ottoboni in his Palazzo Cancelleria. (Ottoboni, appointed a cardinal at age 22 by his uncle, Pope Alexander VIII, spent enormous sums on the production of opera, and even wrote a libretto himself based on the story of Columbus's voyage to America.)

At first the papal throne smiled on opera. In 1669 Pope Clement IX—who, like Cardinal Giulio Rospigliosi, was the librettist of several operas performed at the Palazzo Barberini—authorized Count Giacomo d'Alibert to erect a theater intended for the public performance of operas. This theater, built out of a deserted prison on the banks of the Tiber, Teatro di Tor di Nona, opened in 1671 with operas by two Venetian composers, Francesco Cavalli and Giovanni Antonio Boretti.

It was rough going for the Tor di Nona, however. Four years after its founding it was closed by orders of the new pope who did not smile on opera. It reopened in 1690 (a new pope, of course) only to be closed a half-dozen years later and torn down in 1697. The Romans triumphed once again when it was rebuilt in 1733, but by then it had competition from other theaters. Renamed the Apollo, it was active in the early part of the 19th century, with its *prima*s including Rossini's *Matilde di Shabran* in 1821; Verdi's *Il trovatore* in 1853 and *Un ballo in maschera* in 1859; and Donizetti's *Il duca d'Alba* in 1882, some 42 years after the composer had completed it. Teatro Apollo was demolished in 1889.

Teatro Argentina was built by Duke Giuseppe Sforza-Cesarini in 1732. The 24-year-old Rossini's *Il barbiere di Siviglia* was given its *prima* there in 1816; sad to relate, however, it was booed on

ALMAVIVA

O SIA

L' INUTILE PRECAUZIONE

COMMEDIA

DEL SIGNOR BEAUMARCHAIS

Di nuovo interamente versificata, e
ridotta ad uso dell'odierno teatro
Musicale Italiano

DA CESARE STERBINI ROMANO

DA RAPPRESENTARSI

NEL NOBIL TEATRO

DI TORRE ARGENTINA

NEL CARNEVALE DELL' ANNO 1816.

Con Musica del Maestro

GIOACCHINO ROSSINI.

ROMA

Nella Stamperia di Crispino Puccinelli
presso S. Andrea della Valle.

Con licenza de'Superiori.

The cover of the libretto for the *prima* of Rossini's *Il barbiere di
Siviglia* at Rome's Teatro Argentina on 20 February 1816. (*Almaviva*
was the opera's original title.) Courtesy Teatro dell'Opera di Roma.

opening night! Credible reports by foreign visitors of the era suggest that although the Argentina was at that time among the largest opera houses in Europe, it was neither well maintained nor well decorated. Still in existence (on what is today Via di Torre Argentina), having been restored in 1837 and again in 1971, Teatro Argentina is used on rare occasions for opera presentations today, but has served primarily as a symphony hall since World War II and more recently as a dramatic theater. At first the opera season coincided with Carnival. Later the seasons were extended into late spring. Eventually two smaller theaters—of considerably less importance—opened in Rome for opera: Teatro Pace and Teatro Valle. The latter today is a garishly modernized theater, its principal claim to fame having been the *prima* of Rossini's *Cenerentola* as well as those of five Donizetti operas.

In the 1870s an ambitious real estate speculator named Domenico Costanzi, who had a great passion for opera, dreamed of building a private theater that would be ideal for lyric productions. In 1876 he acquired a tract of land behind the Albergo Quirinale (a hotel in which he also had interests) and founded a society to build the new theater. His was not an easy job, for both politicians and influential Romans raised all kinds of objections: location, size, design, décor, funding, allotment of boxes, and so on. Costanzi was not easily discouraged, fortunately, and so he, along with his architect, Achille Sfondrini, went ahead with the work. Teatro Costanzi thus opened on 27 November 1880 with Rossini's *Semiramide*, and, similar to most opening nights in Rome, the show on stage paled in comparison to the spectacle in the house. An hour before curtain time, there began a long procession of elegant carriages on Via Firenze, bearing the most prominent aristocratic families, foreign dignitaries, and government officers. To the strains of the "Marcia Reale" the royal carriage approached, with "Queen Margherita dressed in a light pink gown trimmed in cerulean blue, a diadem of brilliants arranged in a star in her blond hair."[48]

On the front page of *L'Opinione* on the morning after Teatro Costanzi's opening night, music critic D'Arcais wrote:

What is the future of Teatro Costanzi? . . . Teatro Costanzi . . . will be a meeting place for the most cultured people of high society. Certainly there will also be places for those with smaller pocketbooks (more than there may be presently at

the Apollo). . . . The doubts regarding the possibility of sub-
stituting it for the Apollo, a theater unworthy of a capital city,
I believe have been dispelled. It will come to this only if one
desires that the most beautiful theater in Rome be used for
no more than masked balls or for industrial fairs. It would be
a shame! But, at the same time, I believe that to transport
productions and the public from the Apollo to the Costanzi,
some modifications should be in order. Three tiers of boxes
are not enough for a city like Rome, and two balconies seem
to me excessive. Could not Sfondrini substitute another row
of boxes for the First Balcony?[49]

Teatro dell'Opera di Roma

Teatro Costanzi—which was renamed the Royal Opera and
then Teatro dell'Opera di Roma—originally had, in addition to
main-floor seating, 104 boxes arranged in three tiers plus two balconies, altogether seating some 2293 spectators. The stage was,
for the size of the house, dreadfully small, the foyer equally
cramped and unattractive.

In July of 1888 Teatro Costanzi advertised in *Teatro Illustrato* a
competition it was sponsoring for "an opera in one act—with a
single scene or two at most—on an idyllic, serious, or humorous
theme of the composer's choice."[50] The theater guaranteed that
the three winning works would be produced at Teatro Costanzi.
Pietro Mascagni—then 25 years old—was ecstatic. Within a few
months he drafted *Cavalleria rusticana* and submitted it. As most
of the world now knows, he won first prize. The resounding success it received at its *prima* on 17 May 1890 is an occasion to remember in the history of opera: 60 curtain calls. And within ten
months, this first opera by the then-unknown composer had taken
its place among the repertories of the major European theaters.

Domenico Costanzi passed away in 1898 and his son Enrico
took over the management, developing seasons that were given
over to operettas and equestrian circuses as well as opera. (Enrico Costanzi's first season opened with the world premiere of
Mascagni's *Iris*.) The theater's most illustrious *prima* took place
on 14 January 1900, when Puccini's *Tosca* was unveiled. Mascagni's *Le maschere* was less successful the following year, a work
premiered simultaneously in five other theaters: those in Milan,
Turin, Genoa, Venice, and Verona. Only in Rome did it enjoy any

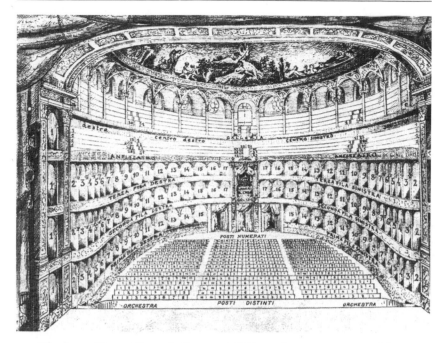

The box office at Rome's Teatro dell'Opera has superimposed box and seat numbers on a 19th-century etching of the theater to help patrons locate their places in the theater. Courtesy Teatro dell'Opera di Roma.

success, and that was likely due to the fact that the composer—who lived in Rome—conducted that presentation.

In 1908 the theater was sold to a syndicate, the Società Teatrale Internazionale, which in its first season demonstrated the international promise of its title, for it opened with Wagner's *Die Walküre*, followed by Verdi's *Aida*, Ambroise Thomas's *Hamlet* (with Titta Ruffo), and then presented for the first time in Italy Claude Debussy's *Pelléas et Mélisande*. From 1911 to 1925 Emma Corelli directed the house, and under her governance many new operas were given, though none of lasting importance.

Following the March on Rome of 1922, Il Duce, Benito Mussolini, dreamed of making Rome once again a great capital city, one having an opera house more beautiful and more important than Teatro alla Scala in Milan. At first he entertained the idea of building an impressive new theater, but by 1926 he had resigned himself to a remodeling and refurbishing of Teatro Costanzi. Thus it was in 1926 that the city of Rome purchased the theater and

131

The *manifesto* announcing Rosina Storchio's first appearance at Teatro Costanzi (today known as Rome's Teatro dell'Opera) during the season of 1917–18. Courtesy Teatro dell'Opera di Roma.

The facade of Rome's Royal Opera House (Teatro Reale dell'Opera)
as it appeared on a postcard dated 1928. Courtesy Teatro dell'Opera
di Roma.

hired Marcello Piacenti as the architect for the remodeling. His resulting plans changed the main entrance from Via Firenze (which
is now on the outside left of the building) to Via Viminale. In order
to do this, the city had to negotiate with the postal ministry, which
owned the small tract of land between the theater and Via Viminale. For this spot the architect designed a beautiful garden piazza that was eventually renamed Piazza Beniamino Gigli. The
entire side of the building facing Via Viminale and the piazza was
redone with large slabs of marble decorated in gold relief with figures in the then-popular Liberty style.

In addition to the cosmetic changes of the exterior, major
changes were also effected inside. Each tier of boxes gained its
own foyer, and the stage space was enlarged to 585 square meters
(7166 square feet) and fitted with movable platforms. Additional
dressing rooms as well as rehearsal rooms were also added, and the
pit lowered and enlarged. Today Teatro dell'Opera seats 1604 patrons in its three tiers of boxes, two large balconies, and orchestra.

Because Teatro Costanzi had by 1926 fallen into a state of disrepair and dinginess from continuous use and little upkeep, it took
the workers a year longer to complete the renovations than originally anticipated; thus it was 1928 before the doors of the house

A postcard of 1932 showing the changes Mussolini requested for the facade of Teatro dell'Opera, a view that includes the "new" Piazza Gigli in front. Courtesy Teatro dell'Opera di Roma.

opened again, and there patrons found a large plaque tacked to the wall immediately above the proscenium arch:

VICTORIO EMANUEL III REGE
BENITO MUSSOLINI DUCE
LUDOVICUS SPADA POTENZINI ROMAE GUBERNATOR
RESTITUIT MCMXXVIII/A VI
[The "A VI" stood for "Year 6" of Fascism.]

The Royal Theater did not immediately become an *ente* as had by this time the theaters of Milan, Genoa, Florence, and Bologna. Instead, Ottavio Scotto was appointed impresario in the old-fashioned manner. The Royal Opera opened on the night of 27 February 1928 with a performance of Boito's *Nerone*. The composer Alfredo Casella voiced the hopes of many a Roman when he said in an interview for the *Christian Science Monitor* of 31 July 1926:

One must be grateful to Mussolini's government for having tackled with such boldness and breadth of vision one of the most difficult problems of the national musical life. One must again hope that this theater may escape as long as possible

134

from the "bureaucratization" which almost inevitably en-
slaves all state enterprises.[51]

Casella's fears were well founded. A year after it was reopened,
the Royal Opera fired Scotto as impresario, placing the theater
directly under the control of the governor of Rome. Thus the Royal
Opera was then an *ente autonomo*.

World premieres under this new organization were hardly more
spectacular than they had been under the old impresario system.
The list includes a number of long-forgotten works, some by long-
forgotten composers. Among the best-remembered works and/or
composers are Ildebrando Pizzetti's *Lo straniero* (1930), Ermanno
Wolf-Ferrari's *La vedova scaltra* (1931), Alfredo Casella's *La donna
serpente* (1932), Ottorino Respighi's *La fiamma* (1934), Franco
Alfano's *Cyrano de Bergerac* (1936), Gian Francesco Malipiero's
Ecuba (1941) and *I capricci di Callot* (1942), Alfredo Casella's *La
rosa del sogno* (1943), Riccardo Zandonai's *Biancaneve* (1951),
Franco Mannino's *La stirpe di Davide* (1962), Sylvano Bussotti's
Fedra (1988), and Lorenzo Ferrero's *Charlotte Corday* (1989).

During the Fascist years, especially during the 1930s and
the early '40s, the seasons leaned heavily toward the German
repertory.

After World War II, when on 2 June 1946 the Italians voted to
abolish the monarchy in favor of a republic, the Royal Opera was
renamed Teatro dell'Opera di Roma. The quality of the productions became a point of contentious discussion, with politicians
blaming the *sovrintendenti*, and the general public, in turn, blaming
the politicians for their manipulations of the *sovrintendenti* and
artistic directors. Surprisingly, there were still a few outstanding
productions during the next 40 years, including such important
20th-century works as Britten's *The Rape of Lucretia* (1949), Hin-
demith's *Mathis der Maler* (1951), Gruenberg's *The Emperor Jones*
(1951), Milhaud's *Cristoforo Colombo* (1954), Roussel's *Bacco e
Arianna* (1957), Hans Werner Henze's *Der junge Lord* (1965),
Gottfried von Einem's *Dantons Tod* (1970), Gian Carlo Menotti's
Help! Help! the Globolinks! (1972), and Philip Glass's *The Civil
Wars* (1984).

Following the appointment of distinguished musicologist and
Rossini Opera Festival impresario Bruno Cagli as artistic director
of Rome's Teatro dell'Opera from 1986 to 1989, the quality of
productions increased considerably. Unfortunately, as he himself

lamented, an artistic director's time and energies are not all necessarily devoted to artistic matters.

> The role of the artistic director in an operatic *ente* is extremely tiring today because of the manner in which an *ente* is organized. The time one can devote to musical things is minimal because of bureaucratic details and union responsibilities—not to mention the extra things—an artistic director is forced to face. The crosses that an artistic director must bear are many, and include the musicians' union as well as strikes—all those non-musical elements; on the other hand, the rewards of the position are great and include many moments of musical satisfaction.[52]

It must be these "rewards" that attracted Gian Carlo Menotti to the position, but in October 1994, the board released him from his contract, complaining he was never in Rome but always in Scotland or Spoleto. With this announcement came the news that Teatro dell'Opera would be closed indefinitely for a major structural overhaul; in the interim, the opera season moves to Teatro Brancaccio, an 1800-seat theater built in 1916.

The Season at Teatro dell'Opera

The season in Rome begins in late November and closes around mid-June; ordinarily there are about seven or eight operas scheduled during the winter season, each presented five or more times. The 1993–94 season (Gian Carlo Menotti's only full season as artistic director) was typical:

Verdi's *Aida*
with Nina Rautio and Giuseppe Giacomini;
conducted by Daniel Oren, with staging by Franco Zeffirelli

Dvořák's *Rusalka*
with Penelope Thorne, Ruthild Engert, and John De Hann;
conducted by Richard Hickox

Puccini's *Manon Lescaut*
with Elena Filipova; conducted by Philippe Auguin,
with staging by Gian Carlo Menotti

Donizetti's *Lucia di Lammermoor*
with Mariella Devia and Vincenzo La Scola;
conducted by Daniel Oren

Rossini's *Zelmira*
with Christine Weidinger, Rockwell Blake, Simone Alaimo,
and Armando Ariostini

Zemlinsky's *Der Geburtstag der Infantin*
conducted by Donato Renzetti,
with staging by Andrei Serban

Prokofiev's *The Love for Three Oranges*
conducted by Donato Renzetti,
with staging by Andrei Serban

Donizetti's *Don Pasquale*
with Giusy Devinu and Renato Bruson;
conducted by Paolo Carignani,
with staging by Gian Carlo Menotti

Leoncavallo's *I pagliacci*
with Cecilia Gasdia; with staging by Franco Zeffirelli

Practical Matters

Except for opening night, which is quite a social and political affair in Rome, tickets—while expensive—are no higher than at any other major theater in Italy.

For information in English (available 24 hours a day, according to the theater management), the telephone number is 06/675. 95725; for reservations not more than 10 days before a performance, the telephone numbers are 06/675.955721 (in English) and 06/675.95720 (in Italian). You can, of course, write the theater for brochures and information, but they are very slipshod in responding to such requests. Neither should you expect miracles over the telephone. Ask the specific questions you want answered and let them respond verbally. If you request that they mail you a brochure, or if they offer to mail a response to your questions, the chances of ever receiving such a brochure or letter are slim indeed. In 10 years of requesting brochures by telephone or mail from Teatro dell'Opera, I have never received one. Should you wish to try your luck, however, the address is Teatro dell'Opera di Roma, Via Firenze 72, I-00184 Rome.

For those who wish to purchase tickets at the box office, the *biglietteria* is located to the left of the front entrance. Hours are from 9:00 A.M. to 4:00 P.M. Tuesdays through Saturdays, and until 1:00 P.M. on Sundays.

For the Armchair Fan

Although there is nothing in print in English, Teatro dell'Opera publishes an interesting 210-page paperback in Italian, *Il Teatro dell'Opera di Roma*, which has excellent photographs both in black-and-white and in color. In spite of its title, however, it is a fragmented account. Divided into chapters, it has a rather interesting and thorough account of Teatro Costanzi, but nothing about the history or structure of the house during the time it was known as the Royal Opera, or later, as Teatro dell'Opera di Roma. Chapters are devoted to both world and Italian premieres from 1881 to 1989, plus a chapter each on the two principal Teatro dell' Opera *primas*: *Cavalleria rusticana* and *Tosca*.

Cacaci, Francesco. 1989. *Il Teatro dell'Opera di Roma*. Ed. Vincenzo Gristomi Travaglini. Rome: Edizioni del Teatro dell'Opera di Roma.

There are several quite good recordings of opera productions in Rome's Teatro dell'Opera. The one of Paisiello's *Don Chisciotte* is a recent recording (1990) and presents an excellent aural picture of the company as it exists today. The recordings of Verdi's *I lombardi* and *Il trovatore* date from 1969 and 1964 respectively, and speak of an earlier age.

Paisiello, Giovanni. *Don Chisciotte*. Nuova Era 6994/95; with Paolo Barbacini, Romano Franceschetto, Maria Angeles Peters, Elena Zilio, Mario Bolognesi, and Bruno Praticò; Orchestra e Coro del Teatro dell'Opera di Roma; conducted by Giorgio Morandi. Recorded live on 13 July 1990.

Verdi, Giuseppe. *I lombardi alla prima crociata*. Butterfly Music BMCD 008; with Luciano Pavarotti, Renata Scotto, and Ruggero Raimondi; Orchestra e Coro del Teatro dell'Opera di Roma; conducted by Gianandrea Gavazzeni. Recorded live, 20 November 1969.

Verdi, Giuseppe. *Il trovatore*. EMI CMS 7 63640-2; with Gabriella Tucci, Giulietta Simionato, Franco Corelli, and Robert Merrill; Orchestra e Coro del Teatro dell'Opera di Roma; conducted by Thomas Schippers. Recorded in 1964.

Teatro Verdi
TRIESTE

The repertory and even the very nature of the season at Trieste's Teatro Verdi—much more cosmopolitan and international in its approach than that of the other major Italian houses—reflects the political vicissitudes of the city itself.

Trieste, under Roman control circa 180 B.C., was later made a colony by Julius Caesar. Then in 948, after the breakup of the Roman Empire, it was granted independence by Lothair II, king of Italy. Captured by the Venetians in 1202, the city constantly agitated for autonomy, and in 1382 Trieste placed itself under the protection of the Habsburg's Leopold III, whose overlordship gradually developed into Austrian possession. A town of almost 6000 inhabitants when it was proclaimed an imperial free port by Charles VI in 1719, Trieste's population had reached almost 160,000 when it was deprived of that privilege in 1891. As the prosperous main port of the Austro-Hungarian Empire, the Austrian census of 1910 showed that two-thirds of Trieste's 750,000 people were Italians (Austrian and Italian subjects); the rest were Slovenes and Croats, other Austrian subjects (including Germans), and foreigners.

The preponderance of Italians provided the basis upon which, in the secret treaty of London in 1915, Britain, France, and Russia agreed to give the city to Italy at the peace settlement. The city was thus occupied by Italian troops in 1918, but its activity as a port dropped by 90 percent because it was cut off by a political frontier from its natural hinterland. The Fascist government, however, poured money into building up the city, including its port, and, in the area of culture, the Italian state government created in 1938 a university in the city and made Teatro Verdi a state opera (*ente autonomo*). Seized in 1943 by the Germans, who intended to keep it as a southern outlet to the sea for the Greater German Reich, Trieste was occupied by Marshal Tito's Yugoslav troops in 1945 and claimed for Yugoslavia. The peace treaty with Italy signed in Paris in 1947 created, instead, the Free Territory of Trieste, to be guaranteed by the United Nations Security Council. In this instance the city of Trieste was divided temporarily into northern and southern zones, the former under United States–British military administration, the latter under Yugoslav administration. This silly division proved completely unworkable and led to some intense political wrangling that involved all concerned parties. Finally the negotiations of 1954 resulted in an agreement that gave all of the southern division and a bit of the northern (518 square kilometers/202 square miles) to Yugoslavia (now Slovenia), and the balance of the northern zone (some 233 square kilometers/91 square miles) to Italy.

Thus while the port city of Trieste belongs to Italy today, and its population is largely made up of ethnic Italians, its earlier cultural and political heritage is still in evidence. After all, Trieste, situated on what was the Yugoslav border, is—as the crow flies—only 97 kilometers (60 miles) from Austria, 194 kilometers (120 miles) from Germany, 242 kilometers (150 miles) from Hungary, and 435 kilometers (270 miles) from Rome!

It is no wonder then that Teatro Verdi's *cartellone* for the 1990–91 season, for example, included, in addition to the standard Italian, German, and French repertory, works from the Croatian, Hungarian, and Yugoslav cultures. Croatia was represented by Ivan Zajc's three-act tragic opera, *Nikola Šubić Zrinjski* and Yugoslavia by *Pittori fiamminghi*, an opera by the Yugoslavian-born composer from Istria, Antonio Smareglia. During the summer International Operetta Festival, a troupe from Budapest brought Imre Kálmán's *Die Zirkusprinzessin* to Teatro Verdi.

The Story of Teatro Verdi

The opera house today known as Teatro Verdi was built by the private initiative of a number of Trieste's wealthier noble families and opened on 21 April 1801 as Teatro Nuovo (New Theater) with a production of Giovanni Simone Mayr's *Ginevra di Scozia*. To distinguish this elegant house from a much inferior but newer theater that was colloquially referred to as the "new theater," the opera house in 1820 adopted the name Teatro Grande. Then, in 1861, when the city purchased the building, it became Teatro Comunale. On 27 January 1901, the very day on which Giuseppe Verdi died, the city council of Trieste officially changed the theater's name and dedicated it to the memory of Giuseppe Verdi, and today it is officially Teatro Comunale "G. Verdi" di Trieste.

Although the theater has had a number of names during the past almost 200 years, its physical appearance has remained essentially unchanged since 1801. The interior, whose design is attributed to Selva, initially resembled that of Teatro La Fenice in nearby Venice. The architect Matteo Pertsch designed the exterior after a sketch of Selva's, and the resulting facade bears a certain resemblance to Milan's La Scala.

The first alterations in the interior were made in 1831 when a new *loggione* (gallery) was installed. Other remodeling and refurbishing work occurred in 1846, when the boxes and proscenium arch were redecorated with Moorish designs. From 1882 to 1884 the theater was closed so that the foundation and structural elements could be checked for their solidity. At the same time the stage equipment was brought up to date. In 1930 the third tier of boxes was eliminated and turned into a *galleria* that became the first balcony, while the earlier *galleria* became the second balcony (as we would use the term in English).

During the decade from 1830 to 1840 Teatro Verdi (at that time still called Teatro Grande) presented such unusual works as Auber's *La muette de Portici* as well as the first Italian productions of Rossini's two "French" operas, *Le Comte Ory* and *Guillaume Tell*. And in 1843 the *Triestani* enthusiastically greeted the theater's first production of Verdi's *Nabucco*, which was followed by *I vespri siciliani*. In 1848 Teatro Verdi presented the world premiere of Verdi's *Il corsaro*, written especially for this theater. Here Verdi's *Aroldo*, evolved from *Stiffelio*, was, in turn, given its world premiere on 16 November 1850.

Over the years a number of works outside the traditional Italian/German/French repertory have appeared on Teatro Verdi's *cartellone*: Dvořák's *Rusalka*, Rimsky-Korsakov's *The Legend of the Invisible City of Kitezh*, Tchaikovsky's *Mazeppa*, Zoltán Kodály's *Háry János*, and Moniuszko's *Halka*. Teatro Verdi's less-familiar French repertory has included Dukas's *Ariane et Barbe-Bleue* and Meyerbeer's *Dinorah*. (Meyerbeer was enthusiastically acclaimed at Teatro Verdi when, in 1824, he personally conducted his *Il crociato in Egitto*.) Unusual Italian repertory has included the Ricci brothers' *Crispino e la comare* as well as works by Zandonai, Respighi, and Wolf-Ferrari. Among 20th-century compositions, operas by Poulenc, Prokofiev, Penderecki, Shostakovich, Janáček, and Menotti have been mounted here.

In the field of conducting, the city of Trieste is justly proud of its native son, Victor De Sabata. In addition to his work, over the years Teatro Verdi has enlisted the services of Gino Marinuzzi, Herbert von Karajan, Hubert Soudant, Evelino Pidò, Spiros Argiris, Daniel Oren, and Roberto Abbado. The list of recent stage directors includes Filippo Crivelli, Giulio Chazalettes, Virgino Puecher, and Gian Carlo Menotti. (Franco Zeffirelli designed the sets and costumes for Teatro Verdi's *La fille du régiment*.)

The current roster of vocal artists includes, among many others, Johanna Meier, Elena Zilio, Katerina Ikonomou, Alessandra Ruffini, Gail Gilmore, Giusy Devinu, Eleanora Jankovic, Lucia Aliberti, Bruce Ford, Giuseppe Sabbatini, Giovanni Furlanetto, József Gregor, Paolo Washington, Robert Tate, and Barry Anderson.

Teatro Verdi is located right at the heart of the old port at Molo Audace (the Bold Pier), though it is the back end—the stage portion—of the theater that faces the waters at Riva Tre Novembre. The patron's entrance to the theater is actually off Piazza dell'Unità at Piazza Verdi, though the theater's mailing address is Riva Tre Novembre 1.

Following its most recent restoration in 1987, Teatro Verdi accommodates 1500 patrons in its two full tiers of boxes, single tier of side-boxes, two balconies, gallery, and main floor. The boxes, of cream color with ornate gold filigree work, are trimmed in red velvet that matches the upholstery of the chairs in the orchestra (stalls/parterre). The frescoed ceiling hints less of its original Moorish decoration than of the classic style of Pompeii. Altogether it is a comfortable theater with excellent acoustics and an always varied and interesting *cartellone*, with each opera produced and brought to the stage with loving care and expert musicality.

According to Nicoletta Cavalieri, the director of external affairs:

> Teatro Verdi offers over 300 programs a year. As an *ente*, it provides an opera season of more than 80 performances and both a fall and spring symphony season as well as other concerts and ballets. In addition to our local season in Trieste, Teatro Verdi always seeks to create a season full of cultural exchanges with neighboring countries.[53]

The multi-talented and hard-working Raffaelo de Banfield, the British-born composer who has been artistic director of Teatro Verdi since 1972, is very astute:

> Though we have presented such important musicians in our productions as Richard Strauss and Herbert von Karajan as conductors, and such singers as Maria Callas, Renata Tebaldi, Giuseppe Di Stefano, and Mario Del Monaco, we have

never given in to the "blackmailings [*ricatti*]" of the "star system," and, instead, have been attentive to reasonably prudent politics in artistic choices.[54]

Trieste has been fortunate in the selection of the experienced Giorgio Vidusso as its *sovrintendente*, a politician-musician who appointed the 27-year-old Chinese Lü Jia as principal conductor at Teatro Verdi and who instituted the Festival Internazionale dell' Operetta in Trieste, a festival devoted to light music and theater. "Will Trieste really become the 'merry heart' of Mitteleuropa?" Vidusso rhetorically asks. He continues in his own English:

> This special form of musical entertainment [operetta] has enjoyed the greatest success in Trieste for well over 20 years, thus becoming an established tradition. . . . According to the programme that has been drawn up by the organizers, the festival is meant to follow the itineraries of Europe's musical theater, thus reflecting the Empire's "merry apocalypse," the caustic wit that developed secretly during the Second World War and the inclination for popular melodrama that was revived by the musical comedy.[55]

The Season at Teatro Verdi

The regular opera season at Teatro Verdi begins in early December and concludes in late May. Generally there are five or more titles on the *cartellone*, each presented about nine or 10 times. The season of 1990–91 is representative:

Mozart's *Don Giovanni*
with Knut Skram, Michail Ryssov, Ana Pusar,
Luigi Petroni, Linda Russell,
and Giovanni Furlanetto/José Fardilha;
conducted by Wolfgang Rennert
(10 performances)

Bellini's *La straniera*
with Lucia Aliberti, Vincenzo Bello, Roberto Frontali,
and Sara Mingardo; conducted by Gianfranco Masini
(10 performances)

Verdi's *Nabucco*
with Fabio Armiliato, Francesca Arnone,
Jonathan Deutsch/Branislav Jatich, Gail Gilmore/
Linda Roark Strummer, and Mihaly Kalmandi/
Eduard Tumagian; conducted by Piergiorgio Morandi
(10 performances)

Massenet's *Werther*
with Giuseppe Sabbatini, Armando Ariostini,
and Chantal Dubarry/Helga Müller Molinari;
conducted by Tiziano Severini
(10 performances)

Donizetti's *Don Pasquale*
with József Gregor/Paolo Washington, Roberto Coviello/
Marco Camastra, Aldo Bertolo/Pietro Ballo,
and Gabriella Morigi/Gemma Bertagnolli;
conducted by Roberto Abbado
(10 performances)

Smareglia's *Pittori fiamminghi*
with Daniel Muñoz/Fabio Armiliato, Carlo Striuli,
and Milena Rudiferia/Rossella Redoglia;
conducted by Gianfranco Masini
(10 performances)

Zajc's *Nikola Šubić Zrinjski*
with the chorus and artists of Teatro Ivan Zajc di Fiume
(1 performance)

The Festival Internazionale dell'Operetta

The International Operetta Festival in Trieste runs from mid-June until late July. The 1991 season, for example, included three operettas: *Wiener Blut*, the three-act operetta constructed by Leon Stein from the music of Johann Strauss (seven performances at Teatro Verdi); Franz von Suppé's three-act *Boccaccio* of 1879 (seven performances at Teatro Verdi); and Imre Kálmán's three-act *Die Zirkusprinzessin* of 1926, performed in the original German (three performances at Teatro Verdi). In addition to these three operettas, the festival included a video presentation at the Museo Revoltella, "Milly allo specchio," a retrospective of Bertold Brecht's songs and dances; "L'ultime canzone" featuring tenor Lajos Kazma in songs of Tosti presented at Caffè San Marco; "Le

144

cetre di Waltraud e Ursula" in sounds of the Vienna of Mozart and the film "The Third Man"; "Cartoline veneziane" with soprano Cosetta Tosetti at Caffè San Marco; "A Song in My Heart" at the Museo Revoltella, featuring Shawna Farrell in songs of Cole Porter, George Gershwin, Jerome Kern, Irving Berlin, and Richard Rodgers; "Festa in Castello" at Trieste's historic shrine, the Castello di San Giusto, featuring Teatro Verdi Orchestra under the direction of its permanent conductor, Lü Jia, with works by Suppé, Offenbach, and Johann Strauss; "Je suis come je suis" with the best songs of Juliette Gréco at Teatro Verdi; and "Operetta in Piazza" in Piazza dell'Unità in front of Teatro Verdi: three evenings with the Municipal Band "G. Verdi" of Trieste in programs of music by von Suppé, Offenbach, Lehár, Kálmán, Balfe, Ivanovici, Morricone, and Boieldieu.

The festival of 1992 included two interesting and unusual operettas: Robert Stolz's *Frühjahrsparade* (sung in Italian as *Parata di primavera*) and Giuseppe Pietri's *Addio giovinezza*, as well as a recital by Helene Delavault.

Practical Matters

Ordinarily, ticket sales for each event begin five days before opening night performances, and, for repeat performances, on the day of the performance. To order tickets from outside Trieste, send a registered letter to Biglietteria del Teatro, Piazza Verdi 1, I-34121 Trieste, or by fax to 040/366.300. Your request by letter should be accompanied by your name, address, and telephone number, as well as the day and date of performance, the opera title, and the desired seat location (including the quantity of tickets), along with a remittance in Italian lire for the cost of the tickets. Ticket orders will be filled in the order received. Telephone orders are accepted from 11:00 A.M. to 1:00 P.M., and tickets must be picked up at the box office by 6:30 P.M. on the day of performance.

The box office of the theater, at Piazza Verdi 1, is open every day, except Monday, from 9:00 A.M. to 1:00 P.M. and from 4:00 to 7:00 P.M. On days of performances, the box office remains open until 9:00 P.M. Will-call tickets must be picked up at the box office at least a half-hour before the performance. No refunds are made.

Ticket prices—while expensive—are the most reasonable of any major house in Italy. Tickets for the summer festival are slightly less costly, but still—by international standards—expensive.

145

For the Armchair Fan

While there are no books on Teatro Verdi in English or Italian, two CDs exist that give a good aural impression of the theater and its productions.

> Bellini, Vincenzo. *La straniera*. Ricordi RFCD 2010; with Lucia Aliberti, Vincenzo Bello, and Roberto Frontali; Orchestra e Coro del Teatro "G. Verdi" di Trieste; conducted by Gianfranco Masini. Recorded in the opera house in 1990.

> Wolf-Ferrari, Ermanno. *Il campiello*. Ricordi RFCD 2014; with Daniela Mazzuccato Meneghini and Carlo Striuli; Orchestra e Coro del Teatro "G. Verdi" di Trieste; conducted by Carlo Bareza. Recorded in the opera house in 1991.

Teatro Regio
TURIN

At the end of Via Roma—that broad, straight street built by the Romans that is today lined with handsome arcades sheltering the windows of luxury shops—stands the Palazzo Reale, the royal palace. Built between 1646 and 1658, its brick facade—rather plain in design—suggests the conservatism and temperate nature of the House of Savoy that, beginning in 1056 with Umberto the White-handed, ruled Turin and its surrounding territory: first the province of Savoie, then Piedmont, and, from the unification of Italy in 1861 to the establishment of the republic in 1945, all of Italy including Sicily and Sardinia.

Through the efforts of Carlo Emanuele III (1732–73), a philosopher-king, Turin was made into "the finest village in the world" in the words of Montesquieu, with one of the monarch's greatest contributions being the establishment in 1740 of a royal theater—Teatro Regio—just to the southeast of the palace itself. With an arcaded front that still stands today, the horseshoe-shaped theater designed by architect Benedetto Alfieri held five tiers of boxes, with the royal box covered by a magnificent and opulent *baldacchino* (canopy). The theater accommodated altogether 2500 patrons, its handsome proscenium opening decorated in neoclassical style with baroque ornamentation. Modeled after the great San Carlo of Naples, Teatro Regio opened on 26 December 1740 with a performance of Francesco Feo's *Arsace*.

During the next 200 years Teatro Regio presented more than

100 *primas* of such works as Johann Christian Bach's first opera, *Artaserse* (1760), Cherubini's *Ifigenia in Aulide* (1788), Meyerbeer's *Semiramide* (1818), Catalani's *Loreley* (1890), Puccini's *Manon Lescaut* (1893) and *La Bohème* (1896), and Zandonai's *Francesca da Rimini* (1914). Then, on the night of 8 February 1936 tragedy struck, and this magnificent theater burned to the ground. The headline of the next morning's *La Stampa* announced, "Teatro Regio Destroyed by a Violent Fire," with the accompanying photograph showing tongues of flame leaping uncontrollably from the windows of the theater's arcaded front. Though the firemen fought bravely, the best they could do was to save one of the foyers and keep the fire from spreading to the adjoining structures of the palace complex. The main floor, built of wood, was completely consumed, as were the tiers of wooden boxes. The stage was a pile of rubble, the roof of it completely destroyed, leaving a great gaping hole. Judging by the press photographs taken the day after the fire, the conflagration had started in the area of the stage and had then moved on to the house.

Between this total destruction by fire and the vagaries of World War II that followed, the *Torinesi* were unable to rebuild and reopen Teatro Regio until 1974. New architect Carlo Mollino retained the original arcaded facade on Piazza Castello and designed a magnificently modern house behind it. The seating capacity was reduced to 1756 seats; the new *sala* contains only one tier of boxes, and this tier is located on the perimeter of the house's elliptical shape. To the architect's credit, this new house not only has excellent acoustics and marvelous sightlines, it has the feel of an opera house, not of a modern hall or auditorium as so many of today's "opera" buildings have. The foyer, on what Americans would call the second floor, is at once modern, spacious, and elegant. "This feeling is generated," Alfieri tells us, "by the large space that we have allowed so that the patrons can move about freely, circulating and intermingling, the whole illuminated by a transparent cupola. Two symmetrical 'bridges' connect this foyer with the theater proper."[56] Teatro Regio triumphantly reopened on 10 March 1973 with Verdi's *I vespri siciliani*, an imposing production, rehearsed by Vittorio Gui, conducted by Fulvio Vernizzi, and produced by Maria Callas (her first production) in collaboration with Giuseppe Di Stefano, with choreography by Sergey Lifar.

The design for the reconstruction of Turin's Teatro Regio. The theater's facade closely resembles the original and masks the modern
design of the house itself. Courtesy Teatro Regio di Torino.

The City of Turin and Its Opera House

Turin, a lively, prosperous town of wide avenues and spacious
squares, lies on the left bank of the River Po and is framed by the
arc of the Cottian and Graian Alps to the north. The symmetry of
Turin's layout is an inheritance from Roman times; its architectural beauty stems from the baroque period. A town of fashionable
women and distinguished-looking men, "the courteous and refined
atmosphere of Turin," the Michelin guide quite aptly states, "is
that of a cultural center distinguished by many bookshops, well-
known newspapers and a large university."[57]

The cultured and educated nature of the *Torinesi* is very much in
evidence when you attend an opera performance at Teatro Regio.
Among the most sophisticated and elegantly dressed audiences I
have encountered in Italian opera houses, the *Torinesi* know, respect, and love their opera, and the management presents for them
some of the most richly varied fare to be found in an Italian *ente*.

"Actually the public that goes to opera is rather homogeneous,"

148

Elda Tessore, Teatro Regio's *sovrintendente* admits. "Some are truly aficionados and are extremely attentive to what is happening both theatrically and musically on stage."[58]

Elda Tessore is that rare phenomenon in the annals of Italian opera, a woman occupying one of the most important executive/administrative posts in opera. In an interview held in association with the 250th anniversary celebration of Teatro Regio in 1991, Tessore indicated her intense desire to reach out to an even wider public.

Over the course of the years, Teatro Regio has had a characteristic that on one side is positive and on the other negative. Substantially, all performances are covered by subscriptions (about 18,000 in a theater that seats 1700) and this is positive because it permits complete coverage, financially, of the productions. There is, however, a negative side. In spite of my love for the subscribers, there is also a risk of completely leaving out the non-subscribers. We need to find a way to permit everyone to be able to go to the box office and purchase a ticket, even at the last moment, without having to pre-book months in advance. On this occasion of the 250th anniversary, I am trying to impress on all *Torinesi* that Teatro Regio is home for everyone and that everyone should at least visit it once.

I am also committed to bringing Teatro Regio closer to the *Torinesi*, to the youth and elderly through collateral initiatives, including ones through the valuable collaboration of musical "associations" and organizations. One such initiative is the exposition that is opening this month for the 250th anniversary of the theater. I can assure you that it is an immense pleasure to see all of the dedication and passion that is going into this project. Because of it, there is a 50 percent possibility that instead of the theater's becoming a museum, it will become a meeting place for the city and its people.[59]

The exposition of which Tessore spoke—"L'arcano incanto" (Mysterious Enchantment)—was a huge exhibit involving some 10 different areas of the theater altogether, each devoted to a different element of opera: original scores, programs, librettos, costume designs, costumes, sketches of stage sets, miniatures, a total of 764 items! The glass-encased diorama of the stage that was located in front of the theater for the pleasure of sidewalk passersby was of very special interest. Periodically it demonstrated through electronics (in miniature) how the newly installed electronic scenery-changing elements and lighting units will function when the installation is completed, the very latest in state-of-the-art electronic manipulation of set pieces, borders, wings, and drops.

Opera in Turin

The production of opera in Turin actually predates the founding of Teatro Regio in 1740. The rise of opera—out of its primitive elements: dances, feasts, and stage interludes—was engendered in Turin as elsewhere in Italy by noteworthy events that were celebrated with great festivities, especially the marriages of members of the royal family. The first "opera" was *Zalizura*, set to music by Sigismondo of Palermo, a composer who was then head of the chamber musicians of Carlo Emanuele I of Savoy. In 1678 music by an unknown composer accompanied *I portici di Atene*, a "joyous feast of fireworks celebrated by the Royal Lady on the River Po." Other spectacles took place at Teatro dei Commedianti, at the ducal palace, and at Teatro delle Feste, the predecessor of Teatro Regio Ducal.[60]

In 1710 Teatro Carignano (named after the other branch of the House of Savoy) was inaugurated. The productions at the Carignano (which still exists as a theater) alternated between plays and operas. Then in 1740 the royal theater, Teatro Regio, opened. Its early seasons included works by Jommelli, Hasse, Traetta, Galuppi, Piccinni, Sacchini, and Cimarosa, among others. In 1798, because of the political realities of the time, the name of the theater was changed to Teatro Nazionale, and an architect was commissioned to demolish the crown decorating the royal box along with its throne chair and replace them with regular seating facilities. The theater closed the next year because of financial difficulties and then reopened in 1801 as the Grand Théâtre des Arts; Giacomo Pregliasco was appointed its impresario, a position he occupied for nine years. Two years later, in 1803, General Jacques-François Menou donated the Théâtre des Arts to the city of Turin, which, in turn, renamed it Teatro Imperiale the following season. Sebastiano Nasolini's *Mitridate* was specially staged during the season of 1805 for the appearance of Napoleon at Teatro Imperiale.

Closed for renovations from 1806 to 1810, the house reopened again under its present name, Teatro Regio. From 1814 to 1838, it staged a series of Rossini operas—some nine titles altogether. Bellini's *La straniera* appeared in 1831, followed by *Norma* in 1833 and *I Capuleti e i Montecchi* in 1836. Donizetti dominated the seasons of 1834 (*Fausta* and *Anna Bolena*) and 1837 (*Belisario* and *Lucia di Lammermoor*).

"After some decades of uneventful administration," Giorgio Pestelli writes in *New Grove*,

> Teatro Regio, especially under the direction of the impresario Depanis, enjoyed a period of vigorous revival: in 1876 Wagner's *Lohengrin*, which had failed at La Scala three years previous, was a great success here, and Turin became a Wagnerian centre; and in 1895 Toscanini conducted the Italian premiere of *Götterdämmerung*.[61]

The 19th century ended brilliantly at Teatro Regio with the *primas* of Catalani's *Elda* in 1880, Puccini's *Le villi* in its 1884 version, *Manon Lescaut* in 1893, and *La Bohème* in 1896. The new century arrived with the Italian *prima* of Strauss's *Salome* in 1906, conducted by the composer, and the world premiere of Zandonai's *Francesca da Rimini* in 1914. In 1911, as part of the celebration for the 50th anniversary of the unification of Italy, Debussy conducted a concert of his own music at the theater.

A rival appeared on the scene in 1925: Teatro di Torino, which took over the former Teatro Scribe. Under the artistic direction of G. M. Gatti, and with the collaboration of Vittorio Gui and Alfredo Casella, it brought back into the repertory such neglected operas as Rossini's *L'italiana in Algeri* and Gluck's *Alceste* and put on the first performances in Italy of Strauss's *Ariadne auf Naxos*, Malipiero's *Sette canzoni*, Ravel's *L'heure espagnole*, and Stravinsky's *Les noces*.

During the period from the fire of 1936 to the opening of the new Teatro Regio in 1973, concerts dominated the *cartellone* in Turin, although the *ente* Teatro Regio did produce operas at other theaters.

Teatro Regio Today

Though some writers have described the new Teatro Regio as being shaped in the traditional horseshoe configuration, this statement must be qualified. For all the importance and success of the true baroque horseshoe configuration, it has one very marked and distinct disadvantage: in those boxes nearest the stage, at that open point of the horseshoe where the ends turn in toward each other as they return to the proscenium opening, there are box seats that not only do not face the stage but actually face somewhat away from the stage. In designing the new Teatro Regio, the architect avoided this by cutting off the horseshoe shape at its widest point, thus offering a truncated ellipse comparable to half an egg. Around the outer edge of this ellipse there is a single row of boxes, some 38 altogether, some seating six, most seating four. The main floor of the house—raked at an excellent level for good sightlines—is divided by elevation into three sections: the front, center, and back, each with comfortable plush chairs arranged in gently curving arcs.

The Season at Teatro Regio

Because today's budgets suggest shorter seasons, Teatro Regio generally offers a *cartellone* of five or six operas and two evenings of ballet. The season begins in late October or early November and concludes between the end of June and mid-July, with each opera presented eight to 10 times. Offerings for the season of 1992–93 were as follows:

Puccini's *La Bohème*
"A special production for young interpreters,"
with Liliana Marzano, Silvia Gavarotti, Roberto Aronica,
Domenico Colaianni, Claudio Ottino, Jorge Vaz De Carvalho,
and Riccardo Ferrari; conducted by Fabrizio Maria Carminati
(13 performances)

Massenet's *Esclarmonde*
with Alexandrina Pendatchanska, Alberto Cupido, and
Michele Pertusi; conducted by Alain Guingal
(8 performances; first performance in Italy)

Puccini's *Manon Lescaut*
with Norma Fantini, Stefano Antonucci, Giuseppe Giacomini,
and Jules Bastin; conducted by Tiziano Severini
(10 performances)

Verdi's *Falstaff*
with Leo Nucci, Bruno Pola, Josef Kundlak,
Madelyn Monti, Lucia Valentini Terrani, and Raquel Pierotti;
conducted by Bruno Campanella
(9 performances)

J. Strauss's *Die Fledermaus*
with Sona Ghazarian, Donald George, Patrick Raferty,
and Sebastian Holecek; conducted by Alfred Eschwé
(8 performances)

Cilea's *Adriana Lecouvreur*
with Raina Kabaivanska, José Fardilha,
and Stefania Toczyska; conducted by Daniel Oren
(9 performances)

Donizetti's *Lucia di Lammermoor*
with Alida Ferrarini, Gregory Kunde, Enrico Cossutta,
and Roberto Servile; conducted by Bruno Campanella
(10 performances)

Only one evening was given over to ballet during the 1992–93 season, that for *Giselle* in a production from the Deutsche Oper Berlin (eight performances). There were four recitals of which one was a joint recital: Cecilia Gasdia, Ruggero Raimondi, Daniela Dessì and Giuseppe Sabbatini, and Marilyn Horne.

There is a small theater in Teatro Regio—Piccolo Regio, which seats 430—which presented a marionette opera for children as well as chamber music, electronic music, and dance programs.

Practical Matters

Teatro Regio placed in service during the 1991–92 season the most up-to-date computerized ticket sales office in Italy. This enables a person to buy tickets quickly and efficiently either by appearing in person at the box office or by mail.

Tickets for Teatro Regio are very expensive, especially for the opening night of the season and opening nights of a run. For special matinées, the price drops to as low as about $20 for any seat in the house.

Except for opening nights, the back center-section seats (the least expensive in the house) do not go on sale until one hour before curtain time. The box office, open daily, except Mondays, from 10:00 A.M. to noon and from 3:30 to 7:00 P.M., is located at the front entrance to the house, on Piazza Castello. Requests by mail must indicate the opera, the date of the performance, and the seat location along with the number of tickets desired. Money for the tickets, payable in Italian lire, may be sent with the order either in the form of an international postal money order or a bank draft. Requests will be filled in the order received. They must arrive not less than 20 days before a performance; confirmation notices will be mailed five days before the performance. Requests should be mailed to Teatro Regio Torino, Piazza Castello 215, I-10124 Turin. Tickets must be picked up at the box office not less than one hour before curtain. For further information (in Italian), the telephone number is 011/88.151; fax 011/8815.214.

For the Armchair Fan

Though nothing has been published in English, there are 2 marvelous books on Teatro Regio in Italian. The first, a magnificently illustrated catalogue of some 839 pages from the 250th anniversary exhibit "L'arcano incanto," provides tables of performances as well as captions for its more than 1000 photographic illustrations (many in color) that most readers unfamiliar with Italian can understand. The other volume, of some 480 pages and illustrated in color, is a history of the theater from its founding in 1740 to its burning in 1936.

Basso, Alberto, ed. 1991. *L'arcano incanto: Il Teatro Regio di Torino 1740–1990*. Milan: Electa.

Gualerzi, Valeria, Giorgio Gualerzi, and Giorgio Rampone. 1992. *Momenti di Gloria: Il Teatro Regio di Torino 1740–1936*. Turin: Teatro Regio di Torino.

For the armchair listener, there are not only two very interesting complete opera recordings available but a marvelous anthology of famous voices that have appeared on the stage of Teatro Regio.

Rossini, Gioachino. *Il barbiere di Siviglia*. Nuova Era 6760/62; with Rockwell Blake, Enzo Dara, Luciana Serra, Bruno Pola, and Paolo Montarsolo; Orchestra e Coro del Teatro Regio di Torino; conducted by Bruno Campanella. Recorded at Teatro Regio, June 1987.

Verdi, Giuseppe. *I due Foscari*. Nuova Era 6921/22; with Renato Bruson, Nicola Martinucci, and Maria Gabriella Onesti;

Orchestra e Coro del Teatro Regio di Torino; conducted by Maurizio Arena. Recorded live, 14 December 1984.

Grandi voci al Teatro Regio: A 250th Anniversary Celebration. Memories HR 4384/85; with Francesco Tamagno, Giuseppe De Luca, Ezio Pinza, Conchita Supervia, Eva Turner, Toti Dal Monte, Maria Caniglia, Aureliano Pertile, Alfredo Kraus, Raina Kabaivanska, Renata Scotto, Carlo Bergonzi, José Carreras, Fiorenza Cossotto; Katia Ricciarelli, Renato Bruson, Lucia Valentini Terani, Rockwell Blake, Luciana Serra, and Enzo Dara. Recorded between 1903 and 1988.

Teatro La Fenice
VENICE

Suspended as it is between sky and sea on some 117 islands, Venice must surely be the most unusual city in the world: 150 streets of water, romantic gondolas, more than 400 bridges arching gracefully over the canals, and magnificent palaces and churches dating back to the 12th century. Truly it is a city of magical days and mystical nights.

As one glides down the Grand Canal in a gondola or on a *vaporetto* (the water-borne Venetian equivalent of a public streetcar or bus), one dreams of glories past. As you pass the Palazzo Vendramin, that rugged structure of 1509, you realize it was here that Wagner spent so many happy hours with his beloved Cosima, and where finally, in 1883, he died in her arms. Continuing on, recall that it was on this very canal that the funeral cortege of Igor Stravinsky, with its flower-bedecked water-hearse, passed in 1971 on its way to the island cemetery of San Michele in the city he loved more than any other. At Piazza San Marco, the Church of the Pietà stands on the water's edge as it has since those days of the early 18th century when Antonio Vivaldi became a violin teacher here, eventually conducting at this orphanage for girls the most famous orchestra in the world and writing more than 50 operas within its confines.

Towering over it all is the doge's palace, the Palazzo Ducale—where Otello (be he Verdi's or Rossini's) supposedly met his fate. And next to the palace stands the Basilica of San Marco, for whose chapel choirs those mighty geniuses of the baroque era—Giovanni Gabrieli and Claudio Monteverdi—wrote such sublime music.

A short walk from Piazza San Marco—leaving from the square's center, on the side opposite the basilica—leads you through narrow passageways and over arching bridges to Campo San Fantin (*campo* is the Venetian word for "square"), where stands perhaps the most charming and exquisite opera house in all the world, Teatro La Fenice.

Built in 1792, it opened with a performance of *I giuochi d'Agrigento* by Giovanni Paisiello, probably the most popular opera composer of the day. Rossini, Bellini, and Donizetti were all helped early in their careers by premieres and performances at La Fenice. When Donizetti, already quite famous in 1843, responded to the management of La Fenice's request that he write a new opera for Carnival 1844 by demanding 30,000 francs, the administration withdrew their invitation to Donizetti and extended it instead to the 30-year-old Giuseppe Verdi. The resulting *Ernani* was a huge success, and Verdi was invited back in 1851 (for which season he wrote *Rigoletto*) and in 1853 (for which he composed *La traviata*).

Ensconced in the Albergo d'Europa (now the Hotel Europa and Britannia) on the Grand Canal, he wrote on the evening after the latter's *prima* to his friend Emanuele Muzio: "*La traviata* last night was a fiasco. Is the fault mine or the singers? Time will tell."

Evidently Teatro La Fenice thought the fault was other than the composer's, for they invited him back for the season of 1857 for which he wrote *Simon Boccanegra*. And Verdi—whose music dominated La Fenice during the last half of the 19th century—was still alive when the youthful Toscanini, still in his 20s, introduced *Falstaff* and *La forza del destino* to Teatro La Fenice and Venice.

Remarkably, Richard Wagner made his last appearance as a conductor at Teatro La Fenice. It was Christmas Eve of 1882, his wife's birthday, and as a present for Cosima, he led his C-Major Symphony (written exactly 50 years earlier) for just a few friends who were present, among them Franz Liszt and Engelbert Humperdinck.

Surely we must agree, even today, with the words of Friedrich Nietzsche: "When I search for a word to replace that of music, I can think only of Venice."

Opera in Venice

Opera arrived in Venice a bit differently than it did in other Italian cities, for during the early years of the 17th century there was remarkably little activity in dramatic music with a few notable exccptions. These exceptions would include the incidental music written by Claudio Merulo for *Le Troiane*, which was performed for the visit of Henri III of France in 1574, and the intermezzi on biblical subjects mounted for the visit of Japanese princes in 1585.

Although it had been the custom during the reign of Doge Grimani (1597–1605) to perform a *favola pastorale* (pastoral fable) three times a year in the courtyard of the doge's palace, these collections of songs and choruses did not constitute an opera in the Florentine sense. True opera, as it was then known, had to await the arrival of Claudio Monteverdi, who was appointed *maestro di cappella* at St. Mark's in 1613, a post he occupied until his death 30 years later. At first he admitted to his old friend and librettist Alessandro Striggio, "My ecclesiastical service [at St. Mark's] has somewhat alienated me from [writing for] the theater."[62]

In 1637, however, as Monteverdi entered his 70th year, the first public opera house anywhere in the world was opened in the parish of San Cassiano in Venice with a performance of *Andromeda* by Francesco Manelli. Within a year Teatro San Moisè opened with Monteverdi's earlier *L'Arianna*, but in the next four years he wrote four new operas, of which we still have the music for two, *Il ritorno d'Ulisse in patria* of 1640 and *L'incoronazione di Poppea* of 1642, the latter written for Teatro Santi Giovanni e Paolo.

It is most remarkable that by the end of the 17th century, Venice had 16 new theaters producing opera, with most of them identified by the name of the parish in which they were located. Incredibly, by the year 1700 these theaters had produced altogether 358 different operas!

Of these 16 theaters, only two remain, the older having opened in 1661 under the patronage of the illustrious Vendramin family. A contemporary French journal—*Mercure Galant*—described it as "very grand, very beautiful, all painted and gilded anew, and among the most important in Venice. It contains five tiers of boxes, 33 in each tier."[63] Originally called Teatro San Salvatore after the parish, it was renamed Teatro Goldoni in 1875. Though used during the post–World War II years as a movie theater, it has more recently been refurbished and used for drama.

The other surviving 17th-century theater, known today as the Malibran, was built in 1678 behind the church of San Giovanni Grisostomo and is the most magnificent of all the Venetian opera houses of that century. Giovanni Bonlini, writing a half-century later described it thus:

It was built within the space of a few months above the ruins of an old building already destroyed by fire with that magnificence appropriate to the house of Grimani. It was once the habitual dwelling of the famous Marco Polo who lived at the end of the 13th century, renowned in every age for his far distant travels. Thus, from a pile of memorable ashes one saw, almost unexpectedly in this great capital and true kingdom of marvels, arise this real phoenix of theatres to the glory of poetry and music, which, with the vastness of its superb structure, was able to rival the pomp of ancient Rome, and which, with the magnificence of its more than regal dramatic display, has now gained the applause and esteem of the whole world.[64]

Though this house once witnessed the *prima*s of operas by Handel and Gluck, it served for many years in the late 20th century as a movie theater. More recently it has been refurbished and used for concerts and recitals. My most recent experience in the theater was a performance of Bellini's *La sonnambula* with June Anderson.

A very complete and detailed description of the theater as it first appeared was given by a Parisian correspondent in Venice, in an article written just five years after the house opened. Speaking of this theater in the parish of St. John Chrysostome, the writer reported it to be

the most beautiful and richest in the city. The auditorium is surrounded by five tiers of boxes, one on top of another, 31 in each tier. They are embellished by sculptural ornaments in low and high relief, all gilded, representing various kinds of antique vases, shells, roses, rosettes, flowers, foliage, and other types of decoration. Below and between each of these boxes are as many human figures depicted in white marble, also in relief and life-sized, holding up the pillars that form the separations between the boxes. *These* are men with clubs, slaves, busts of both men and women, and groups of little children, all placed in such a way that the heaviest and most massive ones are below and the lightest at the top.

The upper part and the ceiling of the auditorium are painted in the form of a gallery, at one end of which, at the side of the stage, are the arms of the Grimani, and above a glorification of some fabulous divinity, surrounded by a flock of winged children who wind flowers into garlands.

158

The stage is 13 *toises* and 3 *pied* [25 meters/82.5 feet] in width, and of proportional height. Its opening is formed by a great proscenium of the height of the auditorium, in the thickness of which are four boxes on each side, of the same symmetry as the others, but much more ornate and rich. In the vault of the proscenium two figures of Fame with their trumpets appear suspended in air, and a Venus in the center caresses a little Cupid.

An hour before the Overture at the theater, the painting of the Venus is withdrawn, and during the Overture a kind of chandelier ornamented with four branches of gold and silver work descends. The chandelier has a height of from 12 to 14 *pied* [3.5 to 4.3 meters/12 to 14 feet], its trunk a great sculptured cartouche of the Grimani coat of arms, with a crown of *fleurs-de-lys* and of rays surmounted with pearls. The chandelier carries four great tapers of white wax, which light the auditorium and remain lighted until the curtain is raised. Then the whole machine vanishes, and the proscenium returns to its original appearance. As soon as the opera is ended, the machine appears again to light the auditorium and to allow the spectators to leave at their ease and without confusion.[65]

It should be remembered that the large number of boxes—altogether 165 in this theater—is an indication that both personal and political business was transacted during a performance. The French ambassador to Venice assured a friend that "all diplomats went to the opera regularly in order to discover secrets that would otherwise remain concealed from them."[66] Thus it is understandable that the doge himself allotted boxes to the heads of foreign missions and personally drew lots to ensure good diplomatic relations through a fair distribution of the best seats and boxes.

Gran Teatro La Fenice

By the end of the 17th century, the city of Venice was known as the Queen of opera since it had seven functioning opera theaters. Again, all were known at that time by the name of the parish in which they were located: the San Salvador (later renamed the Apollo, then the San Luca, and known today as Teatro Goldoni); the San Cassiano; the San Angelo; the San Moisè; and, of course, the three theaters erected by the Grimani family: the San Giovanni Grisostomo (known today as Teatro Malibran), the San Samuele, and the San Benedetto (known today as Teatro Rossini). And it was in the late 1600s that the last but by far the most important of the theaters, Gran Teatro La Fenice, was built.

Before the construction of La Fenice, Teatro San Benedetto was the most elegant and the busiest theater in Venice. Unfortunately it burned to the ground in 1773, and it had hardly been rebuilt when it became involved in a lawsuit between the society that owned the theater and the Venier family that owned part of the land on which it was built. The court decided in favor of the Veniers, and it was then that the society considered building another theater, one even more grand, more beautiful, and more luxurious than the San Benedetto.

At a meeting of the society, 72 voted favorably for the proposed new theater, 28 against. The group then decided on Giannantonio Selva (1753–1816) to head the project and take care of all the necessary day-to-day details. Mario Nani Mocenigo wrote a contemporary account of this event:

> It was decided to acquire land from the School of San Rocco in the quarters of Santa Maria Zobenigo and San Angelo; a building already stood on the property, one used as a private residence, which they arranged to have demolished.
>
> The new theater, the Società decided, should be called La Fenice [The Phoenix], thus symbolizing what had happened to them with their loss of a theater through fire and the arising of a fresh new structure, a thing of even more beauty than the old.[67]

The demolition of the existing structure was begun in June 1790; by April 1792 the new theater was built; and on 16 May it was inaugurated with a performance of Giovanni Paisiello's *I giuochi d'Agrigento*. This was a turbulent period in Venice, and although other opera theaters suffered interruptions in their seasons for various reasons, La Fenice not only kept to its schedule, but in a short time became the most prestigious and famous among the Italian houses and among the most admired and important in the world. By employing the most celebrated composers, famous singers, and elaborate stage settings and costumes, La Fenice has maintained this position for much of its history.

After Paisiello, the most important composer of the day was

Giovanni Simone Mayr, whose opera *Saffo* was the highlight of the 1793–94 season. It was followed by Domenico Cimarosa's *Gli Orazi e i Curiazi*. The new works that then followed appeared with impressive regularity, numerous in title and varied in importance. In these limited paragraphs I can only give a hint of this significant activity.

Gioachino Rossini made his Venetian debut in 1810 at Teatro San Moisè with his delightful comedy *La cambiale di matrimonio* and then dedicated his following 10 operas to Venice, beginning on 6 February 1813 with *Tancredi*, his first opera seria (with the exception of his youthful *Demetrio e Polibio*). He then wrote another two operas for Teatro La Fenice while writing six for other Venetian theaters, the more important of the two for La Fenice being *Semiramide*, which was introduced on 3 February 1823.

Of the 10 important operas by Vincenzo Bellini, two were written for La Fenice: *I Capuleti e i Montecchi*, which opened on 11 March 1830, and *Beatrice di Tenda*, on 16 March 1833.

Gaetano Donizetti was another great Italian composer whose works were heard in Venice beginning with *Enrico di Borgogna*, which opened in 1818 at Teatro San Luca. For La Fenice the composer from Bergamo wrote *Anna Bolena*, first performed in 1830, a production followed by that of his *Lucia di Lammermoor*. Two operas were then written specifically for La Fenice: *Belisario*, first presented on 4 February 1836, and *Maria di Rudenz*, on 30 January 1838. *Belisario* was the last opera presented at Teatro La Fenice before the theater was destroyed by fire on the night of 12/13 December 1836.

The society decided to proceed immediately with the rebuilding of the theater. The important but intricate task was turned over to two brothers—Giovanni Battista and Tommaso Meduna—who were among the most celebrated architects of the day, while Tranquillo Orsi was assigned the task of designing the delicate decorations for the theater.

On the night of 26 December 1837—like its namesake the phoenix—Gran Teatro La Fenice rose from the ashes to yet another life, this time more resplendent with its pink and gilt décor than ever before. It has four tiers of boxes embracing the orchestra (stalls/parterre) in the horseshoe shape and is a house that seats but a thousand people in an intimate atmosphere of elegance. In addition to its porticoed entrance on Campo San Fantin, there is even more splendorous an entrance on the canal for those who arrive by gondola. Complete with 18th-century banquet rooms and an imposing foyer, La Fenice remains one of the pre-eminent opera houses of the world.

Following its reemergence, the name of Giuseppe Verdi dominated the *cartelloni* for the balance of the 19th century. His *Nabucco* was introduced there in 1842, and, following its success, La Fenice commissioned the next five Verdi operas: *Ernani* (9 March 1844), *Attila* (17 March 1846), *Rigoletto* (11 March 1851), *La traviata* (6 March 1853), and *Simon Boccanegra* (12 March 1857). By mid-century, La Fenice had only one serious rival in the world of opera: Teatro alla Scala.

Important restorations were made in the building in an effort to preserve this important historic theater. The first was in 1854, when damage to the ceiling and its decorations was repaired and minor modifications made in the structure itself. Another restoration occurred following the war in 1918 (Teatro La Fenice had been closed from 1915 to 1918).

In 1930 one of the initiatives of the Fascist government in Rome established at Teatro La Fenice the Festival Internazionale di Musica Contemporanea, a project instigated in association with the state government's recently founded Biennale d'Arte.

From 1936 to 1938 Teatro La Fenice was closed for a complete overhaul: decorations, general painting, carpeting, and structural and architectural elements. A major reorganization of the stage area was effected to accommodate new technical equipment, including a modernization of the counterweight system for flying sets and drops, an addition of lifts and traps in the floor, and an updating of the lighting system to the standards of the day. (As of this writing, the lighting facilities are again being renewed, this time to a computer-based system.)

Upon Teatro La Fenice's reopening in 1938 with a performance of Verdi's *Don Carlo* on 21 April, it became an *ente autonomo*. Then, following the war, the theater introduced world premieres of some of the 20th century's most important lyric works: *The Rake's Progress* by Igor Stravinsky, *The Turn of the Screw* by Benjamin Britten, *The Angel of Fire* by Serge Prokofiev, and, in 1960, *Intolleranza* by Luigi Nono. Teatro La Fenice has also been responsible for some important 20th-century revivals, including the first performance of Handel's *Alcina*.

The theater's roster of artists is necessarily a list of the important names in the world of opera: Toti Dal Monte, Enrico Caruso,

Beniamino Gigli, and in more modern times, Luciano Pavarotti, Renata Tebaldi, Renata Scotto, Alfredo Kraus, Gianni and Ruggero Raimondi, Piero Cappuccilli, Montserrat Caballé, Mirella Freni, and Marilyn Horne.

The Season at La Fenice

The opera season in Venice is usually one of the longest in Italy, generally opening in October and concluding in late July with about eight or nine titles on the *cartellone*, each title offered about five times. In addition, there are important recitals, one of the most active symphony seasons in Italy, displays and exhibits, conferences, lectures, and recitals. Frequently the non-operatic events—especially concerts and recitals—are presented at other theaters (Teatro Rossini and Teatro Malibran) and at such classic churches as the Chiesa di San Stae, site of many of the concerts for the Vivaldi 250th anniversary celebration in 1991, and the Chiesa di Santo Stefano.

From December 1991 to December 1992 the *ente autonomo* Gran Teatro La Fenice celebrated its bicentennial with an extremely interesting program. "The point of emphasis of our bicentennial celebration," John Fisher, the Scottish-born artistic director of La Fenice at the time announced to the press, "is underpinned by two values that this theater has always treasured: faithfulness to historical perspective and quality of performance."[68]

Included in the *cartellone* for the bicentennial were operas that had received their world premieres in Venice: Verdi's *Rigoletto* and *La traviata*, Benjamin Britten's *The Turn of the Screw*, and Rossini's *L'italiana in Algeri* and *Semiramide*. The schedule also included works that La Fenice had introduced to Italy, for instance George Gershwin's *Porgy and Bess*, produced as part of the Carnival festivities of 1992. The season also included such important works of the repertory as Verdi's *Don Carlo*, Donizetti's *Lucia di Lammermoor*, Puccini's *Turandot*, and Wagner's *Tristan und Isolde*.

In addition, La Fenice offered three different balletic experiences: performances of *Viktor* by Pina Bausch, a tribute to Maurice Béjart; performances by the Ballet Béjart Lausanne, presented each evening in Piazza San Marco during the first week of September; and an evening of Russian ballet directed by Sergej Vikharev, *primo ballerino* of the Maryinsky Ballet of St. Petersburg. Solo recitals for the season included those by Editha Gruberova, Alfredo Kraus, Dmitri Hvorostovsky, Samuel Ramey, and Marilyn Horne.

The Bicentennial Gala on the evening of 16 May 1992 featured, along with the chorus and orchestra of La Fenice under the baton of Georges Prêtre, Katia Ricciarelli, Marilyn Horne, Samuel Ramey, Neil Shicoff, Mariella Devia, Francisco Araiza, Bernadette Manca Di Nissa, Roberto Scandiuzzi, Lucia Mazzaria, and Raina Kabaivanska, in a program televised all over the world.

Following its fascinating 250th anniversary Vivaldi exhibit, La Fenice mounted such displays for its bicentennial as "Historical Stage Sketches of La Fenice," "Verdi and La Fenice," "Homage to Jean-Pierre Ponnelle," "Rossini and La Fenice," and "Two Hundred Years of La Fenice."

Round-table discussions, a regular feature at Teatro La Fenice, included during this celebratory season "Don Carlo/Don Carlos," "The Moment of *Rigoletto*," "*Tristan und Isolde*: A Venetian Encounter," and "Producing *La traviata*."

Practical Matters

Not only is Teatro La Fenice installing computerized ticketing facilities, it has become the first box office in Italy to accept credit card payments for advance reservations (American Express only). Tickets are as reasonably priced at Teatro La Fenice as they are at any Italian *ente*, roughly equivalent to the prices one would find at the Metropolitan Opera House in New York or at the Royal Opera House, Covent Garden, in London.

The box office, at the front left of the portico entrance to the house, is open daily, except Mondays, from 9:30 A.M. to noon, and from 4:00 to 6:00 P.M. For further information write Biglietteria, Teatro La Fenice, Campo San Fantin, I-30124 Venice; the fax number is 041/522.1768, or you may telephone 041/521.0161 or 521.0336.

For the Armchair Fan

There is a bit of information on opera in Venice in the book *Five Centuries of Music in Venice*, though more specific details are given in the Italian-language booklet *Gran Teatro La Fenice*, published by the theater (and available for purchase at its box office, though the attendants could never find a copy of it whenever I tried to locate it at the box office!).

Landon, H. C. Robbins, and Jo Norwich. 1991. *Five Centuries of Music in Venice*. New York: Schirmer Books.

Campsi, Ugo, et al. 1985. *Gran Teatro La Fenice*. Venice: Teatro La Fenice.

Several recent and important productions at Teatro La Fenice have been recorded and are available. According to *sovrintendente* Dr. Lorenzo Jorio:

Starting with our bicentennial in 1992, we are going to produce, in association with the recording company *Rivoalto*, two compact discs. The first is dedicated to *Le Voci della Fenice* [The voices of La Fenice], edited by Giorgio Gualerzi with Callas, Lauri Volpi, Horne, Sutherland, Pavarotti, Anderson, Cossotto, Ricciarelli, Kabaivanska, Ramey, Scotto, Gencer, Caballé, Freni, Caruso, Tebaldi, Raimondi, and other stars. The second disc will be dedicated to bel canto operas that have been revived in modern times by Teatro La Fenice.[69]

Leoncavallo, Ruggero. *La Bohème*. Nuova Era 6917/19; with Bruno Praticò, Martha Senn, Mario Malagnini, Lucia Mazzaria, Jonathan Summers, Silvano Pagliuca, and Pietro Spagnoli; Orchestra e Coro del Teatro "La Fenice"; conducted by Jan Latham Koenig. Recorded live, January 1990.

Donizetti, Gaetano. *Maria de Rudenz*. Fonit Cetra (LP) LMA 3009; with Katia Ricciarelli, Silvia Baleani, Alberto Cupido, Silvio Eupani, Leo Nucci, and Giorgio Surjan; Orchestra e Coro del Teatro La Fenice; conducted by Eliahu Inbal. Recorded live in Teatro La Fenice, January 1981.

Rossini, Gioachino. *Tancredi*. Fonit Cetra (LP) LROD 1005; with Marilyn Horne, Lella Cuberli, Ernesto Palacio, Nicola Zaccaria, Bernadette Manca Di Nissa, and Patricia Schuman; Orchestra e Coro del Teatro La Fenice; conducted by Ralf Weikert. Recorded live, June 1983.

Handel, George Frideric. *Rinaldo*. Nuova Era 6813/14; with Marilyn Horne, Cecilia Gasdial Ernesto Palacio, Christine Weidinger, and Natale De Carolis; Orchestra La Fenice di Venezia; conducted by John Fisher. Recorded live in Teatro La Fenice, June 1989.

Chapter 3

FESTIVALS

Half the fun of attending a summer festival is the opportunity it presents to experience new and different settings and to get away from traditional concert halls and opera houses. In Italy, festivals often provide a chance to enjoy music *all'aperto*—in the open—with the star-studded sky for a ceiling and for a backdrop perhaps a villa or palace, the calm, still waters of a lake, or even an amphitheater carved out of solid granite by the slaves of Diocletian some 17 centuries ago.

Although some of Italy's summer celebrations are world famous—the pageants of ballet and opera at the Arena in Verona, for example—other festivals are hidden away and little known except by the *cognoscenti*. Musica nel Chiostro (Music in the Cloister) in southwest Tuscany near the village of Batignano is one of the most fascinating of the summer celebrations, a festival that has risen from the decaying remnants of a once-handsome monastery, a building, which, before being totally abandoned, had served as a glass factory during World War II. The story of this rebirth is an interesting one.

In the early 1970s the English set designer Adam Pollock discovered the 17th-century Monastero di Santa Croce and thought it would make an ideal setting for open-air opera. For several summers he worked with a group of English student volunteers repairing the building so that it had adequate living and working quarters for a resident opera company. In 1974 he launched his

167

opera festival, Musica nel Chiostro, with Purcell's *Didone ed Enea*. Then as now, the cast and orchestra were made up of some of the finest young professional instrumentalists and singers—predominantly English—who served the cause of opera without pay, working four weeks simply for the joy of summering in Italy and working with a cast of top-notch artists in a fully professional environment. More recent seasons have included C. P. E. Bach's *Temistocle* of 1732 as well as a newly commissioned opera by the young English composer Stephen Oliver, based on Thomas Mann's short story, "Mario and the Magician" (the locale: the nearby Tuscan seacoast). This *prima* was coupled with a rousing production of Jacques Offenbach's comic satire on court life, *Ba-Ta-Clan*, with each of these works given in a different part of the monastery, its varied walls, balconies, and cloisters serving the cause of lyric art just as Adam Pollock had originally envisaged.

Another small but extremely interesting festival takes place not too far from the old walled city of Lucca: Festival Marlia, named after the site of its founding, the Royal Villa of Marlia built in 962 A.D. Having outgrown the spacious formal gardens at Marlia, the festival now takes place some 40 kilometers (25 miles) north at Bagni di Lucca, a resort known as early as the 10th century as the Baths of Corsena because of its more than 20 salt and sulfur thermal baths. The 1988 festival, for example, was titled "Bonaparte and Byron: Music and Art in Europe During the Second Empire." (Both Bonaparte and Byron had enjoyed the local thermal baths.) Comprised of drama, cinema, concerts, conferences, and opera, the festival offered as a highlight the very first production anywhere of Giovanni Paisiello's *Proserpine*, a lyric-tragedy originally written for the Paris Opéra in 1803. Staged in the courtyard of the stately Villa Ada with Second Empire décor, the opera made clever use of the villa itself as a backdrop thanks to director Lorenzo Mariani. The performance was conducted by Herbert Handt, an American who lives in Lucca and helped found the Festival Marlia in 1977.

A little farther south in Tuscany is the tiny (population 1500) hilltop village of Rosignano, with its towered palace-fortress rising from the peak of the mountain. Its Summer '88 festival included concerts as well as ballet and was a tribute to the late Nino Rota, a composer of international significance.

The excellent exhibition mounted at the Palazzo Marini chronicled Rota's classical association with such artists as Gabriele

D'Annunzio, Igor Stravinsky, Manuel De Falla, and Arturo Toscanini. On display were holographic as well as printed scores of his operas, ballets, oratorios, and songs. There were also displays related to his popular side: film scores, recordings, and the two Oscars Hollywood awarded him. The living tribute was the performance in the village piazza of two of his one-act operas, a worthy recognition of one of this century's most gifted and versatile composers, operas that provided a bit of romance and comedy under the stars.

Opera Barga in Tuscany is another of the smaller summer festivals that, when the budget allows, presents interesting music and opera. The most impressive things about Opera Barga's production of Cimarosa's *Il pittore parigino* during the summer of 1990 (as I noted in my *Opera Canada* review) were the near-perfect intonation and blend of the Orchestra Salieri of Budapest, and the discerning and sensitive musical direction of its conductor, Tamás Pál. The opera was performed in the 17th-century cloister of a Carthusian monastery, the Certosa di Pisa (Charterhouse of Pisa), a setting ideal for an outdoor performance, with the Apennine hills silhouetted in the moonlight behind the baroque facade of the church. The stage design, an ingenious series of self-transforming paintings, was by Gillian Armitage Hunt, an Englishwoman now a long-time resident of Tuscany and the founder of Opera Barga.

There is an almost unlimited variety to these Italian music festivals, something, as it were, for every taste. Out of the more than 170 festivals that take place in Italy each summer, some are devoted to the works of a single composer—the Rossini Opera Festival in Pesaro and the Bellini Festival in Catania, for example. Others are devoted to operetta and opera buffa—e.g., the Festival Internazionale dell'Operetta in Trieste and the Festival dell'Opera Buffa in Sassari. There are festivals dedicated to the bel canto repertory (the Festival della Valle d'Itria in Martina Franca) and to diverse works of the middle-European countries—Italy, Austria, Hungary, the Czech Republic, Croatia, Serbia, and former Yugoslavia—(the Mittelfest in Friuli). There are festivals featuring the greatest of world-class artists (the Ravenna Festival, "the prestigious musical event that seems to project to European heights," Claudia Mambelli wrote in *L'Opera*[1]); and there are others that, despite their topical importance, seem to be mishandled provincial affairs (Puccini Festival in Torre del Lago, "Puccini deserves better. . . . Puccini deserves much more," Sabino Lenoci and Luca Pellegrini wrote in *L'Opera*[2]). Some festivals appear only to disappear (after 40 years of effort, the Verdi Festival did not survive its opening season of 1989); others have been around for more than half a century (the Maggio Musicale Fiorentino was founded in 1933).

The challenge for the visitor is to find the right festival for one's particular interests: starry skies and historic settings; operas and concerts conducted by the great maestros; indoor festivals where both the artists and the public are protected from the elements; or festivals with atmosphere—Mount Etna as a backdrop, or a setting within the courtyard of a Second Empire villa or a recycled monastery. In the following pages you will find 10 of the more interesting and important festivals described in detail; at the end of the chapter, there is a listing of most of the other festivals that feature at least one opera on their annual *cartellone*, along with the whens and wheres of such adventures. Be aware that the Maggio Musicale Fiorentino is discussed in Chapter 2's section on Teatro Comunale in Florence, and both the now-defunct Festival di Caracalla and the Arena di Verona are discussed as spectacles in Chapter 4.

Donizetti e il suo tempo
BERGAMO

Bergamo—the birthplace of Gaetano Donizetti—is a striking city that lies at the foot of the Bergamasque Alps. (In reality it is two cities: the old "upper town" [Città Alta], where the composer was born; and the "lower town" [Città Piana], which is the heart of modern Bergamo.) It is a fascinating city to visit: quiet, peaceful, picturesque, and for the opera fan it provides an opportunity to trace the footsteps of Donizetti all the way from the windowless cellar where he was born on 29 November 1797 to the palace where he died some 50 years and 70 operas later. And a bonus is added for those who visit during the annual festival, Donizetti e il suo tempo (Donizetti and His Time): the chance to hear at least two of the maestro's many operas come alive in fully staged productions at Teatro Donizetti.

Donizetti e il suo tempo was established in 1982 with three objectives in mind: to present the first productions in modern times of forgotten works; to mount works that have not previously been produced in Bergamo; and to stage Donizetti operas in newly authenticated critical editions.

The first festival opened with Donizetti's *La favorita* in its traditional Italian version; 10 years later it was offered in the original French as it was first written for the Paris Opéra, a critical edition prepared by the American musicologist Rebecca Harris-Warrick in association with the Milanese publishing house of G. Ricordi.

By the end of the first decade of the festival, one-third of Donizetti's 70 operas and two pieces for the lyric theater by his mentor in Bergamo—Giovanni Simone Mayr—had been mounted, a list that includes many operas whose names are all but unknown to most. Many of these performances were "firsts" for the twentieth century: *Sancia di Castiglia* in 1984, *Gianni di Parigi* in 1988, *Elisabetta al castello di Kenilworth* in 1989, and *L'assedio di Calais* in 1990. Three other titles were novelties for the theater in Bergamo: *I pazzi per progetto* (1982), *Torquato Tasso* (1986), and *Fausta* (1987).

The Donizetti festival instituted its Donizetti Prize in 1987, awarded to outstanding artists of the bel canto repertory: Leyla Gencer in 1987, Katia Ricciarelli in 1989, and the internationally acclaimed *basso buffo* Enzo Dara in 1991.

Donizetti e il suo tempo takes place each year before Teatro Donizetti's regular lyric season, a month-long program that starts in mid-September and closes in mid-October. With the possible exception of a concert of sacred music that might be presented at one of Bergamo's impressive churches, all operas, concerts, and recitals are presented at Teatro Donizetti. Thus the festival, in essence, is a series of separate events—usually numbering about 10, not counting repeat performances of operas—presented over a four-week interval at the theater. To date no attempt has been made to incorporate exhibits or symposia in the schedule.

The festival is made up of diverse elements. The 10th anniversary edition, for example, opened with a piano and orchestra recital by Enzo Dara, winner of that year's Premio Donizetti. Three performances of *La favorita* followed, in the newly authorized critical edition in French. Several recitals came next: one for oboe and piano featuring pieces by Donizetti, Golinelli, Pascolli, and Schumann; one for flute, violin, and harpsichord with works by Locatelli and J. S. Bach; a recital by Rockwell Blake of arias by Donizetti, Mozart, and Rossini; and a recital by Raina Kabaivanska with arias by Donizetti, Verdi, Puccini, and Cilea. A symphony concert by the Radio Orchestra of Milan conducted by Vladimir Delman followed with music by Haydn and Beethoven. The highly successful and musically entertaining 1988 production of Donizetti's *Gianni di Parigi* then returned for three performances. This second opera production was followed by a concert of sacred choral and instrumental music by Padre Davide of Bergamo to honor the 200th anniversary of his birth, with the performance taking place at the church of San Alessandro in Croce; the festival closed with a program of cantatas by both Mayr and Donizetti presented at the theater.

The operatic productions in Bergamo feature some of the finest young Italian artists of the day, many whose names are little known outside Italy. The better-known names of recent seasons include Susanna Anselmi, Caterina Antonacci, Elena Zilio, Luca Canonici, Giorgio Surjan, and Paolo Coni.

The Season at Teatro Donizetti

The regular opera season at Teatro Donizetti follows the festival and lasts from late October through early December. Ordinarily the season consists of four works, operas frequently presented and/or produced in association with other houses in the Lombard region, most notably Teatro Grande in Brescia and Teatro Ponchielli in Cremona. A recent season was typical; it opened with three performances of Puccini's *La Bohème* featuring the winners of the As.li.co. competition in Alessandria, perhaps Italy's best-known and most qualified apprentice program. The *cartellone* continued with two performances of Bellini's *I puritani*, produced jointly with Brescia and Cremona with a typical regional cast, and two performances of a ballet, *Il vespro siciliano*, choreographed to Verdi's music, a production featuring Carla Fracci and the Philharmonic Orchestra of Piacenza. It closed with two performances of Verdi's *La forza del destino*, produced in association with the theaters in Brescia and Cremona.

The Revival of Donizetti Operas

The real Donizetti renaissance started after World War II in 1948, with the production of several rarities: *Poliuto*, *Betly*, and *Il campanello* in addition to *La favorita* and the *Messa da Requiem*. Organized in 1955 under the title Teatro delle Novità (literally

"Theater of Novelty" but more accurately translated as "Theater of the New"), Teatro Donizetti in the next five years offered productions of works that had disappeared from the active repertory such as *Rita*, *Anna Bolena*, *Maria di Rohan*, *Maria Stuarda*, *L'ajo nell'imbarazzo*, and *Pigmalione* (in concert form). Then followed after an interruption of half a dozen years *Marin Faliero*, *Roberto Devereux*, *Il Giovedì Grasso*, *Belisario*, *Lucrezia Borgia*, and *Parisina*. The presentation of such rediscoveries concluded in 1975 with *Les martyrs*.

Noting the success of festivals throughout Italy, the community of Bergamo sought to establish a better-organized approach to the lyric works of its "patron composer" and, in 1982, organized its first festival, Donizetti e il suo tempo, while at the same time promulgating the three-part formula stated earlier: the presentation of two or three operas each season by Donizetti and/or his contemporaries that would be either firsts for the 20th century, firsts for Bergamo, or firsts of newly devised critical editions. In its opening decade the festival presented some 23 different Donizetti operas. One wonderful discovery, *Gianni di Parigi*, was so popular with the audience in its initial revival in 1988 that it was repeated during the season of 1991.

In 1963 Bergamo celebrated the bicentenary of its other illustrious composer, Giovanni Simone Mayr, the maestro who had been the youthful Donizetti's mentor. For the occasion, Mayr's opera concerning the War of the Roses—*La rosa bianca e la rosa rossa*—was mounted. In the absence of an orchestral score, the work was rescored in the manner of the chief composers of that era: Cimarosa and Paisiello. This reconstruction was remounted for the Donizetti e il suo tempo festival of 1990. (Earlier, in 1984, the first performance in the 20th century of Mayr's *L'amor coniugale* had been presented as part of the festival.)

Fringe Benefits

The ancient Lombard city of Bergamo has several claims to fame besides being the birthplace of Gaetano Donizetti. The *commedia dell'arte* with its colorful, traditional characters originated in Bergamo during the 16th century, and that wonderfully robust peasant dance, the *bergamasque*, also had its birth in the town for which it is named.

Known as Bergonum to the Romans, the city was the center for

173

the Orobi tribe. It then became a Roman city, and after its destruction by Attila, Bergamo was rebuilt and became the capital of a Lombard dukedom. From 1264 it was ruled by the Visconti and in 1428 passed to Venice, under whose rule it remained until 1797. Dominated by the French, Bergamo became Austrian after the fall of Napoleon in 1815, and it became part of the kingdom of Italy in 1859.

Because Bergamo is divided into two parts—the upper and lower cities—a visit to its historical points of interest and Donizetti shrines should be similarly divided. To my mind, it seems more logical to begin in the Città Alta, the upper city, which is historically much older and also the location of most of the buildings associated with the life and death of Donizetti.

There are three ways to reach the Città Alta: a bus from the central piazza goes up Viale Vittorio Emanuele—a rather steep, winding road—which leads to Porta San Agostino, the eastern gate (built in 1575); two funiculars, perhaps more convenient for the visitor, run from Viale Vittorio Emanuele, just before it starts uphill, and terminate at the main square, Piazza Mercato delle Scarpe (Shoemarket Square); or you can walk up the hill on Via Borgo Canale from the northwest part of town, an area known as Borgo Canale, where at No. 14 a plaque marks Donizetti's birthplace (29 November 1797). Though the building is not regularly open to the public, a request to the porter (telephone 237.374), which should include a gratuity, usually gains admission. In a letter to a friend, Donizetti described this spot of his birth:

I was born underground in Borgo Canale. You went down cellar steps, where no glimmer of light ever penetrated. And like an owl I took flight . . . never encouraged by my poor father, who was always telling me: it's impossible that you will compose, that you will go to Naples, that you will go to Vienna.[3]

As it continues up the hill, Via Borgo Canale turns into Largo San Alessandro, which in turn reaches the walls of the Città Alta at Porto Alessandro. Passing through the Piazza Cittadella and following Via San Salvatore, which branches off at its far right corner, you reach Via Arena. A plaque on the wall at No. 18 (behind the basilica of Santa Maria Maggiore) marks this as the house of Bergamo's Giovanni Simone Mayr. Austrian by birth, but Italian by both inclination and adoption, Mayr not only lived most of his life in Bergamo, but contributed greatly to its musical life. Under the auspices of Santa Maria Maggiore he founded two charitable institutions: one for aged musicians and their widows and one for orphans; he also converted the music school of the church into a conservatory. Among his first class of composition students was the nine-year-old son of an indigent family, a youth whose name would become part of the name of the conservatory itself: Civico Istituto Musicale Gaetano Donizetti.

A bit farther down the street from Mayr's house, at Via Arena 9, you will find that very Istituto Musicale (which since 1897 has been divorced from the church and is now sponsored by the community with support from the state). The conservatory accommodates two important institutions: the library (Biblioteca del Civico Istituto Musicale Donizetti), which serves as the center for Donizetti research and is open daily, except Sunday, from 9:00 A.M. to noon and from 2:30 to 6:30 P.M.; and the Donizetti Museum (Museo Donizettiano), open Monday through Friday during the same hours as the library and Sunday by appointment (telephone 237.374). This quite interesting museum contains memorabilia (including a death mask), music manuscripts, first editions, original portraits, musical instruments (including one of the maestro's), and documents.

Via Arena turns into Via Gaetano Donizetti just past Piazza Rosali, and at No. 1 on what is today Via G. Donizetti you will find the home—the Palazzo Scotti—to which Donizetti returned at age 50, already in an advanced stage of insanity (which had probably been brought on, according to the authorities, by syphilis), and the place where he died on 8 April 1848. He was buried at the Valtese Cemetery, but his remains were transferred in 1875 to the basilica of Santa Maria Maggiore, and in 1951, again moved from one part of that church to another for final interment.

The basilica of Santa Maria Maggiore, directly behind the conservatory, has been the center of Bergamo's musical life since 1450, and for nearly 200 years it was the major center in northern Italy for ecclesiastical music. (It was under the sponsorship of this church that Mayr created his two charitable institutions and organized his music conservatory.) The tombs of both Mayr and Donizetti may be found in the church, as well as a plaque commemorating Amilcare Ponchielli, who served as a choirmaster here from 1882 until his death in 1886.

In 1807, a new theater—Teatro di Società—was built in the upper city by a group of dilettantes who wanted a theater in the Città Alta whose repertory would suit their tastes. It was not long before Mayr's operas were dominating the repertory at this then-new theater, and Donizetti's *Enrico di Borgogna* made its first appearance at this house in 1819. Teatro di Società lasted until 1892 when it ceased to function as an opera house and fell into disrepair. Today you will find the structure has become a *trattoria* (a peculiarly Italian type of steam-table restaurant).

While in the Città Alta you should visit two extremely interesting spots having little to do with music or Donizetti: La Rocca (the citadel) and the Colleoni Chapel.

A visit to the Rocca, an awesome tower built in the 14th century, offers a spectacular view of the old town. A short stroll leads you to Piazza Vecchia (the "Old Piazza"), which is the historical center of town, with its Palazzo della Ragione (Palace of Reason) dating from the 12th century, the oldest communal palace in Italy. Started in 1199, it was rebuilt in the 16th century and then restored in 1981. The *duomo* (cathedral) is nearby, but it is, with its mixture of styles and architecture, probably the least important structure in the area. Of more interest is the Colleoni Chapel with its magnificent frescos by Tiepolo depicting the life of John the Baptist. Dating from the 15th century the chapel commemorates Bartolomeo Colleoni, a Bergamasque captain in the service of the Venetian republic. Art historians judge it to be one of the first affirmations of the Renaissance by a Lombard artist.

A tour of the lower city returns you to more modern times, the buildings at its center having a late 19th-century look. The heart of the main square (perhaps a mile down Via Papa Giovanni XXIII, the street that stretches straight out from the train station), Piazza Cavour, is dominated by the Sentierone, a group of marble-arched shops, cafés, and boutiques. Surrounding the square are such monumental structures as the law courts, historic churches, and the chamber of commerce. And just across the street is Teatro Donizetti. The friendly Caffè Donizetti on the right side of the theater offers, of course, espresso, as well as a variety of *gelati*, that special form of Italian ice cream. On the left side of the theater is an intimate little park with white swans floating on its pool, a huge seated statue of Gaetano Donizetti serving as a background.

Originally known as Teatro Riccardi, this theater opened on 24 August 1791 with Piccinni's *Didone*. The house burned to the ground in 1797, but, remarkably, it was rebuilt within two years. During the period from 1801 to 1809 the repertory was dominated by the works of Giovanni Simone Mayr. Following those years, works were staged and conducted by both Bellini and Verdi. The first Italian performance of Meyerbeer's *L'Etoile du Nord* was given in 1879. The repertory also included works by Donizetti and Rossini. In 1897 the theater changed its name to Teatro Donizetti to mark the centenary of the composer's birth.

Designed in the ornate Italian baroque manner, there are in the horseshoe-shaped main *sala* 20 rows in the orchestra (stalls/parterre), which seat some 442 patrons; three tiers of boxes (34 boxes in each tier), accommodating another 300 spectators; and the two galleries, which seat an additional 364 people, for a total capacity of slightly over 1100.

Practical Matters

Tickets for the Donizetti e il suo tempo festival are reasonable in price, with their average cost about half of what you would pay at an *ente*. The least expensive seats in the gallery cost less than $10.

The box office, to the left of the main entrance, is open during the festival from 10:00 A.M. to 12:30 P.M. and from 3:00 to 7:00 P.M. Tickets go on sale the day before each event. For those who wish to order by mail, requests should be sent to Teatro Donizetti, Piazza Cavour 15, I-24100 Bergamo, to arrive by 1 September. Orders will be filled in the sequence in which they are received. The *biglietteria* suggests that alternate dates and seat locations be indicated on postal requests. (Opening nights are almost always sell-outs.) The only form of payment accepted is a postal money order in Italian lire payable to Teatro Donizetti, Bergamo. Confirmed tickets are available for pickup the day of the performance; those tickets not retrieved at least one hour before a performance will be resold and not refunded.

There are 22 hotels in Bergamo that range from the two 4-star hotels—the 90-room Cristallo Palace (Via Ambivieri 35; telephone 035/311.211; fax 034/312.031) and the 150-room Excelsior San Marco (Piazzale della Repubblica 6; telephone 035/232.132; fax 035/222.3201)—to the 11 1-star hotels, the least expensive of which is the Caironi (Via Torretta 6; telephone 034/243.083). For further hotel information, prices, and addresses, write Azienda Autonoma di Turismo at Piazza Vecchia 9 (telephone 034/232.730).

For the Armchair Fan

Little has been published on Donizetti e il suo tempo in Italian and nothing in English. Since there have been no conferences and no symposia, nothing in the way of Donizetti research has been published either. The two principal reference works on the theater and the Donizetti museum are in Italian; on the other hand, William Ashbrook's *Donizetti* is a masterful work in English recalling both the composer's life and providing a detailed description of all his operas. The guidebook is in English and is quite adequate for the general tourist and mentions most of the spots that might be of interest to opera fans.

Donati-Petteni, G. 1930. *Il Teatro Donizetti*. Bergamo: L'Istituto Musicale Pareggiato "Gaetano Donizetti."

Sacchiero, V., ed. 1972. *Il Museo Donizettiano di Bergamo*. Bergamo: Il Museo Donizettiano di Bergamo.

Ashbrook, William. 1982. *Donizetti*. Cambridge: Cambridge University Press.

Gelmi, Beatrice, and Valeriano Sacchiero. 1986. *Bergamo Step by Step . . . A New Practical and Comprehensive Guide of the Town*. 3rd ed. Bergamo: Grafica e Arte Bergamo.

Fortunately for the armchair listener, there are several albums that provide excellent aural pictures of the festival.

Donizetti, Gaetano. *Elisabetta al castello di Kenilworth*. Ricordi/Fonit Cetra RFCD 2005; with Mariella Devia, Denia Mazzou, Jozef Kundlak, Barry Anderson, Carlo Strivli, and Clara Foti; Orchestra e Coro di Milano della RAI; conducted by Jan Latham Koenig. Recorded live in Teatro Donizetti, October 1989.

Donizetti, Gaetano. *Gianni di Parigi*. Nuova Era 6752/53; with Luciana Serra, Angelo Romero, Giuseppe Morino, Elena Zilio, Enrico Fissore, and Silvanna Manga; Orchestra Sinfonico e Coro di Milano della RAI; conducted by Carlo Felice Cillano.

Mayr, Giovanni Simone. *La rosa bianca e la rosa rossa*. Dischi Ricordi RFCD 2007; with Caterina Antonacci, Susanna Anselmi, Luca Canonici, Silvia Mazzoni, Danilo Serraiocco, and Enrico Facini; Orchestra Stabile di Bergamo; conducted by Thomas Bricetti.

The Festival Belliniano
CATANIA

One wonders if Vincenzo Bellini ever thought of Catania—the city of his birth—after he moved north at the age of 17 to study at the conservatory in Naples and then went on to pursue a professional career not only in that city, but still farther north in Milan and eventually in Paris, where he died at age 33. In contrast, Catania has thought a great deal about its most famous native son. The city's largest park—quite magnificently and unusually landscaped —is named Giardino Bellini in his memory; a towering granite statue of the composer stands in the center of Piazza Stesicoro, one of the city's busiest intersections; an opera house was erected in his memory and named after him in 1890; and in 1926, Vincenzo Bellini's birthhouse became a national monument, housing both a museum and a library dedicated to him. In addition, the community of Catania was able to convince the French authorities that the composer's remains should rest in the *duomo* of the city of his birth rather than in Paris's Père Lachaise cemetery, the transfer being effected on 23 September 1876. More recently Teatro Bellini established an annual lyric celebration to honor the famous composer: the Festival Belliniano.

Founded in 1989, the Festival Belliniano is relatively new, although a tradition of producing operas by the "patron composer" of Teatro Bellini stretches back over 100 years. Scheduled before the regular season, the festival starts at the end of September and runs through the first week of October. In spite of the fact that the operas and concerts are presented at Teatro Bellini in the very heart of the busy "old city," the directors have achieved a truly festive atmosphere. All traffic is blocked from the large piazza in front of the theater during the festival, and a special carpet of green grass is rolled out between the monumental fountain in the center of the piazza and the principal entrance to the theater. "Festival Belliniano" is spelled out in large letters of red and white carnations, which together with the green of the background represent Italy's national colors.

A traditional red carpet frames the piazza and leads to the central portal of the theater; huge terra-cotta pots outline the path with flaming bowls of red begonias, pink and yellow chrysanthemums, and lavender and pink phlox. The three streets leading into the piazza are each overarched with portals from stage sets of past productions—principally *Aida*—to form handsome entries to the festive piazza.

Inside the theater there are sprays of fresh flowers mounted on the front of every third box—spikes of red gladiolus and white chrysanthemums to blend with the house's red-velvet and gold décor. And in the spacious *sala ridotta* (the upstairs foyer) special exhibits are mounted. The last time I visited the festival, a display was given over to theatrical jewelry called "Gocciole d'astri" ("dripping stars") because such baubles play an important role in opera: Mefistofele leads Margherita to perdition with a casket of them, while Wolf-Ferrari's *Jewels of the Madonna* and Bizet's *Les pêcheurs de perles* feature them in their titles. Included in the display were famous crowns worn by such Boris Godunovs as Tancredi Pasero at Milan's Lyric Theater during the season of 1946, Nicola Rossi-Lemeni at La Scala in 1953, and Raffaele Ariè in Athens in 1964. The famous Turandot crowns on exhibit included that worn by Maria Callas at La Fenice in 1948, made up of large white ostrich plumes offset by metallic gold and silver rosettes, and that worn by Birgit Nilsson at La Scala during the season of 1970. Of great historic interest was the richly and ornately bejeweled belt worn by Enrico Caruso in 1899 in *Mefistofele* at Teatro Costanza (now Teatro dell'Opera) in Rome and the velvet, turquoise-studded belt worn by Giuseppe Tamagno during the season of 1885 for the first performance of *Otello* at La Scala.

The first Festival Belliniano established the pattern for subsequent years: two bel canto operas per season—one usually well known (Bellini's *I puritani* that opening year), the other infrequently performed (Paisiello's *Nina, o sia La pazza per amore* that first festival). In addition to operas, there are concerts, recitals, symposia, and, as already mentioned, displays and exhibits.

The Story of Teatro Bellini

Teatro Massimo Vincenzo Bellini in Catania, is, in my opinion, the most beautiful and acoustically perfect in the world: acoustically better than San Carlo in Naples and more beautiful than La Fenice. Teatro Bellini's colors and proportions are in perfect harmony, and I never get tired of admiring them. Every time I appear on stage there it is, inevitably—for me—a perfect pleasure.[4]

These words by Beniamino Gigli attest to the glories of Teatro Bellini, a house built in 1890 on one of the most attractive piazzas in the heart of the "old city." Though there had been several theaters in Catania, the citizens—through the city council—decided they wanted a true opera house, and on 26 June 1880 authorized the construction of such an edifice. After 10 years of political wrangling and much tampering with the architectural plans drawn up by Carlo Sada, Teatro Bellini opened on 31 May 1890 with a production of Bellini's *Norma* conducted by Cesare Rossi and featuring Virginia Damerini in the title role.

Over the following century the four popular Bellini operas—*Norma*, *I puritani*, *Il pirata*, and *La sonnambula*—were seldom missing from the schedule for more than a few seasons, and eventually the lesser-known Bellini operas started to appear as well: *Beatrice di Tenda* in 1935 to celebrate the centenary of Bellini's death (remounted during the seasons of 1966, 1975, and 1984); *La straniera* in 1954 (a work repeated in 1971, 1979, and 1988); *I Capuleti e i Montecchi* in 1935 (repeated during the seasons of 1959, 1970, 1978, and 1986); and *Zaira* in 1976 (remounted during the 1990 Festival Belliniano).

Though over three dozen operas in the last 100 years have received their world *primas* at Teatro Bellini, none have achieved fame or fortune, and almost all the composers' names (such as Marchese, Coppola, and Frontini) have practically been forgotten. On the other hand, Teatro Bellini is one of the few theaters in all of Italy (outside of Spoleto, of course) to have mounted operas by Gian Carlo Menotti (most Italians considered him an American composer in spite of his Italian birth and citizenship, at least until he became artistic director of Teatro dell'Opera in Rome in 1992): *La medium* in 1952, *Il console* in 1961, *Amelia al ballo* in 1964, and *La santa di Bleeker Street* in 1992. Other contemporary composers have been well represented at Teatro Bellini, with visits and personal appearances at the theater by Darius Milhaud, Francis Poulenc, and Igor Stravinsky, plus productions of works by Bartók, Dallapiccola, Honegger, Malipiero, Mannino, Nabokov, Orff, Petrassi, Prokofiev, Respighi, and Rota.

The roster of artists who have appeared at Teatro Bellini is filled with legendary names. In 1906, Pietro Mascagni conducted four performances of his *Iris* as well as two of *Cavalleria rusticana*. In 1933, Riccardo Zandonai conducted his own *Gazza amorosa*, and three years later Umberto Giordano was present for the Bellini's

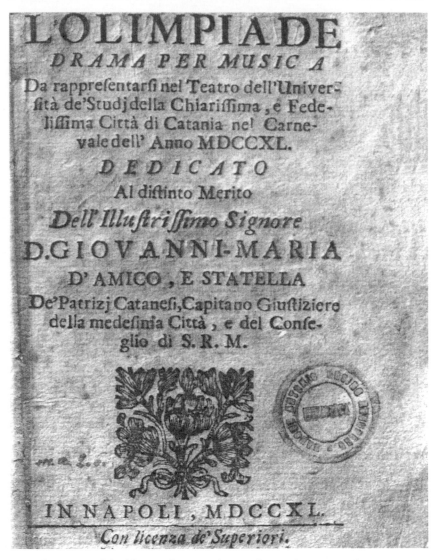

L'OLIMPIADE

DRAMA PER MUSICA

Da rappresentarsi nel Teatro dell'Università de'Studj della Chiariffima, e Fede-
liffima Città di Catania nel Carnevale dell' Anno MDCCXL.

DEDICATO

Al diftinto Merito

Dell' Illuftriffimo Signore

D.GIOVANNI-MARIA

D' AMICO , E STATELLA

De'Patrizj Catanefi, Capitano Giuftiziere
della medefima Città , e del Confe-
glio di S. R. M.

IN NAPOLI , MDCCXL.

Con licenza de' Superiori.

The cover of the libretto for Pergolesi's *Olimpiade* presented in Catania at Teatro dell'Università during Carnival of 1740. Courtesy Teatro Bellini.

production of his *Andrea Chénier*. In 1951, for the 150th anniversary of Vincenzo Bellini's birth, Verdi's *Requiem* was presented for the first time at the *duomo*, with the orchestra and chorus of Teatro San Carlo in Naples, directed by Gabriele Santini with Renata Tebaldi, Ebe Stignani, and Francesco Albanese as soloists. Broadcast performances from Teatro Bellini have included *Norma*, with Maria Callas, Giulietta Simionato, Gino Penno, and Boris Christoff, and *I puritani* with Carlo Tagliabue, Wenko Wenkov, and Boris Christoff, conducted by Ermanno Wolf-Ferrari.

In 1986 Teatro Massimo Vincenzo Bellini (to use its full, official name) became an *ente autonomo regionale*, a newly formed classification that centers the responsibility for the theater's administration on the regional rather than the city government. In this instance, the president of the region appoints a *commissario straordinario* as the administrator. Francesco Paolo Busalacchio, who has served in this position since its creation, glories in the fact that his theater mounts some of the finest lyric works, including, but not limited to, the *Oberon* of Weber, *Salome* of Strauss, *Guglielmo Tell*, *Ernani*, and *Werther*, all legendary titles.

> Our effort must be to bring attention to all forms of musical expression, including modern and contemporary works. Our strong Greek heritage in Sicily must be reflected in our plans, also. We must create, of necessity, an easily adaptable and functional theater in affiliation with the university, the Concert Art Society, and the Dramatic Theater, for example. With such a joint effort we can create for our territory a cultural "carpet," reaching out to offer our rich cultural heritage to all our citizens.[5]

The Season at Teatro Bellini

The traditional opera season commences after the Festival Belliniano and consists of concerts, recitals, ballet, and opera. The lyric portion of the season begins in late October and runs to mid-June and usually consists of seven or eight different operas. The 1991–92 season, for example, opened with Puccini's *La rondine*, followed by Mozart's *Il flauto magico* conducted by Teatro Bellini's artistic director, Spiros Argiris; *La santa di Bleeker Street* staged by Gian Carlo Menotti, its composer; Ponchielli's *La Gioconda*; Verdi's *La traviata* conducted by Christian Badea; Strauss's

Der Rosenkavalier conducted by Spiros Argiris with Renata Scotto as the Marschallin; and *Sophisticated Lady* with music by Duke Ellington presented by the New York Harlem Theater. It closed with *Simon Boccanegra* with Sherrill Milnes in the title role and Christian Badea again on the podium.

Following the regular season, in July Teatro Bellini usually presents two operas "in the open" at Teatro Greco in Syracuse. A recent season featured *Turandot*, with Sophie Larson in the title role and direction, costumes, and stage sets by Sylvano Bussotti; and *Simon Boccanegra*, staged by Gian Carlo Del Monaco and conducted by Christian Badea (Knut Stramm was the Simone this time).

Fringe Benefits

Catania sits on the slope of Mount Etna as it reaches the Ionian Sea. Though this area has been civilized for over 2000 years, the horrific earthquake of 1693 almost completely destroyed the city of Catania; thus what you see in the historic center of town today are wonderful baroque palaces and churches largely constructed in the 18th century, many on the sites of previous structures. A pleasant stroll up Via Etnea from the *duomo* will provide you with a good survey of some of the more characteristic baroque palaces and structures, as well as offer you an opportunity to see some of the city's most fashionable stores.

The imposing baroque *duomo*, founded in 1093, was rebuilt in 1169 and again in the 18th century on a design by Palazzotto. The interior, with its three naves and Latin cross design, is most spacious. There are interesting paintings on the walls, impressive choir stalls carved in walnut by the Neapolitan sculptor Sciopione di Guido in 1588 (with scenes from the life and the martyrdom of St. Agatha), and a richly carved stone doorway with episodes of the Passion. In the Chapel of the Madonna are two beautiful stone tombs containing the remains of some 14th-century Aragonese kings and queens of Sicily. The *duomo* also houses the tombs of many bishops and archbishops, as well as that of Vincenzo Bellini (immediately to the right by the first pillar as one enters the church).

A huge granite statue of Bellini, erected in 1882, stands in the center of Piazza Stesicoro, about 10 blocks up Via Etnea from the *duomo*. Four larger-than-life-sized figures surround the base, characters from Bellini's four most famous operas: *Norma, I puritani, La sonnambula,* and *Il pirata.* Several lines of the most famous arias for these characters are carved in staff notation at the base of the figures.

Another six blocks along Via Etnea bring you to Giardino Bellini, a fascinating park made up of hills and pathways lined by more than 100 varieties of trees—including palm and fig trees—and vast expanses of lawn. One little hillock in the park is crowned by an ornamental, wrought-iron pergola for open-air band concerts; another is crowned with an imposing wooden tea house, and beside a sparkling fountain, a clock and a calendar have been created out of living plants! Although occupying the place of honor, the bronze bust of Vincenzo Bellini is only one of a number of marble and bronze busts that line the path of "Famous Men."

The Museo Civico—the museum in the Bellini birthhouse—is but two blocks up Via Vittorio Emanuele from the *duomo*, facing Piazza San Francesco d'Assisi. The museum is open Monday through Saturday from 9:00 A.M. to 1:30 P.M., and from 8:30 A.M. to noon on Sunday; admission is free. Though the building today is badly in need of surface repairs to its facade and a new paint job, a contemporary etching of the structure shows it to have been quite a respectable lodging at the time of the composer's birth: a palazzo belonging to Mario Gravina e Cruyllas. Rosario and Agata Bellini rented a modest apartment off its inner courtyard with the balcony of the living room facing the *corso* that is today Via Vittorio Emanuele. The six rooms of the museum contain fascinating artifacts from the composer's life, including a number of original manuscripts (both piano/vocal and full scores) and playbills of important performances. Perhaps the most gruesome item is the wooden coffin—complete with flags, decorative hardware, and drapes—in which the composer's remains were transferred from Paris to Catania. His fortepiano as well as several important portraits—all originals—are also on display. Though objects are poorly exhibited because of lack of space and proper lighting, it is a museum well worth visiting.

Practical Matters

The Festival Belliniano has not yet attracted major attention on the international festival circuit; thus ticket prices are probably lower than for any other festival anywhere in the world (when I

The birthhouse of Vincenzo Bellini, as seen in an 18th-century engraving by A. Bonamore. The three-room Bellini apartment is now a museum. Courtesy Teatro Bellini.

was there in 1991, $16 was the top price for a ticket!), but such low prices imply no compromise of quality. With rare exceptions, recitals, chamber music, symphonic concerts, and musical encounters are free of charge.

Festival brochures may be obtained by writing, telephoning, or faxing the festival office (almost no one speaks English at the theater): Festival Belliniano, Teatro Massimo Vincenzo Bellini, Via Perrotta 12, I-95131 Catania; telephone 095/312.020; fax 095/321.830.

Ticket prices for the regular opera season run higher than for the Festival Belliniano but are still a bargain by Italian standards, with the top price usually a bit over $50.

For the Armchair Fan

A wonderful 660-page hardcover book was published to celebrate the 100th anniversary of the founding of Teatro Bellini. Though its text is solely in Italian, much of it is an enumeration of performance dates, titles, and casts that can be easily understood by persons unfamiliar with the language. The book is profusely illustrated with both color and black-and-white illustrations of artists, productions, stage sets, and various bits of Bellini memorabilia, including items from the Bellini museum.

> Danzuso, Domenico, and Giovanni Idonea. 1990. *Musica, Musicisti e Teatri a Catania (dal mito alla cronaca)*. Palermo: Publisicula Editrice.

A recording of Bellini's infrequently performed *Zaira* provides an excellent opportunity to savor the sound of Teatro Bellini.

> Bellini, Vincenzo. *Zaira*. Nuova Era 6982/83; with Katia Ricciarelli, Alexandra Papadjakou, Ramon Vargas, and Simone Alaimo; Teatro Massimo Bellini Chorus and Orchestra; conducted by Paolo Olmi. Recorded live in Teatro Massimo Bellini, 1990.

The Arena Sferisterio
MACERATA

The Arena Sferisterio is both extraordinary and striking in appearance, its neoclassical elegance unequaled in the world of amphitheaters. Over the years it has housed a variety of events *all'aperto*: ball games, horse races, medieval jousts, small *corridas*, and other popular festivals ranging from the hoisting of hot-air balloons to the mounting of operas that it now offers routinely and splendidly each summer in a setting at once impressive and thrilling.

The Story of the Arena Sferisterio

Built at the beginning of the 19th century on the initiative of, and with financial support from, 100 of Macerata's most prominent and wealthy citizens, the Arena Sferisterio was originally intended as a stadium for *pallone*, a favorite sport of the people of Macerata and the surrounding Marche. First developed in the 15th century and popular through the close of the 19th, *pallone* is a game played with a round leather ball, a *sfero* or "sphere," hence the arena's name.

The public is accommodated in a semi-elliptical, open-fronted structure of two levels with Doric columns separating the loges and a stone balustrade capping the top of the building. The original design for the arena by Irmeo Aleandri of San Severino in-cluded a first floor with 52 loges, in the middle of which was the magistrate's loge. Another 52 loges opened off the second floor, and a wide terrace opened off the third. A large arena occupied the center of the project, backed by an imposing wall (which still serves as the back of the stage today). The first stone was laid on 2 October 1820, and the inauguration took place on 5 September 1829.

In the summer of 1921, under the auspices of Duke Pier Alberto Conti of Macerata, an opera was presented for the first time, Verdi's *Aida*, a production with such a successful run that *La Gioconda* was offered the following year. One of the first musical events of major importance to take place in the arena outside the area of opera was a centenary concert by Beniamino Gigli, first presented in 1927 and repeated in 1929. Over the years, other types of ceremonial events attracted such important personages to the Sferisterio as Popes Gregory XVI and Pius IX and Kings Vittorio Emanuele II and III.

The year 1966 marked a pivotal point in the story of opera at the Arena Sferisterio, for in that year the city council had the arena restored and transformed it into a magnificent open-air theater consisting of 104 covered boxes in two tiers; a huge orchestra (stalls/parterre) area; and a large balcony—altogether seating 6000 patrons. The stage itself is impressive: some 82 meters (271 feet) across the front and made up of more than 490 square meters (6000 square feet) of floor space.

The world's most prominent artists have performed at the Arena Sferisterio. During that first season of 1967, Mario Del Monaco appeared in Verdi's *Otello*, and it is interesting to note that today, a quarter-century later, the Arena Sferisterio's *sovrintendente* is that tenor's son, Gian Carlo Del Monaco.

Equally impressive seasons followed, such as that of 1968, opening with *Carmen* in a production featuring Giuseppe Di Stefano as Don José; the second title was *Tosca* with Tito Gobbi as Baron Scarpia. *Turandot* with Birgit Nilsson and Franco Corelli was the artistic peak of the 1970 season, which also offered a *Traviata* with the three Renatos: Scotto, Cioni, and Bruson. All this was followed by *Lucia di Lammermoor* with Renata Scotto and Luciano Pavarotti and a *Bohème* with Franco Corelli. In 1972 Cesare Siepi appeared in the title role of Boito's *Mefistofele* supported by Magda Olivero; *Madama Butterfly* that year featured Leyla

Gencer, Carlo Bergonzi, Cornell MacNeil, and Fedora Barbieri with Giuseppe Patané conducting.

The season of 1977 was outstanding: *La Bohème* with Raina Kabaivanska and José Carreras and *Il trovatore* with Katia Ricciarelli, Carlo Bergonzi, and Renato Bruson. And in 1979 the conductor was forced to encore "E' lucevan le stelle" when Placido Domingo appeared in *Tosca*.

The 1980s were ushered in with operas by Mussorgsky and Wagner and ballets starring Rudolf Nureyev. José Carreras, Montserrat Caballé, and Sesto Bruscantini appeared in *La forza del destino*; the *Barbiere* was a legendary production with Marilyn Horne, Ernesto Palaccio, Enzo Dara, Leo Nucci, and Cesare Siepi.

Worldwide attention was focused on the Arena Sferisterio when Ken Russell produced his scandalous *La Bohème* there in 1984, setting the story of the Bohemians in a German-occupied Paris of both 1914 and 1944, with Mimì a victim of drugs!

The Summer Season

Though it does not call itself a festival, the season of opera at the Arena Sferisterio in July and August of each year is one of the most festive events of the Italian summer. Because of its large seating capacity, the Arena is able to offer for reasonable prices some of the world's finest vocal artists in impressively designed and handsomely mounted productions. One recent summer season, for example, included Mozart's *Don Giovanni* with Sesto Bruscantini (as Giovanni) directed by Gustav Kuhn; Donizetti's *Don Pasquale* (presented in Macerata's 18th-century Teatro Lauro Rossi) with Bruno Praticò directed by Roberto De Simone and conducted by Roberto Abbado; and *Madama Butterfly*, conducted by Elisabetta Maschio, who, according to *L'Opera* magazine, at 27 and largely self-taught as a conductor, "was the first woman to conduct during the summers of music in Macerata, and very likely the first ever to conduct a Puccini opera, in Italy at least." (The magazine's evaluation: "The young conductor emerged victorious.")[6] The young Japanese soprano Yasuko Hayashi sang the title role.

Fringe Benefits

The Marches—or *Le Marche* in Italian—stretch between the hills of the southern Apennines down to the Adriatic Sea. It is a scenic region of mountains and valleys, with great turreted castles standing on high peaks defending passes and roads—silent testament to the region's warlike past. The Marches have passed through numerous hands. First the Romans supplanted the native civilization; then Charlemagne supplanted the Romans and gave the region its name: it was divided into "marks" or provinces, under the rule of the Holy Roman Emperor. An almost never-ending struggle between popes and local lords followed. Cesare Borgia succeeded in wresting control of the Marches from the local suzerains, annexing the region to the papacy of his father, Alexander VI.

Despite being a small city (population 43,000), Macerata, built on a hill between two parallel valleys through which the Chienti and Potenza rivers flow, has always been an active cultural center, the seat of a university since 1290. Built in the 10th and 11th centuries on the ruins of the ancient Helvia Ricina, which had been destroyed by Alaric in 408 A.D., the highest, oldest part of the city is still enclosed by the remains of the city walls. Today only about one-tenth of the town's population lives within the area defined by the old city walls. Nevertheless, it is the area of most interest for the tourist.

The finest building in the old city is the Loggia dei Mercanti (the Loggia of the Merchants), which dates from the first years of the 16th century. The loggia was closed by a papal legate in 1641 to become a bedchamber reached from the adjacent Palazzo del Comune (city hall). Fortunately the three elegant arches and the open loggia above were reopened and restored to their original state in 1905.

For the music lover, the magnificent neoclassical amphitheater, the Arena Sferisterio, just outside the city walls, is the center of interest. (If visiting it in the daytime, try—for a diversion from music—to envision the buffalo jousts that were so popular here at one time!)

While there is not much more of musical interest in Macerata (which is actually a center for grain production and hog and sheep farming), there is a series of interesting museums housed in the old Jesuit Institute next to the 17th-century, late-Renaissance church of San Giovanni: a carriage museum, civic art gallery, and Risorgimento museum as well as the town library. These museums are open Tuesday through Sunday from 9:00 A.M. to noon, with the exception of the Risorgimento museum, which in July and early August is open from 8:30 A.M. to noon; at other times, it is open from 9:00 A.M. to 1:00 P.M. and from 3:00 to 7:00 P.M.; it is closed Saturday afternoons.

Practical Matters

Tickets for opera performances are relatively reasonably priced for a summer festival that features world-class artists, with the top price somewhat under $50 and the lowest around $5.

The *biglietteria* is located at Piazza Mazzini 10, and is open during the season from 10:00 A.M. to 1:00 P.M. and from 5:00 to 8:00 P.M. It may be reached by telephone at 0733/561.464.

For further information on the season, ticket prices, and placing orders, contact Informazione at Piazza Libertà 3, I-62100 Macerata; telephone 0733/40.576 or 49.402. The office is open weekdays from 8:00 A.M. to 2:00 P.M.

There are nine hotels in Macerata, which range from two 4-star hotels—the 51-room Motel Agip (Via Roma 149b; telephone 0733/34.246) and the 21-room Residence Arcadia (Via Padre Matteo Ricci 134; telephone 0733/41.746)—to three 1-star hotels, the least expensive of which is the nine-room Albergo Gioberti (Via Gioberti; telephone 0733/48.903).

For further information on hotels and rates, contact Ente Provinciali per il Turismo, Piazza della Libertà 12, I-62100 Macerata; telephone 0733/45.807.

The Festival della Valle d'Itria
MARTINA FRANCA

"Unusual." That is the word that seems to best describe not only the choices of operas for the Festival della Valle d'Itria but also the architecture found on all sides as you approach Martina Franca, the city where the festival is located, an area rich in *trulli*, those strange white-washed buildings with cone-shaped roofs (more about these later).

Founded in 1975 by Paolo Grassi, who had just retired as music director for the Italian State Radio-Television network, the festival—in his own words—is dedicated "to seeking new ways of presenting Italian bel canto opera from Monteverdi to the beginning of the 19th century"; at the same time, the festival has stressed "the contribution of Neapolitan composers and their city's musical tradition to the world of opera."[7] As the Italian music critic Gian Carlo Landini rightly discerned, "The Festival della Valle d'Itria [is] an event of primarily cultural interest rather than one centered on performance."[8]

Paolo Grassi's following pronouncement is quoted on all festival programs: "The theater remains that which its creators intended it to be: a site where the community reveals itself to itself, the place where a community listens and either accepts or rejects the message."[9]

Though based in the city of Martina Franca in the Puglia region—that very "heel" of the Italian "boot"—the Festival della Valle d'Itria attempts to serve not only its host city, a little hilltop town nearly equidistant from the Gulf of Taranto and the Adriatic Sea (about 40 kilometers/25 miles either way), but many of the surrounding cities and towns: Taranto, Trani, Bari, Alberobello, Locorotondo, and Galatina. Normally two weeks in length, the festival is scheduled from late July to early August and consists of three or four operas of which at least two are fully staged. In addition, there are concerts—both vocal and instrumental—as well as programs of sacred music. Concerti nel chiostro (Concerts in the Cloister) presented late afternoons at the convent of the Salisian order is a very special series of programs with informal concerts of operatic arias and scenes presented in concert format with piano accompaniment by the young scholarship winners who have been studying in the festival's studio program.

With reference to opera productions, there are two venues in Martina Franca: the somewhat plain Teatro Verdi, a traditional early 19th-century opera house that seats about 900 people, and the courtyard of the Palazzo Ducale (the more frequently used venue), which is adapted for concerts and operas during the festival by erecting a series of bleachers on one side, accommodating some 800 patrons, and a stage platform on the other. The acoustics in the courtyard leave much to be desired, as the orchestral sound—without benefit of baffle, shell, or shield—seems diffused, a collection of many separate sounds rather than a blended unity of timbres. Likewise, the human voice seems to lack focus and point in this outdoor ambiance.

The 1991 festival, dedicated to the memory of its founder, Paolo Grassi, presents a good idea of the usual summer offerings. Antonio Vivaldi's *Farnace* was mounted twice at Teatro Verdi in a production by Egisto Marcucci, conducted by Massimiliano Carraro with the Philharmonic Orchestra of Graz, Austria, in the pit and a cast of good regional Italian singers on stage (almost all completely unknown outside Italy). The second fully staged opera was Verdi's *Ernani* presented in the courtyard of the Palazzo Ducale with Vincenzo La Scola in the title role, supported by Daniela Dessì as Elvira and Paolo Coni as Don Carlo, with the Orchestra Internazionale d'Italia in the pit, the Bratislava Chamber Choir from Yugoslavia on stage as the chorus, and Giuliano Carella conducting. The production was by Filippo Crivelli, with a stylized stage set and costumes by Emanuele Luzzati and Luca Antonucci.

An "Omaggio a Meyerbeer" (Homage to Meyerbeer) was offered one evening at the Palazzo Ducale with the Orchestra Internazionale d'Italia directed by Massimo Biscardi, featuring a quartet of vocal soloists—Alessandra Ruffini, Ines Salazar, Giuseppe Morino, and Paolo Coni—who sang arias in concert form from *L'africana*, *Dinorah*, and *Gli ugonotti*.

The Philharmonic Orchestra of Graz, under the baton of Ernest Hoeztl, presented an evening of operatic arias and duets from two of Alessandro Scarlatti's operas—*La Statira* and *Griselda*—on the same program as *Endimione e Cintia*, a cantata for two voices, also by Scarlatti, featuring Maria Cristina Zanni and Francesca Rotondo as vocal soloists.

Concerts of sacred music were presented by the Bratislava Chamber Choir in Alberobello, and "Arias and Nocturnes" (with music by Mozart, Schubert, and Rossini) was presented by a group of vocal and instrumental soloists at the Convent of San Domenico in Martina Franca and at the Greek Church in nearby Locorotondo. Mozart's Mass in C minor, K. 427, was presented in honor of the Mozart bicentennial under the direction of Paolo Carignani with the festival's resident soloists and chorus at the Romanesque cathedrals in Taranto, Trani, and Bari, and at the basilica of Santa Caterina in Galatina.

A concert performance of Delibes's *Lakmé* closed the festival with Alessandra Ruffini in the title role, supported by Giuseppe Morino as Gérald and Bruno Praticò as Nilakhanta; the Orchestra Internazionale d'Italia was in the pit, the Bratislava Chamber Choir on stage, and Carlos Piantini on the podium.

The Story of the Festival

In years past the summer evenings in Martina Franca were quiet ones. It was Paolo Grassi who first came up with the idea of a festival that could offer tourists aesthetically rewarding evenings during their holiday sojourns. Grassi had gone to his parent's home in Martina Franca to rest and relax after a busy season as chairman of the Italian State Radio-Television network (he had earlier served as artistic director of Milan's Teatro alla Scala). As he thought about the possibility of a festival for his hometown, it occurred to him that with his contacts with international artists through both RAI and his earlier years at La Scala, he could produce a 10-day to two-week festival for what it would cost an ordinary theater to present a one-evening program.

From the very first festival in 1975, the emphasis in Martina Franca has been on bel canto, with performances based on texts and scores proven to be authentic and with all works presented in their entirety—no cuts. Thus it was at the Festival della Valle d'Itria that unabridged editions were first mounted in current times of *Tancredi*, *I Capuleti e i Montecchi*, *Fra Diavolo*, *I puritani*, *Semiramide*, *Il pirata*, *L'incoronazione di Poppea*, *Giulio Cesare*, and *La favorita*. There have also been some first performances in modern times including Rossini's *Adelaide di Borgogna* and Traetta's *Ifigenia in Tauride*, both of which brought to light unknown aspects of these works and drew attention from the international music world.

In addition to the public performances in Martina Franca, an important role has been played by musicological events: international round tables, conferences, and concert/conference combinations. Subjects have included "Music and Mass Media," "Traetta and His World," "Tito Schipa of 'The Tenor's Grace,'" and "*I puritani* I and II," referring to the two versions of the Bellini opera. In addition to RAI, which often telecasts and/or broadcasts entire concerts and performances, the festival has also drawn the attention of German and Austrian television.

The list of singers who have performed at the festival is impressive: Renata Tebaldi, Sesto Bruscantini, Magda Olivero, Luciano Pavarotti, Ruggero Raimondi, and Lucia Valentini Terrani. "Martina Franca also takes pride for having served as a 'launching pad' for many successful careers," Rodolfo Celletti, its artistic director, proudly states, "artists such as Lella Cuberli, Martina Dupuy,

Luciana Serra, Dano Ruffanti, Simone Alaimo, Daniela Dessì, Paolo Coni, and Giuseppe Morino among others."[10]

The Concerti nel chiostro recitals are the culmination of the festival's educational program, a course in vocal technique and style conducted by Rodolfo Celletti. In addition, seminars at Martina Franca were inaugurated in 1989 for training future technicians and artists in set design and acting, the programs taught by Maurizio Balò and Egisto Marcucci, respectively.

In 1985—the "European Music Year"—the Festival della Valle d'Itria was awarded the Abbiati Prize as the best musical initiative of the year "for consistency of its offerings in a stimulating cultural environment."

Fringe Benefits

While the Puglia region of Italy traces its history and warfare back to prehistoric times, the city of Martina Franca is fairly young, having been established on Mount San Martino in the 10th century by refugees from Taranto who were trying to escape the Saracens. Four centuries later, Philip of Anjou enlarged the village by building walls and fortifications, erecting 12 square towers and 12 round towers and offering the community a number of franchises, hence the name Martina Franca.

Today the city is a showcase of baroque and rococo styles. The walls and the 24 towers are gone (though four city gates remain), but quaint, narrow, and winding streets are lined with countless homes and palaces whose soft blond stones are carved with marvelous convolutions, their balconies set off by artistically designed wrought-iron balustrades.

The Palazzo Ducale—in whose courtyard festival performances are held—dates from 1668, its architecture attributed to Bernini. Today it serves not only as the festival headquarters in summer, but year-round as the city hall.

Though there are no *trulli* in the center of Martina Franca, the surrounding countryside is filled with them, and no matter which road you take to approach Martina Franca, you will see scores of them. At nearby Alberobello—about 32 kilometers (20 miles) away—there are huge clusters of *trulli*.

And what are *trulli*? They are round, white-washed houses with walls about half a meter (1.5 feet) thick, characterized by ruddy or gray dry-stone roofs whose cone shapes dot the landscape like so

Two *trulli*, with their distinctive conical roofs. Author's collection.

many giant spinning tops. The cone is formed by small limestone slates set in a spiral without mortar to bind them. Though the region's oldest *trulli* date back to the 16th century, this type of construction technique, still in use in this area today, goes back to prehistoric times, and local historians think that it was either from Greece or the Middle East that the *Pugliese* learned it.

Most *trulli* have special decorations such as a sphere or sprouting-leaf figure located at the apex of the cone; paint-daubed religious symbols decorate the slates of some of the older *trulli*, some pagan, many Christian, and even the seven-branched menorah of the Jews.

For a time it was thought that *trulli* were built to avoid taxation, since only "permanent" homes were taxed. According to this now-disproved legend, *trulli*, with their unmortared roofs, were structures easily moved when the tax collector came.

Practical Matters

Transportation is a bit of a challenge for the visitor; an automobile is almost a necessity. The closest train station is in Fasano, which itself is an overnight ride from Bologna down the Adriatic coast. From Fasano you can take a bus (actually two buses, one from the train station to Fasano proper, and another over hill and dale to Martina Franca) or a 30- to 40-minute taxi ride.

There are only three hotels in Martina Franca, so many festivalgoers who have automobiles stay in one of the half-dozen nearby towns. In Martina Franca itself there is the 24-room, 4-star Villa Ducale (Piazza Sant'Antonio; telephone 080/705.055; fax 080/705.104); and two 3-star hotels: the 49-room Hotel Dell' Erba (Via dei Cedri 1; telephone 080/901.055; fax 080/901.658) and the 81-room San Michele (Via Carella 9; telephone 080/705.355). For those who stay in nearby towns—which range from a 15- to 30-minute ride away—a car is a must, as public transportation does not exist for the practical purpose of festivalgoers.

Festival tickets are moderately priced, running generally in the area of $10 to $50 each. The Concerti nel chiostro and the concerts at the cathedral are free of charge.

Reservations may be made by writing to Centro Artistico Musicale Paolo Grassi, Biglietteria, Palazzo Ducale, I-74015 Martina Franca (TA), adding a 10 percent booking fee to the cost of every ticket. Enclose with the order either an international money order in Italian lire or a bank transfer credited to account number 20626720107 of the Banca Commerciale Italiano, Agenzia di Martina Franca, Via Montegrappa 2, under the name "Centro Artistico Musicale Paolo Grassi."

Inquiries may be made by telephone to the Centro Artistico Musicale Paolo Grassi at the Palazzo Ducale during the festival season by calling 080/707.191. Usually someone there speaks English.

For the Armchair Fan

Reading material about the Festival della Valle d'Itria is extremely limited. The only story about it that has appeared in print may be found in a bilingual magazine distributed to tourists.

Rossano, Antonio. 1991. "Musical Miracles: The Valle d'Itria Festival" (in Italian and English). *Follow Me* (Edizione Pugliese) (June): 42–43.

There is a variety of both composers and styles for the armchair listener when it comes to music recorded live at the Festival della Valle d'Itria.

Bizet, Georges. *Les pêcheurs de perles*. Nuova Era 6944/45; with Giuseppe Morino, Alessandra Ruffini, Bruno Praticò, and Eduardo Abumradi; Orchestra Internazionale d'Italia e Coro Filharmonico Slovacco di Bratislava; conducted by Carlos Piantini.

Donizetti, Gaetano. *Maria di Rohan*. Nuova Era 6732/33; with Mariana Nicolesco, Giuseppe Morino, Paolo Coni, Francesca Franci, Vincenzo Alaimo, and Giacomo Colafelice; Orchestra Internazionale d'Italia e Coro Filharmonico Slovacco di Bratislava; conducted by Massimo de Bernart. Recorded live at the Palazzo Ducale, August 1988.

Mercadante, Saverio. *Il bravo*. Nuova Era 6971/73; with Dino di Domenico, Andelisa Tabiadon, Janet Perry, Sergio Bertocchi, and Stefano Antonucci; Orchestra Internazionale d'Italia e Coro Filharmonico Slovacco di Bratislava; conducted by Bruno Aprea. Recorded live at the Palazzo Ducale, July 1990.

Piccinni, Niccolò. *La Cecchina, ossia La buona figliuola*. Memories 3101/03; with Maria Angeles Peters, Giuseppe Morino, Bruno Praticò, Alessandra Ruffini, and Gabriella Morigi; Orchestra Serenissima Pro Arte; conducted by Bruno Campanella. Recorded live at the Palazzo Ducale, July 1990.

The Cantiere Internazionale d'Arte
MONTEPULCIANO

The festival in Montepulciano—the Cantiere Internazionale d'Arte—is always a marvelous assortment of displays, exhibits, concerts, operas, dramas, and "happenings," an exemplification of its title (*cantiere* literally means "yard"), with the entire community a stage upon which multifarious forms of art—on a truly international level—are created. Established in 1976 by Hans Werner Henze, one of the world's most talented and gifted composers, especially in the field of opera, the Cantiere Internazionale d'Arte is, in his own words,

> a center for young artists (singers, actors, instrumentalists, stage directors, conductors, composers, set designers, costumers, etc.) that offers them an ideal situation in which to study and prove their work, both classical and modern, an opportunity to study both old and new methods of making music. They have a need to discover methods—both old and new—through which they can offer the public the chance to feel, understand, and appreciate the very best in music and art.[11]

Montepulciano, a town with a population slightly over 100,000, is magnificently situated upon an isolated mountain that commands a spectacular view of wide, luxuriant valleys on three sides and, on the fourth, the long slopes of the Valle di Chiana. The Piazza Grande—where many of the festival events take place—is one of the most impressive town squares in central Italy.

The Cantiere Internazionale d'Arte takes place from mid-July to early August of each summer and consists of operas; ballet and modern dance; symphonic concerts; chamber music; recitals; and displays and exhibits of paintings, sculpture, and ceramics. The venues include, in addition to the Piazza Grande, the intimate 18th-century Teatro Poliziano, the Temple of San Biagio, the Teatrino di San Biagio, the church of San Francesco, and the *cortile* of the Civic Museum. With few exceptions, three performance events a day are scheduled: the first at 11:00 A.M. (moved on Sunday to noon), the second at 6:00 P.M., and the final concert or event at 9:00 P.M.

A typical festival, the recent XVI Edition opened in Piazza Grande with Hans Werner Henze's newly created "mime drama for actors and dancers," *Labirinto*, a coproduction with the new Munich Theater of Music, with the music of Stomu Yamash'ta and the stage direction of Jonathan Moore. (*Labirinto* was repeated for a second performance a week later.)

The first production in modern times of the original version (first performed in Caserta in 1789) of Giovanni Paisiello's opera, *Nina, o sia La pazza per amore* was then offered on three different evenings at Teatro Poliziano with a young cast of singers, the Collegium Musicum of Bologna, serving as the on-stage chorus, and the newly formed Youth Symphony of Berlin (a Henze creation) in the pit; Markus Stenz, the music director of the festival, conducted.

This was followed by three performances of *Greek*, the first opera written by the young English composer Mark Anthony Turnage, a work first presented at the Edinburgh Festival of 1988.

The concert program was launched in the Temple of San Biagio with Monteverdi's *Selva morale e spirituale*, which is a heterogeneous collection of sacred pieces: a few sacred madrigals for five voices accompanied by two violins or basso continuo, a *canzonette* for three equal voices with and without two violins, a four-voice a cappella mass, a Gloria, Psalms, and a Magnificat. This varied collection of vocal/instrumental works was performed by the combined voices of the Stuttgarter Vocalsolisten from Germany, the Concentus Politianus, and students and teachers from Montepulciano's Community Institute of Music.

The two symphony concerts with the Youth Symphony Orchestra of Berlin—one directed by Henze and one by Stenz—were presented in the church of San Francesco and included *primas* of works by Roderick Watkins, Detlev Glanert, and Hans Werner Henze as well as compositions by Mahler, Haydn, Beethoven, and Stravinsky.

Among the chamber music programs, one entitled "Festival Paisiello" featured works by Mattias Pinscher (the world *prima* of his *Tre omaggi a Paisiello*) along with works by Paisiello and was presented by the students from the Fiesole Music School near Florence at Teatrino di San Biagio. In addition, there were 29 additional concerts of chamber music, including organ recitals, a survey of guitar music from 1500 to today, piano recitals, staff recitals, harpsichord programs, string quartet concerts, and a saxophone quartet from Perugia in concert. Six of the chamber concerts featured works by modern Italian composers, including pieces by Luciano Berio, Bruno Maderna, Salvatore Sciarrino, and Marco Tutino, and one concert offered works by a half-dozen student composers from Montepulciano. The closing concert featured J. S. Bach's Suite No. 3 and Mozart's Mass in C major, K. 258.

The exhibits included such interesting displays of art as "Oggetti a Pendolo" (Objects that Hang, in other words, mobiles) in the courtyard of the Civic Museum. "Puppets for Children of Every Age," featuring students from the Marionette School of Munich's Biennale, was presented twice daily in various locations, mostly courtyards and towers.

The Story of the Festival

Hans Werner Henze, the eldest of six children born into a typical lower middle-class German family in 1926, early demonstrated an equal interest in music, painting, and design; thus it is not surprising that the first festival he organized a half-century later was multifaceted in its approach to art.

Henze's decision to follow the path of music professionally to the exclusion of the other arts was wise.

Showered with more commissions than he could hope to cope with, by his mid-twenties Henze had already achieved the kind of success that most composers dream of in vain. He was, nevertheless, acutely aware of its dangers. His experiences in the late 1930s and during the war years had also left a deep scar, an unease amounting almost to a hatred for his native Germany, which this success could do little to assuage and which he was just beginning to resolve as he approached his fiftieth birthday. And so, lured by the revelatory beauty of Italian art and landscapes, he suddenly decided early in 1953 to abandon Germany for Italy.[12]

As the years passed, Henze's view of his native land tempered a bit, but he was still fascinated by Italy and things Italian. Thus, in 1976, after discovering the beauties as well as the seclusion of Montepulciano, he decided to found a unique festival, one that would allow young artists of every ilk to study, experiment, and perform without the dictates of honoraria being a factor. From the very first, no participant—on any level, in any field—has been paid. The community of Montepulciano, however—with financial assistance from the state, the region, and the province—provides housing and meals for the participants. "Those who decide to work at Montepulciano," Henze cautioned, "agree to this system. They know that Montepulciano is not a commercial festival and agree that the impetus to participate and create comes solely from sociopolitical and cultural objectives."[13]

That the festival has been eminently successful on the artistic level is attested to by such music critics as Roberto Del Nista, who wrote in *L'Opera*, "It's not rhetoric or a cliché to have to note that every opera season of the 'Cantiere di Montepulciano' that we have attended—with the full cognizance of the grounds for which we are constrained to compare these with other kinds of fruitful productions (the '*Entes*,' 'theaters of tradition,' festivals, etc.)—responds to the highest level of quality."[14]

Fringe Benefits

Montepulciano, some 65 kilometers (40 miles) southwest of Florence, is perched on the crest of a hill of volcanic rock some 606 meters (2000 feet) above sea level. Its first inhabitants were refugees from Chiusi, in the valley below, who were fleeing the

Barbaric invasion of the 6th century. First known in the Roman dialect as Mons Politianus, its citizens today are called *Poliziani*, and it is by that name that we know its most famous son, Angelo Ambrogini, as Poliziano, a favorite of the court of Lorenzo the Magnificent and one of the great classical scholars, as well as poet and playwright, of his day.

Montepulciano is an almost perfect miniature of a Renaissance city, a feel that derives from the continuous patronage of the Medici. Because of its strategic location, both the Sienese and Florentines disputed the town's rightful ownership for centuries. Having once gained the upper hand, the Medici sent their finest architects to redevelop the town. A new *duomo* was built that contains a striking funeral monument by Michelozzo Michelozzi, who also designed the Palazzo Comunale (city hall), one of the most impressive buildings to be found in Montepulciano, a structure strongly resembling the Palazzo Vecchio in Florence.

Montepulciano is centered around two main arteries, good streets from which to view and enjoy its glories: Via Roma, beginning at the city gate known as Porta al Prato and winding its way up the hill under a variety of street names, and Via Ricci. The spacious and grandiose Piazza Grande—quite irregular in shape—is situated at the crest of the hill at the very heart of town, the principal center of activities for the Cantiere Internazionale d'Arte.

The most impressive building on this piazza is the Palazzo Comunale, a Gothic building with battlements and a high machicolated tower from which projectiles could be dropped on attacking armies. Remodeled in the 15th century by Michelozzo, the tower provides great views, no less spectacular today than they must have been in the 16th century: to the east three lakes in the distance—Trasimeno, Chiusi, and Montepulciano; to the west three hilltop towns in the middle distance, one rising above another, their ancient battlements glistening in the sun—Pienza, San Quirico, and Montalcino.

Inside the *duomo*, which sits on another leg of the piazza, there is, on the high altar, a rich altarpiece of 1401 by Taddeo di Bartolo of Siena. Across from the *duomo* sits the majestic Renaissance Palazzo Nobili-Tarugi, whose design is attributed to Antonio da Sangallo the Elder, a member of that famous family of artists and sculptors and the artisan responsible for several of Montepulciano's most famous buildings. The palace has a portico and great doorway with semicircular arches; six Ionic columns, standing on a lofty base, support the pilasters of the upper story. Another striking feature of the Piazza Grande is its ancient well, adorned with an admirable sculpture of a lion that supports and holds aloft the Medici coat of arms.

The Temple of San Biagio, where some of the festival events take place, is one of the most significant examples of Renaissance architecture and is the work of Antonio da Sangallo, who designed it to be built over the remains of the earlier *pieve* (parish church) San Biagio. The campanile was in place by 1534, with the principal work on the church finished by 1595. The sculptured cornice and molding work is of special interest.

Whether you experience Montepulciano by walking up and down its curving streets or by visiting the interesting sites and venues of its different festival events, you will find it a visual joy. Among the impressive door-knockers, handsome window ironwork, winding *vicoli* (alleyways), and streetside cafés, the most amusing spot for me in this town is the aged clock tower with its masked Pulcinella striking the hours in front of the church of Sant'Agostino, the Pulcinella a 16th-century gift from a Neapolitan visitor, the church another Michelozzo design.

Practical Matters

Hotel space in Montepulciano is limited, and advance reservations for the Cantiere Internazionale d'Arte period are highly recommended. La Terrazza—on two levels as its name suggests—is a renovated 16th-century residence-turned-hotel (2-star with 16 rooms) only a minute's walk from the Piazza Grande (Via Piè al Sasso 16; telephone 0578/757.440). The 2-star Il Marzocco is located in the center of town; it has 18 rooms (Piazza Savonarola 18; telephone 0578/757.262). The "newer" (that is to say, more recently opened) Albergo Duomo (2-star) has 11 rooms and is located in the historical center of town (Via San Donato 14; telephone 0578/757.473).

Information about the Cantiere Internazionale d'Arte may be had by writing to its office, Cantiere Internazionale d'Arte, I-53045 Montepulciano (SI), or by telephoning 0578/757.089; fax 0578/758.307. There is usually someone in the Cantiere office who speaks English.

For the Armchair Fan

Because of the unique nature of this festival, no written account of it has been published. Two books about the town of Montepulciano will interest the visitor, however. The first is in Italian (the more authoritative and better documented) and the other is a quadri-lingual (Italian, English, German, French) guidebook. Its rather thorough descriptions of each important building or location are in Italian, immediately followed by brief summaries in the other languages.

Cecconi, Valeriano. 1980. *Profili di città etrusche: Chiusi—Chianciano—Montepulciano*. Pistoia: Tellini.

Calabresi, Ilio, Giovanni Garroni, Paolo Barcucci, Lucia Monaci Moran, and Gisella Bochicchio. 1981. *Montepulciano*. Montepulciano: Editori del Grifo.

There has been only one commercial recording issued of a live performance at Teatro Poliziano.

Mascagni, Pietro. *Sì*. Bongiovanni BG 2050/51-2; with Margherita Vivian, Amelia Felle, Marina Gentile, Mauro Nicoletti, Antonio Comas, and Giulio Liguori; Orchestra Sinfonica del Cantiere d'Arte di Montepulciano; Coro Symbolon Ensemble; conducted by Sandro Sanna. Recorded live in Teatro Poliziano, 24 July 1987.

The Rossini Opera Festival
PESARO

Of Italy's more than 150 music festivals each year, the Rossini Opera Festival in the seaside city of Pesaro on the north-central Adriatic coast must surely be the most prestigious, its fare always adventuresome and intriguing, its soloists and conductors selected from the world's finest bel canto artists. And, coupled with the opportunity to enjoy brilliant productions of Gioachino Rossini's operas (which include both the quite familiar and the very rare), you can spend the days at the seaside: sunning, swimming, windsurfing, reading, or relaxing.

Each year the Rossini Opera Festival takes place over the course of approximately two weeks in mid-August, at the very height of the Italian holiday season. The festival includes the presentation of three operas as well as symphonic concerts and recitals devoted to Rossini's music. The three operas usually consist of two new productions and the remounting of a previous festival production. While many of the operas are long-forgotten, almost unknown titles to all but Rossini scholars and fans, the better-known Rossini operas are also included, all in critical editions (more about this later). For example, the 11th Rossini Opera Festival included four performances of *Tancredi* in the Milan version of 1813, presented in the 1500-seat Palafestival (regularly known as the Sports Palace); four performances of *Otello, ossia Il moro di Venezia* produced at the intimate baroque opera house, Teatro Rossini, with its 890 seats divided between the orchestra (stalls/parterre) and four tiers of boxes; and four performances of a double-bill in the 600-seat Auditorium Pedrotti of the Rossini Conservatory of Music: Mozart's first "commissioned" opera written when he was 11—*Die Schuldigkeit des ersten Gebotes*—and Rossini's first "commission," written when he was 18, the delightful comic farce *La cambiale di matrimonio*. In addition to these three evenings of opera, there was a symphonic concert featuring choral works with orchestra performed by the chorus and orchestra of Teatro Comunale di Bologna entitled "Le cantate per i Borboni," with Rockwell Blake and Francesco Piccoli as soloists; a series of four piano recitals (Michele Campanella, Jeffrey Swann, François Thiollier, and Laura De Fusco); a concert by the students of the Accademia Rossiniana, the summer training program of the festival; and three "encounters" with musicologists: Philip Gossett talking about *Tancredi*, Bruno Cagli speaking on *Otello*, and Alberto Zedda discussing "Continuity and Contiguity in the Operas of Mozart and Rossini."

Over the years the Rossini Opera Festival has offered a wonderful variety of works. In addition to those already mentioned, the festival has produced: *Il barbiere di Siviglia, Bianca e Falliero, Le Comte Ory, La donna del lago, Edipo e Colono, Ermione, La gazza ladra, L'inganno felice, L'italiana in Algeri, Maometto II, Mosè in Egitto, L'occasione fa il ladro, Ricciardo e Zoraide, La scala di seta, Semiramide, Il Signor Bruschino, Il turco in Italia*, and *Il viaggio a Reims*, along with concert performances of Rossini's *Stabat Mater* and *Petite Messe Solennelle. Atelier Nadar*, created by Bruno Cagli from the second and third volumes of Rossini's *Péchés de Viellesse*, was also presented, a fully staged and costumed production.

The Story of the Festival

Gioachino Rossini was born on 29 February 1792 in a tiny apartment in a three-story, sandstone-colored brick building (today a Rossini museum) on Pesaro's main business street. Son of a horn player who appeared both with the local town band and in the pit orchestra of the theater, Gioachino moved with his family back to his father's hometown of Lugo when he was eight. Though the composer never took up residence again in Pesaro (he was educated in Bologna and made his career in Venice, Rome, and Milan until he left Italy altogether), he carried with him such fondness for this town of his birth that when he died in Passy, France, on 13 November 1868, he left all his considerable fortune to the municipality of Pesaro, providing they establish a music school named in his honor. That school opened in 1882 and became the Conservatory "Gioacchino Rossini" in 1939.

In addition to the conservatory, the municipality established the Fondazione Gioacchino Rossini in 1940 for the advancement of research and study of matters relating to Rossini. In 1974 the Rossini Foundation, in cooperation and partnership with the Milan publishing house of G. Ricordi, inaugurated a unique enterprise of monumental proportions in the field of music printing: the publication of the complete works of Rossini in critical editions, scheduled to comprise 50 volumes.

The Rossini Opera Festival was founded by the municipality of Pesaro in 1980, the year in which the town's opera house—Teatro del Sole, built in 1637—was completely restored and reopened (it was renamed Teatro Rossini in 1854). At the time it was established, the Rossini Opera Festival was intended to supplement the work of the foundation with theatrical performances. This was the beginning of a complex cultural operation aimed toward the revival of all Rossini's "forgotten" works as well as critical editions of the perennial Rossini "favorites," a joint venture in musicology, theatrical performance, and publishing.

Before it became an *ente autonomo* in 1985, the festival was directly organized for some years by the municipality of Pesaro, which also undertook the greater part of the expenses, with financial assistance from such public and private institutions as the Ministry of Tourism and Entertainment, the regional boards of Pesaro and Urbino, the board of Regione Marche, the Banca Populare Pesarese, the Cassa di Risparmio (savings bank) of Pesaro, and, since 1982, the local industry Scavolini, which immediately became the festival's official sponsor.

Typical of Italian organizations, the festival as an *ente* is politically as well as artistically oriented, though it does better than most to emphasize the artistic element. The board is always presided over by the mayor of Pesaro, while artistic decisions are the responsibility of the *sovrintendente* appointed by the city council (for many years the *sovrintendente* has been assisted by an artistic advisor, the enlightened and tireless Alberto Zedda). The Rossini Foundation guarantees the cultural importance of the festival by taking part in all discussions about the works chosen for performance.

Critical Editions

Because the Rossini Opera Festival is noted for its critical editions of operas—including those presented on stage as well as those offered in printed editions—one could ask, "What is a 'critical edition'?"

Philip Gossett of the University of Chicago, who is not only the editorial director of the publishing committee of the Fondazione Rossini but one of the most important guiding figures behind the festival, explains it all very well:

Critics indifferent to Rossini's music frequently take the existence of multiple authorial versions as evidence that the composer himself was indifferent to his art. But it is essential to understand that the problem of "revision" in Italian opera did not end with Rossini and composers of his generation, nor did it begin there. In the 17th and 18th centuries, operas were usually revised from one set of performances to another, whether by the composer himself (Gluck's versions of *Orfeo*, Mozart's revision of *Don Giovanni*) or, more often, by whatever composer may have been responsible for supervising a set of performances. The practice continues to our own day, as anyone who has worked with contemporary composers can verify. Do operas existing in multiple states have "ideal" versions? Probably not. Whether a theater chooses from among actual versions of which there is compositional authority or assembles from them a contingent performing version to meet particularized needs depends on as many different factors as those that originally gave rise to the versions themselves. To insist mindlessly on either "authority" or "contingency" in opera performance is to trivialize the aesthetic problems posed by an art form in which the scenic realization of a particular work is never a simple matter. . . .

No single set of performances of a musical work, not to mention a play or ballet, can aspire to provide a definitive vision of the work. Critical editions can aspire to be "definitive" (although it is by no means clear that the goal is realistic), performances cannot. Each set of performances, whether one that insists on the authority of an authentic version or one that responds flexibly to the particular contingencies of a theater, provides another view of the work and in doing so deepens our knowledge of that work.[15]

If the matter of developing a critical edition is as nebulous and challenging as Gossett indicates, how is a critical edition derived? Michael Collins, one of the investigative musicologists of the Rossini Foundation, provides some insights from his experience in preparing the critical edition of Rossini's *Otello*.

In view of the fact that we have Rossini's autograph manuscript, the one in which composition took place, the task would seem simple, but it is not. The autograph in some cases presents more than one layer of music, modifications often made for practical rather than artistic considerations, either by the composer or by some later revisionist. To ascertain the definitive form of Rossini's ideas is therefore somewhat like a detective game in which we must seek clues not only in the autograph but in some 16 secondary manuscripts made at copy centers in Naples, Rome, and Venice. Less helpful are the one orchestral score published by Castil-Blaze in Paris (1823–24) and the 17 piano-vocal scores dating from the 1820s to the 1850s, because of editorial decisions that often remove the music far from Rossini's original intentions.[16]

As Collins points out, the resulting critical edition is "perhaps not so stunning as, say, the restoration of the Sistine ceiling, but the goals have been very similar: the restoration of a masterpiece."[17]

Fringe Benefits

Pesaro is a wonderful, friendly city to visit. It dates back to at least the 8th century B.C. and today consists of two principal streets that form its axes: Viale Trieste, which parallels the waterfront and on which about 50 of the town's more than 60 hotels are located, and, branching off Viale Trieste at about its midpoint and at a right angle to it, Via G. Rossini. By staying at one of the beachfront hotels you have the opportunity to swim in the mildly warm waters of the Adriatic, the water peaceful and calm in front of the hotels because of the breakwater that extends along the coast at this point. Most hotels offer, for a small charge, the rental of beach umbrellas and lounge chairs (quite the custom in Italy), and a number of them also maintain their own swimming pools. The summer tradition in Pesaro as well as in other watering spots is to take all meals at the hotel—known as full pension—although the fixed evening hour for dinner (*cena*), 7:30 P.M., precludes arriving on time for the customary 8:30 P.M. curtain since it always takes at least a full hour to serve a meal. Curiously, especially for Italy, a country in which almost everything runs behind time, the patrons for the evening performances at the Rossini Opera Festival have usually already gathered when the doors open at 8:00 P.M. The walk from the beachfront hotels to the three performance centers takes about 30 minutes without hurrying. Taxis, although available, are almost never used by the festival patrons. A daytime stroll down Via G. Rossini (which is called Viale delle Repubblica at the beachfront end) offers some interesting landmarks of considerable importance for Rossini fans.

The Rossini birthhouse is located at Via Rossini 34. At the time of the composer's birth, it was owned by a Spanish don who served at the nearby cathedral of Pesaro. After passing through several hands, this three-story building, built in the late 15th or early 16th century, was purchased in 1891 by the municipality of Pesaro and became a national monument in 1904. Completely restored in 1989, the birthhouse is now open to the public from 10:00 A.M. to noon and from 4:00 to 6:00 P.M. on weekdays, and from 10:00 A.M. to noon on Saturday. There is a small admission charge, and a handsome illustrated catalogue is on sale at the home. In addition to excellent copies of memorabilia, documents, scores, and portraits, the museum displays an original Rossini-owned spinet whose fallboard is engraved: "Luigi Maffei Venezia 1809." The original of the well-known Gustave Doré painting of the composer is also on display.

Turn left on Via Rossini as you leave the birthhouse, and in just two very short blocks you will come to the main square of Pesaro, Piazza del Popolo. On the right you will find the Palazzo Ducale, a magnificent porticoed structure built by Alessandro Sforza between 1450 and 1465 to enlarge the existing town residence of the Malatesta family. Its noble *cortile* commissioned in the 16th century is the setting for one of the most unusual and unique events of the Rossini Opera Festival: Videofestival. There, for seven nights running, visitors can enjoy on a giant video screen the musical "event" of the evening simultaneously with its "live" presentation at Teatro Rossini or the Auditorium Pedrotti or the Palafestival. There is a nominal charge (usually under $5) for admission in the evening to these tele-events. In the daytime one can enjoy the beauties of the palace and courtyard free of charge.

Turn right as you leave the Palazzo Ducale, and a bit farther down (actually two very short blocks) you should make a right turn onto Via Pedrotti to reach the conservatory that stands at the street's end on Piazza Olivieri. The building itself is called the Palazzo Olivieri-Machirelli and dates from the 18th century. (The design is by Gianandrea Lazzarini of Pesaro.) On 31 July 1892 it became the home of the Liceo Musicale Rossini, and at that time a new Salone dei Concerti was constructed on the first floor (actually the second floor in the American way of counting floors), a space dedicated on Rossini's birthday—29 February 1892—with a concert conducted by Maestro Pedrotti. Today the space is known as the Auditorium Pedrotti and is used by the festival for both opera productions and concerts. Lacking air-conditioning, the auditorium—which has excellent acoustics and good sight-lines—becomes dreadfully hot and stuffy during summer evening performances.

The conservatory also houses a museum of Rossini memorabilia, and its library includes, in addition to some of Rossini's manuscripts, others by Donizetti, Morlacchi, Paisiello, etc. There is also an excellent collection of musical instruments—especially keyboards—in the magnificent Marble Salon. The famous statue of a seated Rossini sculpted in bronze by Carlo Marochetti may be seen in the *cortile* of the Palazzo Olivieri-Machirelli. Originally unveiled in 1864, it first graced the piazza of the train station in Pesaro, a gift from the founders of the Bologna-Ancona railway system. The statue was later transferred to its present, more protected location.

Returning to Via Rossini and turning right, you will shortly come to Teatro Rossini, the center of Pesaro's cultural and artistic life. Under the name Teatro del Sole (Theater of the Sun) it opened on 23 February 1637 with a presentation of *Asmondo*, a tragedy whose intermissions were filled with a musical intermezzo by Giovanni Ondedei of Pesaro. The theater underwent major changes and restorations (including enlargements) in the years 1697, 1720, and 1788; in 1804, a restructuring of the front portal took place. Earthquakes in 1916 and 1930 necessitated further structural work, and in 1934 the Fascist *podestà* (governor) of Pesaro condemned the building and authorized yet another restoration. World War II intervened, and the restorative work authorized by the *podestà* was never carried out. In the late 1970s the municipality of Pesaro appropriated funds for this restoration, and on Sunday, 6 April 1980, the completely refurbished Teatro Rossini reopened with a gala concert featuring Luciano Pavarotti accompanied by an orchestra made up of professors from the Conservatory "G. Rossini" conducted by Leone Magiera.

Regarding the Palafestival, the Rossini Opera Festival has effected a rather excellent transformation of the town's Sports Palace so that it can be used for opera productions. The Palazzo dello Sport is a modern edifice with bleachers on all four sides of a large playing area. Ordinarily the palace accommodates about 8000 fans. The festival has cut the interior in half lengthwise, with half serving as stage space and the other half as the seating area. For opera productions only every other row is used for seating so that each patron has plenty of leg room, and plastic, contoured seats without arms are installed for comfort. The seating capacity of the complex is thus reduced from 8000 to 1500!

As for the "stage" half, Pier Luigi Pizzi's production of *Tancredi* in 1991 serves as a superb example of how that space may be used in a most creative and spectacular manner. The permanent cement bleachers at the back were incorporated into a castle wall with pinnacles; a central portal in Gothic shape revealed two enormous wooden doors that were opened for the arrival of Amenaide. The young men of the court in their colorful costumes paraded back and forth along the top of the castle walls with banners flying; behind them, reaching to the ceiling of the Palafestival, was a most realistic cloud-filled sky of azure blue. Beneath the palace, on the ground level, a moat of real water reached from the castle to the audience, and it was in a barge propelled by pages that Tancredi made his fateful entrance down this moat. On both sides of the moat (to the central audience's left and right) were green, grassy fields surrounded by real bushes and growing trees. Argirio's arrival on a caparisoned white stallion, accompanied by two mounted medieval soldiers with lances and shields, impressively marked the opening of the opera.

Practical Matters

As one might expect for a festival of the stature and importance of the Rossini Opera Festival, tickets are expensive, principally because the seating capacity is limited (part of the reason for the charm and intimacy of the operas produced in Pesaro).

Requests for tickets should be sent to Servizio Prenotazioni e Biglietteria, Teatro Rossini, Piazza Lazzarini, I-61100 Pesaro; telephone 0721/33.184. Information services are located at Servizio Informazione, Via Rossini 37, I-61100 Pesaro, which is open every day during the festival from 10:00 A.M. to 1:00 P.M.; telephone 0721/30.161. Management (Direzione e Uffici) may be reached at the same address and telephone; fax 0721/30.979. Hotel reservations are a must and may be placed with Servizio Prenotazioni Albergheria I Associazione Pesarese Albergatori; telephone 0721/68.763 or 67.959.

Generally the attire for festival opera performances is semiformal, with about half of the men dressed in coats and ties. Teatro Rossini is air-conditioned, but the central unit is not powerful enough during the sultry days of the festival period to bring the thermometer down to levels generally enjoyed in most modern air-conditioned buildings. The Palafestival, however, has an adequate cooling system, and the temperature there always seems comfortable during performances. There is neither air-conditioning nor air circulation at the Auditorium Pedrotti, and this is a real challenge to those seriously affected by heat. Of the approximately 50 percent of the men who arrive wearing coats, more than half will have shed them by intermission.

For the Armchair Fan

The literature about the Rossini Opera Festival is quite limited considering its stature and importance.

Il Festival/The Festival. 1989. Pesaro: Rossini Opera Festival. A 4-page pamphlet with a text in both Italian and English giving a very brief history and description of the festival from its origins to the 1990s.

Brancati, Antonio. 1980. *Vicende architettoniche e structurati del Teatro Rossini di Pesaro.* Pesaro: Comune di Pesaro. An account (in Italian) of the history—with descriptions of the various reconstructions—of Teatro Rossini from its establishment in 1637 to the 1980 reopening of the restructured and refurbished theater; excellent black-and-white photographs of the most recent renovation (both before and after its completion) are included.

Rebeggiani, Luca. 1987. "Un'istituzione ricca di fermenti e novità." *L'Opera* (July/August). A very brief history of the Rossini Opera Festival (in Italian) with excellent illustrations in color.

Many of the "discoveries" as well as some delightful lesser-known works are available on recordings made live at the Rossini Opera Festival. An interesting and varied selection for home listening follows.

Rossini, Gioachino. *Il viaggio a Reims.* Deutsche Grammophon 415 498-2; with Cecilia Gasdia, Lucia Valentini Telrani, Lella Cuberli, Katia Ricciarelli, Francisco Araiza, Samuel Ramey, Ruggero Raimondi, Enzo Dara, Leo Nucci, and Giorgio Surjan; Prague Philharmonic Chorus and the Chamber Orchestra of Europe; conducted by Claudio Abbado. This recording was made during performances at the Rossini Opera Festival, Pesaro, 1984.

Rossini, Gioachino. *L'occasione fa il ladro.* Ricordi/Fonit Cetra RFCD 2001; with Luciana Serra, Luciana d'Intino, Raul Gimenez, Claudio Desderi, J. Patrick Raferty, and Ernesto Gavazzi; Orchestra Giovanile Italiana; conducted by Salvatore Accardo. Recorded live in the Auditorium Pedrotti of the Conservatorio di Musica "G. Rossini" in August 1987.

Rossini, Gioachino. *La gazza ladra.* Sony Classical S3K 45850; with Katia Ricciarelli, Bernadette Manca di Nissa, William Matteuzzi, Samuel Ramey, Luciana d'Intino, Ferruccio Furlanetto, and Roberto Coviello; Coro Filarmonico di Praga e Orchestra Sinfonica di Torino della RAI; conducted by Gianluigi Gelmetti. Recorded live during performances in Teatro Rossini, 11–24 August 1989.

213

Rossini, Gioachino. *La scala di seta*. Ricordi/Fonit Cetra RFCD 2003; with Luciana Serra, Cecilia Bartoli, Natale De Carolis, William Matteuzzi, Roberto Coviello, and Oslavio Di Credico; Orchestra del Teatro Comunale di Bologna; conducted by Gabriele Ferro. Recorded live in the Auditorium Pedrotti of the Conservatorio di Musica "G. Rossini" in September 1988.

The Ravenna Festival
RAVENNA

The Ravenna Festival is an extraordinary feast, both for the eye and the ear, for as Jane and Theodore Norman point out in their interesting and authoritative book, *Traveler's Guide to European Art*,

> The lover of Byzantine art will find no place, not even in the East, to compare with Ravenna in the magnificence of its surviving mosaics. . . . Here color and pattern have been exploited for effects that are more beautiful than one would believe possible, . . . an unforgettable experience.[18]

With the opulence of these Byzantine mosaics for a setting, the Ravenna Festival features music conducted by Sir Georg Solti, Georges Prêtre, Riccardo Chailly, and Lorin Maazel; music performed by the Philadelphia Orchestra, the Vienna Philharmonic, the Orchestre National de France, and the Dresden Staatskapelle; opera sung by Katia Ricciarelli, William Shimell, Bernadette Manca Di Nissa, Daniela Dessì, Thomas Moser, Gwynne Howell, Gösta Winbergh, Ann Murray, Samuel Ramey, and Carol Vaness; and, as the pièce de résistance, rarely heard lyric gems at Teatro Alighieri, such as Donizetti's *Poliuto* in a Pier Luigi Pizzi production conducted by Gianandrea Gavazzeni, Cherubini's *Lodoïska* in a Luca Ronconi production directed by Riccardo Muti, and Auber's *La muette de Portici* in a Micha van Hoecke production conducted by Patrick Fournillier.

In recent years the festival has been coupled with a Convegno Internationale—an international convention. In 1991 it centered on "Cherubini and the French School," chaired by Francesco Degrada; the 1992 season offered "Intorno a Rossini [Dealing with Rossini]" sessions culminating in a performance of Rossini's *Stabat Mater* conducted by Riccardo Chailly.

214

Founded in the early 1980s, the Ravenna Festival has grown to be one of the most important in Europe and may be the only festival in Italy that has endeavored to achieve international support by establishing a *fondazione* (foundation). Ravenna's *Amici sostenitori* (Sustaining Members) include Marie Hélène, Baroness De Rothschild of Paris; Lord Charles Forte of London (the Italian-born founder of the British-based Trusthouse Forte hotel chain); Gordon and Ann Getty of San Francisco; Lord Arnold and Lady Netta Weinstock of London; and Gian Maria and Violante Visconti di Modrone of Piacenza. Cristina Mazzavillani Muti serves as honorary president of the board of administration.

The Ravenna Festival, which starts in May and lasts through July, offers diverse musical (and non-musical) elements: opera, symphony concerts, chamber music recitals, lecture/forums, and dramatic readings (the latter in association with its celebration of Ravenna's most famous native son, Dante Alighieri). Altogether the festival includes around 25 different musical events, some—such as opera—in multiple performances. To list the sites of these events is to provide a tourist's guide to the most important artistic monuments of the city—indeed, of the world of Byzantine art.

Before learning of these locations ("Fringe Benefits" of the highest order) and their musical events, it may be helpful to know a bit about the origins of the city. Ravenna actually has little in common with other Italian towns, for it has nothing to do with Renaissance popes and potentates, Guelphs or Ghibellines. It has everything to do with Byzantine emperors and exarchs and the most glorious mosaics in the world, surpassing even those of Constantinople itself. Though little has been heard of Ravenna in the last 1200 years, it was—at its moment of glory—the leading city of western Europe, heir to Rome itself.

The Story of Ravenna

Ravenna, which in classical times was situated on a lagoon, Portus Classis, first rose to prominence during the reign of Augustus. With its Port of Classis, Ravenna lay along a vital trade and conquest route that led to Dalmatia and the Danube. Because of its nearly impregnable setting, surrounded as it was at the time by broad marshes, it soon became Rome's biggest naval base on the Adriatic. The city enjoyed its first moment of glory under the rule of Honorius and his sister, Galla Placidia (425–450 A.D.). Honorius, fearful of a Barbarian invasion, moved the capital of the Western Empire from Milan to Ravenna in 402 A.D., and just in time, for Alaric's sack of Rome followed only eight years later. Galla Placidia ruled when her brother was absent from the city and began to enrich it with churches and monuments befitting the capital of the Western Empire. When the Goths attacked Ravenna, Galla Placidia saved the city by marrying the Gothic king, Ataulf. It seemed to be a successful marriage, with Galla Placidia's riding everywhere with the king, even into battle, and after his assassination, she returned to Ravenna and ruled the city herself until her own death in 450 A.D.

As Dana Facaros and Michael Pauls recount in their fascinating book on Italy,

> In Byzantine times, the greatest gift an emperor could bestow on any dependent town was a few tons of gold and enamel tesserae and an artist. . . . It was the early Christians, with a desire to build for the ages and a body of scripture that could best be related pictorially, who made mosaics the new medium of public art in the 6th century. . . . Using a new vocabulary of images, and the new techniques of mosaic art, they strove to duplicate, and surpass, the sense of awe and mystery still half-remembered from the interiors of pagan temples. Try to imagine a church like San Vitale in its original state, with candles—lots of candles—flickering below the gold ground and gorgeous colors. You may see that same light that enchanted the Byzantines—the light of the Gospels, the light from the stars.[19]

Fringe Benefits

Teatro Dante Alighieri, dating from 1838, is the setting for most of the Ravenna Festival's opera productions. A charming house with gold stucco on ivory-colored woodwork, Teatro Alighieri has an intimate feeling. Designed in the traditional horseshoe configuration, its four tiers of boxes, main floor, and single balcony accommodate 835 patrons.

Historically this theater replaces an earlier one, Teatro Comunitativo (Community Theater); the design of the new house is by Tommaso and Gianbattista Maduna, who only two years earlier had been commissioned to restore and redecorate Teatro La

Fenice in Venice. In September of 1840 the foundation stone was laid, and two years later the theater opened with a production of Meyerbeer's *Roberto il diavolo*.

Recent summer festival seasons at Teatro Alighieri have included performances of Antonio Salieri's *Les Danaïdes* and Gluck's opera *La danza* (1990), Luigi Cherubini's *Lodoïska* (1991), and Donizetti's *Poliuto* and Cimarosa's *Il matrimonio segreto* (1992).

The Rocca Brancaleone was built by the Venetians as a fortress in 1457 during their brief domination of Ravenna. Today the largest portion of the Rocca—the part known as The Citadel—is given over to a beautifully landscaped public garden. Originally it was a village made up of houses, a mill, workshops, and warehouses.

At the northwest corner of the Rocca, four enormous stone towers, each some 15 meters (50 feet) in diameter, mark the corners of an enclosed courtyard, the space into which opera and symphony concerts are tucked in the summer. One corner with its tower and adjacent walls serves as the backdrop of a specially constructed stage mounted on temporary scaffolding and platforms. Opposite this, a series of bleachers that can accommodate 2500 patrons is erected for the audience.

The Rocca has been the setting for Beethoven's *Fidelio* in 1990 with Lorin Maazel conducting (a concert performance) and Daniel Auber's *La muette de Portici* directed by Patrick Fournillier in 1991. During the 1992 season the Rocca was used for concerts by the Vienna Philharmonic under Riccardo Muti and by the Orchestre National de France under Georges Prêtre.

The basilica of San Vitale, an octagonal temple founded by Giuliano Argentario at the behest of Bishop Ecclesius, was consecrated in 548 A.D. by Archbishop Massimiano. It is one of the wonders not only of Ravenna but of the world because of the originality of its structure (its design combines Byzantine and Roman characteristics), the beauty and opulence of its marble (which still remains intact), and above all, its mosaics. The plan actually consists of two octagons, one enclosed within the other. A typically Eastern gallery for women is above the area between the octagons, and a dome covers the central section. The exterior is bare and the bricks exposed, a situation quite typical of Byzantine churches, whose luxurious, resplendent decorations were reserved for the interior.

The basilica of San Vitale has been the festival setting for concerts by the Warsaw Chorus and Orchestra directed by Henryk

Wojnarowski (1990), by the Cappella Istropolitana di Bratislava and the Lehrerchor Villach directed by Jaroslav Krcek (1991), and by the Accademia Bizantina directed by Luciano Berio (1992). The basilica is also used for solo recitals and chamber concerts. During the 1993 festival it was the setting for Dante Alighieri's *Paradiso* in a script by Giovanni Giudici with original music by the contemporary composer, Salvatore Sciarrino.

The basilica of Sant'Apollinare Nuovo, built in the first third of the 6th century, was originally the Palatine Church of Theodoric. All that is left from the original building are the wonderful mosaics, which constitute one of the most extensive pieces of such ancient work still intact today. The processions of the virgins and martyrs are the most typical examples we have of Byzantine style. This basilica has been the setting for concerts by the Accademia Bizantina (1990), the Wiener Kammerensemble (1991), and the Orchestra da camera di Padova e del Veneto (1992).

The basilica of Sant'Apollinare in Classe, about 8 kilometers (5 miles) from Ravenna on what used to be the coastline, was built in the first half of the 6th century according to the wishes of Archbishop Ursicino. It is one of the most perfect of Ravenna's basilicas and is renowned not only for its architectonic structure but also for its mosaics and for the marble tombs of former archbishops that lie along the lateral aisles.

This basilica has been the setting for the Beethoven Ninth Symphony with the chorus and orchestra of the Maggio Musicale Fiorentino conducted by Carlo Maria Giulini in 1990, the Poulenc *Gloria* and Fauré *Requiem* with the Orchestre du Capitole de Toulouse and Coro Orfeon Donostiarra conducted by Michel Plasson (1991), and in 1992, both Rossini's *Stabat Mater* with the chorus and orchestra of Teatro Comunale di Bologna conducted by Riccardo Chailly and the concert given by the Festival Orchestra of Schleswig-Holstein conducted by Sir Georg Solti.

The Franciscan Cloisters—with an entrance situated near Dante's tomb—were part of the monastery built by the Franciscans after the concession of 1261. The Cloister of the Cisterna is made up of 28 pillars (seven on each side), and a beautiful font richly decorated in marble stands in the middle of the grass courtyard. On the west side a tablet bears an inscription commemorating the theft of Dante's bones by monks. This beautiful setting under the stars, with the pillared portico as its backdrop, was used by the Beethoven Quartet (1990) as well as for programs dedicated to Dante by Sylvano Bussotti and Roman Vlad (1991) and by Tonino Guerra, Attilio Bertolucci, and Valentina Cortese (1992).

The church of San Francesco was built by Bishop Neone sometime after 450 A.D. as the Basilica of the Apostles (Peter and Paul). In 1261 the name was changed when this church, along with the house, gardens, and porticos, passed to the Franciscans who, having abandoned it in 1810, returned in 1949. Almost nothing remains of the ancient construction. Partially rebuilt in the 10th, 11th, and 18th centuries, the simple, rustic church that sits at the back of Piazza San Francesco today is essentially the work of Pietro Zumaglini dating from 1793. The spacious piazza in front of the church served audiences in Ravenna well as a setting for the Cherubini *Messa solenne* and the Verdi *Stabat Mater* and *Te deum* by the Orchestra Filarmonica della Scala and Coro Lirico Sinfonico della Scala conducted by Riccardo Muti (1991).

Practical Matters

Tickets for the major events of the Ravenna Festival are always expensive by international standards. For information and brochures about the Ravenna Festival, contact Ravenna Marketing Turistico, Via Corrado Ricci 8, I-48100 Ravenna; telephone 0544/ 395.85; fax 0544/343.09.

There are special weekend packages available consisting of tickets for three performances and hotel accommodations for three nights with full board (one's seating locations, from orchestra to gallery, parallel one's hotel classification—from 4-star to 2-star). There are several tourist agencies in Ravenna that will make reservations for this type of package: Cooptur (Via Salara 36; telephone 0544/372.60), Teodorico Holidays (Via di Roma 102; telephone 0544/530.8220), Orinoco Viaggi (Via Cavina 1; telephone 0544/ 464.630), Viaggi Generali (Via Beatrice Alighieri 9; telephone 0544/331.66), Windtour (Via IV Novembre 39; telephone 0544/ 365.90), Classenese (Via Diaz; telephone 0544.333.47), and Bizantina Viaggi (P. la Marinai d'Italia 8; telephone 0544/531. 755).

The visitor to the Ravenna Festival has a choice of hotel settings. For those who want to do a bit of relaxing on the beach in addition to festivalgoing and sightseeing, the Park Hotel Ravenna, located 12 kilometers (8 miles) from the center of Ravenna, offers a happy compromise. A 4-star hotel, the Park has 146 rooms. For the latest price quotations and reservations, write Park Hotel Ravenna, Viale delle Nazioni 181, I-48023 Marina di Ravenna; telephone 0544/432.743.

For location, the Bisanzio, another 4-star hotel, is excellent, a prime location for festivalgoing, sightseeing, and shopping. It is small and modern and has air-conditioning. For details, the latest rates, and reservations, write Albergo Bisanzio, Via Salara 30, I-48100 Ravenna, or telephone 0544/27.111.

Other choices include the very well-run but simple Hotel Centrale Byron (3-star) with 57 rooms, located only steps from the Piazza del Popolo. Its Liberty-style decorations (Italy's equivalent of art nouveau) offer a change of pace from mosaics (Via IV Novembre 14, I-48100 Ravenna; telephone 0544/22.225). Another choice is the Jolly Hotel, a 4-star, four-story, 75-room "cracker box" of a businessman's hotel built in 1950 (Piazza Mameti 1, I-48100 Ravenna; telephone 0544/35.762). And the 3-star Argentario (closed from December to February) is centrally located and has 34 basic but comfortable rooms (Albergo Argentario, Via Roma 45, I-48100 Ravenna; telephone 0544/22.555). For further information write or call the tourist office, APT, at Via Salara 8, I-48100 Ravenna; telephone 0544/35.404.

For the Armchair Fan

Though there are any number of excellent books with superb illustrations about the mosaic treasury to be found in Ravenna, nothing has been published in English about the Ravenna Festival. A brief article in the Italian magazine L'Opera concerns the early years of the festival.

Rebeggiani, Luca. 1987. "Un festival di atmosfere." L'Opera (July/August): 20–21.

There are opportunities to listen to unusual works that have been produced at the Ravenna Festival.

Donizetti, Gaetano. Alina, regina di Golconda. Nuova Era 033.6701; with Daniela Dessì, Adelisa Tabiadon, Rockwell Blake, Paolo Coni, Andrea Martin, and Sergio Bertocchi; Orchestra Giovanile dell'Emilia Romagna "Arturo Toscanini"; Gruppo Giovanile della Cooperativa "Artisti del Coro" del Teatro Regio di Parma; conducted by Antonella Allemandi. Recorded live in Teatro Alighieri, July 1987.

While the following album was actually taped live during the performance of *Le maschere* in Bologna, it is the same production, cast, chorus, and orchestra that first presented the opera in the Teatro Comunale di Bologna production at Teatro Alighieri for the Ravenna Festival.

> Mascagni, Pietro. *Le maschere.* Ricordi/Fonit Cetra RFCD 2004; with Amelia Felle, Maria José Gallego, Vincenzo La Scola, Giuseppe Sabbatini, Enzo Dara, Angelo Romero, Oslavio Di Credico, Carlos Chausson, and Nelson Portel; Orchestra e Coro del Teatro Comunale di Bologna; conducted by Gianluigi Gelmetti. Recorded live at Teatro Comunale di Bologna, December 1988.

Festival dei Due Mondi/Festival of Two Worlds
SPOLETO

Back in 1958 when Gian Carlo Menotti first arrived in the sleepy little Umbrian town of Spoleto some 160 kilometers (100 miles) northeast of Rome, the townsfolk thought him crazy when he spoke of "organizing a cultural festival to unite people from Italy, America, and other countries all over the world to exchange their ideas and experiences."[20] Provincial in outlook and limited in vision, the *Spoletini* simply could not envision an international festival devoted to music, dance, poetry, and the plastic arts. With a kindly glint in their eyes, they dubbed Menotti *Il matto*—"The Crazy One"—as he walked through the streets and byways of Spoleto organizing and overseeing his first Festival dei Due Mondi/ Festival of Two Worlds (everything about the festival is printed in both Italian and English).

Some 34 years later, on the occasion of Menotti's 80th birthday, the composer playfully chided the local citizenry. At the close of the first act of *Goya*—one of his most recent operas, presented in a revised edition for the festival that year—there is a religious procession that passes through the plaza in Madrid, where this act takes place. The delighted *Spoletini* were amazed on opening night to discover that among the colorfully dressed crowd in the procession, there appeared in torn and tattered clothes *Il matto*—the town fool—led by an equally tattered ragamuffin. Instantly they recognized *Il matto*, their *matto*, Gian Carlo Menotti himself, being led about in the stage procession by his grandson! (He who laughs last?)

Festival dei Due Mondi/Festival of Two Worlds takes place in Spoleto from late June through mid-July and offers daily fare of the most diverse nature. The 34th edition, for example, lasted 19 days, and during that time, 62 different productions were offered: three operas, three ballets, eight dramatic representations, 41 concerts, and seven scientific lectures, plus art exhibitions and Spoleto-cinema, for a total of 200 performances including the projections.

There are 10 theaters in Spoleto, and for the 34th festival they hosted some 250 musicians, chorus members, and soloists; 144 dancers; 40 singers; and 40 actors. Some 92 people were involved in the production of *Three Penny Opera* alone. In all, there were 820 artists actively participating in the festival, plus a staff of 58. (Spoleto has about 40,000 inhabitants, but, during the festival, an estimated half-million visitors pass through the city, and of those, about 100,000 buy tickets for one or more events.)

Since the beginning of the festival, Menotti has succeeded in maintaining a record of fresh ideas and original events. Ken Russell's "unscrupulous" interpretation of *Madama Butterfly* in 1983 caused an uproar; and Philip Glass's *Hydrogen Jukebox*—a setting of texts by the rebellious Allen Ginsberg—caused consternation in 1990. For many years Menotti refused to allow Spoleto to stage any of his own operas: he was already famous and his aim was to present new talent from the "Two Worlds." Once the festival was successfully in operation and accomplishing this purpose, the composer relented and, in turn, directed many of his own creations: *The Medium*, *The Consul*, *The Saint of Bleeker Street*, *La loca*, *Le dernier sauvage*, and *Goya*.

Menotti emphasizes that he chooses young artists for the festival rather than big-name stars whose fees are high and who are usually booked seasons in advance. "Though the artists be young," the maestro stressed, "there is no compromise with quality."[21] Thus, in 1988, *Jenůfa* (a production of the German director Gunter Kramer conducted by Spiros Agiris, the festival's music director at the time) was honored with one of Italy's most prestigious awards for lyric opera, the Premio Abbiati, which stated that this production was an example "of perfect singing and casting."

Throughout its long history, the Spoleto festival has assembled and presented the truly great in the world of art and music. The first festival, in 1958, opened with Visconti's production of Verdi's *Macbeth* conducted by Thomas Schippers; that season also included Jerome Robbins's Ballets U.S.A. dancing *Opus Jazz*. It also saw Henry Moore, Ezra Pound, and Jean Cocteau, all coming at their own expense. In addition, Sir John Gielgud recited George Hyland's *Ages of Man*, and Margot Fonteyn and Rudolf Nureyev danced *Raimonda*.

In its early years Spoleto presented both dancers and dance companies making their first Italian appearances: Alvin Ailey, the aforementioned Jerome Robbins, Maurice Béjart, Paul Taylor, and Merce Cunningham; and, in the field of music, Cathy Berberian, Vinette Carroll, Samuel Barber, Zubin Mehta, Luciano Berio, and Werner Torkanowsky. The roster also included Ben Shawn, Beni Montresor, Robert Rauschenberg, Andy Warhol, and Marcello Mastroianni.

The Story of the Festival

Few today remember that Gian Carlo Menotti visited about 60 Italian towns in central and northern Italy—including Bergamo, Sulmona, and Todi—before selecting the little hillside town of Spoleto as the site for his proposed festival. Egidio Ortona, the former minister of culture at the Italian embassy in Washington (and a close friend of the composer) points out, "Spoleto seemed to Menotti the ideal place. It was conveniently sited; there was the haunting beauty of the buildings, streets, and alleys, and it had not one but two theaters."[22]

Teatro Nuovo (New Theater) dates from 1854, while Teatro Caio Melisso (where Rossini once appeared)—a small theater-turned-cinema and in need of restoration at the time the composer first saw it—was built in 1667. These two houses at first comprised the total public space of the festival. Later, others were adapted for the summer program. In 1963, two large granary storage rooms in the ex-prison at the foot of the Palazzo della Signoria were transformed into Teatro delle sei, the festival's "cellar." The deconsecrated church of San Nicolò became another theater and was inaugurated in 1969 with *Orlando furioso* by Vivaldi in a production directed by Luca Ronconi. The outdoor amphitheater—Teatro Romano—was restored and began hosting concerts and dance programs in 1974. Many other churches and spaces—including the basilica of Saint Euphemia, the *duomo* and its enormous public square (where the huge closing concert is always held), and the Pegasus Room and Villa Redenta—are also important locations for festival events. Today there are 10 such spaces altogether; another site now looms on the horizon. As writer-translator William Weaver states,

> The forbidding Rocca dall'Albornos, the massive fortress named for the wily warrior-cardinal who built it, dominates the hill overlooking Spoleto. Its former inhabitants include such sinister figures as Cesare Borgia and his sister Lucrezia, but in more recent times it was a maximum security prison. From his arrival, Menotti fought to have the prison's few convicts moved elsewhere, so the great spaces inside could be used for happier purposes. At long last, this goal has been reached. The Rocca, now returned to civil life, is in the process of being restored. And the composer is fighting to make sure that at least part of its area is dedicated to the festival, for the fine arts commission is bent on using its half for a museum and for other temporary exhibitions.[23]

The first Festival dei Due Mondi/Festival of Two Worlds took place from 5 to 30 June 1958, with Gian Carlo Menotti as acting president. Artistic direction was entrusted to Thomas Schippers, who also served as music director. John Butler was in charge of dance, José Quintero of drama, and Giovanni Urbani of the plastic arts. The first edition boasted an audience of just over 18,000, with box office sales at about 19 million lire. Today the audience has grown to over 100,000 per season, and the annual budget is set at about 8 billion lire.

The unique feature of the Spoleto festival is the fact that it is the only musical enterprise in the country completely free from political control or influence, a fact guaranteed by the institution of the governing board as a *fondazione* in 1987. "This is the only festival in Italy that doesn't belong to a political party," Menotti proudly states.[24] This leaves artistic decisions in the hands of working artists, not politicians. For example, Menotti dismissed the drama director and appointed a new one, something that would have been impossible at La Scala, which has to keep peace with the unions as well as with all political parties.

What has preoccupied Menotti for several years is the artistic inheritance of the festival he has created. He makes no mystery of the fact that he would like to see Chip, his adopted son, in charge of Spoleto, but only if he can conquer the top post.

I want him to be in control of my name, of my artistic work. This means that whoever wants to perform my works must get Chip's permission and imprimatur. Because Spoleto is licensed to my name and I created it, I want Chip to be involved . . . in the festival, to protect its quality and continuity.[25]

Chip Menotti, a reserved man with gentle manners and a kind smile that hides a real Irish temper, has been Menotti's assistant for the last 20 years. "He has impeccable taste and I trust him. But he is not ambitious," according to the composer. "I would like him to be more so."[26]

Gian Carlo Menotti met Chip in New York in 1961 when the boy auditioned to play Toby in *The Medium*. He now manages Yester, the Menotti home in the hills of Lammermuir in Scotland, where the young Menottis live. Chip has helped his father remodel this palatial estate, where the maestro resides when he is not off directing or administrating operas and opera productions at Rome's Teatro dell'Opera or Festival dei Due Mondi/Festival of Two Worlds in Spoleto.

Fringe Benefits

The town of Spoleto, which dates from prehistoric times, has been a visitor's attraction for years, with tourists stopping off on their way south to Rome along the Flaminia and pausing to admire the glorious *duomo*, the awesome Roman bridge, the quaint medieval streets, and an intriguing variety of churches whose constructions span the centuries. Today a leisurely uphill walk leads you past many spots of historical interest and architectural beauty, locations that in many cases serve as performance venues for the festival.

Enter Spoleto at the bottom of the hill at Piazza Garibaldi or Via Posterna and make your way to Piazza della Torre and up Via Elladio past the magnificent Centro Congressi San Nicolò. The church was constructed in the 14th century, together with the lower church of Santa Maria della Misericordia and the adjacent convent. The San Nicolò is now a beautiful theater, its architectural plan allowing for only one wide and bare aisle ending in a deep polygonal apse, a soaring and harmonious cornice for the modern plexiglass or wooden set designs that have found their way into the ancient stone building.

From the San Nicolò, walk across Via Vaita San Andrea to Piazza Beniamino Gigli and Teatro Nuovo. The theater was constructed from a design by Ireneo Aleandri between 1854 and 1864. Stucco bas-reliefs and medallions of Rossini, Alfieri, Goldoni, and Metastasio decorate the facade. Since 1958, major productions of the Spoleto festival have taken place in this 600-seat, functional, if not noteworthy, theater.

Now walk up Via della Filitteria and Via del Duomo into Piazza della Signoria, where under the arches a small theater specially conceived for drama has been created. It is called Teatro delle sei and seats 80 spectators.

Climb the steps from Piazza della Signoria to Piazza del Duomo, the heart of the city and the festival, and certainly the most spectacular spot in Spoleto. The *duomo* was built during the 12th century and the portico added in 1504. It provides the perfect frame for the closing Concerto in Piazza—the fashionable highlight of the festival—although the acoustics are not as perfect as the setting. A simple wooden structure is erected in front of the beautiful facade, and the stone steps that lead up from the piazza provide seating for 6000.

Piazza del Duomo is also the location of two other spaces: Teatro Caio Melisso and the church of Sant'Eufemia. The Caio Melisso was named after the Spoletian writer and friend of Augustus, Caius Maecenas. At the beginning of the 17th century it was a primitive public playhouse; in 1668 it became a full-fledged theater with four tiers of boxes. The ceiling and the background scenery of the theater were done by Bruschi, who also decorated the central ceiling of the foyer. The theater was reconstructed in the 1870s. Though small—only some 300 seats—it is enchanting in design and gracious in ambiance.

The tiny church of Sant'Eufemia, with its purely geometrical apse, looks upon the stairway that leads to the *duomo*. The church is situated on the grounds of the bishop's residence and is one of the most significant Romanesque works of art in Umbria. It was constructed in the first half of the 12th century, and the interior is more beautiful than the exterior (if that is possible). The vertical development of the aisles and the *matronei* (women's galleries) is in bare white stone, and the altar itself—a rectangular block of white marble inlaid with swirling mosaic designs—is an emblem of simplicity and beauty. Although the Sant'Eufemia is now deconsecrated, it still retains a strongly religious atmosphere, a perfect ambiance for the cycle of chamber music concerts that occur here.

Saunter down the Corso Mazzini and you pass the Cinema Moderno and the Sala Frau. The latter takes its name from the family who founded the furniture firm of Poltrona Frau (*poltrona* means armchair), which sponsored the restoration of this small but intimate space and created its very original seating.

The Corso leads into Piazza della Libertà, which looks down on Teatro Romano. This theater was restored to its present form thanks to pressure from Menotti and the Amici di Spoleto (Friends of Spoleto). It is set up against the ex-monastery of Sant' Agata, which provides a breathtaking background for a stage that has become something of a temple for classical and modern dance.

Practical Matters

One of the most pleasant things about Spoleto is the genuine warmth with which the townsfolk welcome festival visitors (quite in contrast to such festival sites as Salzburg). Though hotel and meal prices may seem high—true throughout all of Italy—the *Spoletini* do not gouge or try to take advantage of their guests.

Hotel space has always been scarce, and early reservations are a must. (The addition of two new hotels in 1990 has somewhat alleviated the situation.) Actually the choices run all the way from the charming Hotel Gattapone—built in the shadow of the imposing Rocca Alborniziana, perched as it is on the edge of the breathtaking precipice from which begins the beautiful Ponte dei suicidi (Bridge of Suicides)—to the newly built, plastic-and-glass, 4-star Albarnoz Palace Hotel. The Hotel Gattapone has but eight rooms, the Albarnoz Palace some 96.

For a complete list of hotels, camping facilities, and telephone numbers of families with rooms to rent in Spoleto and the surrounding area, call or write Azienda di Promozione Turistica di Spoleto, Piazza della Libertà 7; telephone 0743/220.311; fax 0743/46.241.

Tickets for festival events can be purchased in Spoleto at Teatro Nuovo, Piazza B. Gigli (telephone 0743/40.265) from 10:00 A.M. to 1:00 P.M. and from 4:00 to 7:00 P.M. any day except Monday, when it is closed. For information you may telephone 0743/44.097.

Tickets go on sale at the box office of the theater where the performance is to take place one hour before the start of the performance. Seats for Teatro Romano, Sant'Eufemia, Sala Frau, and Teatro Caio Melisso (for the noontime concerts) are not numbered, so arrive early in order to choose a good seat. It is also a good idea to take a cushion along to Teatro Romano as stone steps can become extremely uncomfortable after two hours.

Admission is free to the Spoletocinema at the Cinema Moderno, the scientific meetings, and the Westminster Choir concert in the *duomo* (do not confuse this with the closing concert in front of the *duomo*). Tickets for Friday-evening and weekend shows are extremely difficult to obtain, but it is usually possible to buy tickets for matinées and for performances and concerts during the week without having to reserve them too far in advance.

For those who order by mail, send with the aforementioned required form a bank check in lire (which should include a 10 percent pre-sale charge) made payable to Associazione Festival dei Due Mondi to the Biglietteria Festival dei Due Mondi, c/o Teatro Nuovo, I-06049 Spoleto. Postal money orders and telephone reservations are not accepted. Priority is given on the basis of the postmark, but the festival will not be held liable for any postal delays or disservice. The *biglietteria* will confirm the seats allocated and advise applicants of how and where to collect their tickets; refunds for unavailable seats "will be made promptly."

For further information, one may contact the festival office in Rome, or, during the weeks of the festival, the secretary or box office in Spoleto. The office in Rome is the Uffici del Festival a Roma, Via Cesare Beccaria 18, I-00196 Rome; telephone 06/321.0288; fax 06/320.0747. In Spoleto the secretary may be reached at Teatro Nuovo, telephone 0743/44.097; fax 0743/221.584; box office 0743/40.265.

For the Armchair Fan

Although each edition of the festival publishes a handsome, well-illustrated booklet in Italian and English of some 75 or more pages, this relates only to the current festival. *Spoleto Festivals* has a text in Italian, but since it is filled with photographs and performance details of the various Spoleto festivals—those in Spoleto (Italy), Charleston (now no longer associated with Menotti), and Melbourne (now defunct)—it should present a vivid panorama for the interested. There is also a handsome booklet published to coincide with the 1993 "Il teatro di Menotti in Italia"

exhibit at the Spoleto festival. Filled with excellent color repro-
ductions of stage sets, the text, in Italian, provides performance
venues, dates, and casts. Finally, there is a biography of Menotti
in Italian that gives considerable attention to Festival dei Due
Mondi, complete with excellent black-and-white photographs of
festival activities among others.

D'Amico de Carvalho, Caterina, and Vittoria Crespi Morbio.
1993. *Il teatro di Menotti in Italia*. Rome: Edizioni de Luca.

Fabbri, Lionello. 1987. *Spoleto Festivals: Spoleto, Charleston,
Melbourne*. Rome: Elle Edizioni.

Gruen, John. 1981. *Gian Carlo Menotti*. Trans. Franco Salvatorelli. Turin: ERI Edizioni RAI.

There are recordings that provide a good overview of festival
productions.

Donizetti, Gaetano. *Il duca d'Alba*. Melodram (LP) 002; with
Ivana Tosini, Renato Cioni, Louis Quilico, Vladimiro Gan-
zarolli, Enzo Tei, and Franco Ventriglia; Orchestra e Coro
del Teatro "G. Verdi" di Trieste; conducted by Thomas
Schippers. Recorded live in Teatro Nuovo, August 1959.

Barber, Samuel. *Antony and Cleopatra*. New World Records
NW322/323/324-2; with Jeffrey Wells, Eric Halfvarson, Jane
Brunnell, Kathryn Cowdrick, Esther Hinds, Robert Grayson,
Mark Cleveland, Charles Damsel, and Steven Cole; West-
minster Choir; Spoleto Festival Orchestra; conducted by
Christian Badea. Recorded live in Teatro Nuovo, June 1983.

Menotti, Gian Carlo. *Goya*. Nuova Era 7060/61; with Cesar
Hernandez, Suzanna Guzman, Andrew Wentzel, Penelope
Daner, Howard Bender, Boaz Senator, Daniele Tonini, and
Karen Nickell; Westminster Choir; Spoleto Festival Orches-
tra; conducted by Steven Mercurio. Recorded live in Teatro
Nuovo, 26–29 June and 3, 7, 11, and 13 July 1991.

Taormina Arte
TAORMINA

Taormina is a glorious site for a festival, the view spectacular
from its ancient Greco-Roman amphitheater across the Bay
of Naxos to Mount Etna. The tiny, narrow streets of this prehistoric village—some not six feet wide—are quaint and fascinating.
And as a music festival, Taormina Arte features the very finest
world-class artists; Giuseppe Sinopoli is the music director and

229

his Philharmonia Orchestra from London the resident ensemble.

The town itself, which has just a few over 10,000 inhabitants, sits on a shelf that clings precipitously to the side of a sheer, 3650-meter (12,045-foot) granite cliff, with its hotels and quaint shops perched some 8 kilometers (5 miles) up steep, zig-zagging roads from the beach and train station (an area known as Taormina Giardini).

The French author Guy de Maupassant summed up the significance of Taormina when he wrote in 1885:

> If someone should ask me what to see in all of Sicily if [he] had only one day to spend there, I would answer without hesitation: Taormina. It is only a landscape, but a landscape in which you find everything that seems created on earth to seduce eyes, mind and fantasy.[27]

The subtitle of Taormina Arte is "Rassegna Internazionale di Cinema-Teatro-Musica [International Review of Cinema-Theater-Music]" and reflects the tripartite nature of its programming. Scheduled from late July to mid-September, most of the music events take place at the very height of Taormina's tourist season, the last days of August and early September. Concerts, ballets, and opera performances are given in the 8000-seat Teatro Antico; the annual opera production is part of an ongoing theme, "Opera and Myth," established by Sinopoli in 1991 with Wagner's *Lohengrin* (conducted by Sinopoli and directed by Wolfgang Wagner, the composer's grandson, in a production featuring the Bayreuth Festival Chorus). The series of myths has continued with Richard Strauss's *Elektra* in 1992, directed by Luca Ronconi, and Vincenzo Bellini's *Norma* in 1993. (After all, Bellini was born just 64 kilometers/40 miles away in Catania.)

Guest conductors for the festival's symphony concerts have included Leonard Bernstein directing the Festival Orchestra of Schleswig-Holstein, Gerd Albrecht leading the Hamburg Staatsorchester, and Luciano Berio and Rafael Frühbeck de Burgos conducting the Philharmonia Orchestra. The list of vocal soloists is most impressive and includes sopranos Gabriele Schnaut, Luana Devol, and Sabine Hass; mezzos Hanna Schwarz and Uta Priew; tenors Horst Hiestermann, Warren Ellsworth, Robert Schunk, and Siegfried Jerusalem; and baritone/basses Manfred Schenk, Hans Sotin, Kurt Rydl, and Alfred Muff among others.

230

Because of space limitations (only Teatro Greco is available for music performances), normally only one opera is mounted per season, but the symphony concerts include large portions of operatic fare, including in recent seasons Richard Strauss's *Salome* (complete) and excerpts from Wagner's *Die Meistersinger von Nürnberg* and *Götterdämmerung* and a complete Act I of *Die Walküre*.

The annual Taormina Arte musical slate usually contains four evenings of ballet, three performances of the opera, and four different symphony concerts. The choice of repertory reflects Taormina's unique location with such featured works as Richard Strauss's *Aus Italien* and Mendelssohn's Symphony No. 4, the "Italian." Solo recitals by pianists and violinists are scheduled, and contemporary music is frequently represented. A series of Luciano Berio's works, including his masterpiece, *Sinfonia*, for example, has been given under his baton, while the Italian minimalist composer, Salvatore Sciarrino, was commissioned by Taormina Arte to write a work for viola and orchestra.

As for the related theater and cinema events, there are almost daily offerings throughout July of major movies past and present, with the viewings sponsored jointly by the Rassegna del cinema (Cinema Review), the International Film Festival, and the Settimana del cinema americano (Week of American Movies). The theatrical offerings that take place at various sites in Taormina during the month of August are both locally mounted and co-produced and include both Italian and world *primas*. In 1989 the cinema and theater section awarded its first Premio Europa to Peter Brook for his efforts and achievements in the theater.

The Story of Taormina Arte

As with most Italian communities and festivals, Taormina has suffered the vicissitudes of political interference and factional division, but fortunately, since the establishment of Taormina Arte in 1983, the efforts seem unified in purpose and lofty in ideals. The oldest branch of Taormina Arte is the film wing, the Rassegna del cinema, founded in 1954 by the provincial tourist office. A summer music festival—Estate Musicale—was established in 1962, but foundered after four changes of management, having encountered financial difficulties each time. In 1976 the local tourist office sponsored the Festival Internazionale Teatro Taormina, but in spite of its artistic success, it ended in financial disaster.

231

Consequently Taormina Arte was created to save a series of events in a state of organizational breakdown caused by the discrepancies between the various tourist organizations during the late 1970s (which was also a period of rapid cost increases). The appointment of Gioacchino Lanza Tomasi as artistic director of the music section was a fortuitous one. A musicologist by training, he had been the artistic director of Teatro dell'Opera in Rome for 10 years, and in 1991 assumed the position of artistic director of the opera house in Bologna. The appointment in 1990 of Giuseppe Sinopoli as both resident conductor and music director has given the music wing not only a sense of stability, but a worthy vision of the future.

As Lanza Tomasi frankly admits,

Taormina has always attracted large groups of English and German tourists, so it seems quite consistent to appoint a British orchestra—the Philharmonia—as the resident ensemble and to include a number of German works in the festival's operatic offerings. After all, Wagner loved Italy, visited here frequently, completed his *Parsifal* in Sicily, and died in Venice. Likewise Richard Strauss was enraptured by the beauties of Sicily's magnificent shores and azure-blue water, the mountains and all their glory.

To complete our "international" picture, we have appointed a well-known and much respected conductor—himself a Sicilian—as music director: Giuseppe Sinopoli.

Our approach to music is multifaceted. We want to offer the public the best Italy has to present, while including in our programming the greatest artists and composers and conductors from all over the world. Thus we presented Luciano Berio conducting his *Voci. Folk Songs II* in 1991 while not forgetting the Prokofiev centennial. We have presented Beethoven's Ninth as well as commissioned Salvatore Sciarrino to write a new work for violist Augusto Vismara and orchestra. We also have presented the Electric Phoenix in works by Janequin as well in pieces from The Beatles Collection. We are fortunate to have established a working relationship with Bayreuth. This is a good thing, for Bayreuth turns away about 30,000 ticket requests a season (the Festspielhaus holds something less than 2000, while our Teatro Antico can accommodate at least 8000 patrons at a time). Wolfgang Wagner directed a stunning *Lohengrin* for us in 1991, a production that included the Festival Chorus from Bayreuth."[28]

Taormina has always been a tourist town, and Sinopoli sees the wisdom in providing opera for these visiting guests:

The climate in Taormina is perfect in every way for a festival. For example, Teatro Antico accommodated 4000 spectators an evening for the concert performances of Richard Strauss's *Salome*, which we did in 1990, while during the same summer in the highly cultural city of Milan, Strauss's *Die Frau ohne Schatten* conducted by Wolfgang Sawallisch barely filled half the house at La Scala.[29]

Fringe Benefits

Taormina is a town whose origins are buried in myth and mystery and whose beauty is legendary. It had a period of great splendor around 358 B.C., when Andromache, whose son was Timaeus the philosopher, was elected head of the town, a period that saw the birth of a unique Hellenistic society in Taormina. Siracusian rule was followed by Roman domination, and during the Middle Ages the town came under heavy attack by the Moslems. It became the capital of Byzantine Sicily in the 9th century. Taormina took part in the Sicilian Vespers, and in 1410 became the seat of the Sicilian parliament. Spanish domination of Taormina was succeeded by French occupation in 1675; the city then came under Spanish rule again, this time with Philip V on the throne. The French Bourbons took over in 1734, with their governance lasting until 1861 when Italy was united.

Unique and fascinating parts of this history are to be found everywhere in Taormina: ancient walls and fortifications, magnificent villas, classic open-air theaters. Although the Normans ordained Taormina a seat of tourism because of its geographical location, its magnificent landscapes, and its splendid climate, as well as the wonderful color of its sky, sea, slopes, countryside, trees, and flowers, it would be more correct to say that Taormina was born touristic: many years before the Normans, the *Siculi* had chosen it as their home city, not just because of its political position but for its splendid vistas and wonderful climate. The Greeks, Romans, Byzantines, and Saracens followed in turn; all its conquerors inhabited Taormina for long periods.

In any case, one of Taormina's most important tourists of the last century—Johann Wolfgang Goethe—dedicated exalting pages to the city in his book entitled *Journey to Italy*. But perhaps Taormina is famous as an international tourist center today because of Otto Geleng, a young red-haired Prussian painter. Late in the 19th century Geleng arrived in Sicily (at age 20) in search of subjects; on his way through Taormina he became so fascinated by its splendors that he stopped there. Geleng began to paint everything the town offered: nooks and crannies, ancient villas and fortifications, flowers, gardens, and trees. When his paintings were later exhibited in Paris, neither the critics nor the public would believe that such gorgeous scenes actually existed and fully believed them to be figments of the artist's vivid imagination. Hurt that people were skeptical about the reality of such beauty, he challenged them to travel to Taormina, promising that he would pay everyone's expenses if he were not telling the truth. He went back to Taormina and created its first hotel out of a noble mansion, now called the Timeo Hotel, and that was that! His paintings did reflect absolutely unique natural wonders.

The most important relic of the past as far as the festival tourist is concerned is Teatro Antico. Is it Greek or Roman? This is a question that has always been open to debate among experts and critics. All disputes would end if they would remember Taormina's origins as a Greek *polis* (city/state) and the fact that each and every Greek city had its own theater where tragedies by Aeschylus, Sophocles, and Euripides and comedies by Aristophanes, just to name the most famous authors, were performed. The theater in Taormina is the second largest in Sicily (the one in Syracuse is the largest). In accordance with their well-known ostentatious nature, all the Romans did was to enlarge the theater they thought too small. (And it apparently took decades for them to do that.) It is about 50 meters (165 feet) wide, 120 meters (396 feet) long, and 20 meters (66 feet) high, which means that tens of thousands of cubic meters of stone had to be removed. Further evidence that the theater is of Greek origin is shown by the well-cut blocks of Taormina stone (similar to marble) below the *scene* (pronounced SHEH-neh) of the theater, a typical example of Greek building technique according to archaeologists.

The theater is divided into three main sections: the *scene*, the *orchestra*, and the *cavea*. The *scene*, opposite the *cavea*, is where the actors used to perform. There is now a huge 10-meter (33-foot) portion missing in the center of the *scene*, supposedly caused by attacks during the wars. This serious damage to the theater makes it even more evocative due to the magnificent panorama (the Bay of Naxos and Mount Etna) that can now be seen. According to reconstructions by experts, the *scene* was decorated with two series of columns of the Corinthian order, recognizable by the shape of the capitals and their acanthus-leaf design (the acanthus is a wild Mediterranean plant). The *orchestra* of the theater was the flat clearing in the center that separated the *scene* from the *cavea*. This area was for the musicians, but choruses and dancers also performed there. The word *orchestra*—today meaning a large ensemble of instrumental musicians—comes from this part of the Greek theater. The *cavea* is the series of steps where the spectators were seated. The first and last semicircular steps are some 62 meters (205 feet) and 147 meters (486 feet) long respectively. The steps were carved out of the rock, and in places where there was none, they were built with masonry. The *cavea* was divided into five seating areas called *diazòmata* by the Greeks and *praecinctiones* by the Romans, both meaning "enclosed zones." The theater is thought to have accommodated about 5400 spectators.

No one is certain exactly when the theater was actually erected. Those who believe it was built by the Greeks say it must date from around the middle of the 3rd century B.C., when Hiero was the tyrant of Syracuse. But due to the theater's structural characteristics, some say it was erected by Roman engineers to be used exclusively by Greeks. This would explain all the Greek inscriptions inside the theater. Today this theater—called Teatro Antico to avoid the controversy over whether it is actually Greek or Roman—is still Taormina's main attraction for tourists. And as festivalgoers will discover, the seating plan today is still based on that of the ancient *diazòmata* or *praecinctiones*, with the stage for opera productions being the old *scene*, while the orchestra sits in the *orchestra*. The front center section of the *cavea* has been built up with bleachers containing individually numbered seats, and the two front side and center sections fitted up with plastic, contoured chairs. The upper sections (unnumbered) make use of the original stone benches. Cushions may be rented for performances, especially important for the longer Wagner operas.

Practical Matters

Taormina, wrapped in olive trees, oleander, and jasmine, and aflame with red and purple bougainvillea, is a tourist's town filled with high-quality antique shops, boutiques, and stores featuring the ceramic and metal crafts of Sicily. Its hotels are a bit more expensive than elsewhere in Italy, its visitors a little more elegantly and fashionably dressed, its cultural offerings usually of the highest order.

There are 65 hotels in Taormina that range from the 5-star San Domenico Palace to the 1-star *locanda* Villa Rita. The San Domenico is one of the great hotels of Italy and, naturally, is both extremely elegant and extremely expensive (rooms were just under $500 a night the last time I visited Taormina). The Hotel Mediterranée, a 4-star hotel, is quite typical of the average lodging. It offers air-conditioning and a wonderfully landscaped garden with swimming pool; in addition, it provides minibus service, free of charge, three times a day down the hill to the beach at Mazzarò, where the hotel makes beach umbrellas and lounge chairs available (also free of charge) in front of its "sister," the Lido Mediterranée Hotel.

In speaking of the San Domenico Palace Hotel it becomes difficult to decide whether a description should fall under Taormina History or Hotel Accommodations. Suffice it to say the San Domenico is one of the important wonders of Taormina. Unfortunately its impressive interior can be enjoyed only by guests of the hotel as it is not open to the public. This hotel was once a Dominican monastery, actually the third to be located in Taormina. Its origins and history are related to Damiano Rosso, a Dominican friar who was a descendant of the Altavilla family and Prince of Cerami; after becoming a friar he donated all he owned to the Dominican order in 1430. His antique mansion was therefore turned into Taormina's Dominican monastery. The San Domenico was the first or perhaps the only castle existing in Taormina during the Middle Ages. Some centuries later the estate was given back to Damiano Rosso's heirs who turned it into a hotel. The only part of the former monastery to remain open to worship was the chapel, which, however, was destroyed by bombings on 9 July 1943. The congress hall of the hotel was built on the ruins of the chapel, conserving the remains of the minor altars. The bombings did not damage the rest of the hotel or the 50 cells that were later turned into luxurious hotel rooms. The beautiful cloister and magnificent park, which overlook the sea and have a view of Mount Etna, are the most charming parts of the hotel. A second wing added to the hotel in the 1930s harmoniously reflects the architectural style of the rest of the building and is decorated with many authentic art treasures, sacred vestments and vessels, and paintings by well-known artists.

For a list of hotels in Taormina and nearby Taormina-Mazzarò, where the Lido Mediterranée as well as 23 other beachfront hotels are located, write, telephone, or fax Azienda Autonoma Soggiorno e Turismo di Taormina, Piazza Santa Caterina/Palazzo Corvaja, I-98039 Taormina (ME); telephone 0942/23.243; fax 0942/24.941. A funicular railway connects Taormina with Taormina-Mazzarò.

A festival brochure may be requested by post, telephone, or fax: Taormina Arte, Via Pirandello 31, I-98039 Taormina (ME); telephone 0942/21.142; fax 0942/23.348.

Tickets, which are expensive, may be ordered by mail; for this purpose it is absolutely essential to use the order form included in the festival brochure. After completing it, enclose with it a photocopy of the telegraph money order, in Italian lire, clearly stating that it is payment in full and includes the 10 percent booking surcharge, payable to Taormina Arte. No other form of payment is accepted, neither is partial payment. Requests will be returned to the sender if the official order form is not used or is filled out incompletely. Postal bookings should be sent to Taormina Arte, Ufficio Biglietteria, Via Pirandello 31, I-98039 Taormina (ME). According to the ticket office,

> Seats will be assigned on the basis of the posting date of registered letters. Taormina Arte will not be liable for any postal delay or disservice. The booking office will confirm the reservation of seats. Confirmed tickets can be collected at the ticket office during the festival upon presentation of Taormina Arte's booking confirmation.

Remember that airmail service between either the United States and Italy or the United Kingdom and Italy usually takes about three weeks in each direction, and posting by registered mail is highly recommended.

For those who wish to purchase their tickets in Taormina, the box office is located on the ground floor of the Conference Hall (telephone 0942/626.314), which is open from 10:00 A.M. to 1:00 P.M. and again from 5:00 to 8:00 P.M. during the festival. According to the festival organizers, "a direct line for information service has been organized exclusively to meet your requirements. Information is provided in Italian, English, German, and French."

The audiences at Teatro Antico tend to be stylishly dressed, with most of the men in the center section wearing dark or summer suits. A cool breeze frequently wafts in across the amphitheater from the Bay of Naxos below and makes a coat for men and a light shawl or scarf for women quite welcome. The temperature in September averages 25° Celsius (78° Fahrenheit), with a high of around 28° Celsius (83° Fahrenheit) in the daytime and a low of 19° Celsius (66° Fahrenheit) at night.

For the Armchair Fan

At present there are neither books nor pamphlets on Taormina Arte, nor are there any live recordings commercially available. Artistic director Tomasi plans to offer commercially released video discs, recorded live, starting with the 1994 season.

The Puccini Festival
TORRE DEL LAGO PUCCINI

Visitors to the Puccini Festival at Torre del Lago will find themselves immediately immersed in the countryside that Giacomo Puccini knew and loved so well, especially Lake Massaciuccoli (pronounced mah-sah-CHOOK-koh-lee), with its grassy marshes in which the maestro loved to spend leisurely hours hunting coot and duck or fishing from a boat. The outdoor theater where opera performances take place is literally just across the street from Villa Puccini, where the composer lived most of his life and where he worked on every opera from *La Bohème* to the triptych and *La rondine*.

Established in 1930, the Puccini Festival takes place each year from late July through mid-August, a season that usually consists of three operatic productions plus a few isolated recitals and lecture/seminars. Unlike most other Italian festivals that follow the *stagione* system, the three operas at Torre del Lago alternate night to night, allowing the short-term visitor an opportunity to see and hear all three operas on consecutive, or nearly consecutive, nights if the trip is properly planned.

All operas are given in the specially constructed, outdoor Teatro di Quattromila (Theater of 4000), which accommodates almost 4000 spectators. The stage itself is a raised platform built on the edge of Lake Massaciuccoli. (For a recent *Turandot* production, the lake itself served as a backdrop, with a huge moon made of brass erected on a float, which was anchored in the center of the lake for the nighttime scene.)

During the period when Renzo Giacchieri was artistic director, a rather practical plan was formulated: each production would stay in the repertory for three years, with one new and two returning productions each summer. In addition, he felt that the festival should offer the visitor a chance to savor other works written during the same period in which Puccini was creating his operas. He thus coupled a marvelous production of *Gianni Schicchi* (most effectively set in the Victorian period) with a delightful rendition of Ravel's *L'heure espagnole*.

At the present time there seems to be no fixed policy with reference to repertory. The 1991 season, for example, offered *Turandot* with Ghene Dimitrova in the title role, a fantastical production conducted by the Russian maestro Yuri Ahronovich, with direction, sets, and costumes by Sylvano Bussotti, which came from Teatro Bellini in Catania. The second work on the *cartellone* was *Madama Butterfly*, a production originally directed by Renzo Giacchieri with a cast of principals most of whom are little known even in Italy. Then followed a double bill: *Le villi*, Puccini's first opera, coupled with his last completed opera, *Il tabarro*. Giuseppe Di Stefano appeared in the short spoken part of *Le villi*, while Giuseppe Giacomini sang the role of Luigi in the production of *Il tabarro*. The orchestra of Teatro del Giglio in Lucca was the resident ensemble for the festival.

The 1991 season opened rather inauspiciously with a gala held in Viareggio at Villa Borbone, where the Great Hall accommodates 400 guests. It was a presentation entitled "The 1900s: Paris and Vienna at the Beginning of the 1900s—Music and Poetry" and featured the E.CO Ensemble, soprano Anastasia Tomaszewska Schepis, and television personality/music critic Vittorio Sgarbi. (One review of this lecture/recital was captioned ". . . But Puccini Deserves Better.")[30]

Speaking of repertory, the 34th festival in 1992, by way of contrast, centered around *Edgar*, a coproduction with the Chigiana in Siena, and two new productions: *La Bohème* and *Manon Lescaut*. Faulty management and provincial thinking and planning, along with a lack of adequate direction and finances made it necessary to move the 1993 festival to Viareggio in November, and that at a movie theater. Puccini *does* deserve better!

Puccini and His "Ivory Tower"

Giacomo Puccini was a quiet, shy man who much preferred to spend an afternoon playing cards with a few fishermen or hunters from around his lakeside home to dining at lavish banquets in palaces with society and nobility (though he became quite accustomed to the latter as his fame spread).

Born in Lucca, he trained at the Conservatory "G. Verdi" in Milan, where his first opera, *Le villi*, was produced. It was followed by *Edgar* and then the highly successful *Manon Lescaut*.

With the income from *Manon Lescaut*, Puccini was able to keep a youthful pledge: to redeem the family home, a small apartment, in Lucca, which had been sold after his mother's death. "I care about the four cracked walls, the disjointed beams, and even the ruins of my home," he had written earlier to a friend. "I will redeem my home, of that you can be sure."[31]

Puccini shied away from settling in Lucca himself, however, because of the manner in which the city and its citizens responded to his elopement with Elvira Gemignani (their marriage had to wait, by Italian law, until 10 months after the death of her husband; it eventually took place in 1904). The composer felt he had found the ideal spot at Torre del Lago, a remote fishing village on the edge of Lake Massaciuccoli some 8 kilometers (5 miles) from Lucca en route to Viareggio on the Tyrrhenian seacoast. It was a small, unpretentious village, the lake itself surrounded by fishermen's huts made of bog grass and not inaccurately described by Illica—Puccini's best-known librettist—as a "swamp."

When the composer first discovered it in 1884, the village, according to Puccini's own count, consisted of "120 inhabitants and 12 houses."[32] At first he rented a modest home from one of the caretakers of a large estate; as his income increased, Puccini moved to a more elaborate villa, one he rented from Count Grottanelli of Siena. Eventually he was able to start construction on his own home, Villa Puccini, and in 1900 he, Elvira, and their son Antonio moved in. Ecstatic over "his" lake and the new villa, Puccini wrote to a friend that this was "supreme bliss, paradise, Eden, Emphrean, my ivory tower, spiritual vessel and royal palace."[33]

The Story of the Puccini Festival

The Puccini Festival was founded in 1930. "Puccini was dead six years," Luciano Alberti, former artistic director of the festival, writes in his own English.

> He had dreamed of staging his operas beside his home on the lake. We have famous letters, much cited (and with good reason) in the milieu of Torre del Lago. Torre del Lago's festival is not, then, one of those affairs which are born overnight beside a spa. It was born beside the tomb and home of Puccini.[34]

The festival's first theater arose in the flat space between Villa Puccini and the lake, an area still known as Piazzale Puccini. A temporary, barn-like structure was erected for the stage and temporary benches placed around the piazza for seating. Produced by the Carro di Tespi Lirico ensemble, *La Bohème*—the festival's very first presentation—was conducted by Pietro Mascagni. The following year the repertory was enlarged to two operas: *Madama Butterfly* and a repeat of *La Bohème*, this time featuring Beniamino Gigli as Rodolfo.

During the Fascist period, only one festival took place, that of 1937, which was a concert rather than an opera; Licia Albanese was one of the featured soloists of that event.

In 1949, on the occasion of the 25th anniversary of the death of Puccini, *La fanciulla del West*—a production from Rome's Teatro dell'Opera—was presented, starring Maria Caniglia in the title role. After a brief hiatus, the festival started up again in 1952 with a concert, and then in 1953, opera productions appeared on the slate again: *Madama Butterfly* (1953), *Turandot* and *Manon Lescaut* (1954), and *La Bohème* and *Tosca* (1955). Soloists in the 1950s included Magda Olivero, Giuseppe Campora, Antonietta Stella, Giuseppe Di Stefano, Rosanna Carteri, and Ferruccio Tagliavini.

By the 1960s the theater—still located in Piazzale Puccini—had new benches for the patrons, and the stage space at the edge of the lake had been enhanced by a new platform (the old barn-like structure had been done away with) with temporary pillars on it that at least suggested a proscenium arch. Among the outstanding soloists of that decade were Luciana Bertoli, Gino Bechi, Rolando

Panerai (in a production from Palermo's Teatro Massimo), Mario Del Monaco, and Tito Gobbi. The conductors included Oliviero De Fabritiis and Ermanno Wolf-Ferrari (the latter in a production of *Butterfly* from Florence's Teatro Comunale).

Since 1971 the Puccini Festival has continued without interruption. Artists of the 1970s included Nicola Rossi-Lemeni (a soloist in Puccini's *Messa di Gloria* in its first public performance), Placido Domingo, Raina Kabaivanska, Renata Scotto, Luciano Pavarotti, Katia Ricciarelli, José Carreras, Franco Corelli, Maria Chiara, Mariela Devia, and Olivia Stapp.

During the 1970s the theater was moved from the central piazza—Piazzale Puccini, which now remains basically open—a bit to the north, to an area still on the edge of the lake but with tall rows of trees surrounding the space on three sides. A small footpath leads from Piazzale Puccini to the theater proper, Teatro di Quattromila. (Festival announcements as well as the staff and performers refer to it more colloquially as Teatro all'Aperto.)

Artists of the 1980s and '90s include Rosalind Plowright, Victoria de Los Angeles (in a recital), Eva Marton, Cathy Berberian (in a chamber concert), Giuseppe Taddei, Cecilia Gasdia, Gail Gilmore, and Monserrat Caballé.

In 1985 the administration of the festival (the mayor of Viareggio and a board of directors appointed by the city council) tried to establish a firmer foundation for the festival, soliciting plans for a new "permanent" theater. They appointed a new artistic director in the hopes of establishing a more stable schedule of operas and productions without having to borrow those from Palermo, Rome, and Florence. Though Carlo Alberto Ferrari, mayor of Viareggio, stated unequivocally that a new theater rendering homage to Puccini would soon be a reality, nothing of a concrete nature has been accomplished except for a handsome architectural sketch by Galileo Chini of a projected new theater. In 1994, to celebrate the 70th anniversary of Puccini's death and the 40th anniversary of the Festival Pucciniano, the name was officially changed to Puccini Festival and the Teatro di Quattromila completely renovated.

Fringe Benefits

Festival guests will enjoy a visit to Torre del Lago Puccini and the Villa Puccini, but I would offer one word of caution. Today Torre del Lago consists of more than the "120 inhabitants and 12 houses"

Puccini found in 1884. Rather it is, in summer, a bustling holiday resort village filled to brimming with vacationers. A kiosk located between Villa Puccini and the lakeshore displays postcards and cheap plaster busts of the composer, and such other intrusions as the Bar Liù and the Ristorante Butterfly flourish nearby. The noise from the portable radios at the public campsite immediately in back of the festival theater is quite plainly heard at softer moments during performances of the operas, a condition the festival committee and tourist office in Viareggio annually pledge to correct.

The center of attraction for the musical visitor—other than the performances themselves—is Villa Puccini, which stands lakeside at the center of Piazzale Puccini, a mausoleum-cum-museum. After the composer died at the clinic in Brussels, he was temporarily buried in the Toscanini family plot in Milan while his son Antonio had the Villa Puccini properly consecrated by the church and the former dining room fitted up as a mausoleum. His father's remains were then interred at Villa Puccini, as were Elvira's when she died in 1930, and, in turn, Antonio's, and eventually Rita's (Antonio's wife).

Villa Puccini, at Piazzetta Puccini 266, is still owned by the family; the composer's granddaughter, Simonetta Puccini, lives on the first floor (the second story by the American system of reckoning). Open daily in the winter from 9:00 A.M. to noon and from 2:00 to 5:00 P.M., and in the summer from 9:00 A.M. to noon and from 3:00 to 7:00 P.M., the villa employs a porter, an old family retainer, who waits to guide small groups (never more than 25) through the house for a nominal fee.

The downstairs of this two-story villa is just as it was in the days when the composer worked in the front room on the old upright Forster piano, creating *Bohème*, *Butterfly*, the *trittico*, and *Rondine*. Adjacent to this is the sports room, where all the maestro's old hip boots and waders still stand ready for him, his rifles carefully stacked on the racks at the side of the room.

Practical Matters

Because hotel space is, for all practical purposes, non-existent in Torre del Lago Puccini, festivalgoers may need to stay either in Viareggio, some 8 kilometers (5 miles) west on the seacoast, or in Pisa, some 25 kilometers (16 miles) to the south. As public transportation is not a practical solution, a car is a must in either case.

There are two hotels in Torre del Lago Puccini, but both are generally booked a year or two in advance by families planning to enjoy a seaside holiday in August. The 1-star Andrea Doria has 15 rooms (Via Marconi 55; telephone 0585/341.007); the 1-star Butterfly has 10 rooms (Via Belvedere Puccini 24; telephone 0684/341.024). Your best bet, however, will probably be to contact the tourist office in Viareggio, which lists some 195 officially registered hotels: Azienda Autonoma di Cura Soggiorno e Turismo, Viale Carducci 10, I-55049 Viareggio (LU); telephone 0684/42.233.

Tickets for performances at Teatro di Quattromila are reasonably priced for an Italian festival and may be ordered by mail or purchased at the Festival Office at Piazzale Belvedere 4. For festival brochures and further information on ordering tickets, contact the office by mail or telephone (0585/340.235 or 350.567 or 350.568) or fax (0584/350.562).

For the Armchair Fan

The best reference on the history of the Puccini Festival—a very short and sketchy account at best, but at least it appears in both English and Italian—may be found in the annual festival book of 1985. Regarding Villa Puccini, my own account of the composer and his home is illustrated with gorgeous color photographs by Angelo Ceresa.

> Domenici, Lisa, Alberto Paloscia, Paolo Menichini, and Vivian Hewitt. 1985. *31° Festival Pucciniano*. Torre del Lago Puccini: Pubblicazione dell'Ufficio Stampa del Festival Pucciniano.
>
> Rossi, Nick. 1990. "Puccini at Home." *Opera Now* (August/September): 34–39.

No commercial albums have been recorded live at Torre del Lago.

Other Festivals

Listed below are some of the more regularly scheduled festivals held throughout Italy; each generally features at least one opera as part of the festival. The listing is by town or city, with the province and the region indicated in parentheses. The title of the festival is given in italics, followed by the venue.

Tickets for most of the festivals listed below are comparatively cheaper than for operas at *entes*. Such festival tickets range from inexpensive (less than $10) to expensive ($50 or more). A moderately priced ticket will run between $20 and $40.

Agliè (TURIN/PIEDMONT)

Festival Musica in Scena
Castello di Agliè
Agliè (TO)

> Venue seats 700; season: August; one opera; inexpensive.

Barga (LUCCA/TUSCANY)

Opera Barga Festival Lirico Internazionale
Parco di Villa Gherardi
Via Acquedotto
Barga (LU)

> Venue seats 500; season: August; one opera; moderate.

Batignano (GROSSETO/TUSCANY)

Musica nel Chiostro
Monastero di Santa Croce
Batignano (GR)

> Venue built 1621; seats 300; season: July and August; two operas; moderate.

Bolzano (BOLZANO/TRENTINO–ALTO ADIGE)

Bolzano Estate
Teatro Walther von der Vogelweide
Via Seiliar 1
Bolzano

> Venue built 1967; seats 544; season: August; one opera; moderate.

Cortona (AREZZO/TUSCANY)

Rinascita Cimarosiana
Teatro Signorelli
Piazza Signorelli
Cortona (AR)

> Venue built 1857; seats 400; season: July; one opera; no charge.

Fano (PESARO/MARCHE)

Stagione Lirica Estiva
Corte Malatestiana
Piazza XX Settembre
Fano (PS)

> Venue built 15th century; seats 1200; season: July and August; three operas; moderate.

Fermo (ASCOLI PICENO/MARCHE)

Festival Lirico Sinfonico
Arena "Villa Vitali"
Viale Trento
Fermo (AP)

Venue built 1850; seats 1500; season: July and August; four operas; moderate.

Ivrea (TURIN/PIEDMONT)

Festival Musica in Scena
Piazza Ottinetti
Ivrea (TO)

Season: August; two operas; moderate.

L'Aquila (L'AQUILA/ABRUZZO)

Festival Miami-Aquila
Teatro San Filippo
Via dell'Oratorio 6
L'Aquila

Venue built 18th century; seats 200; season: July; one opera; inexpensive.

Livorno (LIVORNO/TUSCANY)

Comitato Estate Livornese
Teatro Comunale di Villa Mimbelli
Via S. Jacopo in Acquaviva
Livorno

Venue built 1979; seats 660; season: July; one opera; moderate.

Naples (NAPLES/CAMPANIA)

Settimane Musicali Internazionali
Teatro Mercadante
Piazza del Municipio
Naples

Venue built 1780; seats 640; season: June; one opera; moderate to expensive.

Novara (NOVARA/PIEDMONT)

Stagione Estiva
Quadriportico della Canonica
Vicolo Canonica
Novara

Venue seats 650; season: June and July; three operas; moderate.

246

Pamparto (CUNEO/PIEDMONT)

Festival dei Saraceni
Chiesa Parrocchiale di S. Biagio
Pamparto (CN)

Venue built 1648; seats 500; season: July; one opera; no charge.

Perugia (PERUGIA/UMBRIA)

Sagra Musicale Umbra
Teatro Comunale Morlacchi
Piazza Morlacchi
Perugia

Venue built 1781; seats 800; season: September; one opera; moderate.

Pompeii (NAPLES/CAMPANIA)

Panatenee Pompeiane
Teatro Grande
Pompei Scavi
Pompeii (NA)

Venue built 5th century B.C.; seats 3000; season: September; one opera; moderate.

Rosignano Marittimo (LIVORNO/TUSCANY)

Festival di Castiglioncello
Piazzetta del Museo
Rosignano Marittimo (LI)

Season: August; one opera; inexpensive.

San Gimignano (SIENA/TUSCANY)

Stagione Lirica all'Aperto
Piazza del Duomo
San Gimignano (SI)

Season: July; one opera; moderate.

Sassari (SASSARI/SARDINIA)

Festival dell'Opera Buffa
Teatro Verdi
Via Politeama
Sassari

Venue built 1890; seats 900; season: December; four operas; moderate.

Siena (SIENA/TUSCANY)

Settimana Musicale Senese
Teatro dei Rinnovati
Piazza del Campo
Siena

Venue built 1560; seats 570; season: August; one opera; moderate.

Syracuse (SYRACUSE/SICILY)

Festival Internazionale delle Arti Barocche
Palazzo Beneventano del Bosco
Syracuse

Venue built 15th century; season: July; one opera; moderate.

Tagliacozzo (L'AQUILA/ABRUZZO)

Festival di Mezza Estate
Chiostro di San Francesco
Tagliacozzo (AQ)

Venue built circa 1500; seats 400; season: August; one opera; inexpensive.

Terni (ROME/LAZIO)

Operaincanto
Teatro Comunale "G. Verdi"
Corso Vecchio 23
Terni (ROMA)

Venue built 18th century; seats 1000; season: September; four operas; inexpensive.

Trapani (TRAPANI/SICILY)

Luglio Musicale Trapanese
Villa Margherita
Viale Regina Margherita 1
Trapani

Venue seats 1500; season: July; two operas; moderate.

Turin (TURIN/PIEDMONT)

Settembre Musica
Teatro Carignano
Piazza Carignano 6
Turin

Venue built 1715; seats 700; season: September; one opera; inexpensive.

Chapter 4

SPECTACLES

Italians have always loved the theater. To trace the origins of either the theaters or the Italians' fondness for them, however, is to delve into the remotest pages of history.

> The origin and development of the primitive structures (probably no more than a mound of earth!) came about so that the public could see the performances. From these homely beginnings the Greek and later the Roman theaters grew into complex and stately structures.[1]

Today the remnants of the most stately of these arenas and amphitheaters serve the cause of music well. On the island of Sicily, opera may be seen during the summer months at the Greek theater in Syracuse, an amphitheater dating from the 5th century B.C. and one of the largest—134 meters (442 feet) across—and best-preserved theaters of the ancient world. The amphitheater in Taormino (described in Chapter 3) dates from the Hellenic period—the 3rd century B.C.—and is one of the most idyllic settings imaginable for opera in the summer. The Valley of Temples at Agrigento, beautifully situated on a hill overlooking the southern coast of Sicily, is the scene for the summer Panatenee Pompeiane, its operas selected from those originally presented in Pompeii. The Doric temples of Agrigento, which date back to the 5th through 1st centuries B.C., provide a classic setting for opera *all'aperto*.

On the mainland, the remnants of the Roman temple at Fiesole (circa 80 B.C.), a summer retreat 8 kilometers (5 miles) into the hills above Florence, offers a historical setting for the operas and ballets presented by L'Estate Fiesolana each summer. Teatro Romano in Benevento—a city in the middle of Italy, halfway between Naples on the Tyrrhenian Sea and Bari on the Adriatic Sea—is one of the largest Roman theaters still in existence. Built in the 2nd century B.C. during the reign of Emperor Hadrian, it was restored by Caracalla. Today it serves as the setting for a summer opera festival that generally consists of three different operas, each given twice.

By far the most impressive site, however, is the Arena di Verona, a handsome survivor from the 1st century A.D., an amphitheater that has been the setting for outdoor opera since 1913. As for Rome, the capital of that ancient empire, its *terme* (baths)—as the Baths of Caracalla were first called—were a unique festival setting for many years.

For today's summer visitor to Italy, these ancient sites provide wonderful spectacles to see, hear, and enjoy.

The Baths of Caracalla
ROME

The Baths of Caracalla are one of the glories of ancient Rome. Begun by Septimus Severus in 206 A.D. and inaugurated by his son Caracalla 11 years later, they were able to accommodate 1600 bathers at a time, with the structures serving, as M. E. Sheafer described them in her *Marvels of Ancient Rome*, as "immense club houses."[2] These baths continued in use until the Goths destroyed the aqueduct in the 6th century.

> The complex consisted of a central block housing the various baths and, some way off, an enclosure with gymnasiums, halls, offices, and libraries. Between these two were gardens.
>
> The enclosure, composed of porticoes with small rooms behind (for dressing rooms and shops), covered a square whose sides were 330 meters [1089 feet] long, with two large symmetrical apses for additional gymnasiums and a hall for cultural gatherings and lectures. An exedra, shaped like the elongated half-*cavea* of a stadium, was situated in the center . . . and used for theatrical performances. Beside the stadium were the Greek and Latin libraries.[3]

The Baths of Caracalla in a late 18th-century engraving. Courtesy Teatro dell'Opera di Roma.

The former *calidarium*—a large hot-room in which the atmosphere was moistened by a tub of hot water with which the bathers doused themselves—served as a setting in summer for the performance of opera. Some idea of the size of this area can be judged from the fact that in a performance of *Aida*, with a cast of hundreds on stage, there was still room for a four-horse chariot to be driven on stage, turned around, and driven off again.

"An unforgettable experience in one of the world's most unique corners," is the way the *Giornale d'Italia* described the evening when more than 8000 patrons enjoyed the first performance of an opera on that stage on 7 August 1937.[4]

> The spot has the potential of suggesting the unreal. Truly the glorious silence of centuries past breathes of Cyclopean ruins, illuminated by the light of dreams, made to sing with the divine melodies of Donizetti, consecrated with the love for the grand and the beautiful.[5]

Such was the florid language of the music critic who wrote of that first performance of opera at the Baths, a production of Gaetano Donizetti's *Lucia di Lammermoor*.

251

This outdoor gala was Il Duce's idea according to *La Tribuna*, "brought to life and realized by His Excellency Piero Colonna, Governor of Rome."[6]

Recalling the enormous success that the Arena di Verona was having with outdoor opera, Mussolini dreamed of developing in the capital city of Rome his own center for summer productions of opera. Toward this goal he encouraged an experiment: three performances of Donizetti's *Lucia di Lammermoor*, to be offered *all' aperto*. As Il Duce saw it, the indoor seating capacity at Teatro dell'Opera was limited to somewhat less than 2000 patrons per performance and could not begin to accommodate the number of summer visitors who wanted tickets. Coupled with this was the fact that in those pre-air-conditioning days, Teatro dell'Opera became unbearably hot in summer. Yet another of Mussolini's concerns dealt with employment for the opera's chorus and orchestra, many of whom sailed for America in July and August to make money and "live the good life" (*guadagnarsi da vivere*), according to *La Tribuna*.[7] This same article went on to praise the zeal with which Mussolini's committee had tackled the experiment. "Within a few days, through their ardor and fervor, their tirelessness and dedication, they created a truly Roman theater, a grand modern theater located between the enormous and miraculous walls of the Baths of Caracalla for those spectacular performances."[8]

As for the so-called silence of the ages that once was a part of the atmosphere at the Baths of Caracalla, one now heard the noise of Rome's heavy traffic. And instead of operas' being staged where there actually was a Roman theater in the original complex, a temporary theater was created from the *tepidarium* (the large hall of temperate atmosphere meant for the cooling-down of bathers), which was fitted with chairs to accommodate 8000 spectators.

For opening night in 1937, the music critic of the *Giornale d'Italia* believed, "everything was done from the heart to make this project a success, a triumph of technical aspects, and all for the glory of the spirit. Thus *Lucia* . . . has consecrated an auspicious theater for the masses."[9]

The production of *Lucia di Lammermoor* was directed by Oliviero De Fabritiis and the title role sung by Toti Dal Monte, who was assisted by the greatest tenor of the day, Beniamino Gigli. The cast also included the baritone Luigi Montesanto, bass Ernesto Dominici, soprano Maria Huder, and tenor Nino Mazziotti.

This experiment was so successful that the first official season was scheduled for the following year. For acoustical reasons the positions of the stage and public were reversed, with the stage placed on the *calidarium* and the audience seated in the garden. In addition, dressing rooms and storage spaces were built for the occasion.

The official opening took place on 30 June 1938 in the presence of Benito Mussolini, with the audience estimated at over 20,000 and the cast for *Lucia* this time including Beniamino Gigli, Gina Cigna, Ebe Stignani, Gilda Alfano, Armando Borgioli, and Nicola Moscona, with direction by Vincenzo Bellezza. A performance of Boito's *Mefistofele* followed and featured Nazzareno De Angelis, who, although 57, was the leading interpreter of the title role. Then De Fabritiis returned for an *Aida* that established that work as *the* showpiece par excellence for the Baths (as it had proven to be for the Arena di Verona); Bellezza directed a *Lohengrin* featuring a young Tito Gobbi; and from 26 July to 4 August, Pietro Mascagni conducted performances of his own *Isabeau* with Gina Cigna in the lead. The initial season closed on 15 August (a much-venerated holiday in Italy, *ferragosto*) with the fourth performance of *Turandot* starring Magda Olivero.

As the seasons progressed, the major names in the world of opera appeared on the *cartelloni*: Giacomo Lauri Volpi, Giuseppe Di Stefano, Gabriella Tucci, Giulietta Simionato, Giulio Neri, Maria Callas, Boris Christoff, Renata Tebaldi, Nicola Rossi-Lemeni, Ferruccio Tagliavini, Rosanna Carteri, Franco Corelli, and Mario Del Monaco among others.

In 1991 the sponsoring institution, the *ente autonomo* Teatro dell'Opera, decided to call the summer season a festival, naming the initial offering the I° Festival di Caracalla in honor of the 50th season of summer opera at the Baths of Caracalla. As in the past, the season ran from early July to the end of August. It offered 10 performances of *Aida*, eight of *Nabucco*, and four of *Rigoletto*, in addition to five evenings of the ballet *Zorba the Greek*, 25 "Concerts of Soloists from the Theater of Opera," and a single program by the Royal Philharmonic of London.

Luca Pellegrini, one of the music critics on the staff of *L'Opera*, Italy's most important opera magazine, asked a question in the title of his review of this "new" festival: "Did the summer bring a change?"[10] (The summer offerings at the Baths had become an in-joke among the *cognoscenti* of Rome who viewed the whole thing as a commercial enterprise of dubious quality designed for tourists

Terme di Caracalla

GOVERNATORATO DI ROMA - TEATRO REALE DELL' OPERA
STAGIONE LIRICA - A. XVI

Sabato 9 Luglio 1938 - A. XVI - ore **20,45** precise

PRIMA RAPPRESENTAZIONE

AIDA

Opera in quattro atti (sette quadri) di A. GHISLANZONI
Musica di GIUSEPPE VERDI

(Prop. G. Ricordi e C.)   INTERPRETI PRINCIPALI   (Prop. G. Ricordi e C.)

Maria Caniglia   **Beniamino Gigli**   **Ebe Stignani**
Aida   *Radames*   *Amneris*

Benvenuto Franci   **Nicola Moscona**   **Ernesto Dominici**
Amonasro   *Ramfis*   *Il Re*

Un messaggero: Nino Mazziotti - Una sacerdotessa: N. N.

Sacerdoti - Sacerdotesse - Ministri - Soldati - Capitani - Funzionari - Schiavi

DANZE - Coreografia di BORIS ROMANOFF - Prima ballerina assoluta: ATTILIA RADICE

Primi ballerini: Guglielmo Morresi - Filippo Morucci

Maestro Concertatore e Direttore

OLIVIERO DE FABRITIIS

Maestro del Coro: GIUSEPPE CONCA
Regista: HERBERT GRAF - Direttore dell'allestimento scenico: PERICLE ANSALDO
Realizzatore delle luci: Ettore Salani
Direttore musicale del palcoscenico: Luigi Ricci - Altro maestro del coro: Oscar Leone
Altri registi: Bruno Nofri - Oscar Saxida Sassi
Maestri sostituti:
Giuseppe Bertelli - Emilio Casolari - Simone Cuccia - Francesco Molinari Pradelli - Corrado Muccini
Mario Panunzi - Nicola Rocci - Nino Stinco
Maestro rammentatore: Armando Petrucci - Maestro della Banda: Augusto Pittoni
Bozzetti e scene di Nicola Benois - Costumi del Teatro Reale dell'Opera - Mobili ed attrezzi della Ditta Rancati

---

(compresa la tassa erariale) PREZZI (compresa la tassa erariale)

Poltrone numer. **25**   Poltrone numer. **15**   Primi Posti **8**   Secondi Posti **4**
d'Orchestra L.   di Platea L.   di Platea L.   NON NUMERATI   di Platea L.   NON NUMERATI

Norma per la vendita e validità dei biglietti
Orario di vendita al BOTTEGHINO del TEATRO REALE dell'OPERA

L'orario feriale e festivo per la vendita dei biglietti al Botteghino del Teatro è il seguente:
dalle 8,30 alle 12,30 e dalle 16,30 alle 20,30.
Nei giorni di spettacolo il Botteghino del Teatro rimarrà aperto ininterrottamente dalle
8,30 alle 20,30; però la vendita dei biglietti per la rappresentazione della sera stessa, sara sospesa alle
16,30 precise per essere ripresa dalle 18 in poi alle Biglietterie situate presso le Terme di Caracalla.
Dalle 16,30 alle 20,30 saranno venduti al Botteghino del Teatro i soli biglietti per gli
annunziati spettacoli successivi.

Orario di vendita ai chioschi rionali
Piazzale S. GIOVANNI, Piazza FIUME, Piazzale FLAMINIO, Piazza SONNINO (Trastevere).
L'orario di vendita nei suddetti chioschi rionali è il seguente:
Dalle ore 8 alle 13,30 e dalle 16 alle 20,30.
S'intende che nei giorni di rappresentazione l'orario pomeridiano è limitato soltanto alla vendita
dei biglietti per gli spettacoli successivi, poiché dalle 18 in poi i biglietti per lo spettacolo della
sera stessa, possono essere acquistati alle Biglietterie presso le Terme di Caracalla.
Il biglietto è valido soltanto nella sera dello spettacolo per la quale esso viene acquistato e
non è rimborsabile.
Qualora la recita sia sospesa dopo l'inizio il biglietto va considerato interamente usufruito.

**L'ingresso alle Terme di Caracalla verrà aperto alle ore 18,45 - Iniziato lo spettacolo
verrà sospeso l'accesso ai posti, sino all'intervallo fra un quadro e l'altro**

Tip. Nava e C. - Roma

A *manifesto* for the performance of *Aida* at the Baths of Caracalla on 9 July 1938, featuring Maria Caniglia as Aida, Ebe Stignani as Amneris, Beniamino Gigli as Radames, and Nicola Moscona as Ramfis; Oliviero De Fabritiis conducts, with staging by Herbert Graf. Courtesy Teatro dell'Opera di Roma.

who know little about opera.) His response, from his own English translation for the International Edition of *L'Opera*:

> Did the summer [ever] bring a change! Because it must be admitted in all frankness that the new production of *Nabucco* at Caracalla, after a pompous and very predictable *Aida* (preceded by a clever and entertaining historic procession through the center of Rome), was sufficiently spectacular and visually alluring. . . . [This was] a proud, noble, stimulating, imposing, and imaginative *Nabucco*.[11]

Unfortunately, the change was short-lived. Under the reform government elected in 1994, minister of culture and environment Domenico Fisichella (a member of Silvio Berlusconi's Forza Italia party) declared that, starting with the summer of 1994, there would be no more opera performances at the Baths of Caracalla. Citing damage to the complex from heavy equipment, vibrations, and the wear and tear of some 200,000 spectators a summer, Fisichella stated that the Baths had witnessed their last opera production. Time will tell.

Arena di Verona
VERONA

Verona, a city of 790,000 inhabitants, is nestled in an S-curve of the River Adige, at the foot of the Lessini mountains, not too distant from Lake Garda. The city was founded in prehistoric times on a shallow spot along the river—now the site of the Ponte Pietra or Stone Bridge—where the merchants on the salt and amber route from the Adriatic to Germany could wade across. Possibly founded by the Veneti,[13] the site was of such great importance during the Roman era that it became a Roman town in 49 B.C. Little Rome—as Roman Verona was justly called—was a walled city of temples and basilicas, leafy trees and pleasant squares, with a theater and an amphitheater. For two centuries it enjoyed a vitality seen in few other cities. The years of peace came to an end in 312 A.D., when Pompeianus, general of Maxentius, was defeated and killed near Verona by Constantine. By the 4th century Verona was Christian, and in the middle of the 5th it became the capital of Theodoric's Ostrogoth kingdom before becoming a Longobardic dukedom and the seat of Pepin, king of Italy under the Carolingian empire.

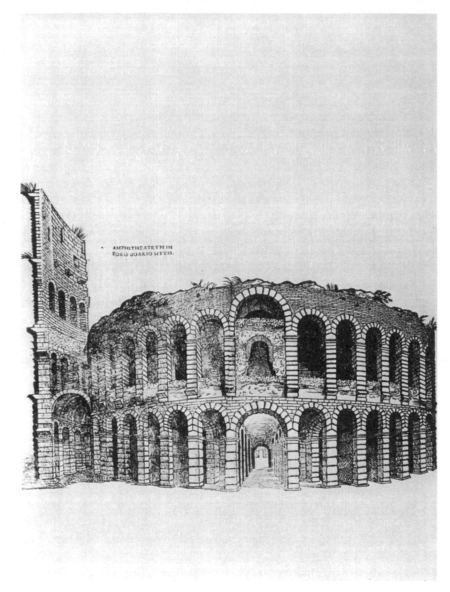

The Arena di Verona seen in an early print that probably dates from the 17th century. Courtesy Arena di Verona.

256

The pleasure-loving Romans created two public centers of entertainment in Verona while the town was under their sway. The Roman theater dates back to the time of Augustus and, along with a similar theater in Trieste, is the best preserved in the Venetian region. Built during the 1st century B.C., the Roman theater was uncovered early in the 19th century beneath some religious buildings and private homes; restorative work was started in 1834.

The Roman amphitheater, built in the 1st century A.D. and popularly called the Arena, lies just outside the walls of the Roman town. The *ala* (wing) is all that remains of the outer wall, which probably collapsed during the earthquake of 1117. During the Middle Ages the amphitheater was the setting for duels, and later for tournaments, bullfights, races, and theatrical events. The Arena originally accommodated 30,000 spectators (one and a half times the population of the city when it was built), and the interior seating has been restored several times, the first effort dating from the 15th century. Among the largest amphitheaters in the Roman world—152 meters (502 feet) long by 128 meters (422 feet) wide and 30 meters (99 feet) high—it can accommodate some 22,000 spectators in its 43 rows of seating today, but because one end of the Arena serves as a stage for the summer opera season, the seating capacity is thus reduced to 16,600 seats.

Because of the Arena's excellent acoustics for outdoor performances, it was first used for opera in 1913 when *Aida* (the veritable warhorse of outdoor theaters) was produced with Tullio Serafin on the podium; it was presented eight times that season, during the second and third weeks of August. The following year *Carmen* appeared for two performances, and in 1919, during World War I, Ponchielli's *Il figliuolo prodigo* opened on 31 July and played for 16 performances. Seasons devoted to two titles began in 1920 when Verdi's *Aida* (seven performances) and Boito's *Mefistofele* (eight performances) were given.

Though *Aida* leads the record at the Arena di Verona—a total of 34 productions as of 1994, amounting to 285 overall performances of the work—this opera seldom appeared on the *cartelloni* in the early years. Those seasons included the following operas: 1921, Saint-Saëns's *Samson et Dalila* and Mascagni's *Il piccolo Marat*; 1922, Wagner's *Lohengrin* and a double-bill consisting of Leoncavallo's *Pagliacci* and *Il carillon magico*, a "commedia mimosinfonico" by Riccardo Pick-Mangiagalli; 1923, Massenet's *Le roi de Lahore* and Bellini's *Norma*; 1924, Wagner's *Parsifal* and Giordano's *Andrea Chénier*; 1925, Rossini's *Mosè* and Ponchielli's *La Gioconda*; and 1926, Boito's *Nerone* and Verdi's *Il trovatore*.

During the late 1920s and through the '30s the fare was still quite diversified and included such titles as Spontini's *La vestale*, Mascagni's *Isabeau*, von Flotow's *Martha*, Mussorgsky's *Boris Godunov*, Wagner's *Die Meistersinger von Nürnberg*, Rossini's *Guglielmo Tell*, Meyerbeer's *L'africana* and *Les Huguenots*, Catalani's *Loreley*, and Zandonai's *Giulietta e Romeo*. At the same time the big Verdi operas as well as a few of Wagner's music dramas were also on the *cartelloni*: *Aida*, *Rigoletto*, *La forza del destino*, *Un ballo in maschera*, *Il trovatore*, *Otello*, *Nabucco*, and *Lohengrin* and *Tannhäuser*. Puccini was represented by *Turandot*, *Tosca*, and *La Bohème*.

Following World War II (there were no opera seasons from 1940 to 1945) the *cartelloni* generally included three operas, a ballet, and a symphonic concert. *Aida* seldom disappeared, and such other staples of the repertory as *Carmen* (nine seasons) and *Turandot* (six seasons) were frequently offered.

There is a breathtaking custom at the Arena that has thrilled audiences season after season. As twilight hovers over the amphitheater, a signal is given and everyone lights a candle and holds it in the air. It is a truly ecstatic experience to see this old Roman arena illuminated by some 16,000 candles, an apt introduction to a magical evening of opera under the starry Veronese sky.

The distinguished conductor Gianandrea Gavazzeni recalled earlier seasons, when he was first employed there as a deputy:

> At that period there was as yet no established opera company and the 1930 and 1931 seasons were organized by the Trade Fair and by Onofrio Zenatello, brother of the famous tenor and owner of the Hotel Accademia. The performances were conducted by Giuseppe Del Campo, a musician of great authority. . . . The program included, along with the more familiar *La forza del destino*, *Guglielmo Tell*, and *Mefistofele*, two unusual choices, *Boris Godunov* in 1930 and *Die Meistersinger* in 1931. The orchestra was both large and of superlative quality: the orchestra of La Scala supplemented by the best players from Verona and the region of the Emilia, and Vittore Veneziani's Scala chorus supplemented by an excellent Veronese group led by Ferruccio Cusinati. Excluding the very first historic *Aida* (1913) under Tullio Serafin, these seasons turned out to be two of the most successful ever. . . .

The stage director for *Boris* was Alexander Sanine, a fiery Russian who later died in poverty in a Roman hospital. Particularly powerful effects (of movement and violence) were created in the scenes of Boris's coronation and the Kromy revolt. At the first performance it was a particularly beautiful evening, and at the very moment of Boris's death a shooting star traced an impressive arc and plunged behind the Arena. Sanine immediately jumped up onto the stage and, like a character out of a Russian novel, his face lined with tears, shouted: "What a stage-director the Creator is."[14]

The Arena di Verona Today

Since the establishment of the Arena di Verona as an *ente autonomo* in 1936, it has become, in reality, two different theaters offering two different seasons. In summer the *ente* produces three operas, a ballet, and a symphony concert at the 16,600-seat Arena; in winter the *ente* produces four operas at Teatro Filarmonico, a traditional baroque theater built in 1732 that seats but 1600.

A major change in administration took place in 1991 during the Arena's 60th festival. The two able musicians who had artistically guided it for four years departed, *sovrintendente* Francesco Ernani to become the new *sovrintendente* at the refurbished Teatro Carlo Felice in Genoa and artistic director Carlo Perucci for serious health reasons. Together these men had built up both the reputation and the quality of performance at the Arena until the attendance figures topped 600,000 for 1990. The two replacements were both men in their 30s: Maurizio Pulica, former councillor (*assessore*) for the arts in Verona, became *sovrintendente*, and Lorenzo Ferrero, a "composer of the most recent generation,"[15] the artistic director.

Pulica, as *sovrintendente*, was immediately inundated with financial problems and a strike for higher pay.

> I not only have all the financial problems of the other *enti lirici* [Pulica commented shortly after his appointment], I have the additional responsibility of, in fact, supervising two theaters that have diverse problems. My payroll grows from 400 in winter to 1200 in the summer, and the state subsidy is growing less all the time. . . .
>
> It becomes evident to me that, with reference to Teatro

Filarmonico, we will need to share productions in the future. Next season [1992–93] for example, we'll do a coproduction with Salzburg and one with Covent Garden. Then, after the summer festival, we'll go to Japan for the second time; we'll take *Turandot* to Tokyo.[16]

Worried that the new artistic director was a young composer of "modern persuasion," music critic Daniele Martino asked Ferrero whether one could expect rock and jazz on the stage at Verona in an effort to make financial ends meet. Ferrero's response:

It is true that I, as a composer, confirm the important musical language of rock in contemporary music, but I am scandalized by stupid suggestions such as "Cocciante [a pop singer] in opera . . ." and the like. It is one thing to absorb the language (for example, Glass, Adams, Pärt, Boulez) but another thing to put common commercial music on the lyric stage. The public isn't stupid. They can listen to Raiuno [the government-sponsored radio station that broadcasts commercial rock]. As for jazz, that's a different story. We already have jazz in such works as Stravinsky's *Ebony Concerto*.[17]

Modern programming at the Arena relies on those works that best lend themselves to outdoor performances: in 1990, *Aida* (15 performances), *Tosca* (12 performances), and *Carmen* (10 performances); in 1991, *Nabucco* (13 performances), *Rigoletto* (12 performances), and *Turandot* (12 performances); in 1992, *Aida* (16 performances), *Don Carlo* (11 performances), and *La Bohème* (13 performances); in 1993, *Carmen* (13 performances), *Aida* (five performances), and *La traviata* (18 performances); and in 1994, *Norma* (eight performances), *Otello* (11 performances), *La Bohème* (11 performances), and *Aida* (15 performances).

Practical Matters

The Arena is located on Piazza Bra in the heart of Verona and is unmistakable. (*Bra* comes from the Old German word *breit* meaning wide.) Inside the Arena, one end is given over to the stage, while public seating is divided into two principal sections: the 43 rows of stone benches from the original Roman amphitheater, which accommodate patrons in a great, sweeping semi-circle;

and the orchestra (stalls/parterre), the center of the arena, which has been fitted up with a sloping wooden platform on which chairs have been placed.

Unlike most Italian theaters, the Arena di Verona uses the repertory system of scheduling, thus it is possible to hear two different operas on consecutive evenings in town, and for the visitor who spends four nights, there is the possibility of taking in all three operas. Tickets are moderately expensive.

The ticket office is located at Arcovolo 6 dell'Arena (the sixth arch of the Arena itself). The telephone number there is 045/596.517. General information about the seasons may be had from the Information Office, Ente Arena, Piazza Bra 28, I-37121 Verona.

Chapter 5

THE REGIONAL THEATERS

In Italy, it seems, every other hamlet, village, and town north of Rome has its own opera house. Some theaters may seat less than 200, others more than 2000. Some date back to the late 16th century, others were built in this century. In the late 19th century, towns such as Pisa were proud of having three principal houses busy at the same time producing operas, and along that 154-kilometer (95-mile) stretch of the Italian Riviera that reaches from Ventimiglia on the French border to Genoa, there were more than 40 active opera houses.

Not all these theaters have opera seasons today, unfortunately. During the Depression, a number of these houses were turned into motion picture theaters. As Harvey Sachs relates in *Music in Fascist Italy*:

> In 1936 Italians spent nearly as much on opera tickets (25,000,000 lire for 2223 performances) as on admission to sports events (26,000,000) or to the spoken theater (31,000,000); but the cinemas took in 439,000,000 lire— more than five and a half times the combined total of the other entertainments.[1]

With the advent of television following World War II and a simultaneous resurgence of interest in cultural events, the republic tried to encourage the preservation of Italy's cultural heritage, es-

263

pecially its tradition of opera. It was a struggle, however. In 1967 the legislature passed a law in which regional theaters were subsidized "for the musical, cultural and social well-being of the country"[2] and provided substantial sums of money to support this law. Unfortunately a disastrous theater fire in Turin led the government's safety commission to establish new safety standards for all public auditoriums. This new law forced almost every house to create additional fire exits and completely rewire buildings, all at staggering costs. (The Turin fire had been caused by faulty wiring.) This meant the closing of each theater in order to make such renovations. Because the rewiring and the construction of fire escapes (whether wholly within the theater or through its exterior walls) meant major structural changes for buildings, most theater boards used the opportunity to completely redo their edifices with new structural supports, new plaster, new paint, and redecorations, and the addition to their stages of not only more dressing and rehearsal rooms but new, up-to-date equipment for the fly galleries so that scenery could be more quickly and efficiently moved on and off stage, all in addition to new switchboard systems to handle the electric rewiring. Some houses closed as early as the mid to late 1970s for these repairs and modifications, others waited for the 1988 deadline. Thus, today, the visitor to Italy has an opportunity to see most of the regional houses within a decade or two of their complete redecoration, with the gilded stucco work pristine and fresh, the upholstery and drapes on the boxes—usually of velvet—unblemished. Unfortunately, there are still a few wonderful early houses that will apparently remain closed indefinitely because the owners—in most cases the communities themselves—have not had sufficient funds to remodel them. One thinks, for example, of the intimate little 19th-century Teatro Comunale in Bibbiena, a town of less than 2000 in the Casentino Valley south of Florence, which is still closed. Similarly, in Livorno, the great port on the Tyrrhenian Sea and a well-to-do city of some 170,000 inhabitants, the acoustically near-perfect Teatro Goldoni, which dates from 1847, remains closed indefinitely, the theater still condemned, its opera productions either staged in movie palaces or, in the summer, *all' aperto*.

Today's visitor to Italy will discover that in addition to the *enti autonomi* described in Chapter 2, there are 24 government-supported regional houses known as *teatri di tradizione*. There are also a host of small, independent opera houses not grouped under any general name. For the purposes of this chapter, I have included both the *teatri di tradizione* and the non-aligned houses under the rubric Regional Theaters; a rather detailed description of eight of the *teatri di tradizione* (those in Brescia, Cremona, Jesi, Lucca, Mantua, Parma, Pisa, and Reggio Emilia) is offered, in addition to some of the more interesting non-aligned community theaters with opera seasons (Lugo, Savona, and Vicenza). Following these detailed descriptions is a list of other *teatri di tradizione* and a number of additional independent regional houses, a list indicating the year in which the theaters were built, their seating capacity, locations and postal addresses, the number of operas usually presented each season, and the period of that season.

Exactly what are the *teatri di tradizione*? The expression literally means traditional theaters but is used in Italy today as a generic term for a group of theaters so designated by the government, theaters for the most part located in secondary Italian cities.

In contrast to the *enti autonomi*, which are actually state-owned theaters, the *teatri di tradizione* are locally owned and administered. However since a goodly portion of their funds come from the state government, some restrictions are placed on the administrative and artistic direction of such houses. The law states

> 1) all vocal artists must be Italian nationals; 2) the orchestra can have no less than 45 members who are Italian nationals (exceptions are made for chamber works); 3) the State Ministry of Tourism and Entertainment is authorized in case of a proven emergency to employ foreign singers in primary roles, such foreign singers not to exceed 25 percent of the singers employed for the entire season; further, such foreign artists must have been employed in artistic activities in Italy for not less than five years.[3]

Even though the State Ministry of Tourism and Entertainment no longer exists, this law is still on the books and observed, requests for "emergency relief" from the law being referred to whatever office at the time is administering the state subsidy of money. The amount of money the state provides these *teatri di tradizione* must then be approved by the central commission for music. Special financial bonuses are offered for the production of a new opera by an Italian composer; for the first local performance of such a work; for the remounting of an opera by an Italian that has not been staged for 20 years; and for the preparation of performance materials for an unpublished Italian opera.

The Story of the Regional Houses

As the visitor will discover, most of the Italian regional houses—with a few notable exceptions—are theaters constructed in the 18th and 19th centuries, usually of baroque design, with tiers of boxes shaped in horseshoe configuration around the *platea* (orchestra/stalls/parterre). The ornamentation is more often than not intricate, delicate, and a feast for the eye.

Teatro Comunale dei rassicurati in Montecarlo is a typical example of a small house in a small community. Built in 1750, the combined seating in its boxes and on the main floor is 180. The theater is located in a mountaintop community of less than 2000 inhabitants just north of Lucca in the foothills of Tuscany. The local town council had the theater completely restored in 1973: walls reinforced, a new fire escape added, all new electrical wiring, with the theater completely replastered, redecorated, and refurbished. Since the community is too small to sponsor an opera season of even one title, Montecarlo is dependent on the availability of productions passing through that area. In 1988 stage director Aldo Tarabella sponsored a lyric workshop in Montecarlo, and as a terminal project (with financial support from the Rota Foundation) produced a double-bill: Nino Rota's *I due timidi* and *La notte di un nevrastenico*. In 1990, a student production of Mozart's *Bastien e Bastienne* helped celebrate the Mozart bicentenary.

If the theater in Montecarlo is among the smallest in Italy, that in Bari is one of the largest. Bari is a city of 350,000 inhabitants on the central Adriatic coast of Italy. Its opera house, Teatro Petruzzelli, built in 1903, accommodated a few more than 2000 patrons in its two tiers of boxes, large balcony, and gallery, in addition to the main floor. A fire of undetermined origin during the fall season of 1991 (arson is suspected) has closed this rather gaudy house designed in the over-ornate style of the late 19th century (elsewhere it would be called Victorian). As a *teatro di tradizione*, Teatro Petruzzelli receives the largest portion of its 9 billion-lira ($75 million) budget from the state government. With this budget it mounted five major opera productions a year with such world-class artists as Katia Ricciarelli, Olivia Stapp, Silvano Carroli, William Matteuzzi, Giovanni Furlanetto, Giuseppe Sabbatini, and

Anna Caterina Antonacci. Conductors included Daniel Oren, Massimo De Bernart, and Daniele Gatti.

Since the burned-out Teatro Petruzzelli is privately owned, the theater board is trying to hold the owners to their rental contract which states that, in case of fire, "work on the renovation of the theater must begin within one year and be completed in less than three."[4] Work began on the reconstruction in 1993 while the opera season was held in a tent theater dubbed Teatro Bari; work on the main theater is scheduled for completion in 1995.

It is interesting to note that during the summer of 1993, when the honesty-in-government searches were going on in Italy,

> one of the more bizarre cases in the 17-month saga of cor-ruption scandals [involved] Fernando Pinto, one of Italy's most respected theater directors, [who] was taken into cus-tody after Mafia informers alleged that he brought in the criminal organization to burn down his own theater in the southern port of Bari so that he could skim funds from a restoration appeal.[5]

The towns and villages where regional houses are located—both the *teatri di tradizione* and the independent ones—use their the-aters not only for opera, but as concert halls for symphonic pro-grams, chamber music, and recitals and as theaters for dance and, most importantly, for spoken drama, which Italians call prose the-ater. Though one could pick any one of the more than 30 very ac-tive regional houses for an example, I have chosen Modena, for no reason other than that it represents the town where both Mirella Freni and Luciano Pavarotti have their roots. Modena is a city of 150,000 inhabitants located 37 kilometers (23 miles) north of Bo-logna. Built in 1841, its Teatro Comunale, which seats 1100, was restored and refurbished in the late 1980s and today accommo-dates an opera season that runs from January to May, a ballet sea-son from January to May, a symphony season from October to May, and a season of plays from October to April.

The 1992 opera season in Modena offered Verdi's *La traviata* (four performances); a double-bill of Pergolesi's *La serva padrona* and Cimarosa's *Il maestro di cappella* (two performances); Mas-cagni's *L'amico Fritz* (four performances); Rossini's *La pietra del paragone* (three performances); and Wagner's *Parsifal*, given a sin-gle performance in concert form. The theater's ballet season in

1992 included five productions, each offered one or two times: *Black and White* by the Desrosiers Dance Theatre; *Coppelia* by Aterballetto (the regional company of Emilia Romagna); *Charlot danse avec nous* by the Ballet National de Marseille Roland Petit; *Pyramyde-el Nour* and *Mozart Tangos* by the Ballet Béjart Lausanne; and *Rubies* and *Verdiana* by Les Ballets de Monte-Carlo.

The 1991–92 symphony season opened with the RAI Orchestra of Milan, followed by concerts by the Academy of Ancient Music of Moscow, the La Scala Orchestra of Milan, the Vienna Philharmonic, seven different concerts by the "Arturo Toscanini" Symphony Orchestra of Emilia (a series that included Beethoven's first four symphonies as well as the Ninth and the *Missa solemnis*), the Stuttgart Philharmonic Orchestra, the Württembergisches Kammerorchester Heilbronn, the Danish National Radio Orchestra, and the Helsinki Philharmonic Orchestra. Chamber concerts and recitals included the Frans Bruggen/Gustav Leonhardt/Anner Bijlsma trio, the Swingle Singers, the Kronos Quartet, Trevor Pinnock's The English Concert, the Hungarian Chamber Choir, the Strasbourg Percussion Ensemble in association with the Gregg Smith Singers (a concert of music by Xenakis, Cage, Varèse, and Stravinsky), and Chick Corea and the Elektric Band.

The dramatic theater season presented 12 different plays, each offered two or three times in an interesting and varied *cartellone* that included (all in Italian, of course) Shakespeare's *Twelfth Night*, Molière's *The Imaginary Invalid*, Beth Henley's *Crimes of the Heart*, Alan Ayckbourn's *In the Kitchen*, Ed Graczyk's *Jimmy Dean Jimmy Dean*, Pirandello's *Six Characters in Search of an Author*, Cocteau's *Les enfants terribles*, Goldoni's *Two Venetian Twins*, Fiastri and Vaime's *Group Photo with Cat*, Calderon de la Barca's *Life Is a Dream*, the 1990 prize-winning *Sacco pazzo* by Franceschi, and *The Theater of Song*, a series of songs and monologues by Giorgio Gaber and Sandro Luperini.

The visitor will discover that some of the smaller communities of Italy—particularly those of under 5000 inhabitants—have a busy dramatic theater season even if there appears to be no opera. Such communities usually have concerts and recitals, too, including soloists from the lyric theater. The reason for the lack of opera on their *cartelloni* should be obvious: cost. Though the state furnishes some money for most opera seasons, even if the theater is not a *teatro di tradizione*, less and less money is available as the years progress, and the concept of private financing and private sponsorship is one just gaining acceptance in Italy. Piacenza, for example, a community of 100,000 located 72 kilometers (45 miles) south of Milan, now proudly displays on the cover of its season announcements as well as in its programs the names of its two large donor/supporters: Banca del Monte di Parma and Coop, a grocery store chain.

For the visitor who wishes to enjoy the beauties of these marvelous regional opera houses and experience wonderful operatic performances, I suggest checking in the most recent copy of *L'Opera*, where, at the back of the magazine, the *cartellone* for the month is given for each Italian house, including the *enti autonomi*, festivals, the *teatri di tradizione*, and independent regional and local theaters.

In bocca al lupo as we say in Italian, an expression used backstage just before the curtain rises to start the show. Literally it means "in the mouth of the wolf," but in essence it wishes a person good luck.

Teatro Grande
BRESCIA

Brescia is a picturesque old Roman town of about 230,000 inhabitants located 64 kilometers (40 miles) from Verona on the road from Milan to Venice. Surrounded by gardens, and lying at the foot of the Lombardian Alps not far from Lakes Garda and Iseo, Brescia boasts countless Roman ruins dating from the early Empire. In addition, it holds more recent masterpieces: handsome Renaissance palaces and churches and Teatro Grande. First established in the early 18th century, Teatro Grande is in the very heart of town on Corso Zanardelli. Imposing and impressive, it is certainly an edifice that visually lives up to its name "Grand."

Situated at the center of a convex curve of buildings on the north side of Corso Zanardelli—now a cobblestone pedestrian street—the theater's pillared facade is made up of alternating bands of golden brown and white marble. Its grand staircase, three banks of wide marble steps, leads through an atrium decorated with murals of Tragedy and Comedy to the 18th-century Sala delle Statue (Hall of Statues). Supported by Ionic columns capped by a balustrade ornamented with stucco-work of a classical pattern, 16 larger-than-life-sized statues of legendary Greek figures look down from on high. A huge brass chandelier, converted from gas to elec-

The facade of Brescia's Teatro Grande as seen in a print dated 1828 by Luigi Donagani. Courtesy Teatro Grande di Brescia.

tricity, brilliantly illuminates this entrance hall that leads on the left to the main *sala* or auditorium and straight ahead to the *ridotta*, just possibly the most fascinating and resplendent foyer of any opera house in the world.

Built between 1761 and 1769 in rococo style, with hints of both the orient and the occident in its design, this foyer—some 9 by 18 meters (31 by 59 feet) in dimension—is four floors in height, capped by a magnificently frescoed ceiling depicting three scenes of classical Greece: "The Triumph of Apollo"; "Minerva Leading Agriculture"; and "Mercury and Art." Square, inlaid columns of red Verona marble support two galleries and a balcony, each opening directly off the *sala* at the appropriate level to accommodate patrons who wish to stroll and be seen during intermissions. In addition to mirrors, the walls of the second and third levels are decorated with remarkable *trompe l'oeil* frescos depicting 18th-century theater patrons: a group of stylishly dressed operagoers drinking tea; bewigged cavaliers courting charming young ladies; noblemen reading librettos; and even a lady's maid carrying the family poodle.

The *sala* is breathtaking with its gold-on-white rococo decorations, four tiers of boxes, and a gallery rising from the sides of the

horseshoe-shaped orchestra (stalls/parterre). Four allegorical figures appear in the decoration: Tragedy, Music, Comedy, and
Dance. The ornately frescoed ceiling is divided into eight radiating
segments framed in gold; these, in turn, are overlaid with 12
medallions depicting the Greek gods of mythology, poetry, and
music. A royal box rises above the *sala*'s main doorway, framed in
gold and hung with red velvet tapestries. A *retropalco*, a separate
cloak room with mirrors, is assigned to each box.

The Story of Teatro Grande

The first theater in Brescia was built in 1658 by the Collegiate
Church of San Antonio Viennese and was called, quite appropriately, the Collegio dei Nobili. The first documented performance
occurred in 1677; then followed a series of religious programs as
well as classes in music, singing, and recitation, with the patrons
probably coming from the local convent.

The first public theater was established in 1664 by an impresario named Antonio Barzio in one of the halls of the Accademia
degli Erranti, the space now occupied by Teatro Grande's Hall of
Statues. The first recorded performance of an opera was the musical drama by Giovanni Faustini, *Eritrea*, set to music by Francesco Cavalli, "organist of the Basilica of San Marco in Venice" (as
contemporary program notes inform us).[6]

By 1740 the Accademia degli Erranti decided that the theater
needed a main hall or *sala*; it took six years to complete. Forty
years later the Accademia wanted it redecorated in a contemporary
style, and so it was redone with neoclassical ornamentation. During this period the theater was administered by the Accademia
degli Erranti under the proprietary interest of the regent; the boxes
were owned by the wealthy and noble families of Brescia, with the
season of music, opera, and plays arranged by an impresario.

Between 1776 and 1778 the present *ridotto* was created out of
the old academy hall. Politics then intervened as Brescia became
part of the Subalpine Republic under the French from 1797 to
1799. As the French left, the Austrians entered. When, in turn, the
French reoccupied the city, the theater—which the French had
used for balls and banquets—underwent its most profound
change: the construction between 1805 and 1810 of the theater as
we know it today. It reopened in 1811 with the *prima* of Giovanni
Simone Mayr's *Il sacrifizio d'Ifigenia*. Though the present lavish

271

stucco decorations were added in 1860, this in no way interfered with the superb acoustics of this essentially wooden hall.

Through the years the visual beauty of the house has never waned, but the opera seasons have failed to reach international importance. Teatro Grande's golden moment in opera history occurred in 1904, when, a few months after the *prima* of Puccini's *Madama Butterfly* suffered its notorious fiasco in Milan, the newly revised score—in three acts instead of two—was highly acclaimed by the Brescian public. (Arrigo Boito was a member of that audience.)

The Season at Teatro Grande

Brescia's opera season begins in mid-October and lasts until early December, with the *cartellone* generally made up of three or four titles, each opera offered three times. The season of 1989, for example, opened with Puccini's *Tosca* in a production borrowed from Genoa with sets, costumes, and direction by Attilio Colonnello and with Elena Mauti Nunziata as Floria Tosca, Mario Malagnini as Mario Cavaradossi, and Giorgio Zancanaro as Baron Scarpia; Gianfranco Masini conducted. The second production was offered in association with As.li.co., the opera-apprentice program in Milan, with sets and costumes from Teatro Massimo in Palermo: Niccolò Piccinni's *La Cecchina, ossia La buona figliuola*. Verdi's *Simon Boccanegra* followed, in a production first mounted in Florence, with Antonio Salvadori in the title role, Maria Chiara as Maria Boccanegra, and Ezio Di Cesare as Gabriele Adorno; Angelo Campori conducted. The season closed with a double bill: the world premiere of *La finta luna*, by the contemporary Brescian 12-tone composer Giancarlo Facchinetti, and Domenico Cimarosa's hilarious and tuneful *Il maestro di cappella* with Alfredo Mariotti as the maestro; Marcello Rota conducted.

Tickets at Teatro Grande are expensive. The box office is on Corso Zanardelli, to the immediate right of the grand staircase (at street level). Correspondence should be directed to Teatro Grande, Via Paganora 19/a (the stage entrance), I-25100 Brescia. The telephone number is 030/424-00.

Teatro Comunale "Amilcare Ponchielli"
CREMONA

When the Cremonese decided in 1870 to rename their opera house after one of their own Cremona-born composers, they bypassed the name of Claudio Monteverdi, that great genius of the baroque era who effectively founded opera as we know it today, in favor of Amilcare Ponchielli, who today is remembered only for his seldom-performed opera, *La Gioconda*.

Be that as it may, Teatro Comunale "A. Ponchielli" is a center of cultural life in Cremona, a city known more for its violin makers—Amati, Stradivari, and Guarneri—than for its opera. Located at Corso Vittorio Emanuele 52, the theater is but a short walk from Cremona's famous city hall and well-known cathedral. The theater's neoclassical portico, supported by four Ionic columns, extends a bit into the *corso* since it was originally used as a porte cochere. Engraved on its entablature is "*Sociorum Concordia: Erexit a MDCCCVII*," the name of the society that founded the theater and the date of its construction.

The *sala* is in the traditional horseshoe shape, with three tiers of boxes surmounted by a balcony and a gallery. The theater seats 350 in the boxes, 400 on the main floor, 110 in the balcony, and 140 in the gallery, for a total of precisely 1000 spectators. Trimmed with gold stucco on ivory-painted wood, the boxes are draped in wine-red velvet to match the upholstery of the chairs on the main floor.

The Story of Cremona's Opera House

It was in the year 1747, shortly after young Wolfgang Amadeus Mozart visited Cremona, that Marchese Giovanni Battista Nazardi—quite likely inspired by that visit—first envisioned a "grand theater" for Cremona. A cultured nobleman with an ardent passion for music, Nazardi wanted a lyric theater for the city similar to those he had visited in Milan, Mantua, and Brescia. He proposed a "public theater" to be financed and supported as a *condominiale* (condominium), a "casino di conversazione," where for the price of admission, people could enjoy the opera on stage, visit with their friends, and play *tarocchi* or *scacchi* or other games of chance. Nazardi's friend the Marchese Giuseppe Lodi Mora owned an ancient palace near the Po Gate to the city, a building

The portico marks Cremona's Teatro Ponchielli in this 19th-century print. Though the buildings that flank it look the same today, the street itself is now a busy thoroughfare. Courtesy Teatro Ponchielli di Cremona.

that had been rebuilt several times during various wars when it was needed as a garrison. It was decided to demolish the old palazzo to make room for the opera house. Built essentially of wood, this new edifice had three tiers of boxes and, according to contemporary authorities, excellent acoustics. It opened at the beginning of Carnival, 26 December 1747, and was christened Teatro Nazardi.

Then came Napoleon and the fire of 1806. A new society was then formed to sponsor the rebuilding of the theater, and its name was changed to Teatro Concordia. It reopened on 26 October 1808 with a performance of Ferdinando Paër's "dramma giocosa," *Il principe di Taranto*, which, in turn, was followed by another "dramma giocosa," Gaetano Marinelli's *Il trionfo d'amore*, composed especially for the occasion. This second structure had not been entirely finished when it was pressed into use; there were, for example, no panes of glass in the window frames, and the icy-cold December air swept through the theater and across the main floor into the boxes. Nevertheless, the seasons progressed with such works as Paisiello's *I zingari in fiera*, Cimarosa's *Gli amanti comici*,

274

Pavesi's *Elisabetta regina d'Inghilterra*, and Simone Mayr's *Ginevra di Scozia*.

In addition to opera, Teatro Concordia hosted such important musical events as Niccolò Paganini's concert of 1811 until fire swept through the theater once again in 1824, during a run of Rossini's *L'italiana in Algeri*. Reconstruction work began immediately under the supervision of an architect named Luigi Voghera, and by the next Carnival season, the house—basically as we see it today—was reopened with a performance of Rossini's *La donna del lago*.

The years that followed saw the changing tastes of the times, for at first the *cartelloni* offered works by Rossini, Ricci, Valier, and Bellini. Then followed operas by Meyerbeer, Mercadante, Verdi (the early *Nabucco*), and Donizetti (*Lucia*). In 1856 Teatro Concordia presented the world premiere of Amilcare Ponchielli's first opera, *I promessi sposi*, an operatic setting of one of Italy's greatest literary masterpieces, Manzoni's *The Betrothed* (to use the usual English translation). Because of the success of this opera in Cremona, Ponchielli was engaged as the permanent conductor and director of Teatro Concordia. In 1870, upon his death, the theater was renamed in his honor.

The decline of the house and its seasons of opera began after the reunification of Italy, although bit by bit the theater was modernized with the substitution of electric for gas lighting, the introduction of a central heating system, and so on. As motion pictures became popular, Teatro "A. Ponchielli" served as a cinema.

Following World War II, when the theater was used for wartime benefits, an effort was made by two societies—the Società Concerti and the Amici dell'arte Famiglia artistica—to reinstate seasons of opera. After a general refurbishing and redecoration of the house in 1958, Verdi's *Un ballo in maschera* heralded the return of lyric music. Then in 1986, after 240 years as a condominium, the theater was purchased from the boxholders by the Community of Cremona for just under $2 million. Thus today the house is owned by the city that administers it as a *teatro di tradizione*. It is no longer used as a movie house, but hosts such important non-operatic events as the performance of Vivaldi's *The Four Seasons* programmed for the 250th anniversary of Antonio Stradivari's death, featuring Salvatore Accardo using a different one of his own Stradivari for each of the four concertos. The solo artist was accompanied by an orchestra made up exclusively of Stradivari violins, violas, and violoncellos.

Ordinarily the theater opens in September with the Festival of Cremona; the traditional opera season follows from October to November. From November to May there is a series of plays, and from December to May a program of ballet. From December to April the annual symphony season occurs, and in April, Cremona Jazz. Cinzia Maneredini of the theater's press office estimates that there are about 110 musical programs a year in the theater.

The Season at Teatro Comunale "A. Ponchielli"

The opera season in Cremona boasts a *cartellone* that usually includes three or four titles, each opera presented about three times. The 1989 season, for example, opened with Niccolò Piccinni's *La Cecchina, ossia La buona figliuola* in a production mounted by As.li.co.; sets and costumes were from Teatro Massimo in Palermo. *Tosca* followed in a production from Brescia that featured Elena Mauti Nunziata (Tosca), Mario Malagnini (Cavaradossi), and Giorgio Zancanaro (Scarpia), with Gianfranco Masini conducting. The season closed with Cremona's own production of Verdi's *Simon Boccanegra* directed by Virginio Puecher, with Angelo Campori conducting a cast headed by Antonio Salvadori (Boccanegra), Maria Chiara (Maria), and Ezio Di Cesare (Gabriele Adorno).

Ticket prices at Teatro Comunale "A. Ponchielli" are moderate. Reservations are accepted by telephone (0372/407.273) during box office hours: weekdays, except Mondays, from 4:00 to 7:00 P.M. The box office is located to the left of the front entrance of the theater at Corso Vittorio Emanuele 52, I-26200 Cremona.

Teatro "G. B. Pergolesi"
JESI

The colorful and dramatic scene painted on the curtain of the opera house in Jesi is a vivid portrayal, "The arrival of Frederick II at Jesi." Painted in 1850 by Luigi Mancini, a local artist, the scene recalls the return of the German emperor Frederick II of Hohenstaufen, who was born in Jesi in 1194. Quite in contrast, the inscription carved in marble over the main entrance to this theater honors the other world-famous person who had his origins in Jesi, composer Giovanni Battista Pergolesi, who was born there in 1710.

276

Jesi itself is a quiet, bucolic town today, visually reflecting the atmosphere of the medieval city it once was with its 14th-century battlements and fortified walls surrounding the town. Located in the Marches off the Adriatic coast some 30 kilometers (19 miles) inland and southwest of Ancona, Jesi—with a population of 42,000—maintains one of the most celebrated opera houses in the area.

The facade, which faces Piazza della Repubblica, reflects the theater's sober neoclassic design, a three-story palazzo whose ground-floor exterior of marble is marked by a series of nine arched portals surmounted by two levels faced in Roman brick and patterned with neoclassic windows outlined in white marble.

The *ridotto* (foyer) is in a tasteful neoclassic vein and consists of fluted Corinthian columns surmounted by gold capitals. The walls are of blue-and-beige-veined marble, offset with large, gold-framed paintings of pastoral scenes. The intimate *sala*, which seats only 700, is a marvel of gold stucco on wood of an eggshell hue, with three tiers of boxes and a gallery rising above the plush velvet seats of the horseshoe-shaped main floor. The coffered ceiling is highly ornamented with abstract designs of neoclassic origin and scenes from Greek mythology, all of which lend the hall an air of quiet elegance and dignity.

The Story of Teatro "G. B. Pergolesi"

As Giovanni Annibaldi carefully pointed out in his history of Teatro Pergolesi published in 1882,[7] the records of that theater were poorly kept, with far more pages missing than preserved, making an accurate and detailed history impossible to reconstruct. It is known that as early as 1562 musical programs as well as dramatic works with incidental music were presented at the Palazzo Comunale (town hall) and in the oratorio of the Congregazione dell'Oratorio di San Filippo Neri. The first actual theater in Jesi, established in 1731 as a *condominiale*, was Teatro del Leone (Theater of the Lion). Two times a year (for the opening of Carnival and for the September fair) operas were mounted, mostly "dramme giocosi" by composers of the Neapolitan school; both comic and tragic plays were also offered at the theater.

The first recorded performances were for the fair of 1732, two melodramas entitled *Amor e fortuna* and *Nel perdono la vendetta*. Neither the names of the librettists nor those of the composers have survived. The record then skips to Carnival 1734, when *Alessandro nell'Indie*, with music by Gaetano Maria Schiassi, was performed.

The present building, originally called Teatro della Concordia, is first mentioned in a document dated May 1798, which speaks of a house to open in a more central location than that of the Leone. The original plans for the new house, the work of Francesco Maria Ciaffoni, were greatly modified by the chamber architect Cosimo Morelli. The early *cartelloni* were made up of "dramme giocosi" by Piccinni, Anfossi, Guglielmi, and Cimarosa. The records of May 1798, for example, list Cimarosa's *Il principe spazzacamino* and *La capricciosa corretta* as part of the inaugural season, though it must be admitted that no trace of these two Cimarosa scores has ever been found. It is interesting to note that the casts included Anna Guidarini, a soprano from Pesaro who was to become the mother of Gioachino Rossini.

The following season included such titles as *Il vecchio geloso* by Felice Alessandri, *La moglie capricciosa* by Giuseppe Gazzaniga, *Le due gemelle* by Pietro Alessandro Guglielmi, *La scuola de' gelosi* by Antonio Salieri, and *L'amor costante* and *Il ritorno di Don Calandrino* by Domenico Cimarosa.

Several evenings of historical interest have taken place at Teatro "G. B. Pergolesi." On the evening of 21 May 1799, a celebration in honor of Napoleon Bonaparte was given, including a cantata for two voices with choral and orchestral accompaniment composed for the occasion by Nicola Zingarelli, the celebrated maestro di cappella of the basilica of Loreto. For the visit of His Holiness Pope Pius IX in 1848, the theater offered a cantata by Clitofonte Dini. "That evening when the curtain rose," the local paper reported, "there was deafening applause. . . . There on stage —at its center—was a bust of Pius IX adorned with banners of all the Italian states, that of Lombardy, which is now under Austrian rule, veiled in black. And above all this, the [Italian] tricolor."[8]

To honor Gaspare Spontini, who was born in a tiny suburb of Jesi in 1774, the theater mounted on 3 October 1875 a special production of his *La vestale* to belatedly mark the centennial. At the same time, memorial plaques were unveiled at the town hall and in the atrium of the theater.

Finally, in 1880, after years of effort, the name of Teatro della Concordia was changed to Teatro "G. B. Pergolesi" to honor the 170th anniversary of his birth. A special performance of that composer's *Stabat Mater* was conducted by Nicola Mancini to mark the occasion. (The official proclamation of this name-change was not documented until 30 September 1883 because it had to be signed by all members of the *condominiale*, administrators of the condominium, and related associations of Jesi.)

In the summer of 1892, Teatro del Leone was destroyed by fire, leaving Teatro "G. B. Pergolesi" the site for not only opera and musical events but the setting for plays and other dramatic productions.

Closed in 1925 because its roof and ceiling needed repairs, the theater reopened in September 1927 with a performance of Verdi's *Aida*, in an opera season sponsored by the Società Teatrale. *Aida* was followed Umberto Giordano's *Fedora*, Pietro Mascagni's *L'amico Fritz*, and the ballet scene from Gounod's *Faust*.

The theater was used for a time as a cinema, a crisis that was somewhat alleviated when the town government intervened and sponsored the Compagnia dell'Opera Lirica Italiana, offering a 1931 season consisting of Mascagni's *Cavalleria rusticana* paired with Leoncavallo's *I pagliacci* and both Verdi's *Rigoletto* and *La traviata*. Closed during World War II, the "Pergolesi" reopened in 1947 with Puccini's *Tosca* and Giordano's *Andrea Chénier*. In 1960 the theater was completely restored and refurbished to celebrate the 250th anniversary of Giovanni Battista Pergolesi's birth, the opening event on 1 September marked by a performance by the Camerata Accademia of the Mozarteum in Salzburg of music by Pergolesi, Bach, Handel, and Mozart. This was followed by performances of Vivaldi's *La Sena festeggiante* and Purcell's *Dido and Aeneas* in a production from Aix-en-Provence.

In September 1953, a 19-year-old Renata Scotto made her operatic debut as Cio-Cio-San in Puccini's *Madama Butterfly* at the theater. She was received there with warm and energetic applause in the role that was to become her hallmark and later wrote in her autobiography about the charm of this theater and the enthusiasm of its audiences.

Finally, on 3 May 1968, the theater achieved what had been its goal for many years: it became a *teatro di tradizione*, a theater recognized by the state as one of the important regional houses of Italy. It celebrated the occasion with a performance of Verdi's *Otello* featuring Mario Del Monaco as Otello and Antonietta Cannarile as Desdemona. Giuseppe Morelli conducted, while Del Monaco's son, Gian Carlo Del Monaco, directed. By 1976 Mozart had made it to Jesi for the first time when his *Così fan tutte* was given a stellar production.

The Season at Teatro "G. B. Pergolesi"

The opera season in Jesi takes place in October and November of each year, with its *cartellone* usually consisting of three operas and a ballet, three performances of each. A recent season, for example, opened with *Aida* in a production by Beppe De Tomasi, conducted by Filippo Zigante with a cast headed by Antonella Banaudi, Mario Malagnini, Elisabetta Fiorillo, and Giorgio Zancanaro. Adolphe Adam's ballet *Giselle* followed, succeeded in turn by Mozart's *Le nozze di Figaro*, directed by Giampaolo Zennaro and conducted by Roberto Paternostro. The season closed with Rossini's *Il barbiere di Siviglia*, with a cast including Bruno De Simone, Adelina Scarabelli, Maurizio Comencini, and Silvano Pagliuca. Klaus Arp conducted; Gianni Gualdoni directed.

Ticket prices at Teatro Pergolesi are quite reasonable. Information may be obtained about the *cartellone* from the box office, where reservations may also be placed. The box office is located at the front of the theater, Piazza della Repubblica 9, I-60035 Jesi (AN). The box office telephone number is 0731/538.355.

Teatro del Giglio
LUCCA

To visit Lucca for the opening of the opera season is to experience one of the most exciting and thrilling events Italy has to offer. The unique festivities begin on the eve of the Festa della Santa Croce (13 September), with the start of the opera season on the following Friday evening. The Festa itself is a reenactment of an incident that took place in Lucca a thousand years ago. A crucifix with the features of Jesus Christ reputedly carved by Nicodemus had been brought back to Italy from the Holy Land by Bishop Gualfredo on a ship without sails or a crew. After landing near La Spezia, the bishop had the crucifix, the Volto Santo (Holy Visage), transported by ox cart to the church of San Frediano in Lucca. According to the faithful, a miracle then occurred: the statue removed itself to a nearby field where subsequently the *Lucchese* built their cathedral of San Martino.

To celebrate the Festa, all the old palaces, churches, and buildings in the center of town, including Teatro del Giglio, are outlined in the evening by thousands of flickering votive candles attached to the buildings so that they outline doorways, arches, and windows and even define the corners of buildings and the shapes of the roofs and eaves. Known as the Luminaria di Santa Croce, these eyes of flickering light give the city a fairy-tale-like atmosphere.

There is a processional on the same evening as the Luminaria that commemorates the movement of the statue from the church to the site of the cathedral. Bishops, clerics, and nuns; police and firefighters; Swiss Guards in striped tights complete with helmets and spears; and teenagers in jeans, jackets, and American sweat-shirts—all bearing candles, banners, and emblems of the Roman Catholic Church—move from the church of San Frediano to the cathedral of San Martino. As one American reporter chronicled it,

> In this symbolic transport of relics from one church to the other, marchers are both festive and solemn, proudly unreg-ulated yet showing communal pride. They also help explain in their own way the joys and sorrows of opera *all'italiana*, when disorganization seems to frustrate and fertilize.[9]

The Story of Teatro del Giglio

Theatrical activity in Lucca began as early as 1600, with pro-ductions that—as elsewhere—were presented in the great salons of the palaces belonging to important princes and dukes. Two prin-cipal theatrical centers emerged in Lucca: the Palazzo de' Borghi and the Palazzo Pretorio, the latter (now known as the Palazzo del Podestà or Hall of the Governor) a Renaissance building begun in 1494. Its handsome open *loggia* may still be seen today on Piazza San Michele.

On 19 August 1672, the Board of the Republic of Lucca com-missioned a committee to explore the possibility of building a pub-lic theater. They decided on a site, one occupied by the Jesuit con-vent and church of San Girolamo, an order that had recently been suppressed by Pope Clement IX. Teatro Pubblico (as it was first named) opened there on 14 January 1675 with a solemn ceremony followed by the performance of two operas: *Attila*, by Pietro An-drea Ziani, and *La prosperità di Elio Seiano*, by Antonio Sartorio. The new theater offered opera twice a year, at Carnival and in au-tumn, coinciding with the Festa della Santa Croce.

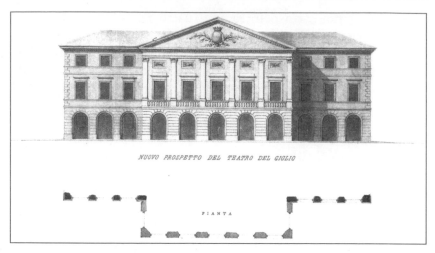

NUOVO PROSPETTO DEL TEATRO DEL GIGLIO

PIANTA

Cesare Lazzarini's sketch for the facade of Lucca's Teatro del Giglio.
(*Pianta* indicates plants.) Courtesy Teatro del Giglio di Lucca.

Fire destroyed Teatro Pubblico 13 years after it opened, and again in 1692. Two brothers, architects Cesare and Giovanni Lazzarini, were engaged to redesign the theater, a building that when completed looked essentially as it does today. Known briefly after the French arrived in Lucca as Teatro Nazionale, it was decided that Maria Luisa di Borbone, the sovereign of Lucca by proclamation of the Congress of Vienna, should choose a new name for the house when it reopened in 1819. The *sovrintendente* proposed three possibilities: Teatro San Luigi, the saint of Duchess Maria Luisa's name day; Teatro del Giglio, referring to the flower on the coat of arms of the House of Borbone; and Teatro Alfieri in honor of the Italian playwright. The duchess selected "del Giglio," and Teatro del Giglio it has remained.

Teatro del Giglio is a free-standing building on the southeast side of Piazza del Giglio in the heart of town, diagonally opposite the ducal palace across Via Vittorio Veneto. Of simple, classic design, the facade is in three sections, with the central section thrusting slightly into the piazza, as it originally served as a porte cochere made up of five round arches. The symmetrical side sections, each with a portal and two windows on the ground level, are faced with large slabs of gray stone. The upper two stories are of plaster painted in the traditional ocher, with the windows trimmed in white.

The *sala*, decorated in a light beige with floral trim painted in delicate pastel shades of sage green and rose, consists of three tiers of boxes in the traditional horseshoe design, with a gallery added above them in 1958 to provide additional seating. Both the sightlines and the acoustics are excellent in the boxes. The royal box—used in turn by princes, dukes, governors, and members of the royal family—is spacious and seats 16. Each tier also contains two special boxes (numbers 1 and 20) that are part of the elaborate proscenium arch and overlook the stage (these are known as *barcaccia* in Italian). The intimate main floor, the *platea* (known in the 16th century as the *piazza* when it contained only movable benches for the commoners) contains but 15 rows. Today the house altogether seats 750 patrons.

It was here at Teatro del Giglio that Rossini's *Guglielmo Tell* had its Italian *prima*, and both Verdi and Donizetti presided over their own operas. And, of course, it was here that Puccini had his beginnings.

The Season at Teatro del Giglio

The opera season in Lucca starts at the same time each year: the Friday following the Festa di Santa Croce (13 September). The *cartellone* usually includes three titles, with each opera presented three times. A recent season, for example, opened with Mozart's *Don Giovanni* in a production by Claudio Desderi, based on his work at the Scuola di Musica di Fiesole (a production that traveled, along with the other Da Ponte operas of Mozart, rather widely throughout central Italy). Then followed a double-bill: Donizetti's *Il campanello* coupled with Puccini's *Gianni Schicchi*. The Donizetti featured Angelo Nosotti, Fernanda Costa, Alessandra Zapparoli, and Stefano Antonucci in a production directed by Filippo Crivelli and conducted by Angelo Cavallaro. *Gianni Schicchi* was cast with Rolando Panerai in the title role. The season closed with Rossini's *Aureliano in Palmira* in a production directed by Beppe De Tommasi and conducted by Giacomo Zani.

Zani, who was artistic director of Teatro del Giglio for many years, explained the manner in which he chose the repertory.

We have a small budget with which we must mount three productions and offer, altogether, nine evenings of theater. Thus, in order to assure financial stability, we always schedule at least one or two of the "popular" operas [*La Bohème* and *Il barbiere di Siviglia* in 1989, for example], and then to serve our art and to maintain interest throughout Tuscany and all of Italy in our theater, we try to stage a little-known or infrequently performed work of importance [e.g., Alfredo Catalani's *Edmea* in 1989].[10]

Ticket prices at Teatro del Giglio in Lucca are moderate. The box office, at the front right of the theater on Piazza del Giglio, is open during the opera season from 10:00 A.M. to noon and from 4:30 to 6:30 P.M. daily, except Sundays. For information (in Italian) by telephone, the number is 0583/461.47 or 492.089. The mailing address of the theater is Piazza del Giglio, I-55100 Lucca.

Teatro Rossini
LUGO

Teatro Rossini in Lugo (population 19,000) is one of the oldest opera houses in the Romagna region of Italy (built in 1761), one of the smallest of the Italian theaters regularly sponsoring an opera season (448 seats), and one of the most charming and intimate lyric houses to be found anywhere in the world of opera. It is also a theater closely associated with its namesake, for the composer's father, Giuseppe Rossini, came from Lugo and undoubtedly played horn and trumpet in this very house before moving to Pesaro. It is also quite likely that Giuseppe first met his future wife—the composer-to-be's mother—when she, Anna Guidarini, a *seconda soprano*, sang at the opera house in Lugo. As for the composer himself (who was born in Pesaro), he was 10 or 11 when his father moved the family from Pesaro back to Lugo, where the boy lived for four years before moving on to the conservatory in Bologna for musical studies.

Teatro Comunale in Lugo, as this theater was first known, was an early champion of Rossini's music, offering productions of most of his early operas soon after they had had their *primas* (*prima* dates are in parentheses):

1814, *Tancredi* (1813)
1815, *L'italiana in Algeri* (1813)
1818, *La gazza ladra* (1817)
1820, *La cenerentola* (1817)

1821, *Il barbiere di Siviglia* (1816) and *Il turco in Italia* (1814)
1822, *La donna del lago* (1819) and *Adelaide di Borgogna* (1817)
1823, *Eduardo e Cristina* (1819)
1825, *Semiramide* (1823)
1828, *Otello* (1816)
1831, *Matilde di Shabran* (1821)
1838, *Mosè* (1827)

One wonders how some of the larger operas were mounted on such a small stage as that in Lugo. The seasons today lean heavily to bel canto and contemporary chamber operas. Antonio Taglioni, the artistic director, astutely notes,

> The challenge of organizing a program for a theater such as the Rossini is the opportunity it provides for the theater to become a "chamber music theater" for the Emilia Romagna region. For this purpose, I think ideal works are to be found among: a) *opera buffa* and *opera giocosa* of the 1700 and 1800s (works by Pergolesi, Cimarosa, Paisiello, and Mozart on to Rossini and Donizetti); b) *opera seria* of the 1600 and 1700s (works from Monteverdi to Gluck, including Haydn and Mozart, to cite only the greatest). The type of musical theater works that Teatro Rossini does best—because of the size of its stage, its pit, its house—calls for small companies (five to six singers), either without chorus or with a chorus of only 10 to 15 singers and an orchestra of not over 45 players.[11]

Recent seasons have offered unusual fare that meets these criteria: 1987, Leonardo Vinci's *Catone in Utica* (the first performance of the work in contemporary times, and the opera that opened the house in 1761) and Baldassare Galuppi's *Il mondo della luna*; 1988, Gaetano Donizetti's *Le convenienze ed inconvenienze teatrali*, his *I pazzi per progetto*, and Ferdinando Paër's *Achille*; 1989, Antonio Salieri's *La locandiera* and Gaetano Donizetti's *Betly, ossia La capanna svizzera*; 1990, Raffaello de Banfield's *Una lettera d'amore di Lord Byron* (written in 1955) and Felice Lattuada's *Le preziòse ridicole* (written in 1929); and 1991, Niccolò Jommelli's *Didone abbandonata*.

The Story of Teatro Rossini

The earliest record of an opera performance in Lugo is dated 1641, when Giovanni Battista Guarini's *Il pastor fido* was presented at Teatro Pavaglione, the Roman amphitheater that is still in use today for summer performances of grand opera (it seats 4800). By 1758 it was decided that Lugo needed an enclosed theater, and in August 1759 the new theater—its structure not yet quite complete—opened to the public with a cello recital followed in turn by gala balls and performances of intermezzi. With a desire to finish the theater, the committee turned to Antonio Galli (known as Il Bibiena), *the* theater authority, to complete the work. Finished by 1761, the building's inauguration was celebrated with Metastasio's *Catone in Utica* with music by Leonardo Vinci.

Teatro Comunale di Lugo (as it was first known) is a free-standing building with a most unpretentious exterior; it is a gable-roofed, rectangular three-story building whose plain, plastered facade is broken up by four simulated pillars. The *sala* was originally bell-shaped and made up of four tiers of boxes with 17 boxes on each full tier (the first tier has but 16 boxes because of the entrance portal for the main floor). The fourth tier of boxes was constructed so that it could be used as a balcony; a *loggione*—a gallery for standees—is located a level higher and can accommodate 80 people. The *sala* is 12 meters (40 feet) long by 10 meters (33 feet) wide.

As with most Italian houses, changes, remodeling, and repairs took place from time to time over the years. In 1812 the mechanical elements on the stage were improved and modernized, and in 1819 the curve of the boxes was changed from bell-shaped to the traditional horseshoe curve we see in the theater today. In 1840 the first oil lamp for the *sala* was hung, a magnificent brass fixture manufactured in Vienna and refitted for gas in 1860 and for electricity in 1895. Today it shines as resplendent as ever.

On 21 February 1859, the community council of Lugo changed the name of the theater to Teatro Rossini "to honor and acclaim that celebrated fellow-citizen."[12] In 1863, elegant velvet-cushioned chairs were installed for the first time on the main floor, and in 1914 new dressing rooms were built.

The *cartelloni* over the years have included works by Cimarosa, Mayr, Mercadante, Meyerbeer, Pacini, and Donizetti. Verdi was heard for the first time at Teatro Rossini in 1845, when both his *I*

Lugo - Teatro Comunale

The exterior of Lugo's Teatro Rossini as seen in a postcard dating
from about 1910, when it was known simply as Teatro Comunale.
Courtesy Teatro Rossini di Lugo.

due Foscari (1844) and *I lombardi* (1843) were part of the season.
Puccini was ushered into the house during the season of 1896
when his *Manon Lescaut* (1893) was conducted by Vittorio Man-
gardi, one of La Scala's principal conductors. *La Bohème* (1896)
followed during the season of 1899.

Following World War II, Teatro Rossini was turned into a movie
theater (a not-uncommon fate at that time in Italy for opera
houses). As such, it fell into a state of disrepair until it almost became unusable even as a cinema. Thanks to the Lions and Rotary
Clubs of Lugo, it was decided in the early 1970s to completely restore the theater. After more than a decade and a half of work—re-
inforcing the building itself; adding the newly required steel fire escapes; restoring the wooden boxes and stuccoed frescos to their
original beauty; and a sizeable effort in modernizing the stage with
not only updated mechanisms for the fly galleries that control the
raising and lowering of set pieces, but with all new electrical wiring
and lighting equipment—Teatro Rossini di Lugo joyfully reopened
on 27 August 1986.

287

The Season at Teatro Rossini

The opera season in Lugo begins in January of each year, with a *cartellone* of from one to three titles, depending on budgeting restrictions. Each production is offered three times. There is a summer/fall season sponsored at the Arena del Pavalgione, a season that usually includes the grand operas (*Manon Lescaut* and *La traviata* in 1987; *Carmen* and *Tosca* in 1988; and *Aida* in 1989) in productions that come mostly from the Arena Sferisterio in Macerata.

Tickets for Teatro Rossini are moderately priced. Information on the season and ticket reservations may be obtained at the Ufficio Teatro, Piazza Trisi 1, I-48022 Lugo (RA) or by telephoning 0545/330.37 or 243.61; fax 0545/328.59. The street address of Teatro Rossini is Piazza Cavour, I-48022 Lugo (RA).

Teatro Sociale and Teatro Bibiena
MANTUA

Mantua is a wonderful city for the opera fan to visit, for in addition to two very different but very special opera houses, there are the landmarks associated with *Rigoletto* as well as the ducal palace where Monteverdi produced his first opera.

Although all the guidebooks and taxi drivers in Mantua can direct you to Rigoletto's house (Piazza Sordello 23), and bus drivers en route to Verona always point out the causeway down which Sparafucile had his hideout, all references to *Rigoletto* in Mantua are postcard fantasies, for Piave's libretto (based on Victor Hugo's *Le roi s'amuse*) originally concerned the French court, with Rigoletto the court jester of King Francis. The Austrian censors, afraid after the unrest of 1848 of any slight against the monarch's character, forced Verdi and Piave to change the locale from France to Mantua, even though the libretto and most of the music had already been written!

The plaque on the wall at the Hall of Mirrors in the ducal palace, however, is fact, not fiction. This plaque—painted directly on the wall—reads:

Ogni Venere Di Sera Si Fa Musica Nella Sala Degli Specchi/ Cl. Monteverdi al Card. Ferdin. Gonzaga Da Montova/Il 22 Giugno 1611

Every Friday evening there is music in the Hall of Mirrors
Gallery/
Claudio Monteverdi to Cardinal Ferdinand Gonzaga of Man-
tua/22 June 1611

Monteverdi not only performed as one of the seven string players at the court in Mantua, he composed for all occasions. In 1607,
in the grandiose and inspiring Hall of Mirrors, his first opera—
what one could call the first opera of the genre we know—*Orfeo*,
was performed for the duke and his court. Apparently the new
form so fascinated and impressed the guests that Monteverdi was
encouraged to write two more works—*Arianna* and *Mascherata
dell'ingrate*—for the occasion of the festive wedding celebrations
for Francesco Gonzaga and Margarita of Savoy in 1608. In addition, as Leo Schrade related in his biography of the composer,

A few days after the first performance of *Arianna*, on June 2,
Guarini [the poet] presented his comedy *Idropica*. With various other Mantuan composers, Monteverdi was called upon
to contribute to this production. According to custom, four intermezzi and a *licenza* [a prologue dedicated to a nobleman]
were needed. Gabrielo Chiabrera provided the poetry for all.
The music of the prologue was composed by Monteverdi.[13]

The performance took place in the Teatro delle Corte of the
ducal palace, a room now used as a warehouse. Don Federico Follino, chronicler of the Mantuan court under Vincenzo, reported,

After the cardinals, princes, and ambassadors were seated,
the traditional trumpet fanfare was sounded from the center
of the stage. After they had played it the third time, the huge
house curtain opened suddenly. One saw clouds on stage that
were so cleverly constructed that they seemed to be real. Underneath, waves could be seen surging back and forth. Then
the head of a woman gradually emerged from them. It was
Manto who had founded the city of Mantua. Slowly she arose
and moved to a small island where she stood in the rushes.
The trumpets having now stopped playing, she sang to the
accompaniment of instruments set up behind the scene with
such sweetness that all her listeners were carried away.[14]

The facade of Mantua's Palazzo Accademia in a 19th-century lithograph. The church of Santa Maria del Popolo on the right was torn down in 1891. Author's collection.

As one 20th-century writer opined, "One sometimes wonders how this new art form 'opera' would have survived its childhood diseases without the healthy treatment given it by Monteverdi."[15]

Of Mantua's two theaters, Teatro Scientifico is the older, designed and built by Antonio Galli Bibiena for the Accademia Virgiliana—founded in 1767 to honor Virgil, who had been born in Mantua—to house its orchestra of 18 players. The theater opened in 1769, and the following year, on 16 January, the young Mozart gave a concert here on his first journey to Italy. Located at Via dell'Accademia 47, this magnificent bell-shaped hall with four tiers of boxes (the lowest incomplete, with only four center boxes, and the upper tier given over to a gallery) seats 400. Today the theater is more frequently used as a concert hall than one for opera, but it is still a feast for the eye and ear, with superb acoustics. Following its restoration, the hall has been known as Teatro Bibiena.

The newer theater is Teatro Sociale, built on Piazza Folengo in 1822 to a design by Luigi Canonica. The fall of Napoleon brought the Austrians back to rule in Mantua until the unification of Italy in 1866, and Teatro Sociale was one of the few creative efforts of this rather lackluster period in the city's history.

A free-standing building on Corso Vittorio Emanuele, Teatro Sociale is of traditional neoclassic design, in essence, a Greek temple with a pillared portico. The interior, in horseshoe shape, is made up of three tiers of boxes, above which rise two balconies, one above the other, with the theater seating 1300 patrons.

*Serie delle Compoſizioni muſicali da eſeguirſi nell' Accademia
pubblica Filarmonica, la ſera del dì 16. del corrente
Gennajo, in occaſione della venuta dell' eſpertiſſimo
giovanetto Sig. Amadeo Motzzart.*

1. Sinfonía di compoſizione d'eſſo Sig. Amadeo.
2. Concerto di Gravecembalo eſibitogli, e da lui eſe-
   guíto all'improvviſo.
3. Aria d'un Profeſſore.
4. Sonata di Cembalo all'improvviſo, eſeguíta dal Gio-
   vine, con variazioni analoghe d'invenzion ſua,
   e replicata poi in tuono diverſo da quello in cui
   è ſcritta.
5. Concerto di Violino d'un Profeſſore.
6. Aria compoſta, e cantata nell' atto ſteſſo dal Sig.
   Amadeo all'improvviſo, co' debiti accompagna-
   menti eſeguíti ſul Cembalo, ſopra parole fatte
   eſpreſſamente; ma da lui non vedute in prima.
7. Altra Sonata di Cembalo compoſta inſieme, ed eſeguíta dal medeſimo ſopra un motivo muſicale,
   propoſtogli improvviſamente dal primo Violino.
8. Aria d'un Profeſſore.
9. Concerto d'Oboè d'un Profeſſore.
10. Fuga muſicale compoſta, ed eſeguita dal Sig. Ama-
    deo ſul Cembalo, e condotta a compiuto termi-
    ne ſecondo le leggi del Contrappunto, ſopra un
    ſemplice tema per la medeſima, preſentatogli all'
    improvviſo.
11. Sinfonía dal medeſimo concertata con tutte le parti
    ſul Cembalo ſopra una ſola parte di Violino, po-
    ſtagli dinanzi improvviſamente.
12. Duetto di Profeſſori.
13. Trio, in cui il Sig. Amadeo ne ſonerà col Violino
    una parte all'improvviſo.
14. Sinfonía ultima di compoſizione del ſuddetto.

The printed program for Wolfgang Amadeus Mozart's concert of 16
January 1770 at the Palazzo Accademia. The *espertissimo giovanetto*
was just days shy of his 14th birthday. Author's collection.

The Season at Teatro Sociale

The opera season in Mantua takes place in October and November each year, with the *cartellone* generally offering four titles with two or three performances of each. A recent season, for example, opened with *Les Contes d'Hoffmann*, a production from the Galas Lyriques of Paris. Then came the eternal pair, the Mascagni/Leoncavallo *Cavalleria rusticana* and *I pagliacci* directed by Giampaolo Zennaro and conducted by Sandro Sanna. *Carmen* followed in a production featuring Anna Di Mauro as Carmen and Gianfranco Cecchele as Don José; Patricia Panton directed; Sandro Sanna conducted. The season closed with Umberto Giordano's *Andrea Chénier* with Aldo Filistad in the title role.

Ticket prices at Teatro Sociale are quite reasonable. Teatro Sociale is located at Piazza Folengo 4, and the offices—for information and reservations—may be found at Corso Umberto I 2/b, I-46100 Mantua. The telephone number is 0376/362.739.

The Season at Teatro Bibiena

Teatro Bibiena is under the governance of the Ente Manifestazioni Mantovane, which establishes the regular concert series as well as the operas given from time to time in this wonderful setting.

In 1973 Claudio Monteverdi's *Orfeo* directed by Claudio Gallico, with stage direction by Filippo Crivelli, was presented. In 1974 Gallico conducted a performance here of Paisiello's *Nina, o sia La pazza per amore*, directed by Ruggero Rimini as part of the Mantua City Festival. In 1980 Mozart's *La finta semplice*, prepared by As.li.co., was conducted by Antonello Allemandi and directed by Gabriella Sciutti, while in the following year, the same team produced Offenbach's *Orphée aux enfers*.

For information on the season and ticket prices, write Ente Manifestazioni Mantovane, Via Escheria 19, I-46100 Mantua; telephone 0376/323.849.

Teatro Regio
PARMA

The *Parmigiani* are justly proud of the opera tradition in their city and have long held the reputation of being among the world's most discriminating audiences when it comes to the lyric theater. In *Il Teatro Regio*, Maurizio Corradi-Cervi writes:

Parma has always shown a singular passion for the theater, starting with the days of Imperial Rome when the first and only theater at that time in Emilia was built in Parma. Discovered in 1843 near the Church of San Uldarico, excavations [of the theater] revealed huge marble columns (purple, antique yellow, African stone, etc.) as well as statues, inscriptions and two theatrical masques that adorned the proscenium.[16]

In 1846 an amphitheater was discovered, one that proved to be, when fully excavated, the largest in Emilia. Then followed "the silence of the medieval night" (to again quote Corradi-Cervi)—the 13th to 15th centuries—when only speeches and sacred pageants were presented.

In the early 16th century the first actual theater company was formed by the Accademia Amorevoli. Then in 1545, when the Farnese, who ruled Parma, decided to present brilliant spectacles of dance and dramatic works in Piazza Grande, the possibility of building an enclosed theater first arose.

At the request of Duke Ranuccio II, architect Gian Battista Aleotti da Argenta was dispatched to Vicenza to observe Palladio's Teatro Olimpico. He was then to return to Parma to build an even grander, more imposing theater of wood. It was to be erected near the Hall of Arms in Palazzo Pilotta, the ducal palace. (It was called Pilotta as games of *pilotta* [fives] were played in its courtyards.) The resulting edifice—Teatro Farnese—was indeed grand in size: it accommodated 4500 spectators. Opening on 21 December 1628 for the wedding festivities of Odoardo Farnese and Margherita de' Medici, the theater commissioned for the occasion a work from Claudio Monteverdi. The resulting *Mercurio e Marte* was a splendidly flashy spectacle in which the bridegroom himself and a troupe of horses joined the giant cast; it concluded with a mock sea fight. As one account related,

Mercury and Mars fought with sea monsters over the fate of heroes and lovers. Neptune's tide, flooding the arena to the depth of two feet [60 cm], was finally allayed by Jupiter, who descended from above in a machine with a retinue of a hundred. [A] Florentine eyewitness, reporting back to the secretary of the Grand Duke, felt mostly fear that the theater would collapse, because in addition to the machines, the performers, and an audience of 4000, . . . "the hall had also to sustain the weight of water that rose more than half a yard [45 cm]."[17]

Teatro Farnese was frequently used for the wedding festivities of Farnese and Bourbon dukes. The last show staged in that theater—on 6 October 1732—was occasioned by the entrance of Charles I of Bourbon into Parma; the theater has since been dark although it has always been a tourist attraction. An American bomb landed squarely on the roof of the Palazzo Pilotta on the night of 13 May 1944, and the explosion that followed left Teatro Farnese a heap of rubble. Carefully restored after the war, it is open today for tourists who visit the palace (open weekdays, except Mondays, from 9:00 A.M. to 2:00 P.M. and on Sundays and holidays from 9:00 A.M. to 1:00 P.M.). Visitors should be aware that even though Vicenza's Teatro Olimpico was the model for Teatro Farnese, the latter looks considerably different because Aleotti da Argento designed the stage for movable scenery that could slide on and off via tracks in the floor rather than opting for the fixed-scene perspective of Teatro Olimpico.

In 1674 another theater was built, Teatro della Rocchetta, which had 85 boxes and a large stage. Eleven years later Ranuccio I built Teatro del collegio dei nobili, where many celebrated performances were given, and in 1689, Ranuccio II had the Teatrino di corte erected especially to accommodate the performance of opera. Teatro Ducale, commissioned in 1688 by Ranuccio II, was a much larger theater that accommodated 1200 patrons in its 112 boxes and four balconies. Inaugurated with Bernardo Sabadini's opera, *Teseo in Atene*, it closed in 1828 with a performance of Rossini's *Zelmira*.

Though judged by contemporaries as some of the largest and best theaters to be found in Italy at the time, all the 18th-century theaters in Parma were demolished between 1822 and 1832 for reasons not quite clear.

The Story of Teatro Regio

Parma's current opera house, Teatro Regio at Via Garibaldi 16, opened in 1829 with a work especially commissioned from Vincenzo Bellini, *Zaira*. (Unfortunately it was a fiasco and caused the most violent audience reaction in the house's history.) Originally known as Nuovo Teatro Ducale, the theater was renamed Teatro Regio in 1849 following the first war of independence. It had been built on the initiative of Maria Louise of Habsburg, the emperor's daughter, who had been forced to marry Napoleon. (She had been the glamorous ruler of Parma since 1814, when the Congress of Vienna awarded her the duchies of Parma, Piacenza, and Guastalla.)

Designed by architect Nicola Bettòli, the theater took eight years to build (1821–29). Located between the convent of San Alessandro on the south and Palazzo Ducale on the north (now the provincial administration office), the gable-roofed theater on Via Garibaldi is 37 meters (122 feet) wide, 84 meters (277 feet) deep, and 30 meters (99 feet) high. Its facade is solemn and imposing, with 10 Ionic pillars delineating the ground floor, above which rise two additional floors, the middle with five neoclassical windows and the upper with a large fan window.

The *sala* was originally of elegant simplicity according to contemporary etchings and paintings. In 1853 it was redecorated to the style we see today, with the frescoed ceiling dominated by figures from antiquity. A huge bronze astrolamp, taller than 4.5 meters (15 feet) and weighing 1100 kg (2425 pounds), hangs in the center. Made at a staggering cost in Paris, the chandelier is dominated at its center by three statues: Tragedy, Comedy, and Dance. (Electric lighting replaced the illuminating gas in this fixture in 1890; electricity for the stage was installed in 1907, and throughout the rest of the house in 1913.)

The brilliantly painted house curtain is the work of G. B. Borghesi, "The Triumph of Athena or The Triumph of Wisdom," an allegorical painting that includes such figures as Hercules, Orpheus (playing his lyre), and Athena encountering Pindar, Homer, Virgil, Dante, and Ovid. At the base of the curtain we see the muses: Tragedy, Comedy, and Dance. The *sala* itself, in the horseshoe configuration, is made up of four tiers of boxes, a balcony, and a gallery, altogether accommodating some 1440 patrons. The stage is quite large: 40 by 35 meters (132 by 116 feet). It was during renovations effected in 1907 that the pit for the orchestra was constructed.

In Parma, the repertory of the 18th century had centered around French and Italian composers: Tommaso Traetta, Christoph Willibald Gluck, Jean Philippe Rameau, Giovanni Paisiello, Giuseppe Sarti, and Ferdinando Paër (who was born in Parma in 1771). For his visit in April 1785, for example, Gustave III of Sweden was entertained with Claudio Monteverdi's *Orfeo*; *Zémire e Azor*, by André-Ernest-Modeste Grétry; and a ballet, *Aci e Galatea*, by Francesco Bianchi.

But during the 19th century, Verdi dominated the *cartelloni*. Although he submitted his first opera, *Oberto*, to Teatro Regio, it was turned down as too great a risk. It was not until 31 May 1843 that a Verdi opera actually entered the repertory, *Nabucodonosor* —now known by its contraction, *Nabucco*—with Giuseppina Strepponi (who was later to become Verdi's second wife) as the prima donna. Over the ensuing years, Teatro Regio has produced 23 of Verdi's 26 operas, slighting only the early *Un giorno di regno*, *Il corsaro*, and *Stiffelio*. These *cartelloni*, however, were not limited to Verdi, for they regularly scheduled operas by Rossini, Donizetti, and Bellini. During the decade 1830–40, for example, they presented 69 titles, including 17 by Rossini, 15 by Donizetti, and 12 by Bellini. Other composers represented during the 19th century included Mercadante, Pacini, Nicolai, and Peri. The works of Giacomo Puccini first entered the repertory in the latter part of the century.

The Season at Teatro Regio

It appears that budget restrictions are starting to cut back the number of works given at Teatro Regio. While the season of 1990–91 offered a ballet and five titles (Rossini's *La cenerentola*, Verdi's *Alzira*, Tchaikovsky's *Eugene Onegin*, Massenet's *Manon*, and Donizetti's *Lucia di Lammermoor*), the 1991–92 *cartellone* carried a ballet and only three opera titles (Verdi's *Luisa Miller*, Puccini's *Madama Butterfly*, and Donizetti's *L'elisir d'amore*).

The opening of the season in Parma coincides with the beginning of Carnival and runs until mid or late April. Each title is presented three to four times, and opera tickets are quite expensive. Teatro Regio is the first theater in Italy to accept ticket reservations via home television sets equipped with Videotel, a system of special channels available in certain European countries. Those outside Italy may call or write the box office (weekdays from 9:30 A.M. to 12:30 P.M. and 4:30 to 7:00 P.M.) at 0521/218.910 or 218.912. The address is Teatro Regio, Via Garibaldi 16, I-43100 Parma.

Teatro Comunale "G. Verdi"
PISA

Pisa, though known primarily for its leaning tower, has attracted a wide variety of artists over the centuries. In the 1850s Alexander Borodin—destined to become an illustrious chemist by profession and a stalwart member of that Russian group of composers known as The Mighty Five—lived in Pisa for three years. During this time he played in the orchestra of Teatro dei Ravvivati and served as organist for the cathedral's Cappella Musicale, thus learning much about Italian opera and sacred music.

Christoph Willibald Gluck lived for a time on the outskirts of Pisa in an area known as San Giuliano Terme. While there, he worked on *Il Tigrane* to a libretto by Carlo Goldoni (who also lived in Pisa). Gino Dell'Ira points out in *I teatri di Pisa*, "[Gluck] composed an opera set in the villages of this area that involved peasants and country girls, a work made up of sonnets and dances—something that had plainly never been done in European theaters."[18]

The *Pisani* are eminently proud of their theaters and title their *ente* "I teatri di Pisa" (the theaters of Pisa). The lyric panorama in this old city centers around three edifices. The first, Teatro dei Costanti, opened in 1773 with a performance of Niccolò Piccinni's *Il giocator*,[19] and was subsequently renamed Teatro dei Ravvivati, then Teatro Ernesto Rossi. Although the building still exists, its classic three tiers of boxes and a balcony rise today above abandoned automobiles (it is now used as an indoor junkyard for old cars). Teatro Rossi closed its doors in 1929 as an opera house with a performance of Rossini's *Il barbiere di Siviglia*. The second theater, the Politeama Pisano, opened in 1865 with a performance of *Crispino e la comare* by Federico and Luigi Ricci; the last opera performed in this theater before it was bombed during World War II, on 31 May 1942, was Rossini's *Il barbiere di Siviglia*, featuring Toti Dal Monte as Rosina. The third, Teatro Comunale "G. Verdi," is the current opera house, a theater inaugurated as Regio Teatro Nuovo (Royal New Theater) on 12 November 1867 with a production of Rossini's *Guglielmo Tell*.

Opera in Pisa

The opera annals of Pisa are filled with notices of grand celebrations and interesting incidents. One of the city's first celebrations was for the visit of the Bey of Algiers on 21 February 1831, when Nicola Vaccai's *Giulietta e Romeo* was produced at Teatro Rossi. The following year the Rossi produced Bellini's *La straniera* with a cast of "ugly voices" (to quote the local music critic).[20] City police were called in to quell the disturbance caused by an unruly crowd, who noisily complained about the bad casting. The police ended up arresting an even dozen of these rioters. In 1833 the police had to be called once again during a run of Donizetti's *L'elisir d'amore* because the audience was noisily complaining about the pedestrian nature of the performance.[21]

The waters of the overflowing Po River inundated the orchestra (stalls/parterre) of Teatro Rossi in December 1867. Repairs and refurbishing took three years, with the theater reopening in the autumn of 1870 with Bellini's *Norma*. The house was forced to close again in 1872 for major structural work, a project that took six years. It was then used more and more as a dramatic theater for plays, and less and less for opera. Teatro Rossi closed its operatic wing after the season of 1929.

The establishment of Teatro Politeama Pisano in 1865 meant that its operatic offerings frequently duplicated works mounted at Teatro Rossi. Scheduling was basically conservative at the Politeama: Bellini, Donizetti, Rossini, and Verdi. Then in 1931 Pietro Mascagni arrived in Pisa, and in November of that year he conducted four performances of his *Lodoletta*. He returned the following May to direct three performances of his *Pinotta*, coupled with his *Cavalleria rusticana*.

On 4 May 1932 the City of Pisa officially changed the venue for their opera season to Teatro Verdi. As had happened earlier between the Rossi and the Politeama, the operatic repertory of the Verdi overlapped that of the Politeama. The official status granted the Verdi in 1932 helped alleviate that duplication.

The repertory at Teatro Comunale "G. Verdi" has always been conservative, with the 1932 season, for example, offering two titles: *La traviata* (three performances) and *Madama Butterfly* (three performances). Highlights of the theater's seasons would include that of 1935, when Ottorino Respighi conducted four performances of his *La fiamma* and Gina Cigna and Ebe Stignani appeared in *Norma*. In 1936 Riccardo Zandonai conducted three performances of his *La farsa amorosa*, with a cast headed by Iris Adami Corradetti. Zandonai returned in 1939 to conduct four performances of his most celebrated work, *Francesca da Rimini*. Cloe Elmo appeared as Carmen in 1940, Tito Schipa as Nemorino in *L'elisir d'amore* in 1942. That same year Ferruccio Tagliavini appeared as Frederico in Cilea's *L'arlesiana*. Mario Del Monaco made his house debut as De Grieux in *Manon Lescaut* in 1944; and Tito Gobbi had his house debut the following season as Giorgio in *La traviata*, which was followed in the same season by his appearances as Rigoletto and Figaro (in *Il barbiere di Siviglia*). Maria Callas made her only appearance in Pisa as Floria Tosca in 1950.

Teatro Comunale "G. Verdi" Today

Though the need to bring Teatro Comunale "G. Verdi" up to current Italian safety standards with reference to wiring and fire escapes closed the building in 1985 for three years, the music lovers of Pisa were not content to sit it out. The board of the theater scheduled the opera season in October, when the weather was still rather mild, and arranged for opera productions to be presented in Teatro Tenda, literally a "tent theater," a 900-seat house of canvas that usually accommodated rock concerts.

In 1989 the refurbished Teatro Comunale "G. Verdi" reopened with a production of a commissioned work, Roberto De Simone's *Mistero e processo di Giovanna d'Arco*. The renovated theater, the work of architect Massimo Carmassi, attempted to return the theater to its original beauty while adding those steel fire escapes and other details required by law. As attested by the local paper, the most favorable result "was occasioned by Carmassi's love of architecture and his keen knowledge about three important aspects of the total project that he most successfully solved: architecture, restoration, and interiors."[22]

In the traditional horseshoe configuration, the Verdi has three tiers of boxes above which rise two balconies. These together with the orchestra (stalls/parterre) accommodate 922 patrons. During the most recent refurbishing, the original colors were restored to the *sala*: the upholstered chairs covered in velvet of a golden yellow ocher, the exact color that had been revealed by period samples, and the balustrades of the boxes garnished with a plaster stucco painted in ocher and gold tones.

The Season at Teatro Comunale "G. Verdi"

The opera season in Pisa begins in late September and extends to mid-November. Two to four performances of each title are given, and seasons usually include between three and four operas. The 1989 season, in addition to De Simone's opera, offered Verdi's *Un ballo in maschera* and Puccini's *La Bohème*. The 1991 season—in celebration of the Mozart bicentennial—offered *Le nozze di Figaro* and *Così fan tutte* in productions from Claudio Desderi's Mozart seminar at the Scuola di Musica di Fiesole; in addition the theater offered *Don Pasquale* in a production from Teatro Comunale of Modena and Handel's *Rinaldo* in a production from Teatro "Romolo Valli" in Reggio Emilia.

Ticket prices at the Verdi are moderate. Information (in Italian) may be had by telephoning 050/542.434 or 542.476 or 541.864. The box office is located at Via Palestro 40, I-56100 Pisa. During the season it is open daily, except Sundays and holidays, from 9:00 A.M. to noon and from 3:30 to 5:30 P.M. On performance days the box office is open one hour before curtain.

Teatro Municipale "Romolo Valli"
REGGIO EMILIA

Teatro Municipale "Romolo Valli," the municipal theater in the ancient Roman city of Reggio Emilia about 145 km (90 miles) north of Bologna on the route to Milan, is quite possibly the most elegant of all the gems in the Italian collection of opera houses. Spaciously located on the crest of a knoll at the southern end of the huge Giardini Pubblici (public gardens) in the heart of Reggio Emilia, the theater faces Piazza della Vittoria and Piazza Martini with vast, well-tended lawns surrounding its handsome granite facade. Inaugurated in 1857, the free-standing Teatro Municipale rises in front from three granite steps and is supported by 12 columns that form a portico, the two sides of which are connected to two arcades. The upper part is divided by 14 Ionic pillars that alternate with 13 windows. (The heraldic shield of the municipality of Reggio Emilia is located over the central window.) The top of the facade is ornamented with 14 statues representing (from left to right) Tragedy, Vice, Glory, Drama, Virtue, Truth, Education, Pleasure, Fable, Jest, Dance, Caprice, Comedy, and Sound. Another 14 statues, a mixture—an exhibition as it were—of historical and literary figures placed beside others more strictly associated with the theatrical world, adorn other parts of the edifice. Altogether these figures not only serve a highly decorative purpose, but offer what could almost be described as a shop window calling attention to the marvels within, for the pleasure and education of the public.

The Operatic Tradition in Reggio Emilia

When fire destroyed Reggio Emilia's most important theater in 1851, Teatro Cittadella, which had been built in 1741, the community pooled its resources and constructed a building that was at the same time grandiose and unique in design. Placed in a more central location than the fire-ravaged Cittadella, the new building became not only the artistic center of Reggio Emilia but was physically located at the heart of the community. The main *sala* is horseshoe-shaped, has excellent acoustics, and is richly decorated in white and gold plasterwork. There are four tiers of boxes rising above the orchestra (stalls/parterre) and an upper balcony, altogether accommodating about 1200 patrons. The ancient ducal box, which later became the royal box, has been maintained and is now used for important visiting guests.

The operatic tradition in Reggio Emilia, however, predates Teatro Municipale. Constructed in 1857, it actually divides, as it were, the past (the era of the duchy of the Este family) from the beginning of the new, unified state. While none of today's frequently performed operas originated here, the pages of Teatro Municipale's archives reveal some interesting even if now-forgotten *primas*: Vivaldi's *Siroe re di Persia* (1738), Porpora's *Didone abbandonata* (1725), and Piccinni's *Demofoonte* (1761). Some of the first performances of operas by Gluck, Rousseau, and Hasse were also presented at this theater. Stendhal, in his recollections of Italy, referred to his enjoyment of opera in Reggio Emilia as one of the most important of his Italian experiences.

It is interesting to note how scene changes were made in this theater before its most recent backstage renovation. In the official history of the theater published by the Archivo del Teatro Municipale, we read:

Scene changes were accomplished by a system of movable wings: the wings were blocked in several slits in the wooden floor and were moved by fixing them to rail-mounted trucks in the trap room [under the stage]. This antique equipment cannot be utilized today, owing to the changes in scenery techniques and theatrical fittings, but is worthy of mention in

that it confirms the elaborate functionality of Teatro Municipale from the time it was built. Other devices of this type
include the winches and drums positioned on the two grids
extending [from] the roof, bearing fly bars and ensuring
scenery movement; the two tiers of gangways, projecting balconies delimited by robust rails to which the scenery ropes
can be fixed [tied off], connected to each other by spiral stair-
cases; the fly galleries [the walkways above the stage] en-
abling the stage space to be crossed; the wells, cavities
formed in the outside walls, within which the stone counter-
weights are able to slide; the metal pipes permitting verbal
communication from the first and second gangways to the
stage personnel. Besides these structures and mechanisms
for scenery operation, there are still other machines for special scenic effects: the machine that reproduces the sound of
lightning, located near the organ and consisting of a series of
planks in walnut wood that are positioned in a fan shape and
hinged at one end; the rain machine, located on the first gang-
way on the eastern side of the stage and consisting of a large
wooden wheel covered in sheet metal with a container of lead
balls fixed to its edge; the thunder machine, parallel-piped
shaped body resting on toothed wheels, within which slide
wooden balls. The organ, made in 1815 by Luigi Montesanti
of Mantua, is installed on the left part of the stage.

The above-mentioned systems are of immense historical
value, but have since been replaced with other modern equipment for theater operation, such as the production booth
with electronic equipment controlling the scenic lights; the
sound booth, with transmission and registration [recording
capabilities], listening and call possibilities from various
zones of the theater; a closed-circuit TV system; orchestra
pit extension and the installation of an elevating forestage.[23]

Following more than two decades of the Fascist regime, the city
of Reggio Emilia has successfully accomplished the return of Teatro Municipale to a central position in its cultural life. Apart from
a brief summer holiday, Teatro Municipale is open year-round and
today offers an average of 260 evenings of opera, ballet, symphony
concerts, chamber music, recitals, and plays each year. Exhibitions are frequently presented in the lobbies of the first two floors
adjacent to the entrance halls, displays that are concerned with

the history of the Italian and foreign theater; set and costume design, musical manuscripts, biographies and research, and special exhibits devoted to individual composers and their creations.

The Season at Teatro Municipale

The opera season begins in early January and lasts for about five or six months and usually consists of about five productions, each presented three to five times. Recent seasons have included such unusual but outstanding operas as *Il cappello di paglia di Firenze*, an absolutely hilarious and tuneful comic opera by Nino Rota of "The Godfather" fame (his film scores won two Oscars for "The Godfather" I and II). Staged, costumed, and designed by Pier Luigi Pizzi, it was for me not only the highlight of the 1988 season but one of the most enjoyable evenings I have spent in an opera house. The Italian critics praised it with such words as "fresh," "elegant," and "ironic."

That 1988 season, as an example of the offerings of Teatro Municipale, also included the tried and true, with an *Aida* featuring Maria Chiara in the title role, supported by Nicola Martinucci as Radames, Cesare Siepi as Ramfis, and Bruno Pola as Amonasro, conducted by Donato Renzetti; Mozart's *La clemenza di Tito* with Gösta Winbergh in the title part, supported by Silvia Mosca as Vitellia, Adelina Scarabelli as Servilia, and Martine Dupuy as Sesto, conducted by Peter Maag, with sets, costumes, and direction again by Pier Luigi Pizzi; Rossini's *Il Signor Bruschino* with Bruno Praticò, Patrizia Pace, and Claudio Desderi, conducted by Maurizio Benini; and a colorfully spectacular production of Rimsky-Korsakov's *La fiaba dello zar Saltan* in a Luca Ronconi production, conducted by Vladimir Fedoseev. The season closed with the ever-popular *Madama Butterfly*, conducted by Yoshinori Kikuchi.

Other seasons have included such infrequently performed works as Rimsky-Korsakov's *Il gallo d'oro* in a production from the Mussorgsky Theater of St. Petersburg; Rameau's *Hippolyte et Aricie*, a joint production with the Paris Opéra, the Aix-en-Provence Festival, and Opéra Lyon; Benjamin Britten's *Albert Herring* in a Glyndebourne Touring Opera production; and Handel's *Rinaldo* (one of that opera's first contemporary revivals) in a Pier Luigi Pizzi production.

Ticket prices range from reasonable (gallery seats) to expensive (prime locations on opening nights). The box office is located

on the left of the entrance to the theater, and brochures announcing the season may be had by writing to Teatro Municipale "Romolo Valli," Piazza Martiri VII Luglio, I-42100 Reggio Emilia. The
telephone number is 0522/434.244; fax 0244/466.05.

Teatro Comunale Chiabrera
SAVONA

If you have a predilection for little-known 18th-century opera,
Teatro Comunale Chiabrera in Savona—a town of 76,000 inhabitants some 45 kilometers (28 miles) west of Genoa on the Italian
Riviera—is the place to visit. Here each fall, Teatro dell'Opera
Giocosa—a producing ensemble made up of early-opera buffs—
offers a season of little-known, seldom-performed works. Since
they began in 1979, they have produced the following operas at
Teatro Chiabrera in Savona (with limited repeat performances
given at Teatro dell'Opera del Casinò Municipale in San Remo):

Giuseppe Apolloni (1822–1889)
L'ebreo

Domenico Cimarosa (1749–1801)
Il pittore parigino
Il convito
Gli Orazi e i Curiazi
L'italiana in Londra
Il fanatico burlato

Carlo Coccia (1782–1873)
Caterina di Guisa

Gaetano Donizetti (1797–1848)
Le convenienze ed inconvenienze teatrali
Torquato Tasso
L'esule di Roma
Il furioso nell'isola di San Domingo

Baldassare Galuppi (1706–1785)
Il mondo della luna
L'amante di tutte

Nicola Antonio Manfroce (1791–1813)
Ecuba

Giovanni Paisiello (1740–1816)
Il barbiere di Siviglia
Elfrida
Nina, o sia La pazza per amore

Giovanni Battista Pergolesi (1710–1736)
Il maestro di musica
La serva padrona
La contadina astuta

Federico (1809–1877) and Luigi (1805–1859) Ricci
Crispino e la comare

Gioachino Rossini (1792–1868)
Il Signor Bruschino
Aureliano in Palmira
Il turco in Italia
La gazzetta
Ciro in Babilonia
Torvaldo e Dorliska

Tommaso Traetta (1727–1779)
Le serve rivali

Giuseppe Verdi (1813–1901)
Un giorno di regno

Antonio Vivaldi (1678–1741)
Farnace

For those who are anxious to hear how these operas sound, many of them have been recorded at Teatro Chiabrera by Bongiovanni Dischi of Bologna. Though they have the shortcomings of live performances—audience noise on occasion, the sounds of singers crossing the wooden stage, and, once in a while, an off night for a singer—they are a valuable way to become acquainted with these minor masterpieces of opera buffa and bel canto opera. Those available on CD are listed in the discography at the end of this chapter.

Teatro dell'Opera Giocosa

Founded as a private, nonprofit corporation in 1956, Teatro dell'Opera Giocosa della Città di Genova (to use its full title)—a performing entity, not an edifice—has its offices now at Teatro Chiabrera. Its purpose, as mentioned earlier, is solely to produce and present "early Italian operas not found in currently existing editions,"[24] though many of these operas have been edited and published since the Giocosa first presented them and are currently available in print.

Teatro Giocosa chooses its conductors wisely, with recent seasons including as music directors Massimo De Bernart, Umberto Benedetti Michelangeli, and Giacomo Zani. Among the soloists, there have been such excellent young Italian singers as Anna Caterina Antonacci, Stefano Antonucci, Simone Alaimo, Ezio De Cesare, and Fernanda Costa. Stage directors have included Beppe De Tomasi, Filippo Crivelli, Lorenza Codignola, Luca Verdone, and Paolo Carignani.

Teatro Comunale Chiabrera

While the first recorded theater activity in Savona took place in 1583 (a comic masque), it was not until 1853, when the current theater was built, that opera was established on a firm basis in the city. The project was approved by Vittorio Emanuele II on 9 February 1850, and building commenced immediately. Named after the great Italian poet Gabriello Chiabrera, who was born in Savona in 1552 and died there in 1637, Teatro Chiabrera was established as a condominium with boxes owned by individual families. The city, then a community of 18,000, maintained the theater and pledged "to present not less than 30 performances of melodramas or dramatic works each year."[25]

In this handsome building of white marble, classical in design, the *sala* was decorated in red velvet. Of traditional configuration, there were three tiers of 20 boxes, each in a horseshoe curve, surmounted by a gallery known colloquially as *paradiso*. The stage, considering the size of the house (713 seats), was quite large (approximately 25 by 17 meters/83 by 57 feet), and the painting on the house curtain by Gaetano Borgo Carati of Savona depicted "The Apotheosis of Gabriello Chiabrera in Paradise." The theater opened on 1 October 1853 with a production of Verdi's *Attila*, which was followed on the same program by a ballet, *La Spiritina*, with music by Luigi Astolfi.

Near disaster struck on the next evening. As the *Gazzetta Piemontese* of Turin reported on 3 October 1853:

A glass-plate photograph (note the cracks in the plate) of Teatro Chiabrera taken in 1860. The theater looks today exactly as it did over 130 years ago though modern automobiles replace the carriages in this view. Courtesy Teatro Chiabrera di Savona.

Yesterday evening at the new Teatro Chiabrera in Savona, after the ballet *La Spiritina* had begun, the great chandelier of 50 oil lamps (and weighing more than 900 kilograms [almost a ton]) . . . broke loose . . . from the ceiling and came crashing down, stopped only about 3 meters (10 feet) from the center of the main floor by its emergency cord. This flash of light quickly cleared the theater.[26]

Following the incident, the director of the theater assured the public that the house would henceforth be illuminated by candles placed on the fronts of the boxes. (The enormous astrolamp now in the theater was installed in 1883 and first rigged to burn olive oil, regular lamp oil being considered too odoriferous; it was re-rigged for illuminating gas in 1886 and for electricity around the turn of the century.)

Teatro Chiabrera was closed during the season of 1854–55 due to a cholera epidemic. Following that, the seasons moved ahead regularly. The 19th of March 1882 was a historic occasion for the theater (which, at the time, was one of more than 40 opera houses that dotted the Italian Riviera): Giuseppe Verdi and his wife, Giuseppina Strepponi, made a brief visit after paying their respects at the tomb of Chiabrera.

Tragically, on the night of 19–20 April 1883 the theater burned, but the community immediately initiated steps to restore Teatro Chiabrera to its pristine beauty, and the house reopened for Carnival 1886 with *Aida*, which was followed by *Carmen* and *La forza del destino*. Then, at 6:30 A.M. on 23 February 1887, an earthquake struck the region, killing more than 150 and injuring hundreds of others (at least 10 people died in Savona alone). The balance of the season—in honor of those killed and wounded—was then canceled.

Teatro Chiabrera also successfully survived—thanks to the local firefighters—36 incendiary bombs dropped by the British on the theater on 23 October 1942. Having weathered the war, the theater was closed in 1952 for total restoration, and it remained dark until the 1964 season. The house was devoted primarily to dramatic theater after it reopened, until opera again took its rightful place starting with the 1979 season when Teatro Giocosa of Genoa appeared in Savona to sponsor the largest part of the annual *cartellone*.

The Season in Savona

Today as in the 19th century, Teatro Chiabrera offers a season of opera, symphonic concerts, recitals, and plays. The 1991–92 season, for example, offered two operas: four performances of Rossini's *Aureliano in Palmira* (produced by Teatro Giocosa) and five performances of Verdi's *La traviata* (a coproduction with Teatro Comunale of Treviso and Teatro Sociale of Rovigo). The *cartellone* also included five orchestra concerts, four chamber concerts, and five recitals. The dramatic theater—always the most active branch in Italian houses—presented 10 plays in a total of 41 performances.

The opera season takes place in October and November, and the *cartellone* usually includes (depending on the budget) from one to three 18th-century operas produced by Teatro Giocosa along with one standard opera. Tickets are moderately priced. For information and reservations, write Teatro dell'Opera Giocosa, Piazza Diaz 2, I-17100 Savona. Payment in Italian lire must be made by International Check or Eurocheck. (There is a surcharge of Lit. 2000 for each ticket ordered.) The box office telephone number is 019/820.409 or 821.490, with the office open Tuesday through Friday from 9:00 A.M. to 1:00 P.M.

Teatro Olimpico
VICENZA

The spirit of Andrea di Pietro dalla Gondola, known as Palladio, permeates the town of Vicenza, where he was born and where he created his most famous monument to the theater. (Vicenza is a community of a little under 120,000 inhabitants, 68 kilometers/42 miles from Venice on the road to Milan.) Palladio (1508–1580) was the last great architect of the Renaissance, the author of a monumental, four-volume treatise on architecture, and the designer of one of the most amazing theaters in the world, Teatro Olimpico. He was the creator of the Palladian style, which is characterized by pilasters and columns of composite structure on a colossal scale and an attic often surmounted by statues and trophies. His works of noble design, just proportion, architectural rhythm, and logical vertical order have assured him lasting fame.

Palladio's last work, the incredibly wondrous Teatro Olimpico, is his vision of an ancient Roman theater. The stage, elaborate and permanent, is made entirely of stucco and wood. It consists of superimposed niches, columns, and statues, and its streets are painted in *trompe l'oeil*. The house or auditorium is a semicircular one, reconstructed according to Palladio's interpretation of a description by Vitruvius and based on ancient theaters still in existence.

Although Teatro Olimpico was completed by Palladio's pupil Vincenzo Scamozzi (1552–1616), its most fascinating feature, the illusionary scenery of architecture in false perspective, is almost certainly from Palladio's design. . . . Palladio had been experimenting with theatrical design for 40 years before he was commissioned to do this theater. Rejecting the newly developed square auditorium and proscenium arch, he tried to re-create a Roman theater, with a semicircular auditorium and a permanent stage setting.[27]

The proscenium stage front and set of Teatro Olimpico as seen in Plate III of G. Monternari's folio of 1733, *Del Teatro Olimpico di Andrea Palladio in Vicenza*. Courtesy dell'Assessorata alla Cultura del Comune di Vicenza.

Teatro Olimpico was inaugurated in 1584 with a performance of Sophocles's *Oedipus Rex*. As theater critic Jacques Burdick notes, Teatro Olimpico "gives us a fine idea of the Italian *teatro stabile* [established or permanent theater], the forerunner of the European opera house of a century and a half later."[28]

Though Teatro Olimpico is open to the public for a small entrance fee from 9:30 A.M. to 12:30 P.M. and from 3:00 to 5:30 P.M. (2:00 to 4:00 P.M. from mid-October to mid-March) daily, except Sundays and holidays, it is more thrilling to enjoy a performance in this historic spot.

The Season at Teatro Olimpico

The season in Vicenza includes concerts and classical plays as well as opera. The season of 1991, for example, included three concerts by Claudio Scimone's I Solisti Veneti; two concerts by the Orchestra Città di Vicenza directed by Umberto Benedetti Michelangeli; six evenings of ballet; four concerts of chamber music; and the classical plays *Agamennone* of Alfieri, *La finta serva* of de Chamblain de Marivaux, and *Bérénice* of Racine. Mozart's *Mitri-*

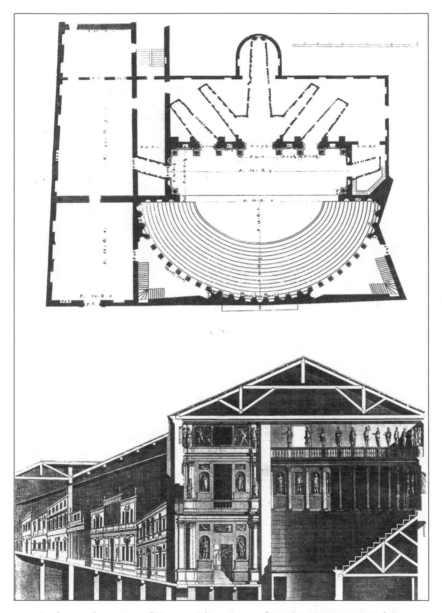

A plan and section of Teatro Olimpico as found in O. Bertotti's folio of 1776, *Le fabbriche e i disegni di A. Palladio* (The Buildings and Designs of A. Palladio). Courtesy dell'Assessorata alla Cultura del Comune di Vicenza.

An engraving of 1847 showing Napoleon being welcomed to Teatro Olimpico by Ottavio Trento, a local dignitary. Courtesy dell'Assessorata alla Cultura del Comune di Vicenza.

date, re di Ponto was the opera, and it featured Rockwell Blake, Lella Cuberli, Bernadette Manca Di Nissa, and Adelina Scarabelli in a Jean-Pierre Ponnelle production (from Venice's Teatro La Fenice) conducted by Roderick Brydon. The 1991 season extended from May through October, with the opera closing the season.

Other recent seasons have included, in the field of opera, Cavalli's *Calisto* and Gluck's *Paride ed Elena* (1989) and Mozart's *Le nozze di Figaro* (1990).

Teatro Olimpico accommodates 350 patrons, and ticket prices for opera are quite moderate. The theater itself is located at Largo Goethe 3, but information and booking arrangements are handled by the Agenzia Viaggi "A. Palladio," Contra Cavour 16 (VI), I-36100 Vicenza; telephone 0444/546.111 or 543.615. The box office at the theater is open a half hour before each performance.

Other *Teatri di Tradizione*

In the following list, the name of the town or city is followed by its province and region in parentheses. The name of the theater is given as registered officially with the Italian government, but the entire name is not always employed in announcements and on programs.

Ardenza (LIVORNO/TUSCANY)

Comitato Estate Livornese
Piazza Civica 1
Ardenza (LI)

Season: July; one opera. Various theaters are used, including Teatro Comunale di Villa Mimbelli, Teatro Quattro Mori, and Teatro la Gran Guardia in Livorno.

Bari (BARI/PUGLIA)

Ente Artistico Teatro Petruzzelli
Corso Cavour
Bari

Built 1903; seats 2100; season: February to May; four operas. Due to a fire of unknown origin—arson is suspected—eight days after the 1991–92 season opened, performances have been transferred to Teatro Piccinni and a tent theater, Teatro Bari, pending the reconstruction of Teatro Petruzzelli.

Bergamo (BERGAMO/LOMBARDY)

Civico Teatro "Gaetano Donizetti"
Piazza Cavour 14
Bergamo

Built 1791; seats 1164; season: September to November; four or five operas.

Como (COMO/LOMBARDY)

Teatro Sociale
Via Bellini 3
Como

Built 1813; seats 1100; season: November and December; three operas.

Cosenza (COSENZA/CALABRIA)

Teatro Comunale "Alfonso Rendano"
Piazza XV Marzo
Cosenza

Built 1895; seats 950; season: October to December; three operas.

Ferrara (FERRARA/EMILIA ROMAGNA)

Teatro Comunale
Rotonda Foschini 4
Ferrara

Built 1787; seats 990; season: January and February; three operas.

Lecce (LECCE/PUGLIA)

Teatro Politeama Greco
Via XXV Luglio 30
Lecce

Built 1884; seats 988; season: March; three operas.

Macerata (MACERATA/MARCHE)

Teatro Arena Sferisterio
Piazza N. Saur 2
Macerata

Built 1820; seats 4000; season: July and August; three operas.

Modena (MODENA/EMILIA ROMAGNA)

Teatro Comunale
Corso Canal Grande 85
Modena

Built 1841; seats 1100; season: January to May; five operas.

Novara (NOVARA/PIEDMONT)

Teatro Coccia
Via Fratelli Rosselli 4
Novara

Built 18th century; seats 1200; season: June and July; three operas.

Piacenza (PIACENZA/EMILIA ROMAGNA)

Teatro Municipale
Via Verdi 41
Piacenza

Built 1804; seats 1056; season: December to March; six operas.

Ravenna (RAVENNA/EMILIA ROMAGNA)

Teatro Alighieri
Via Gordini 27
Ravenna

Built 1852; seats 835; season: July and August; one to three operas.

Rovigo (ROVIGO/VENETO)

Teatro Sociale
Piazza Garibaldi 14
Rovigo

Built 1818; seats 910; season: September to December; five operas.

Sassari (SASSARI/SARDINIA)

Teatro Verdi
Via Politeama
Sassari

Built 1890; seats 1091; season: November; three operas, plus an additional three operas during the Festival dell'Opera Buffa in December.

Other Theaters

Adria (ROVIGO/VENETO)

Teatro Comunale
Piazza Cavour 13
Adria (RO)

Built 1935; seats 1350; season: September; two operas.

Aosta (AOSTA/VALLE D'AOSTA)

Cinema Teatro "G. Giacosa"
Via Xavier de Maistre 15
Aosta

Built 1892; seats 530; season: February; two operas.

Arezzo (AREZZO/TUSCANY)

Teatro Petrarca
Via Monaco
Arezzo

Built 1833; seats 800; season: October; one opera.

Barletta (BARI/PUGLIA)

Teatro Comunale "G. Curci"
Corso Vittorio Emanuele 69
Barletta (BA)

Built 1872; seats 500; season: November; two operas.

Benevento (BENEVENTO/CAMPANIA)

Teatro Romano
Benevento

Built 2nd century A.D., seats 2000; season: June and July; three operas.

Campobasso (CAMPOBASSO/MOLISE)

Teatro Savoia
Via Pepe 5
Campobasso

Built 1925; seats 750; Conservatory "Lorenzo Perosi" produces one opera in June.

Cesena (FORLÌ/EMILIA ROMAGNA)

Teatro Comunale "Alessandro Bonci"
Piazza Guidazzi
Cesena (FO)

Built 1846; seats 770; season: November; one opera.

Chieti (CHIETI/ABRUZZO)

Teatro Marrucino
Piazza Valignani
Chieti

Built 1818; seats 520; season December; three operas.

Foggia (FOGGIA/PUGLIA)

Teatro Comunale "Umberto Giordano"
Piazza Battisti 21
Foggia

Built 1828; seats 728; season: November; two operas.

Messina (MESSINA/SICILY)

Teatro Vittorio Emanuele
Via Garibaldi
Messina

Built 1852; seats 1024; season: March to June; six operas.

Montecarlo (LUCCA/TUSCANY)

Teatro Comunale dei Rassicurati
Via Carmignani 14
Montecarlo (LU)

Built 1750; seats 200; season: May; one or two operas.

Sulmona (L'AQUILA/ABRUZZO)

Teatro Comunale
Via dei Sangro
Sulmona (AQ)

Built 1933; seats 800; season: December; four operas.

Terni (TERNI/UMBRIA)

Teatro Comunale "Giuseppe Verdi"
Corso Vecchio 23
Terni

Built 1782; seats 1000; Operaincanto season: September; two operas.

Urbino (PESARO/MARCHE)

Teatro Sanzio
Corso Garibaldi
Urbino (PS)

Built 1853; seats 650; season: November; one opera.

Vercelli (VERCELLI/PIEDMONT)

Teatro Civico
Via Monte di Pietà 15
Vercelli

Built 1730; seats 817; season: November and December; two operas.

Discography

Titles of operas are given as they appear on the CD and do not always agree with listings in the *New Grove Dictionary of Opera*.

Teatro Sociale   COMO
Bellini, Vincenzo. *La sonnambula*. Nuova Era 6764/65; with Mariella Devia, Luca Canonici, Alessandro Verducci, and Elisabetta Battaglia; Orchestra Sinfonica di Piacenza; conducted by Marcello Viotti. Recorded live on 4, 6, and 10 November 1988.

Teatro Giordano   FOGGIA
Giordano, Umberto. *La cena delle beffe*. Bongiovanni GB 2068/69-2; with Marco Chingari, Fabio Armiliato, Rita Lantieri, and Giovanna Manci; Orchestra Sinfonica di Piacenza; conducted by Gian Paolo Sanzogno. Recorded live on 14 December 1988.

Teatro "G. B. Pergolesi"   JESI
Pergolesi, Giovanni Battista. *Adriano in Siria*. Bongiovanni GB 2078/79/80-2; with Susanna Anselmi, Daniela Dessì, Ezio Di Cesare, and Gloria Banditelli; Orchestra da Camera dell'Opera di

Roma; conducted by Marcello Panni. Recorded live on 20 December 1986.

Teatro La Gran Guardia   LIVORNO

Mascagni, Pietro. *Lodoletta*. Fonè 88F 16-36 2 CD; with Aureliana Beltrami, Clara Betner, Renata Villani, Luciano Saldari, and Fernando Lidonni; orchestra not indicated; conducted by Graziano Mucci. Recorded live on 2 October 1960.

Mascagni, Pietro. *Il piccolo Marat*. Fonè 88 F 17-37 2 CD; with Nicola Rossi-Lemeni, Virginia Zeani, and Umberto Borsò; orchestra not indicated; conducted by Oliviero de Fabritiis. Recorded live on 26 October 1961.

Teatro del Giglio   LUCCA

Catalani, Alfredo. *Dejanice*. Bongiovanni GB 2031/32-2; with René Massis, Maria Luisa Garbato, Carla Basto, and Ottavio Garaventa; Orchestra Lirico Sinfonica del Teatro del Giglio di Lucca; conducted by Jan Latham-Koenig. Recorded live on 6 September 1985.

Catalani, Alfredo. *Edmea*. Bongiovanni GB 2093/94-2; with Graziano Del Vivo, Maurizio Frusoni, Angelo Nosotti, and Marco Chingari; Orchestra Lirico Sinfonica del Teatro del Giglio di Lucca; conducted by Massimo De Bernart. Recorded live in September 1989.

Cimarosa, Domenico. *Gli Orazi e i Curiazi*. Bongiovanni GB 2021/22-2; with Daniela Dessì, Katia Angeloni, Tai-Li Chu Pozzi, Mario Bolognesi, and Simone Alaimo; Coro del Teatro dell'Opera Giocosa, Orchestra Sinfonica di San Remo; conducted by Massimo De Bernart. Recorded live on 2 November 1983.

Teatro Rossini   LUGO

De Banfield, Raffaello. *Una lettera d'amore di Lord Byron*. Ermitage ERM 403; with Elena Zilio and Sylvie Valayre; Orchestra Sinfonica dell'Emilia Romagna "A. Toscanini"; conducted by Gianfranco Masini. Recorded live in January 1991.

Donizetti, Gaetano. *Betly*. Bongiovanni GB 2091/92-2; with Maurizio Comencini, Susanna Rigacci, and Roberto Scaltriti; Coro del Teatro Rossini di Lugo; Orchestra Sinfonica dell'Emilia Romagna "A. Toscanini"; conducted by Bruno Rigacci. Recorded live in January 1990.

Donizetti, Gaetano. *Le convenienze teatrali*. Bongiovanni GB 2091/92-2; with Maria Angeles Peters, Roberto Scaltriti, and Domenico Trimarchi; Coro del Teatro Rossini di Lugo; Orchestra Sinfonica dell'Emilia Romagna "A. Toscanini"; conducted by Bruno Rigacci. Recorded live in January 1990.

Lattuada, Felice. *Le preziose ridicole*. Hermitage ERM 404; with Ezio Di Cesare, Sylvie Valayre, Adriana Cicogna, and Roberto Servile; Coro del Teatro Rossini di Lugo; Orchestra Sinfonica dell'Emilia Romagna "A. Toscanini"; conducted by Gianfranco Masini. Recorded live in January 1991.

Salieri, Antonio. *La locandiera*. Nuova Era 6888/89; with Alessandra Ruffini, Gastone Sarti, and Oslavio Di Credico; Orchestra Sinfonica dell'Emilia Romagna "A. Toscanini"; conducted by Fabio Luisi. Recorded live on 22, 24, 26, and 28 November 1989.

Teatro Regio   PARMA

Donizetti, Gaetano. *L'elisir d'amore*. Nuova Era 6725; with Chris Merritt, Adelina Scarabelli, and Sesto Bruscantini; Coro del Teatro Regio di Parma; Orchestra Sinfonica dell'Emilia Romagna "A. Toscanini"; conducted by Hubert Soudant. Recorded live in March 1988.

Teatro Verdi   SASSARI

Hasse, Johann Adolph. *La serva scaltra*. Bongiovanni CB 2101-2; with Bernadette Lucarini and Giorgio Gatti; Gruppo Strumentale dell' Orchestra Sinfonica di Sassari; conducted by Gabriele Catalucci. Recorded live in December 1989.

Piccinni, Niccolò. *La pescatrice*. Bongiovanni GB 2073/4-2; with Marinella Pennicchi, Maria Luisa Garbato, Maurizio Comencini, and Giorgio Gatti; Orchestra Sinfonica di Sassari; conducted by Carlo Rizzi. Recorded live on 26 November 1988.

Teatro Chiabrera   SAVONA

Apolloni, Giuseppe. *L'Ebreo*. Bongiovanni GB 2089/90-2; with Simone Alaimo, Fernanda Costa, Dino Di Domenico, and Armando Caforio; Coro Francesco Cilea; Orchestra Sinfonica di San Remo; conducted by Massimo De Bernart. Recorded live on 29 and 31 October 1989.

Donizetti, Gaetano. *L'esule di Roma*. Bongiovanni 2045/46-2; with Simone Alaimo, Cecilia Gasdia, and Ernesto Palacio; Coro dell'Opera Giocosa; Orchestra Sinfonica di Piacenza; conducted by Massimo De Bernart. Recorded live on 14 October 1986.

Donizetti, Gaetano. *Il furioso all'isola di San Domingo*. Bongiovanni GB 2056/7/8-2; with Stefano Antonucci, Luciana Serra, and Luca Canonici; Coro Francesco Cilea; Orchestra Sinfonica di Piacenza; conducted by Carlo Rizzi. Recorded live on 10 November 1987.

Donizetti, Gaetano. *I pazzi per progetto*. Bongiovanni CB 2070-2; with Leonardo Monreale and Susanna Rigacci; Orchestra Sinfonica dell'Emilia Romagna "A. Toscanini"; conducted by Bruno Rigacci. Recorded live in December 1988.

Donizetti, Gaetano. *Torquato Tasso*. Bongiovanni GB 2028/29/30-2; with Ambrogio Riva, Simone Alaimo, Luciana Sera, and Ernesto Palacio; Professori d'orchestra e artisti del coro del Teatro Comunale dell'Opera di Genova; conducted by Massimo De Bernart. Recorded live on 16 October 1985.

Paisiello, Giovanni. *Nina o sia La pazza per amore*. Bongiovanni GB 2054/55-2; with Patrizia Orciani, Mario Bolognese, and Alessandro Verducci; Coro Francesco Cilea; Orchestra Sinfonica di Piacenza; conducted by Marcello Panni. Recorded live on 22 November 1987.

Ricci, Federico and Luigi. *Crispino e la comare*. Bongiovanni GB 2095/96-2; with Roberto Coviello, Daniela Lojarro, and Simone

Alaimo; Coro Francesco Cilea; Orchestra Sinfonica di San Remo; conducted by Paolo Carignani. Recorded live in November 1989.

Rossini, Gioachino. *La gazzetta*. Bongiovanni GB 2081/82-2; with Franco Federici, Gabriella Morigi, and Armando Ariostini; Coro Francesco Cilea; Orchestra Sinfonica di Piacenza; conducted by Fabio Luisi. Recorded live on 14 November 1987.

Teatro Sociale di Amelia   TERNI

Franchi, Carlo, and Pasquale Anfossi. *Il barone di rocca antica*. Bongiovanni GB 2081/82-2; with Ugo Benelli, Milena Josipovich, and Giorgio Gatti; Orchestra Giovanile In Canto-Terni; conducted by Gabriele Catalucci. Recorded live on 10 September 1988.

Morlacchi, Francesco. *Il barbiere di Siviglia*. Bongiovanni GB 2085/86-2; with Alessandra Ruffini, Maurizio Comencini, Giorgio Gatti, Romano Franceschetto, and Aurio Tomicich; Orchestra Giovanile In Canto-Terni; conducted by Gabriele Catalucci. Recorded live in September 1989.

Pasquini, Bernardo. *La forza d'amore*. Bongiovanni GB 2067-2; with Bernadette Lucarini, Alessandra Rossi, and Enzo Di Matteo; Orchestra da Camera dell'Associazione "In Canto"; conducted by Fabio Maestri. Recorded live on 10 September 1987.

Pergolesi, Giovanni Battista. *San Guglielmo duca d'Aquitania*. Bongiovanni GB 2060/61-2; with Kate Gamberucci, Susanna Caldini, and Giorgio Gatti; Orchestra da Camera della Provincia di Terni; conducted by Fabio Maestri. Recorded live on 18 December 1986.

Scarlatti, Domenico. *La dirindina*. Bongiovanni GB 2026-2; with Alessandra Rossi and Renato Girolami; Complesso da Camera dell'Associazione Filarmonica Umbra; conducted by Fabio Maestri. Recorded live on 5 August 1985.

Chapter 6

THE LA SCALA
THEATRICAL MUSEUM

The ghosts of operas past and present haunt the rooms of the La Scala Theatrical Museum, rooms filled with portraits, posters, and programs; with manuscripts, scores, batons, and stage models; with musical instruments, costumes, and masks. As John Russell, former chief art critic for the *New York Times*, observed,

> For this visitor, the most enjoyable place in all Milan is the little museum in the opera house of La Scala. This is not because it has great art. It hasn't. Nor is it because it is a model of imaginative presentation. It isn't. The Scala museum is in many respects a mix of esthetic freak show and musicological tag sale. Setting out to count the number of objects in one showcase, I gave up in the low three figures. As for the level of indifferent art and ramshackle presentation, it may well be as high as in any museum in a major city in Europe.[1]

Altogether it is a fascinating and, at times, awesome collection, theatrical history in its raw state—"unedited, unordered, unprocessed, uncombed and unbrushed, but made up of prime quality material."[2]

The rooms that make up the museum resemble much more those of an elegant 18th-century private apartment than the type of plain, rectangular rooms usually associated with a dusty museum. At La Scala there are marble-framed doorways, inlaid tile and parquet wood floors, wallpapered walls, and Corinthian columns of marble, capped with gilt capitals. And though the guide book (which may be purchased at the door) offers a generic title for each of the 11 rooms, the display is really a hodgepodge, a fascinating pack-rat collection of memorabilia of composers, singers, conductors, dancers, actors, and actresses.

Nestled in the corner of a side room, for example, is a glass case containing a jumble of Verdi mementos, but *what* mementos!—the original manuscript of the *Requiem*; a fading sheet of paper on which a youthful Verdi had noted the expenses of his first trip to Milan; the passport he was given as a student, signed by Marie Louise, the widow of Napoleon, in Parma; the maestro's own rehearsal pocket watch; Verdi's letter to Boito announcing the fact that he had completed *Otello*; and King Umberto I's telegram of congratulations on Verdi's 80th birthday. To the side of this case is another in which the tiny portable spinet that introduced the eight-year-old Verdi to music sits on display. It was purchased by his father secondhand and retrieved possibly from some neighbor's attic (spinets were long out of vogue). One of the keys has been removed and rests on the top of the case, revealing an intriguing handwritten statement on its underside:

> I, Stefano Cavalletti, replaced these levers and stirrups and readjusted the pedals [Cavaletti uses archaic terms for the key and plectrum mechanism] which labor I perform as a gift, having seen how well-disposed is the young Verdi to learn to play this instrument; that is enough to satisfy me completely. Anno Domini 1821.[3]

Some of the items on display in the museum recall precious moments in the history of music. The autographed photograph that Claude Debussy gave to Arturo Toscanini reminds us that it was as chief conductor at La Scala that Toscanini introduced *Pelléas et Mélisande* to Italian audiences. And the rather plain walking stick of the redoubtable ballet master Enrico Cecchetti makes one think of when he must have kept time (and order) by tapping it on the floor for his legendary classes.

Musicians have not been served well by portrait artists, and the majority of paintings hanging on the museum walls are of dubious quality but in many instances are the only record we have of the physical appearance of such illustrious sopranos in the history of

Among the La Scala Theatrical Museum's collection of little-known portraits of well-known musicians is this engraving of Verdi dated 1842, when he was working on *Nabucco*. Author's collection.

opera as Giuditta Pasta, Giulia Grisi, Giuseppina Grassini, and Isabella Colbran (who appears in her portrait in what 18th-century artists conceived to be Grecian robes, playing a lyre). Portraits include those of the bass Ignazio Marini and Luigi Zamboni, the baritone who first sang Figaro in Rossini's *Il barbiere di Siviglia*. Puccini's oil portrait by Arturo Rietti is certainly a much more faithful and sympathetic portrait than that of Amilcare Ponchielli by Eleuterio Pagliano. As for Umberto Giordano, there is only a rather gruesome-looking bronze cast of his right hand to remind one of the creator of *Andrea Chénier*.

One of the most amazing items in the collection is the menu from which Giuseppe Verdi ordered dinner on the very last evening of his life, 27 January 1901. He had been staying just down the street from Teatro alla Scala at the Grand Hotel, and the menu was quite a formidable one for a man in his 88th year. In addition to appropriate wines, it begins with a julienne of slivered vegetables in puff pastry, followed by a grilled trout *maître d'hotel*. Then follows a sirloin of beef with vegetables *jardinière*, then a warm pâté of game and a dish of asparagus. To these are added young turkey roasted on a spit, raspberry *gelato* (ice cream), and an assortment of pastries. Incredible!

Visiting the Museum

Though Teatro alla Scala is a handsome and imposing building that frames one side of Piazza La Scala, the entrance to its museum, unquestionably the finest opera museum in the world, is drab and nondescript and a bit difficult to locate without guidance. It is just to the left of the porticoed section of the house, where an arcaded sidewalk is set back from the street. The first doorway under this arcade is the entrance. Though it looks much more like a service entrance, and all that is visible when you look through the open door is a quite common set of office-building stairs, this is the spot. A brass plaque by the door states it all quite plainly: *Museo del Teatro alla Scala*.

The museum is open weekdays from 9:00 A.M. to noon and from 2:30 to 6:00 P.M., and on Sundays and holidays from 9:30 A.M. to 12:30 P.M. and from 2:30 to 6:00 P.M. The admission charge is about $5; the 84-page illustrated guide book (available in English) costs about $10.

There is a passageway from the museum (just behind the entrance table where you pay your admission fee) that leads across the second-floor foyer of the opera house to one of the boxes. Usually this door is open so museum visitors can look inside the *sala* itself; a rehearsal is sometimes in progress, which makes it all the more fascinating. At times, and for completely unexplained reasons, the door of the box is locked. Do not ask the guard why, for his answer is inevitably, "It's always locked." Rather, if you wish to see the *sala*, simply slip him a Lit. 10.000 note, and miraculously the door will open.

Conversely, during a performance in the theater, the passageway to the museum is open at intermissions, and one can, during those intervals, take a quick look—free of charge in this case—at the displays.

Within the museum, Room One is dedicated to composers, with paintings and sculptures portraying Paisiello, Paër, Massenet, Mayr, and Wagner as well as a younger group: Puccini, Boito, Mascagni, and Cilea. Mixed among the composers are portraits of the editor Sonzogno and the playwright and librettist Luigi Illica. An intriguing collection of documents and memorabilia of conductors Arturo Toscanini and Victor De Sabata occupies a prominent place in the room. And, for no comprehensible reason, there is in this room a spinet with 45 keys dated 1667 made by Francesco Guaracino, with the painting on its lid representing Judith triumphantly brandishing the head of Holofernes before the Jews.

Room Two could be called the Porcelain Room, for a variety of porcelain pieces are on display—both of Italian and foreign origin—depicting the history of the performance arts: masks from the *commedia dell'arte* and statuettes of actors, dancers, and musicians. On the wall is the well-known Iganni painting of Teatro alla Scala, which dates from 1852, showing a view of the theater from down the street (Piazza La Scala had yet to be created). Below the La Scala painting hangs an engraving of Milan's Teatro Ducale, destroyed by fire in 1776. Though having nothing to do with porcelain, the other walls are covered (in quite random fashion, I must add) with such important portraits as that of Barbaja, the famous 19th-century impresario of Teatro San Carlo in Naples; Virginia Vasselli, Donizetti's wife; and Maria Callas.

The room of the exedra, Room Three, is the most homely and intimate of them all and dedicated for the most part to famous singers of the past (the glass case in the middle is an exception, a continuation of the porcelain exhibit).

The collection of theater archeology forms a separate grouping in Room Four and is perhaps the only one of its kind in the world. The numismatic section contains the most important collection known of the medals with inscribed edges known as *contorniati*, 166 pieces altogether, as well as Greek and Roman coins numbering several hundred, limited to those with designs depicting public games or entertainment. The *contorniati*, the guide book explains, are so called "because the name of the emperor is inscribed around their edges (*contorni*)."[4] The face of each medal shows the head of the emperor, while the back depicts a scene from a theatrical performance. It is "still unknown just what purpose was served by these medals, and scholars and historians still seek to determine their precise function."[5] They were coined between 356 and 420 A.D. and constitute one of the most vivid records of the Roman theater.

The collection of vases and urns is also dedicated to those painted with theatrical scenes and portrayals of dancers. One very important piece is a large cup (*skyphos*) made of terra cotta with red figures in Cuma style (350 B.C.). It shows a crude wooden stage upon which actors stand in the costumes of Hercules and Hermes along with a veiled woman. In the same glass case you can see tokens used for admission to the ancient theaters. Other displays show bronze and terra-cotta statuettes portraying actors in performance and theatrical masks (both functional and ornamental), along with dolls, musical instruments, and a variety of utensils.

If you are a Rossini fan, you will find Room Five fascinating. In addition to a large bust of the composer by Marrocchetti, you will discover Rossini's contract from Teatro Argentina in Rome for *Il barbiere di Siviglia* as well as the maestro's eyeglasses and the key he used to tune his fortepiano. There is also an autographed photograph dedicated to Barbara and Carlotta Marchisio, the celebrated sisters who sang in his *Semiramide*. Though the room is dedicated to Rossini, other composers invade the space in hodgepodge style, such as Paisiello, whose portrait—a copy most likely, but a good one—painted by Madame Vigée-Lebrun in Naples during 1791 hangs in this room. Nearby is a portrait of Donizetti as well as a sketch of him made a few days before his death. Singers occupy the room, too: Rosina Storchio painted as Madama Butterfly and a portrait of Bertinotti-Radicati, the first woman allowed on the papal stage (1798). A glass display case contains a cast of

Chopin's hand along with smaller portraits and miniatures of Bellini and Zingarelli, locks of both Bellini's and Mozart's hair, and a fan that belonged to Rosina Storchio.

Rooms Six and Seven are devoted to Giuseppe Verdi, and, in addition to the memorabilia already described, portraits of the three most important people in Verdi's life adorn the walls. Even if not great art, they reveal to us the physical appearance of these pivotal figures in the maestro's career: a kindly picture of Antonio Barezzi, who gave the young Beppino (later they called him Verdi; he was never called Giuseppe) his first music lessons and became a second father to him, then a father-in-law, and yet later Verdi's closest and dearest friend; Marghcrita Barezzi, Antonio's daughter, who became Verdi's first wife; and Giuseppina Strepponi, the soprano who later became the second Signora Verdi.

Room Eight is dedicated to dance and ballet, with its displays including a slipper that belonged to Fanny Elssler. You become aware, as you look at it, that the slipper is without the usual padding, as the *en point* position, on tiptoe, was yet to be introduced.

On the walls are sketches by Prampolini for *The Miraculous Mandarin* by Béla Bartók, a painting by Gonin that brings to life memories of ancient celebrations of Carnival, and an important painting by Bachenis of musical instruments. A bust of the famous choreographer Salvatore Viganò, much admired by Stendhal, is the work of the sculptor Bartolini and stood originally on the choreographer's tomb.

Two Venetian paintings of the 18th century are of great documentary interest, for both represent dance lessons. In the first you will see a bowed instrument accompanying the dancers' movement, a custom that was to continue up to the time of Degas. In the large cabinet are props used by the tenor Fusati, a costume for Falstaff that belonged to Mariano Stabile, the costume for Rigoletto worn by Carlo Galeffi, the costume for the Mefistofele of Nazareno de Angelis, and Giulietta Simionato's costume for Cenerentola.

On the left as you enter Room Nine, the last on the second floor of the museum and one dedicated to the dramatic theater, is a large portrait of Eleonora Duse by Wolkoff, next to the smaller one by Kaulbach, who painted the actress in the costume of Froufrou. Nearby is Sarah Bernhardt, and in the small display case, a cast of the hand of Eleonora Duse. On the far wall are two portraits of Carlo Goldoni, a bust of Schiller, and portraits of the comic playwright Marco Praga, of Adelaide Ristori in Schiller's *Mary Stuart* (one of her most famous interpretations), and of Ernesto Rossi in the role of Kean.

Room Ten is decorated with multicolor terra-cotta pieces from the 18th century depicting the characters of the *commedia dell'arte*: Pantalone, Florindo, Rosaura, the Doctor (who can also be seen in a small painting from the 1600s attributed to Carracci), Brighella, and Harlequin. The piano in this room belonged to Franz Liszt and was the one he used during his stay in Gardone Riviera.

Room Eleven is the Library of the Performing Arts and was inaugurated on 30 May 1954, founded with 40,000 volumes bequeathed to the museum by the theater critic of *Corriere della Sera*, Renato Simoni, in order to found a center for theater studies in honor of his mother, Livia. Today the library has more than 100,000 volumes and is the only one of its kind, both for the quality of its texts and for its specialization. All volumes are catalogued and available for research.

In the center of the room is a glass-enclosed display that allows one to compare the original proscenium of La Scala by Piermarini, which dates from 1778, with the circa-1835 restoration made necessary by the accumulation of candle soot, the work of Sanquirico. You can also see a miniature of the overhead stage apparatus before the fly gallery on the stage was modernized. On the walls are some examples from the museum's large collection of scenography; most other sketches for stage sets and costumes are tucked away in storage boxes because of their voluminous nature.

The History of the Museum

The La Scala Theatrical Museum, though certainly not the only museum devoted to opera or music, is definitely the finest and most comprehensive collection of opera and music memorabilia, portraits, books, and sketches to be found. Its origin came about through a fortuitous series of circumstances.

A poster was printed in 1911 announcing an auction to take place in May at the Hôtel Drouot in Paris of a collection of operatic and theatrical memorabilia by an antiquarian named Jules Sambon. On 23 April, with only a week left before the auction, a group of distinguished La Scala patrons and noble Milanese gathered at the theater to consider the possibility of buying the collection *in toto* and establishing a theatrical museum in the opera

CATALOGUE

DES

ANTIQUITÉS

VASES PEINTS, TERRES CUITES
MARBRES, BRONZES, IVOIRES, MONNAIES GRECQUES ET ROMAINES
MÉDAILLONS CONTORNIATES, CAMÉES ET INTAILLES

OBJETS D'ART

DU MOYEN AGE ET DES TEMPS MODERNES

TABLEAUX — PASTELS

Dessins — Aquarelles — Miniatures

PORTRAITS D'ARTISTES DRAMATIQUES, COMÉDIENS
CHANTEURS, CANTATRICES, MUSICIENS, DANSEURS ET DANSEUSES

La Malibran Garcia, par Louis PEDRAZZI
H.-L. Le Kain, pastel par Mᵐᵉ LABILLE-GUIARD

SUJETS DIVERS

Miniature-portrait de Joséphine Grassim, par QUAGLIA

FAIENCES & PORCELAINES

JEUX, INSTRUMENTS DE MUSIQUE, COSTUMES
Sculptures en Marbre et en Bois, Terre cuite

Le tout composant la

Collection Théâtrale de M. JULES SAMBON

ET DONT LA VENTE AUX ENCHÈRES PUBLIQUES AURA LIEU A PARIS

HOTEL DROUOT, Salles Nᵒˢ 9 & 10 réunies

Les Lundi 1ᵉʳ, Mardi 2 et Mercredi 3 Mai 1911, à 2 heures

ET SALLE N° 9

Du Jeudi 4 Mai au Lundi 8 Mai 1911, à 2 heures

COMMISSAIRE-PRISEUR : Mᵉ F. LAIR-DUBREUIL, 6, rue Favart.

EXPERTS

MM. PAULME et B. LASQUIN Fils | MM. ROLLIN et FEUARDENT
10, rue Chauchat   rue Grange-Batelière, 11 | 4, rue de Louvois, 4

EXPOSITIONS, SALLES Nᵒˢ 9 ET 10

PARTICULIÈRE : *Le Samedi 29 Avril 1911, de 1 heure 1/2 à 6 heures*
PUBLIQUE : *Le Dimanche 30 Avril 1911, de 1 heure 1/2 à 6 heures*
Entrée par la rue de la Grange-Batelière.

A poster announcing the Paris auction held in May 1911 of the "Collection Sambon," the purchase of which established the La Scala Theatrical Museum. Author's collection.

LA DAFNE

D'OTTAVIO

RINVCCINI

Rapprefentata alla Serenifs. GRAN DVCHESSA
DI TOSCANA

Dal Signor Iacopo Corfi.

IN FIRENZE
APPRESSO GIORGIO MARESCOTTI.
M D C.
Con Licenza de' Superiori.

The cover of the libretto for *Dafne* by Ottavio Rinuccini,
dated 1600, from the La Scala Theatrical Museum's Biblioteca Livia Simoni. Author's collection.

house in Milan. This group of important men included Duke
Uberto Visconti di Madrone; Professor Ludovico Pogliaghi; com-
poser/librettist Arrigo Boito; the newspaper critic from *Il Secolo*,
Signore Borsa; Senator Mangili; Count Leopoldo Pullé; Dr. Gino
Modigliani, the director of the collection of the Library of Brera in
Milan; and Carlo Vimercati. Thanks to the intervention of the Italian government brought about by Boito, and through the gen-
erosity of 50 citizens of Milan, funds were pledged so that the collection could be purchased intact at the auction.

The museum officially opened on 8 March 1913 with a solemn
ceremony in the foyer of the theater, the speakers including

Modigliani, who, by this time, had become superintendent of fine arts. Through the years there have been many donations to the museum, the largest and most important of which was the bequest of the Livia Simoni library.

Established on the concept of "*a living museum*, one that contributes with sensitivity to the ongoing diffusion of culture, free to commit itself to investigating the entire gamut of performing arts,"[6] the museum has sent displays and exhibits to Russia, Canada, the United States, Argentina, Singapore, Australia, Japan, Sweden, Denmark, Austria, Switzerland, Poland, and England.

Chapter 7

OPERA FOR CHILDREN

It was like a hundred children's audiences I had seen before: kids playfully hitting each other over the head with rolled-up programs, teachers hushing the incessant chatter of energetic youngsters, one or two boys trying surreptitiously to read Mickey Mouse comic books, and even a paper airplane (again courtesy of the printed program) sailing down from the balcony. And then the music began, magic music, for the audience was at once quiet and attentive, and remained that way until the final note some 45 minutes later. The time? The place? The occasion? A performance of Pergolesi's opera, *La vedova ingegnosa*—the story of an "ingenious widow"—at Piccolo Teatro in Florence, by way of the city's Musica per la scuola (Music for the School) program.

"Music for the School" in Florence

One of two outstanding programs involving opera for young people (the other is in Milan), Florence's Music for the School program—the older of the two—typically involves around 40 different concerts each year in the main auditorium of Teatro Comunale, close to 10 dress rehearsals of the Maggio Musicale Fiorentino Orchestra open to children, more than 100 lecture-recitals by vocal and instrumental artists in the classrooms, and an opera such as *La vedova ingegnosa*. Operas are given in Piccolo Teatro, a wonderful little theater of 500 seats with good acoustics and excellent sightlines, a performance hall made out of rehearsal space adjoining the main auditorium of Teatro Comunale.

Florentine public school children from ages six to 18, as well as those from the outlying areas of Tuscany, are invited each year. ("The music they get in their regular school curriculum is, at best, skimpy," Stelio Felici, the director of the program relates.[1]) Each child pays about $1 for a ticket. The initial response for the Pergolesi opera was so great that the run had to be extended from 10 to 14 performances. Each child receives preparation for the opera experience, with booklets covering the story and history of the opera prepared by Teatro Comunale and made available to classroom teachers. Then, just before the performance, a young member of the artistic staff steps before the curtain and briefly chats with the young audience about the difference between arias and recitatives, and what to expect musically.

What a marvelous way to prepare an opera for children: assemble the best cast, use a major orchestra in the pit, choose the finest director available, and spare no expense on spectacular stage settings and lavish costumes. The choice of *La vedova ingegnosa* was a felicitous one, a production that was an absolute delight to see and hear. The story itself concerns a lonely widow who feigns illness to gain the attention of her new neighbor, an eligible doctor. He—in turn—is only a "doctor" for purposes of wooing the widow. Though the music may or may not actually be by Pergolesi, it is an engaging, tuneful score.

Why stage an opera such as *La vedova ingegnosa* instead of one of the so-called children's operas—*Cinderella* or *Hansel and Gretel*? This I asked Talmage Fauntleroy, the American stage director who had produced it. He replied,

> *The Ingenious Widow* is short—a bare 45 minutes without cuts—and children's attention spans are very short. It's important to have a work that captures their interest immediately and holds it throughout the show, otherwise beautiful melodies and the work of earnest artists singing on stage go for naught.
>
> Also, *La vedova ingegnosa* is a story filled with wit and humor, and children love to laugh and giggle. That's one of the reasons why I cast two mimes as *commedia dell'arte* characters, to add more inherent humor and fun to the show. And—best of all—Pergolesi's opera is filled with wonderful

arias and duets. After all, it's music that opera is really all about.[2]

Brilliantly directed by Fauntleroy, the action was always lively but stylish, always humorous but appropriately restrained within the parameters of the traditional *commedia dell'arte*. Soprano Giovanna Santelli, who sang the widow with a bright soprano voice, was fresh from appearances at Venice's La Fenice in *Orphée aux enfers*. *Basso buffo* Franco Boscolo, known for his interpretations of such roles as Gianni Schicchi and Dr. Bartolo, was the properly intimidated doctor who courted the widow. The extravagant sets (an 18th-century parlor and a luxuriant garden complete with two fountains and a rippling stream) and the sumptuous costumes (high baroque in style) were the creation of Raffaele Del Savio, head of the scenic department at Teatro Comunale. A chamber orchestra listed in the program as the Piccolo Orchestra Fiorentino was made up of members of the Orchestra Maggio Musicale Fiorentino and was directed by Marcello Guerrini.

As the curtain closed on the performance, thunderous applause burst forth from the audience of children. I realized at that moment that these youngsters—to quote the final line of the widow on stage—"felt a tingle that was the first sign of love." In this case, a love of opera.

Milan's "La Scala for Children"

A more recently established program than the music and youth program in Florence, La Scala per i bambini (La Scala for Children) in Milan is also more oriented in its totality toward staged productions than its counterpart in Florence.

Each year a bona fide opera is offered as part of the program. Two such operas of recent seasons have featured children on stage as well as in the audience: Kurt Weill's *Der Jasager* and Hans Werner Henze's *Pollicino*. The latter featured a cast made up primarily of children. With a libretto by Giuseppe Di Leva, the story of this "fable in music" is derived from fairy tales by Collodi, the Brothers Grimm, and Perrault and concerns children who are abandoned in a forest by their impoverished mother and father. The cast includes Pollicino and his six brothers (all children); their father and mother (an adult soprano and tenor); seven animals of the forest (all of whom are children save the wolf, who is a bari-

335

A *manifesto* for the performance of Benjamin Britten's *L'arca di Noè*
from the first season (1986–87) of Milan's La Scala per i bambini
program. Author's collection.

tone); two terrible ogres (represented by a baritone and a mezzo performing in *sprechgesang*); and their children, Clotilde and her six sisters (all children).

Kurt Weill's *Der Jasager*, written for school performance in Berlin (its original production was conducted by a child), was successfully presented by La Scala for Children (in Italian, of course) for audiences of children between the ages of 11 and 14 (21 performances altogether in one season alone in La Scala's intimate 400-seat Teatro Piccolo). The Children's Chorus of the La Scala Opera, along with tenors and basses from the Milan Conservatory of Music choir, made up the on-stage chorus. The chamber orchestra in the pit consisted of instrumentalists from Milan's venerable City School of Music. With the exception of two adult parts sung by members of the La Scala Opera Studio, the soloists were children between the ages of seven and 13 and amounted to about 20 youngsters altogether.

The programs for even younger audiences are equally fascinating. A few seasons ago, as I entered Teatro dell'Elfo, I found the audience already transfixed by the action on stage. A colorfully uniformed soldier marched erectly—perhaps a bit stiffly—across the boards to the sound of a jazzy little march tune. The devil, dressed in red complete with forked tail and pointed ears, welcomed him with open arms. The music in the orchestra pit swelled to a climax, and the great velvet curtain swiftly closed on the tableau. Immediately the audience burst into shouts and applause— even loud whistles and raucous screams. The scene was from Igor Stravinsky's *A Soldier's Tale*, but this was not an average Teatro alla Scala audience in Milan, nor was it a traditional La Scala cast on stage. The oldest member of the enthusiastic audience was only 12, the youngest but eight! And the characters on stage were not well-known international opera stars, but fanciful marionettes, created by Luigi Veronese especially for these productions, all part of La Scala per i bambini.

This program is headed by two musically knowledgeable, resourceful, and inventive young men, Sylvano Lupetti and Gregorio Sangiovanni. While the idea of presenting musical theater experiences for the young is neither new nor novel, La Scala's approach is. After the performance, Lupetti told me,

> You see, the tradition in the past has been to take musico-dramatic works written for an adult public and—if these operas

have stories even remotely connected with the world of children (such as Humperdinck's *Hansel und Gretel* or Rossini's *Cenerentola*)—schedule a single performance for children of all ages in the opera house during the work's regular run.

The problems with these kinds of presentations are manifold. The works are much too long for most children. Then, the story Rossini used in his *Cinderella*, for example, is not the same version most children know so well. And an opera house filled with two or three thousand children! Have you ever heard the noise level when two to three thousand children try to sit still and be quiet? It may not bother the average parent, but for the artists on stage, it is certainly disconcerting.[3]

Sangiovanni went on to clarify,

What we try to do at La Scala is to select short works that in performance are well within the attention span of children, pieces of unquestionable musical value by master composers, but which have an immediate appeal for young audiences. We're also aware that what appeals to a four-year-old is not the same work that will appeal to a 14-year-old. And most important, we schedule our productions not at Teatro alla Scala with its almost 2000 seats, but in small intimate theaters and concert halls.[4]

To understand what these two men are saying, one has only to look, for example, at the program of their fifth season: 20 performances of Francis Poulenc's opera, *The Story of Babar, the Little Elephant*, staged with clever, colorful puppets at Teatro di Porta Romana for children from three to six years of age; a marionette version of Felix Mendelssohn's *A Midsummer Night's Dream* for children between the ages of nine and 13 given 12 performances at Teatro dell'Elfo; and Léo Délibes's ballet *Coppélia* mounted by the students of the La Scala School of Dance at Teatro Smeraldo for six performances for children between the ages of six and 13.

Because it is anticipated that children will return year after year to La Scala per i bambini as they are growing up, the repertory varies each season, usually consisting of an opera production, a ballet, and a work—not necessarily designed in its original form for a staged presentation—mounted with marionettes or puppets. And from year to year, the age brackets alternate: for example, the opera one year will be designed for three- to six-year-olds, the next for six- to nine-year olds, and the following season for nine- to 13-year-olds.

When works such as the ones I have described in detail are presented in carefully prepared productions (as regularly occurs with La Scala's children's program), the future of music theater looks promising indeed. As Lupetti proudly proclaims, "Nothing less than the best!"[5]

For the Armchair Fan

The complete libretto of *Pollicino*, along with a cassette of the 1989 production of it at La Scala, has been published. Colorfully illustrated with artwork for children (including how to make their own sets and costumes with a little cardboard, glue, paper, and paint), the text unfortunately is only in Italian. (The second side of the cassette tape contains only the orchestral accompaniment, for classes and groups who wish to perform the work themselves.)

Henze, Hans Werner. *Pollicino*. Ricordi 135438; with Silvestro Sammaritano and Nella Verri; Coro di voci bianche della Scala; Orchestra della Civica Scuola di Musica di Milano; conducted by Cesare Alfieri.

Poulenc, Francis. *Babar the Elephant* (in English). Nimbus NI 5342; with John Amis, narrator; Leslie Howard, piano.

The recording of Weill's *Der Jasager*, a "school opera" dating from 1930, is sung in German; the accompanying booklet is bilingual. The CD also includes another of Weill's operas for young people, *Down in the Valley* (in English), a "folk opera" written at the request of the opera department at the University of Indiana at Bloomington.

Weill, Kurt. *Der Jasager* and *Down in the Valley*. Capriccio 60 020-1; with (in *Jasager*) Tobias Schmeisser, Hilke Helling, and Ulrich Schutte; (in *Down in the Valley*) Ilana Davidson, Marc Acito, Donald Collup, James Mabry, and Donald P. Lang; Fredonia Chamber Singers, State University of Buffalo; Strings of Westfälisches Kammerorchester; conducted by Willi Gundlach.

Chapter 8

OPPORTUNITIES FOR YOUNG SINGERS

There are a number of unique benefits as well as pleasures to be gained by the young singer who is able to spend some time in Italy. First and foremost, a stay in Italy provides an ongoing, daily opportunity to hear the rhythm and placement of the Italian language, an experience so necessary for those who wish to sing opera in Italian, particularly recitatives, with naturalness and ease. Time spent in Italy—especially away from the major tourist centers— also gives the young artist an opportunity to understand something of the culture and spirit of the people upon which the stories of so many Italian operas are based. And, of course, for those who plan to perform on the international circuit, a visit offers a chance to see how Italians organize their seasons, select their casts, conduct their rehearsals, and pay their artists.

Italy provides a number of different opportunities for young artists. There are workshop/apprentice programs, master classes, and competitions and contests. And in each of these main categories a number of varied programs are designed for incipient and professional artists at various levels of development. For those who would gain the most out of an Italian adventure, it would be wise to select that experience carefully with reference to entrance requirements and the would-be participant's current level of achievement. As Talmage Fauntleroy, founder and artistic director of Studio Lirico in Cortona, cautions:

All competitions (*concorsi*) offer a singer the occasion for evaluation; and perhaps the opportunity to be heard by artistic directors, conductors, etc. In addition, they offer a reason to spend some time in Italy; and a chance to win money, contracts, and/or recognition. Winning first place is not always the only reason for participating in any contest. It is important that the singer have his or her goals clearly in mind and also that he or she know the nature, level, and expectations of the vocal competition. One should know something about the general level of the contestants. Age restrictions are good indicators of level, as is the amount of the award. It can be damaging if a singer presents his/herself for any audition before he/she is ready.[1]

One of the important concerns for a young singer who visits Italy to participate in a program is the cost of food and housing. In the early 1980s, Italy was one of the bargain centers of Europe. No more! Today Italy is in many ways the most costly country in Europe. While prices seem to be edging up each year, the following figures—quoted in lire or in U.S. dollars—should provide an approximate guide for the young artist.

Italian hotels—except for a few 5-star deluxe establishments—are rather spartan by U.S. standards: simple, unadorned rooms without televisions (except possibly in 4-star hotels), with air-conditioning in summer minimal to non-existent (again, with the exception of 4-star hotels) and heating in winter also minimal. Almost all Italian hotels in the 1- to 3-star category offer rooms with and without baths. (A bath usually increases the room rate about 33 percent.) In the less expensive hotels a bath usually means an open shower head tucked into one corner of the bathroom along with a wash basin, toilet, and bidet. Rooms without baths usually—even in the least expensive hotels—have a wash basin with hot and cold running water and a bidet. In these instances, a true bathroom with a shower and tub is available down the hall without extra charge.

Italian hotels are rated by stars; the most expensive, the deluxe hotels, are rated as 5-stars. Most American tourists on a budget stay at 2- and 3-star hotels, while students on minimal budgets usually opt for 1-star hotels. While prices vary from year to year and city to city, the range runs roughly from Lit. 20.000 a night for a single without bath to Lit. 500.000 a night at a 5-star hotel (with bath, of course).

In addition to hotels—all of which are listed with the official tourist office, the Ente Nazionale Italiano per il Turismo (which publishes an annual guide that lists exact prices: *Annuario Alberghi d'Italia*)—there are *locanda*s, similar to country inns, a step below 1-star hotels and thus a bit less expensive. There are also youth hostels throughout Italy that provide dormitory-type accommodation for something less than Lit. 25.000 a night.

For those establishments listed as *pensione*s (literally "boarding houses," though many no longer serve meals), the equivalents are as follows: 3-star hotel/first-class pensione; 2-star hotel/second-class pensione; and 1-star hotel/third-class pensione. These facts and figures, along with the following hotel quotations from Cortona (in the province of Arezzo in Tuscany), are from the official brochure published by the tourist office in 1993.

In a smaller town such as Cortona, where I served as the administrative director of Studio Lirico up until 1992, prices are somewhat lower than in the large tourist cities, with a 4-star hotel costing Lit. 72.000 for a single with bath; a 3-star hotel Lit. 55.000 with bath; a 2-star hotel Lit. 30.000 without bath and Lit. 43.000 with bath; and a 1-star hotel Lit. 21.000 without bath and Lit. 27.000 with bath. The youth hostel ran Lit. 15.000 per night, while the convent charged Lit. 25.000 per night for a bed, some in single rooms, others in double rooms, all without baths.

To assist travelers, almost every major Italian city has a booth in the train station marked *Alberghi* (hotels), a city agency that will assist you in locating a vacant room for a night or longer. These agencies do not make a surcharge, though generally they request up to 50 percent of the first night's lodging in cash to hold the room. The agency will give you a receipt, which you then present at the hotel for credit toward your first night's bill. Most Italian cities and towns that attract tourists also have a special office to provide hotel information either by telephone, by post, or in person via brochures of each city. Whether the Azienda Autonoma di Soggiorno (Local Tourist Information Office), Ente Nazionale Italiano per il Turismo (Official State Travel Agency), or Ente Provinciale per il Turismo (Provincial Tourist Office), these offices—all more frequently known and identified by their acronyms: AA, ENIT, and EPT—are ready to help. For those seeking information before arriving in Italy, write the Italian State Tourist Office, 630 Fifth Avenue, New York, New York 10111, or in the United Kingdom, the Italian State Tourist Office, 201 Regent Street, London W1R 8AY.

Workshop and Apprentice Programs

Some of the workshop and apprentice programs in Italy are designed for young professionals (e.g., the Monteverdi project in Fiesole, the Bottega in Treviso, the Accademia Rossiniana in Pesaro) while others are more oriented toward advanced vocalists at career-entry level (Studio Lirico and the Accademia Musicale Chigiana, for instance). Still others provide a typical American university experience, staffed by Americans from the parent university, as in the case of the New York University program.

The following paragraphs describe in detail a number of interesting and varied programs that provide opportunities for young artists to study opera in Italy. There are those that lead to workshop and professional performances of either entire operas or opera scenes: Talmage Fauntleroy's Studio Lirico in Cortona, Claudio Desderi's program at the Scuola di Musica in Fiesole, and Peter Maag's Bottega in Treviso. Others provide vocal coaching and literature: the New York University program at Gubbio, the Accademia Musicale Chigiana in Siena, the Bel Canto Foundation program in Siena, and the Sessioni Senese per la Musica e l'Arte in Siena.

Studio Lirico
CORTONA

Founded in 1982 by Talmage Fauntleroy, a member of the Metropolitan Opera directing staff and former director of opera at the state conservatory of music "Pietro Mascagni" in Livorno, Studio Lirico, jointly sponsored by the University of South Carolina and the city of Cortona, is

> an international four-week intensive opera study program located in Cortona, an Etruscan hilltop town in the province of Arezzo located midway between Rome and Florence. Advanced singers attend classes in Italian language and culture, Italian diction, classes in stage movement and characterization, and vocal interpretation and style in the Italian repertory; they also receive individual coaching in diction and participate in rehearsals on stage of the opera being prepared for performance. All participants are assigned a role from the Italian repertory around which all class work is built, a role

The cover of the 1993 Studio Lirico brochure, which announced six *Musica a mezzogiorno* (noontime concerts), two *concerti lirici* (opera recitals), and the first performance in modern times of Domenico Cimarosa's one-act *farsa per musica*, *L'impresario in angustie*. Author's collection.

that they will present in a workshop production at the conclusion of the four-week program in a public performance.[2]

Studio Lirico is open to advanced students and young singers at the career-entry level. In addition to young artists from the United States, Studio Lirico encourages participation by qualified singers from all countries, including Italians. Fauntleroy suggests that

> the participation by young Italian artists provides a more complete cross-cultural musical experience as well as offering a better overview of opera training programs and career entry opportunities on the international level. Furthermore, it provides non-Italian participants an opportunity to study and prepare Italian operatic literature alongside native Italian-speaking colleagues (a tremendous experience in itself!).[3]

The Studio Lirico program takes place during June and July each summer, with classes, coaching sessions, and rehearsals scheduled according to the Italian custom: six days a week (Monday through Saturday) for approximately six hours a day—from 10:00 A.M. to 1:00 P.M. and from 4:00 to 7:00 P.M. The staff includes outstanding artist/teachers from both Italy and elsewhere who are professionals in the operatic field and/or respected instructors at Italian conservatories and schools of music.

The culminating *concerti lirici* (recitals of operatic scenes and selections) and opera performances are given in the *cortile* (courtyard) of the 13th-century Palazzo Casali and in the 400-seat classical opera house, Teatro Signorelli. Outstanding past productions have included the Italian *prima* of Mario Castelnuovo-Tedesco's *L'importanza di esser Franco*, the first performance in modern times of Handel's *Muzio Scevola*, as well as such traditional fare as Cimarosa's *Il matrimonio segreto*, Mozart's *Le nozze di Figaro* and *Così fan tutte*, and Rossini's *Il cambiale di matrimonio*. Studio Lirico is now launched on a special program called Rinascita Cimarosiana—Cimarosa Reborn—with the performance each summer of a Cimarosa opera that has not been performed since the early 19th century: *L'impresario in angustie* in 1993, *Il convito* in 1994, and *I sdegni per amore* in 1995, for example.

Financially each student is responsible for his/her own transportation, food, and housing in Cortona, although the administrative staff of Studio Lirico will provide assistance in locating rooms in private homes, youth hostels, or hotels.

For further information, a brochure, and an application, write Talmage Fauntleroy, Director of Opera, School of Music, University of South Carolina, Columbia, South Carolina 29208. The telephone number is (803) 777-2458, and fax, (803) 777-6508.

Scuola di Musica di Fiesole
FIESOLE

In 1988 the world-famous baritone Claudio Desderi established an unusual opera program at the Scuola di Musica di Fiesole, a privately owned and operated music school in Fiesole, a hillside community about 8 kilometers (5 miles) from the heart of Florence. Desderi, who had made his debut at the Edinburgh Festival of 1969 in Rossini's *Il Signor Bruschino* and who, since 1990, has been the artistic director of the *ente* I teatri di Pisa, decided to work directly with young singers in the preparation of roles for a specific opera. His initial program was known as the "Progetto Mozart–Da Ponte/Teatro e Musica (Mozart–Da Ponte Project/Theater and Music)." Over a period of three years Desderi turned his attention to the preparation of one opera a year: *Le nozze di Figaro, Don Giovanni,* and *Così fan tutte.* Then, during the Mozart Year 1991, multiple casts were selected from the best participants, and performances of the operas were then given at some of Italy's important opera houses, including Teatro Comunale in Ferrara, Teatro Verdi in Pisa, Teatro Manzoni in Pistoia, Teatro Solvay in Rossignano Solvay, and the summer festival in San Gimignano.

The program was so successful that in 1992 Desderi launched a new three-year initiative—"La vocalità di Monteverdi (1992–1994)/Libertà nel rigore musicale [The Vocal Character of Monteverdi (1992–1994)/Freedom in Rigorous Music]"—in honor of the 350th anniversary of Monteverdi's death. Again, a different opera was approached each year: *L'incoronazione di Poppea* (1992), *Il ritorno d'Ulisse in patria* (1993), and *Orfeo* (1994).

Because of Desderi's commitments as a singer at the Royal Opera House, Covent Garden, and elsewhere, as well as his conducting activities in Pisa, the working sessions in Fiesole stretch over a considerable period of time and require the participant to be available accordingly. For example, the selection of participants for the 1992 *L'incoronazione di Poppea* program lasted from 5 to 12 March for those who had previously enrolled in the Mozart project; auditions for new participants took place from 12 to 17

347

April. Workshop sessions and rehearsals were scheduled from 18 to 27 June, and the final sessions took place from 10 to 20 October. Stage rehearsals for those participants who were selected for public performance followed on schedules established by each of the participating theaters.

Those auditioning for the workshop are expected to know from memory the entire role for which they are auditioning. The annual deadline for applications is 28 February.

Transportation, housing, and meals are the complete responsibility of the participants. Since public buses run rather frequently from Florence to Fiesole (about a half-hour ride), the opportunities for reasonably priced housing are much better in Florence than in the rather elite community of Fiesole (the old summering spot of the Florentine nobility).

For further information, brochures, and an application, write Segreteria della scuola, Scuola di Musica di Fiesole, Via delle Fontanelle 24, I-50016 San Domenico di Fiesole (FI). The telephone number (from 9:00 A.M. to noon and from 4:00 to 6:00 P.M.) is 055/599.994.

The New York University Music Program
GUBBIO

Since 1990, New York University, in cooperation with Gubbio's Amici della Musica, has offered a multifaceted, five-week, graduate-level music program in the medieval city of Gubbio in Umbria, a fascinating 2300-year-old city about a three-hour drive from Rome. The summer program, which takes place from mid-July to mid-August, offers both master classes as well as credited courses for the New York University graduate music program. The master classes "consist of non-credit private lessons . . . as well as preparations for productions and concerts."[4] The graduate program is an extension of that offered on the New York City campus.

The opera studio (course number E85-2063) is under the direction of Bissy Roman, who has studied at the Bucharest and Leningrad Conservatories and the Santa Cecilia Academy in Rome; currently she is a part-time professor of voice on the New York City campus. For the Gubbio Festival she has produced both Mozart's *Lo sposo deluso* and *Impresario*.

The opera studio provides an opportunity for singers to study major operatic roles. Development and study in all aspects of opera training are covered with special emphasis upon the character role. Stage productions highlight the course's activities.[5]

The opera studio meets from 3:30 to 6:30 P.M. during the first two weeks and from 4:00 to 6:30 P.M. in the third to fifth week. The Gubbio Festival opera production is presented on the final Saturday and Sunday evenings of the course.

The opera studio offers three credits toward the New York University graduate degree. The university assists in the housing arrangements, which include monasteries, seminaries, and hotels, some of which provide meals.

For further information, brochures, and applications, write Dr. Esther Lamneck, Department of Music and Music Professions, SEHNAP/New York University, 777 Education Building, Washington Square, New York, New York 10003. The telephone number is (212) 998-5424, extension 855441.

Accademia Rossiniana
PESARO

Since 1989 the Rossini Opera Festival in Pesaro has sponsored the Accademia Rossiniana each August, a

studio dedicated to interpretive problems concerned with the performance of Rossini's music, open to singers, professionals of the theater, and interested students. The studio takes place each summer during the preparation period for the festival and is centered around the Rossini voice; *bel canto* (its history, development, ideals); the dramatic problems of Rossini operas; and concepts of critical editions and modern interpretations.

The program is made up of theoretical lessons, practical exercises, attendance at festival rehearsals, encounters with the festival soloists and directors, and, ultimately, participation in a concluding Accademia recital. A certificate of participation is awarded at the conclusion of the Accademia.[6]

349

The Accademia Rossiniana 1991, with a registration deadline of 15 May, was held, for example, from 12 to 27 August, with the sessions running from 10:30 A.M. to 1:00 P.M. and from 4:30 to 7:00 P.M., six days a week. Sessions included those by Sergio Segalini ("Identifying the Rossini Voice"), Will Crutchfield ("The Rossini Style of the 1800s"), Philip Gossett ("The Lessons of the Critical Editions/The Authentic Versions"), Bruno Cagli ("Aspects of Rossini Dramaturgy"), Paolo Fabbri ("Musical Aesthetics in Italy at the Time of Rossini"), and Maurizio Volo ("Phonic Aspects of the Singing Voice"). Individual coaching sessions for the final *concerto* (concert/recital), visits to rehearsals, and both formal and informal encounters with the festival soloists, conductors, and stage directors were offered in addition to the seminars. "The program is fundamentally structured around the needs of the participating singers," according to Gianfranco Mariotti, the *sovrintendente* of the festival. "The course lasts about 15 days and is gratis. The only cost to the participant is that of food and lodging in Pesaro."[7]

For further information, brochures, and an application, write Rossini Opera Festival, Accademia Rossiniana, Via Rossini 37, I-61100 Pesaro. The telephone number is 0721/619.27.

Accademia Musicale Ottorino Respighi
ROME

With the blessing of Pope John Paul II, the stewardship of honorary president Sir Yehudi Menuhin, and the motto "Pro mundo uno," the Accademia Musicale Ottorino Respighi (AMOR) of Rome sponsors in Assisi and Orvieto a series of master classes in music each summer. In 1992, for example, the Finnish soprano Kim Borg offered a master class from 21 July to 2 August in Assisi devoted to "Lieder, Opera, and Oratorio Singing," and from 6 to 18 August in Orvieto, Giuseppe Di Stefano offered "Opera Singing" and Gerhard Kahry of Vienna lead "Acting and Staging for Opera Singers." Applications are due by 31 May each year, and accommodations at the academy are "compulsory for all master class participants."[8]

For further information, a brochure, and an application, write Segretaria Promozionale, Accademia Musicale Ottorino Respighi, Centro Internazionale di Formazione Musicale, Via Villa Maggiorani 20, I-00168 Rome. The telephone number is 06/30.53. 171; fax, 06/30.50.117.

Accademia Musicale Chigiana
SIENA

According to the official program booklet,

The Accademia Musicale Chigiana—which was founded by Count Guido Chigi Saracini in 1932—organizes every summer, with the collaboration of internationally renowned teachers, music master classes for young musicians from all over the world. Besides the master classes, many other musical activities take place in this period: seminars, concerts performed both by teachers and by the students, meetings, and the Settimana Musicale Senese [Siena Music Week], a festival founded in 1939, [for the purpose of conducting] important research in the music of the past and present.[9]

Students attending the Accademia Musicale Chigiana are divided into active students and auditors. Those who wish to be active students in vocal music must be not more than 30 years old if a soprano or tenor, or 34 years old if a mezzo-soprano, baritone, or bass. For admission to the course, "candidates shall perform three arias of their repertoire and pass two elimination examinations: one at the beginning of the course and the other during the seven following days."[10] No more than 15 active students are admitted to this course, which has had such instructors as Shirley Verrett and Carlo Bergonzi. These master classes usually take place from about mid-July to late August.

There are a limited number of scholarships available, all awarded on the "recommendation of the jury of the competition."[11] Three are courtesy of the Associazione Amici dell'Accademia Chigiana; one is bestowed upon a soloist or ensemble, who will give in return a concert at donor G. B. Scarafia's home. A fifth scholarship, financed with Accademia Chigiana funds, is awarded to the winners of the International Singing Competition "Francisco Viñas" (for information on this competition, write Segreteria del Concorso, Bruch 125, 08037 Barcelona, Spain).

Applications for the Accademia Musicale Chigiana are due on 1 April each year. "All active students who have attended lessons regularly will be granted attendance certificates. Diplomas of Merit and Honour may also be granted."[12] Courses in the Italian language may be arranged through Siena University for Accademia Chigiana for an additional fee.

For further information, a brochure, and an application write Segreteria, Accademia Musicale Chigiana, Via di Città 89, I-53100 Siena. The telephone number is 0577/46.152; the fax, 0577/288.124.

Sessioni Senese per la Musica e l'Arte
SIENA

Founded in 1972, the Sessioni Senese per la Musica e l'Arte is a non-profit organization registered in Connecticut that, in association with the University of Siena, "offers seminars and concerts in Tuscany, Italy. . . . The program is open to graduates, teachers, undergraduates, professionals, and qualified visitors, 19 years of age and above."[13] About 50 students participate each summer.

SSMA (the acronym by which they represent themselves)

offers coaching in performance practice by well-known artist-faculty from leading American and Italian universities in strings, woodwinds, brass, voice, guitar, piano, and composition, plus opportunities to perform vocal and instrumental music in concerts in formal and informal settings in various towns in Tuscany.[14]

The vocal performance practice class (course number MV 111) offers from one to three credits or a certificate. These sessions include coaching, acting, and audition techniques, excerpts from operas and musicals emphasizing performance interpretation repertory, . . . [and] performance in concerts and workshops."[15] The summer session of 1992 extended from 16 July to 18 August; the vocal instructor was Anastasia Tomaszweska, whose credits include engagements with European opera companies.

The deadline for applications is 15 May each year. Costs are calculated in the American manner on the number of credit hours. The minimum is two courses for the summer, the maximum four; in addition to vocal performance, classes include chorus, composition, conducting, early music and baroque ensemble, survey of art music, and Italian language.

SSMA offers an attractive comprehensive package for students that includes

cultural trips, courses, concerts, and travel, etc. The City of Siena offers many special considerations to participants enrolled in the program. Participants will be housed at the Piccolo Teatro Pensione "S. Teresa" and in a comfortable pensione near the university and will be provided with breakfast and lunch, as well as meals at the best local *trattorias*.[16]

For further information, brochures, and an application, write Sessioni Senese per la Musica e l'Arte, 595 Prospect Road, Waterbury, Connecticut 06706. The telephone number is (203) 754-5741; the fax, (203) 754-0180.

La Bottega
TREVISO

Teatro Comunale in Treviso, a charming and picturesque city about 30 kilometers (19 miles) north of Venice, has sponsored the Bottega (literally "shop") each year since 1989. It is

an international laboratory for young singers and musicians directed by Peter Maag. [The Bottega], sponsored by the city, has made this Swiss conductor's dream a reality by providing young talent from all over the world—selected through the famous Toti Dal Monte International Singing Competition that is always held in Treviso—the opportunity in the month of June to make their debuts and launch their careers.

The Bottega, in fact, is not an academic course, but truly and properly *official* theater, where young singers and conductors can directly experience the production of an opera.[17]

Indeed, Bottega productions have been presented as part of the Lirica Autunno Musicale Trevigiano, a festival held each fall in Treviso.

During past years Maag has produced all three of the Mozart–Da Ponte operas and, in 1992, Rossini's *Il turco in Italia*. In 1994, to honor the 250th anniversary of the death of Carlo Goldoni, Maag scheduled two almost unknown 18th-century one-act comic operas set to texts of Goldoni: *Pamela nubile* by Pietro Generali, and *Pamela maritata* by Giuseppe Farinelli. Maag has been assisted by outstanding vocal coaches over the years: Leyla Gencer and Regina Resnik.

The casting for the Rossini opera—as with all the others—was arranged through the Toti Dal Monte competition, also held in

The cover of the 1991 brochure announcing Treviso's Bottega under the direction of Peter Maag, which that year included the preparation and performance of Verdi's *Falstaff*. Author's collection.

Treviso, which took place that year from 23 to 29 June, with announced prizes of Lit. 78.000.000. The roles filled through the competition were as follows: (age limit 30) Donna Fiorilla, Don Narciso, and Zaida; (age limit 33) Selim, Don Geronio, and Prosdocimo. The contestants first took part in an audition, presenting two arias—of their own choice and in any language—that were not from the opera in the competition. They then took part in an audition relevant to the opera in competition as requested by the panel of judges, with these selections sung entirely from memory and in Italian.

The competition itself is divided into stages: 1) preliminaries in which contestants sing one or both of the arias of their choice, and one or more excerpts from the opera in competition, according to the desires of the panel of judges; 2) quarterfinals in which contestants sing whatever is requested from the prepared material as indicated by the panel of judges; 3) semifinals in which contestants sing excerpts from the opera in competition, solo or in groups, and may be heard more than once at the panel's discretion; and 4) the finals in which the panel will announce the cast.

The winners will be called to sing their respective roles in from four to six recitals of the opera in competition. The rehearsals begin around the last week of August and the production opens between October and December. The winners are also requested to make themselves available for 10 days during the month of July. Winners of the competition are paid. For example, in the Rossini opera, the scale was Lit. 3.500.000 for the roles of Selim, Donna Fiorilla, Don Narciso, Prosdocimo, and Don Geronio, and Lit. 2.000.000 for the role of Zaida.

In addition to the fees earned by those who are cast in the production, five study grants are available. In addition, a reimbursement of expenses is given to those contestants admitted to the semifinals, and a further reimbursement to those who reach the finals.

For further information on the Toti Dal Monte International Singing Competition, see the list of *concorsi* (contests) that concludes this chapter. For more on the Bottega, write Ente Teatro Comunale di Treviso, Corso del Popolo 31, I-31100 Treviso. The telephone number is 0422/410.130; the fax, 0422/522.85.

355

Italian Conservatories

For the singer who wishes to study voice and opera over an extended period of time, there are the Italian conservatories of music for those who speak and understand Italian. (A language course at an Italian university might be in order first for those whose language skills do not yet permit easy comprehension.) A language examination is given to all non-Italians who enroll in conservatory courses.

While Italians lament that the conservatories are not what they once were, the level is still quite high. The big difference between the American and British approach to opera on an educational level and that of the Italians concerns the relative emphasis of theory versus performance. In only the most rare instances does an Italian conservatory ever produce or mount an opera on stage. Rather, Italian conservatory students study the theory and history of opera production. Upon graduation from the conservatory, they expect to go directly to an opera house for a professional contract, for there are no community opera theaters, or amateur, semi-professional, or touring opera companies, and the conservatories themselves are not equipped to produce operas. Rather, voice students take a required course in *arte scenica* in which they talk about and study character development and dramaturgy. Most American and British students are amazed at the depth of knowledge young Italians have about opera—its history, its music, and its composers (including such—to foreigners—obscure composers of opera as Mercadante, Galuppi, Sacchini, and the Ricci brothers).

Because of the placement of the Italian language, Italians tend to be natural singers and need little work in the placement of the voice. For this reason, voice lessons at the conservatories tend to focus more on breath control, repertory, and interpretation than on vocal production. And, because the voice maestros are Italians themselves, they frequently are unfamiliar with the placement problems foreigners have and how to correct and assist them.

Those who would consider enrolling in an Italian conservatory should write directly to the appropriate institution for information on costs, courses, and staff. Though the enrollment fees have been increasing a little each year, the cost of a year's program at a conservatory is very reasonable since it is state supported.

The following is a list of the 57 state conservatories of music (*conservatori*), which are located in the principal cities, and another

356

16 *istituti musicali pareggiati* (equalized institutions), which serve some of the regional cities as the equivalent of a conservatory.

Conservatori (Conservatories)

Conservatorio Statale di Musica "Agostino Steffani"
Via Garibaldi 25
I-31033 Castelfranco Veneto; telephone 0423/495.170

Conservatorio Statale di Musica "Alfredo Casella"
Via dell'Annunziata 1
I-67100 L'Aquila; telephone 0862/221.22

Conservatorio Statale di Musica "Antonio Scontrino"
Via G. Cesare 12
I-91100 Trapani; telephone 0923/635.47

Conservatorio Statale di Musica "Antonio Vivaldi"
Via Parma 1
I-15100 Alessandria; telephone 0131/533.63

Conservatorio Statale di Musica "Arcangelo Corelli"
Via Laudamo 9/11
I-98100 Messina; telephone 090/719.610

Conservatorio Statale di Musica "Arrigo Boito"
Via del Conservatorio 27
I-43100 Parma; telephone 0521/282.320

Conservatorio Statale di Musica "Arrigo Boito"
Piazza Dante 1
I-46100 Mantua; telephone 0376/246.36

Conservatorio Statale di Musica "Arrigo Pedrollo"
Contra' S. Domenico 33
I-36100 Vicenza; telephone 0444/514.706

Conservatorio Statale di Musica "Benedetto Marcello"
Palazzo Pisani
I-30124 Venice; telephone 041/522.5604

Conservatorio Statale di Musica "Carlo Venturi"
Via Quartieroni 10
I-25047 Darfo-Boario Terme (BS); telephone 0364/51.904

Conservatorio Statale di Musica "Cesare Pollini"
Via Eremitani 6
I-35100 Padua; telephone 049/87.50.648

Conservatorio Statale di Musica "Claudio Monteverdi"
Piazza Domenicani 19
I-39100 Bolzano; telephone 0471/978.764

Conservatorio Statale di Musica di Adria
Viale Maddalena 2
I-45011 Adria (RO); telephone 0426/216.86

Conservatorio Statale di Musica di Brescia
Corso Magenta 50
I-21100 Brescia; telephone 030/455.19

Conservatorio Statale di Musica di Novara
Via Monte San Gabriele 19
I-28100 Novara; telephone 0321/312.52

Conservatorio Statale di Musica di Rovigo
Corso del Popolo 241
I-45100 Rovigo; telephone 0425/222.73

Conservatorio Statale di Musica di Salerno
Via S. De Renzi 62
I-84100 Salerno; telephone 089/231.977

Conservatorio Statale di Musica "Domenico Cimarosa"
Via Circumvallazione
I-83100 Avellino; telephone 0825/306.22

Conservatorio Statale di Musica "Egidio R. Duni"
Via Duomo 2/13
I-75100 Matera; telephone 0835/222.915

Conservatorio Statale di Musica ex Collegio La Salle
Via La Vipera
I-82100 Benevento; telephone 0824/204.84

Conservatorio Statale di Musica "Felice E. dall'Abaco"
Via Massalono 2
I-37100 Verona; telephone 045/800.2814

Conservatorio Statale di Musica "Francesco Cilea"
Via Affaccio
I-88018 Vibo Valentia (CZ); telephone 0963/591.335

Conservatorio Statale di Musica "Francesco Cilea"
Via Georgia 16
I-89100 Reggio Calabria; telephone 0965/213.08

Conservatorio Statale di Musica "Francesco Morlacchi"
Via Fratti 14
I-06100 Perugia; telephone 075/638.43

358

Conservatorio Statale di Musica "Gesualdo da Venosa"
Via Anzio
I-85100 Potenza; telephone 0971/460.56

Conservatorio Statale di Musica "Gioacchino Rossini"
Piazza Olivieri 5
I-61100 Pesaro; telephone 0721/336.70

Conservatorio Statale di Musica "Gioacchino Rossini"
Corso Cavour 68
I-63023 Fermo (AP); telephone 0734/282.17

Conservatorio Statale di Musica "Giovan Battista Martini"
Piazza Rossini 2
I-40126 Bologna; telephone 051/221.483

Conservatorio Statale di Musica "Giovan Battista Martini"
Piazza Guidazzi 9
I-47023 Cesena (FO); telephone 0547/286.79

Conservatorio Statale di Musica "Giovanni Pierluigi da Palestrina"
Via Baccaredda
I-09100 Cagliari; telephone 070/494.048

Conservatorio Statale di Musica "Girolamo Frescobaldi"
Via Previati 22
I-44100 Ferrara; telephone 0532/342.97

Conservatorio Statale di Musica "Giuseppe Nicolini"
Via S. Franca 35
I-29100 Piacenza; telephone 0523/384.345

Conservatorio Statale di Musica "Giuseppe Tartini"
Via C. Ghega 12
I-34132 Trieste; telephone 040/300.87

Conservatorio Statale di Musica "Giuseppe Verdi"
Via Mazzini 11
I-10123 Turin; telephone 011/530.78

Conservatorio Statale di Musica "Giuseppe Verdi"
Via del Conservatorio 12
I-20122 Milan; telephone 02/701.854

Conservatorio Statale di Musica "Giuseppe Verdi"
Via Cadorna 4
I-22100 Como; telephone 031/263.321

Conservatorio Statale di Musica "Giuseppe Verdi"
Via Roma 19
I-12100 Cuneo; telephone 0171/693.148

Conservatorio Statale di Musica "Jacopo Tomadini"
Piazza 1° Maggio 29
I-33100 Udine; telephone 0432/502.755

Conservatorio Statale di Musica "Licinio Refice"
Viale Roma
I-03100 Frosinone; telephone 0775/850.384

Conservatorio Statale di Musica "Lorenzo Perosi"
Viale Principe di Piemonte 2/A
I-86100 Campobasso; telephone 0874/900.41

Conservatorio Statale di Musica "Luigi Canepa"
Viale Umberto 28
I-07100 Sassari; telephone 079/236.377

Conservatorio Statale di Musica "Luigi Cherubini"
Piazza Belle Arti 2
I-50122 Florence; telephone 055/210.502

Conservatorio Statale di Musica "Luisa D'Annunzio"
Via L. Muzii 7
I-65100 Pescara; telephone 085/421.2070

Conservatorio Statale di Musica "Nicolò Paganini"
Piazza Verdi 13
I-19100 La Spezia; telephone 0187/320.43

Conservatorio Statale di Musica "Nicolò Paganini"
Via Orazio Comes 26
I-70043 Monopoli (BA); telephone 080/742.159

Conservatorio Statale di Musica "Nicolò Paganini"
Via Albaro 38
I-16145 Genoa; telephone 010/350.747

Conservatorio Statale di Musica "Nicolò Piccinni"
Via Brigata Bari 26
I-70124 Bari; telephone 080/347.962

Conservatorio Statale di Musica "Santa Cecilia"
Via dei Greci 18
I-00187 Rome; telephone 06/678.4555

Conservatorio Statale di Musica "Santa Cecilia"
Via S. Marco
I-04100 Latina; telephone 0773/480.173

Conservatorio Statale di Musica "S. Giacomantonio"
Via Isonzo 69
I-87100 Cosenza; telephone 0984/231.88

Conservatorio Statale di Musica "S. Pietro a Majella"
Via San Pietro a Majella 35
I-80134 Naples; telephone 081/459.255

Conservatorio Statale di Musica "Tito Schipa"
Via Ciardo 2
I-73100 Lecce; telephone 0832/644.267

Conservatorio Statale di Musica "Umberto Giordano"
Via Madonna della Libera
I-71012 Rodi Garganico (FG); telephone 0884/950.23

Conservatorio Statale di Musica "Umberto Giordano"
Piazza Negri 13
I-71100 Foggia; telephone 0881/746.87

Conservatorio Statale di Musica "Vincenzo Bellini"
Via Squarcialupo 45
I-90133 Palermo; telephone 091/580.921

Conservatorio Statale di Musica "Vincenzo Gianferrari"
Via Pernici 8
I-38066 Riva del Garda (TN); telephone 0464/539.69

Conservatorio Statale di Musica "Vincenzo Gianferrari"
Via S. Maria Maddalena 16
I-38100 Trento; telephone 0461/310.97

Istituti Musicali Pareggiati (Equal Music Institutes)

Istituto Musicale Pareggiato "A. Tonelli"
Via S. Bernardino da Siena 10
I-41012 Carpi (MO); telephone 059/649.285

Istituto Musicale Pareggiato "Achille Peri"
Via Antonio Allegri 9
I-42100 Reggio Emilia; telephone 0522/368.44

Istituto Musicale Pareggiato "Beniamino Gigli"
Via Pintucci Cavalieri 12
I-62019 Recanti (MC); telephone 071/981.434

Istituto Musicale Pareggiato "G. Puccini"
Via F. Cavallotti 19
I-21013 Gallarate (VA); telephone 0331/790.202

Istituto Musicale Pareggiato "Gaetano Braga"
Piazza Verdi
I-64100 Teramo; telephone 0861/358.66

Istituto Musicale Pareggiato "Gaetano Donizetti"
Via Arena 9
I-24100 Bergamo; telephone 035/237.374

Istituto Musicale Pareggiato "G. L. Malerbi"
Via Emaldi 51
I-48022 Lugo (RA); telephone 0545/242-01

Istituto Musicale Pareggiato "Giovanni Paisiello"
Via Mascherpa 10/A
I-74100 Taranto; telephone 099/792.206

Istituto Musicale Pareggiato "Giulio Briccialdi"
Via Manassei 6
I-05100 Terni; telephone 0744/549.603

Istituto Musicale Pareggiati "Giuseppe Verdi"
Via di Roma 33
I-48100 Ravenna; telephone 0544/223.73

Istituto Musicale Pareggiato "Luigi Boccherini"
Piazza S. Ponziano
I-55100 Lucca; telephone 0583/413.72

Istituto Musicale Pareggiati "Orazio Vecchi"
Viale Berengario 49
I-41100 Modena; telephone 059/237.378

Istituto Musicale Pareggiato "Pietro Mascagni"
Via Marradi 116
I-57100 Livorno; telephone 0586/808.4501

Istituto Musicale Pareggiato "R. Franci"
Via Garibaldi 42
I-53100 Siena; telephone 0577/280.766

Istituto Musicale Pareggiato "Vincenzo Bellini"
Corso Umberto 84/85
I-93100 Caltanissetta; telephone 0943/200.78

Istituto Musicale Pareggiato "Vincenzo Bellini"
Via Vittorio Emanuele 282
I-95124 Catania; telephone 095/316.454

Vocal Competitions

There are some 20 official vocal competitions in Italy open to non-Italian students. This chapter concludes with a list of them, together with addresses, age requirements, and such information as each has made available.

In general, the major competitions are fair and basically honest, though in such a small country as Italy, voice teachers are bound to know personally some if not all of the judges for any single competition. In one of the cities a few years ago, first prize was to be the assignment of the leading role in an important revival of a Mascagni opera. Strangely enough, the name of the leading lady was announced in the opera programs and publicity announcements before the contest had even taken place. This may be somewhat embarrassing, but not too terribly unusual in Italy.

For the record, let it be said that the most trustworthy competitions include the Mario Del Monaco contest in Castelfranco Veneto, the Cascina Lirica in Cascina, and the Callas in Rome.

Buona fortuna!

Concorsi (Competitions)

Adria

Concorso internazionale biennale di canto
c/o Associazione Società Concerti "A. Buzzolla"
Via Alberto Mario 11
I-45011 Adria (RO)

Sponsored by the Società Concerti "Antonio Buzzolla"; founded in 1966; held at Teatro Comunale di Adria; biennial; age limit: over 18 and under 35; applications due 10 days before the contest; takes place in late April and/or early May.

Prizes include a final concert at Teatro Comunale di Adria plus a Lit. 3.000.000 first prize, Lit. 2.000.000 second prize, and Lit. 1.000.000 third prize. In addition, there are three scholarships of Lit. 1.000.000 and eight of Lit. 50.000.

"Finalist prize winners . . . will be recommended to major Italian and foreign theaters, to lyric agencies, to RAI [Italian State Radio/Television], and to various lyric associations and similar organizations."[18]

Busseto

Concorso internazionale per "Voci Verdiane"
Piazza G. Verdi 10
I-43011 Busseto (PA)

Sponsored by the city of Busseto; founded in 1960; held at Teatro Verdi; annual; age limit: sopranos and tenors, 30—mezzos, baritones, and basses, 32; applications due 10 days before the contest; takes place in mid-June.

Prizes include a first prize of Lit. 7.000.000 plus participation in a concert at the Arena di Verona and automatic entrance in the Premio Carlo Alberti Cappelli contest; a second prize of Lit. 2.000.000 plus the

AMM.NE COMUNALE
di A D R I A

AMM.NE PROVINCIALE
di R O V I G O

ASSOCIAZIONE CONCERTI « ANTONIO BUZZOLLA »
A D R I A

« VILLA MECENATI » donazione m° Ferrante e Rosita Mecenati dal 1977 sede degli omonimi:
Conservatorio Statale di Musica ed Associazione Concerti « Antonio Buzzolla ».

XIª EDIZIONE

Concorso Internazionale Biennale di Canto

per aspiranti alla carriera lirica
« FERRANTE MECENATI »
———— Dotato di Lit. 13.000.000 di Premi ————

Patrocinio e Contributo
Ministero del Turismo e dello Spettacolo - Regione del Veneto

Collaborazione
Conservatorio Statale di Musica « Antonio Buzzolla » - Adria

ADRIA (RO) - Italia - Teatro Comunale - 29 e 30 APRILE - 1 e 2 MAGGIO 1992

The cover of a brochure announcing the 1992 edition of Adria's
Concorso Internazionale Biennale di Canto (Biennial International
Singing Competition). Author's collection.

Premio Giacomo Lauri-Volpi for *una voce verdiana* of merit; there are also the Premio Raffaele Arié for a bass of merit (Lit. 2.000.000) and the Premio Tullio Marchetti for a tenor "of particular merit" (Lit. 1.000.000).

In addition, the singers that take part in the training course for the two companies participating in the festival will be chosen from the competing candidates. For example, two Verdi operas were staged by Carlo Bergonzi at Teatro Verdi in Busseto. All costs relating to the organization of the course are sustained by the organizing body.

Cascina

Concorso lirico internazionale Cascinalirica
Associazione Cascinese Amici della Musica
Cascina (PI)

Sponsored by the Associazione Cascinese Amici della Musica; founded in 1976; annual; age limit: 30; applications due in May; takes place in June.

Prizes include a recording opportunity (of opera excerpts with piano accompaniment) for the first five winners, in lieu of cash prizes.

Castelfranco Veneto

Concorso internazionale per cantanti lirici "Mario Del Monaco"
Piazza Giorgione 22
I-31033 Castelfranco Veneto (TV)

Sponsored by the Associazione Amici della Musica Lirica "Mario Del Monaco"; founded in 1985; held at the Conservatorio di Musica "A. Steffani"; annual; age limit: 35; applications due in mid-July.

Prizes include a first prize of Lit. 4.500.000, a second prize of Lit. 3.000.000, a third prize of Lit. 2.000.000, a fourth prize of Lit. 1.500.000, a fifth prize of Lit. 1.000.000, and other prizes and concerts.

Cento

Concorso internazionale per voce liriche premio "Giuseppe Borgatti"
c/o Teatro Comunale Borgatti
Corso Guercino
I-44042 Cento (FE)

Sponsored by Teatro Comunale Borgatti; founded in 1981; held at Teatro Comunale Borgatti; biennial; age limit: men, 35—women, 32; applications due in July; takes place in September.

Cosenza

Concorso internazionale per cantanti "Stanislao e Giuseppe
    Giacomantonio"
Piazza XV Marzo
I-87100 Cosenza

Sponsored by Teatro Rendano; founded in 1987; held at Teatro Rendano; annual; age limit: sopranos, 30—tenors, 32—mezzos and baritones,

COMUNE DI CASTELFRANCO VENETO   PROVINCIA DI TREVISO

ASSOCIAZIONE AMICI DELLA MUSICA LIRICA
"MARIO DEL MONACO"

con il contributo
Regione Veneto
Cassamarca

Concorso Internazionale per Cantanti Lirici
International Competition for Opera Singers
Concours International pour Chanteurs d' Opera
Internationaler Sängerwèttbewerb
Concurso Internacional para Cantantes Liricos

MARIO DEL MONACO

CASTELFRANCO VENETO (Italy) 29 Luglio - 2 Agosto 1992

The cover of a brochure announcing the 1992 edition of the "Mario Del Monaco" International Competition for Opera Singers. Author's collection.

35; applications due 12 May; takes place in June.
Prizes are announced annually.

Enna

Concorso internazionale "Francesco Paolo Neglia" per cantanti
c/o Comune di Enna
Assessorato alla Pubblica Istruzione
I-94100 Enna

Sponsored by the city of Enna; founded in 1962; held at Teatro Comunale Garibaldi; age limit: 35; applications due by the end of June; takes place in July.

Prize winners are assigned roles in an opera to be presented as part of the Stagione Lirica del Teatro Rendano di Cosenza.

Ercolano

Concorso internazionale "Città di Ercolano" per cantanti lirici
Via Madonna della Salute
Ercolano (NA)

Sponsored by Zonta International Area Napoli; founded in 1983; age limit: 35; applications due by 12 April; takes place in late April.

Livorno

Concorso internazionale di canto per voci Mascagnane
Piazza Attias 37
I-57125 Livorno

Sponsored by the Associazione di Studi ed Iniziative Mascagnane; founded in 1989; annual; age limit: between 18 and 35; applications due 15 April; takes place in April or May.

Lucca

Concorso internazionale di canto "Giacomo Puccini" per voce nuove
c/o Fondazione "Giacomo Puccini"
Corte San Lorenzo 9
I-55100 Lucca

Sponsored by the Fondazione "Giacomo Puccini"; founded in 1975; held at Teatro del Giglio; applications due 10 days before the contest; takes place in November.

Mantua

Concorso internazionale per giovani cantanti lirici "Ismaele Voltolini"
c/o Club Amici della Musica
Via Accademia
I-46100 Mantua

Sponsored by the Club Amici della Musica; founded in 1981; held at Teatro del Bibiena; applications due 15 days before the contest; takes place in September.

Novara

Concorso internazionale di canto "Carlo Coccia"
c/o Ente Musicale Novarese
Via Prina 3
I-28100 Novara

Sponsored by the Ente Musicale Novarese "Carlo Coccia"; founded in 1982; held at the Civico Istituto Musicale Brera; age limit: between 18 and 40; applications due 15 September; takes place in late September.
Prizes include a workshop and public performance in Novara.

Parma

Concorso internazionale per giovani cantanti lirici "Premio G. Verdi"
  e "Premio Lino Chezzi"
c/o Associazione Culturale Corale Verdi
Vicolo Asdente 8
I-43100 Parma

Sponsored by the Associazione Culturale Corale Verdi; founded in 1964; held at Teatro Regio; age limit: between 18 and 36; applications due by the end of May; takes place in June and/or July.
Prizes will be announced at contest time.

Rome

Concorso internazionale "Maria Callas" voci nuove per la lirica
Viale Mazzini 4
I-00195 Rome

Sponsored by Radiotelevisione Italiana; held at the Conservatorio "G. Verdi" in Milan; biennial; age limit: 30 to 32; applications due by the end of April; takes place in October.
Prizes are announced biennially.

Siena

Concorso internazionale "Ettore Bastianini" per giovani cantanti lirici
c/o Associazione Amici della Musica "Ettore Bastianini"
Via Montanini 132
I-53100 Siena

Sponsored by the Associazione Amici della Musica "Ettore Bastianini"; founded in 1977; held at Teatro Comunale dei Rinnuovati; biennial; age limit: 36; applications due 10 days before the contest; takes place in April.
Prizes are announced biennially.

Sulmona

Concorso internazionale di canto "Maria Caniglia"
c/o Associazione Musicale "Maria Caniglia"
Vico dei Sardi 7/9
I-67039 Sulmona (AQ)

Sponsored by the Associazione Musicale "Maria Caniglia"; founded in 1983; held at Teatro Comunale; annual; age limit: between 18 and 35; limited to sopranos and mezzo sopranos; applications due 15 days before the contest; takes place in early October.

Terni

Concorso internazionale di canto
Via Manassei 6
I-05100 Terni

Sponsored by A.T.E.M. Briccialdi; founded in 1985; annual; no age limit; applications due 1 September; takes place in September.

Treviso

Concorso internazionale per cantanti "Toti Dal Monte"
c/o Teatro Comunale
Corso del Popolo 31
I-31100 Treviso

Sponsored by the Ente Teatro Comunale Treviso; founded in 1969; held at Teatro Comunale; annual; age limit: sopranos and tenors, 30— mezzos, baritones, and basses, 33; applications due 1 June; takes place in late June.

Prizes include participation in La Bottega, conducted by Peter Maag, with roles assigned in a specific opera presented publicly at Teatro Comunale in Treviso between October and November, and possibly at other theaters for which singers will be paid Lit. 3.500.000 for each major role and Lit. 2.000.000 for minor roles. Other recitals may be scheduled.

Vercelli

Concorso internazionale di musica "G. B. Viotti"
c/o Società del Quartetto
Casella Postale 127
I-13100 Vercelli

Sponsored by the Organizzazione Manifestazioni Viottiane; founded in 1950; held at Teatro Civico; annual; age limit: 32; applications due between 15 September and 30 November; takes place between October and December.

Prizes are announced annually.

Verona

Premio internazionale di canto "Carlo Alberto Cappelli"
c/o Ente Autonomo Arena di Verona
Piazza Brà 28
I-37121 Verona

Sponsored by the Ente Autonomo Arena di Verona; founded in 1987; held at Teatro Filarmonico; limited to winners of the International Singing Competition of the Federation des Concours Internationaux de Musique; applications due 1 August; takes place in August.

NOTES

Chapter 1

1. Ottolenghi 1990, 3–201, passim.
2. *La Repubblica*, 5 May 1989, 29.
3. Jamieson 1990, 21.
4. ANELS 1989, tables 1 through 8.
5. Ottolenghi 1990, 83–103.
6. Jamieson 1990, 21.
7. Ibid.
8. Ibid.
9. Ibid., 20.
10. Ibid.

Chapter 2

1. Sachs 1987, 57.
2. Ibid., 58.
3. Quoted in *Musica e scena*, 11 November 1926, 1.
4. Sachs 1987, 62.
5. Quoted in *La nuova italia musica*, 1 January 1932, 32.
6. Charleston, S.C., interview, 28 May 1993.
7. Wise 1988, 30.
8. Ibid.
9. Ibid.
10. Ottolenghi 1991, 121, 161, 247.
11. Lenoci 1991, 53.
12. Trezzini 1987, 62.
13. Ibid., 66.
14. Annacchini 1987, 47.
15. Hussey 1963, 126.
16. Ibid.
17. Rostirolla 1982, 62–63.

18. Ferrari 1989, 12–13.
19. Milan interview, 12 February 1988.
20. Personal observation.
21. Strunk 1950, 365.
22. "Teatro Comunale" 1932, 1.
23. Rubboli 1990, 54.
24. Ibid.
25. Ibid., 48.
26. Pougin 1881, 10.
27. Pedemonte 1987, 40.
28. Ibid.
29. Ibid.
30. Ibid., 42.
31. Altavilla 1987, 32.
32. Ibid., 32.
33. Ibid., 33–34.
34. Ibid., 34.
35. Ibid.
36. Ibid., 41.
37. Grout 1985, 229.
38. Ibid., 233.
39. Altavilla 1988, 6.
40. Stendhal 1970, 153.
41. Ibid., 154.
42. Levarie 1963, 122–123.
43. Ubaldo Mirabelli to author, 1 October 1991.
44. Rubino 1990, 18.
45. Ibid.
46. Pellegrini 1991, 19.
47. Keates 1985, 41.
48. Cacaci 1989, 15–16.
49. D'Arcais 1880, 12.
50. "Incoraggiamento ai giovani compositori italiani" 1888, 1.
51. Casella 1926, 18.
52. Moretti 1990, 48.
53. Nicoletta Cavalieri to author, 9 October 1991.
54. Raffaelo de Banfield to author, 9 October 1991.
55. Banfield 1991, 9.
56. Basso 1991, 694–695.
57. *Michelin: Italy* 1981, 244.
58. Lenoci 1991, 53.
59. Ibid., 53–54.
60. Casella 1954, 604.
61. Pestelli 1980, 263.
62. Arnold 1985, 38.
63. *Mercure Galant*, March 1683, 271.
64. Bonlini 1730, 37.
65. *Mercure Galant*, March 1683, 250–252.
66. Worsthorne 1954, 11.
67. Mocenigo, quoted in *Gran Teatro La Fenice* 1985, 3.

68. Rome press conference, 18 July 1991.
69. Ibid.

Chapter 3
1. Mambelli 1990, 56.
2. Lenoci and Pellegrini 1991, 37–38.
3. Zavadini 1948, 679.
4. Danzuso and Idonea 1990, 217.
5. Orselli 1988, 41.
6. Carafoli 1991, 30.
7. Rossano 1991, 42.
8. Landini 1991, 42.
9. Di Giuseppe 1991, 7.
10. Martina Franca press conference, 1 August 1991.
11. Montepulciano interview, 21 July 1991.
12. Henderson 1980, 391.
13. Henze 1989, 1.
14. Del Nista 1991, 124.
15. Gossett 1991, 29–31.
16. Collins 1988, 35.
17. Ibid., 41.
18. Norman 1959, 270.
19. Facaros and Pauls 1988, 436.
20. Spoleto interview, 30 July 1991.
21. Ibid.
22. Ortona 1991, 2.
23. Weaver 1991, 29, section XX. Copyright 1991 by The New York Times Company. Reprinted by permission.
24. Spoleto interview, 30 July 1991.
25. Ibid.
26. Ibid.
27. Maupassant 1951, 382.
28. Taormina interview, 10 September 1991.
29. Taormina press conference, 11 September 1991.
30. Lenoci and Pellegrini 1991, 39.
31. Greenfield 1980, 73.
32. Ibid., 74.
33. Gara 1958, 201.
34. Alberti 1985, 11.

Chapter 4
1. *I teatri italiani* 1970, 27.
2. Sheafer 1956, 334.
3. Cacaci 1991, 21.
4. "Spettacolo indimenticabile in una cornice unica al mondo" 1937, 1.
5. Ibid.
6. "Un'idea di Mussolini" 1937, 1.
7. Ibid.
8. Ibid.
9. "Spettacolo indimenticabile in una cornice unica al mondo" 1937, 1.

10. Pellegrini 1991, 114.
11. Ibid.
12. *Terme di Caracalla—Teatro dell'Opera Roma: I° Festival di Caracalla* 1991, 21.
13. Stanghellini 1991, 8.
14. Gavazzeni 1987, 13.
15. Martino 1991, 9.
16. Franchi 1991, 9.
17. Martino 1991, 9.

Chapter 5
1. Sachs 1987, 64.
2. *Gazzetta Ufficiale* 1967, 1.
3. Ibid., 6.
4. Fabris 1992, 4.
5. *International Herald Tribune*, 9 July 1993, 16.
6. Frati et al. 1985, 112.
7. Annibaldi 1882, 1.
8. Tosi 1988, 93.
9. Holland 1989, 80. Copyright 1989 by The New York Times Company. Reprinted by permission.
10. Lucca interview, 15 September 1986.
11. Taglioni 1988, 150, 151.
12. Rossi 1916, 19.
13. Schrade 1950, 239.
14. Follino 1587, folio A4.
15. Levarie 1963, 78.
16. Corradi-Cervi 1962, 5.
17. Levarie 1963, 129.
18. Dell'Ira 1987, 7.
19. Ibid. This authorized history lists *Il giocatore* by Piccinni; the full title is *L'astratto, ovvero Il giocator fortunato* (1772), also known as *Il giocator fanatico per il lotto*.
20. Ibid., 15.
21. Ibid., 16.
22. Romanelli 1991, 82.
23. Mussini 1982, 48.
24. Cantù 1990, 56.
25. Aiolfi n.d. (1984?), 41.
26. Ibid., 51–52.
27. Rothenstein 1968, 3080–3081.
28. Burdick 1974, 45–46.

Chapter 6
1. Russell 1990, 15. Copyright 1990 by The New York Times Company. Reprinted by permission.
2. Ibid.
3. Personal observation.
4. Fioravanti 1989, 47.
5. Ibid.
6. Ibid., 8–9.

Chapter 7
1. Florence interview, 10 February 1985.
2. Florence interview, 15 February 1985.
3. Milan interview, 12 May 1987.
4. Ibid.
5. Ibid.

Chapter 8
1. Rossi 1991, 10.
2. Brochure, *Studio Lirico* 1993, 1.
3. Columbia, S.C., interview, 8 February 1992.
4. Esther Lamneck to author, 23 January 1992.
5. Ibid.
6. Gianfranco Mariotti to author, 15 February 1992.
7. Ibid.
8. Brochure, *Festa musica pro mundo uno/Assisi, Orvieto* 1992, 2.
9. Brochure, *Accademia musicale Chigiana: Siena* 1992, 1.
10. Ibid., 29.
11. Ibid., 21.
12. Ibid., 29.
13. Brochure, *Sessioni Senese per la Musica e l'Arte* 1992, 1.
14. Ibid.
15. Ibid.
16. Ibid.
17. Brochure, *Lirica Autunno Musicale Trevigiano* 1991, 8–9.
18. Lucio De Piccoli to author, 5 February 1992.

BIBLIOGRAPHY

Aiolfi, Renzo. N.d. (1984?). *Il Teatro a Savona: 1583–1984*. Savona: Comune di Savona.

Alberti, Luciano. 1985. "The Puccini Seasons at Torre del Lago." In *31° Festival Pucciniano*. Torre del Lago: Ufficio Stampa del Festival Pucciniano.

Altavilla, Gianni. 1987. "Il Teatro San Carlo di Napoli." *L'Opera* (November).

———. 1988. *Il Teatro di San Carlo: Duecentocinquanta anni di storia*. Naples: L'Ufficio Stampa e Relazioni Esterne del Teatro di San Carlo.

ANELS (Associazione Nazionale Enti Lirici e Sinfonici). *Tabella Riassuntiva* (Tables 1–9). Rome: 1989.

Aniasi, Aldo, et al. 1992. *La Scala, 1967–91: La cronologia completa degli spettacoli degli ultimi 25 anni con tutti gli interpreti*. 2 vols. Milan: Teatro alla Scala.

Annacchini, Davide. 1987. "Il Teatro Comunale di Bologna." *L'Opera* (June): 47–53.

Annibaldi, Giovanni. 1882. "La storia segreta del Teatro Pergolesi." In *L'architettura teatrale nelle Marche*. Jesi: Cassa di Risparmio di Jesi.

Annuario Musicale Italiano. 1990. Vols. 1 and 2. Rome: CIDIM (Comitato Nazionale Italiano Musica).

Arnold, Denis. 1985. "Venice." In *New Grove Dictionary of Music and Musicians*. Ed. Stanley Sadie. London: Macmillan Press Ltd.

Arruga, Lorenzo. 1976. *La Scala*. Trans. Raymond Rosenthal. New York: Praeger Publishers.

Ashbrook, William. 1982. *Donizetti*. Cambridge: Cambridge University Press.

Banfield, Raffaelo de. 1991. *Festival Internazionale dell'Operetta Estate 1991*. Trieste: Mosetti.

Basso, Alberto, ed. 1991. *L'arcano incanto: Il Teatro Regio di Torino 1740–1990*. Milan: Electa.

Bonlini, Giovanni. 1730. *Le glorie della poesia e della musica*. Venice: Modesto Fenzo.

Brancati, Antonio. 1980. *Vicende architettoniche e structurati del Teatro Rossini di Pesaro*. Pesaro: Comune di Pesaro.

Burdick, Jacques. 1974. *Theater*. New York: Newsweek Books.

Cacaci, Francesco. 1989. *Il Teatro dell'Opera di Roma*. Ed. Vincenzo Gristomi Travaglini. Rome: Edizioni del Teatro dell'Opera di Roma.

———, ed. 1991. *Terme di Caracalla*. Rome: Atena.

Calabresi, Ilio, Giovanni Garroni, Paolo Barcucci, Lucia Monaci Moran, and Gisella Bochicchio. 1981. *Montepulciano*. Montepulciano: Editori del Grifo.

Campsi, Ugo, et al. 1985. *Gran Teatro La Fenice*. Venice: Teatro La Fenice.

Cantù, Alberto. 1990. "Il Teatro Chiabrera di Savona." *L'Opera* (December): 52–56.

Carafoli, Domizia. 1991. "Le smanie amorose dei 'Don.'" *L'Opera* (September): 28–30.

Casella, Alfredo. 1926. Interview. *The Christian Science Monitor* (31 July): 18.

———. 1954. "Turin." In *Grove Dictionary of Music and Musicians*. 5th ed. New York: St. Martin's Press.

Cecconi, Valeriano. 1980. *Profili di città etrusche: Chiusi—Chianciano—Montepulciano*. Pistoia: Tellini.

Celletti, Rodolfo, and Marco Contini. 1992. *Grandi Voci alla Scala: Da Tamagno alla Callas*. 2 vols. Milan: Teatro alla Scala.

Collins, Michael. 1988. "Toward a Definitive Otello: Evidence From the Manuscripts." In *Otello*. Pesaro: Fondazione Rossini.

Corradi-Cervi, Maurizio. 1962. *Il Teatro Regio*. Parma: Edizione del comune.

D'Amico de Carvalho, Caterina, and Vittoria Crespi Morbio. 1993. *Il teatro di Menotti in Italia*. Rome: Edizioni de Luca.

Danzuso, Domenico, and Giovanni Idonea. 1990. *Musica, Musicisti e Teatri a Catania (dal mito all cronaca)*. Palermo: Publisicula Editrice.

D'Arcais. 1880. "Qual'è l'avvenire del teatro Costanzi?" *L'Opinione* (28 November): 12.

Dell'Ira, Gino. 1987. *I teatri di Pisa (1773–1986)*. Pisa: Giardini editori e stampatori.

Del Nista, Roberto. 1991. "Ariadne and the Minotaur." *L'Opera* (September): 50–51.

Di Giuseppe, Franco, ed. 1991. *Festival della Valle d'Itria*. Fasano: Grafischena.

Domenici, Lisa, Alberto Paloscia, Paolo Menichini, and Vivien Hewitt. 1985. *31° Festival Pucciniano*. Torre del Lago Puccini: Pubblicazione dell'Ufficio Stampa del Festival Pucciniano.

Donati-Petteni, G. 1930. *Il Teatro Donizetti*. Bergamo: L'Istituto Musicale Pareggiato "Gaetano Donizetti."

Fabbri, Lionello. 1987. *Spoleto Festivals: Spoleto, Charleston, Melbourne*. Rome: Elle Edizioni.

Fabris, Dinko. 1992. "Il Petruzzelli può rinascere ma lotta contro il tempo." *Giornale della Musica* (October): 1, 4.

Facaros, Dana, and Michael Pauls. 1988. *Italy*. Chester, Connecticut: Globe Pequot Press.

Ferrari, Luigi. 1989. Premessa (Preface). *Un'idea dell'Opera*. Bologna: Grafis Edizioni.

Festival/The Festival, Il. 1989. Pesaro: Rossini Opera Festival.

Fioravanti, Giorgio, ed. 1989. *La Scala Theatrical Museum Guide*. Milan: L'Atelier del Libro.

Firenze: rassegna mensile del Comune. 1932.

Follino, Don Federico. 1587. *Descrittione delle solenni cerimonie fatte nella coronatione del Sereniss. Sig. Il Sig. Vincenzo Gonzaga. IIII Duca di Mantova, e di Monferrata II. [etc.]*. Folio A4. Mantua.

Franchi, Susanna. 1991. "Le idee del sovrintendente Pulica." *Giornale della Musica* (May): 9.

Frati, Vasco, Ruggero Boschi, Ida Gianfranceschi, Maurizio Mondini, Franco Robecchi, and Carlo Zani. 1985. *Il Teatro Grande di Brescia: Spazio urbano forme istituzioni nella storia di una struttura culturale*. Brescia: Teatro Grande.

Gara, Eugenio, ed. 1958. *Carteggi Pucciniani*. Milan: Ricordi.

Gavazzeni, Gianandrea. 1987. "Gli anni dell'Arena." In *Arena di Verona: 65 Festival dell'Opera Lirica*. Verona: Ente Lirico Arena di Verona.

Gazzetta Ufficiale. 1967. Rome: Editrice Nazionale.

Gelmi, Beatrice, and Valeriano Sacchiero. 1986. *Bergamo Step by Step . . . A New Practical and Comprehensive Guide of the Town*. 3rd ed. Bergamo: Grafica e Arte Bergamo.

Gossett, Philip. 1991. "Tancredi in Milan: Authority and Contingency in Italian Opera." In *Tancredi*. Pesaro: Fondazione Rossini.

Gran Teatro La Fenice. 1985. Venice: Teatro La Fenice.

Greenfield, Howard. 1980. *Puccini*. New York: Putnam.

Grout, Donald Jay. 1985. *Breve storia dell'opera*. Trans. Caterina D'Amico de Carvalho. Milan: Rusconi Libri S.p.A. Originally published as *A Short History of Opera*, 2nd ed., New York: Columbia University Press, 1965.

Gruen, John. 1981. *Gian Carlo Menotti*. Trans. Franco Salvatorelli. Turin: ERI Edizioni RAI.

Guadagnola, Pasquale. 1989. *Un'idea dell'Opera*. Bologna: Grafis Edizione.

Gualerzi, Valeria, Giorgio Gualerzi, and Giorgio Rampone. 1992. *Momenti di Gloria: Il Teatro Regio di Torino 1740–1936*. Turin: Teatro Regio di Torino.

Henderson, Robert. 1980. "Hans Werner Henze." In *New Grove Dictionary of Music and Musicians*. London: Macmillan Press Ltd.

Henze, Hans Werner. 1989. *Che cosa significa "Cantiere Internazionale d'Arte" di Montepulciano?* Montepulciano: Cantiere Internazionale d'Arte.

———. 1991. *Pollicino*. Milan: G. Ricordi.

Hirst, David. 1989. "Teatro Comunale di Bologna." *Opera Now* (September): 8–10.

Holland, Bernard. 1989. "Drama On and Off Stage for a Catalani Rarity." *New York Times* (17 September): 80.

Hussey, Dyneley. 1963. *Verdi*. London: J. M. Dent & Sons Ltd.

"Incoraggiamento ai giovani compositori italiani." 1888. *Il Teatro Illustrato* (July): 1.

International Herald Tribune. 1993 (9 July): 16.

Iovino, Roberto. 1991. *Il Carlo Felice: Due volti di un teatro*. Genoa: Sagep Editrice.

Jamieson, Nigel. 1990. "Imbroglio: Why opera in Italy appears to be in an ongoing state of crisis." *Opera News* (8 December): 20–21.

Keates, Jonathan. 1985. *Handel: The Man and His Music*. London: Victor Gollancz Ltd.

Lamarque, Lucio. 1983. *La nuova enciclopedia della musica Garzanti*. Milan: Garzanti Editore s.p.a.

Landini, Gian Carlo. 1991. "Tra Vivaldi e Meyerbeer." *L'Opera* (September): 42–44.

Landon, H. C. Robbins, and Jo Norwich. 1991. *Five Centuries of Music in Venice*. New York: Schirmer Books.

La Scala Theatrical Museum Guide. 1989. Milan: Museo Teatrale alla Scala.

Legge 14 agosto 1967, n. 800: Nuovo ordinamento degli enti lirici e delle attività musicale. 1967. Rome: Gazzetta Ufficiale (16 September).

Lenoci, Sabino. 1991. "Restituire il Regio ai torinesi!" *L'Opera* (May): 53–55.

———, and Luca Pellegrini. 1991. ". . . ma Puccini merita di più." *L'Opera* (September): 37–39.

Levarie, Siegmund. 1963. *Musical Italy Revisited*. New York: Macmillan Company.

Mambelli, Claudia. 1990. "Cartellone d'élite." *L'Opera* supplement 36 (June): 56–57.

———. 1991. "Nel nome di Cherubini." *L'Opera* (July/August): 34–35.

Marinelli Roscioni, Carlo, ed. 1987. *Il Teatro San Carlo: La cronologia 1737–1987*. Naples: Casa Editrice Napoli.

Martino, Daniele. 1991. "Due trentenni nell'Arena." *Giornale della Musica* (May): 9.

Martinez, Corrado. 1980. *Il Teatro Massimo: 40 anni di attività artistica dalla costituzione dell'ente autonomo 1936–1975*. Palermo: Edizioni Priulla.

Maupassant, Guy de. 1951. *Correspondance inédite de Guy de Maupassant*. Ed. Artine Artinian. Paris: Ollendorf.

Mercure Galant (March 1683): 1.

Michelin: Italy. 1981. London: Michelin Tyre Co. Ltd.

Moretti, Fausta. 1990. "Desidero solo fare musica." *L'Opera* (July/August): 48–49.

"Musica a Terme di Caracalla." 1937. *La Tribuna* (28 July): 1.

Musica e scena (11 November 1926): 1.

Mussini, Pietro, ed. 1982. *Il Teatro Municipale di Reggio Emilia*. Reggio Emilia: Teatro Municipale "R. Valli."

Norman, Jane and Theodore. 1959. *Traveler's Guide to European Art*. New York: Appleton-Century.

Nuova italia musica, La (1 January 1932): 32.

"Opera lirica a Terme di Caracalla." 1937. *Il Giornale d'Italia* (8 August): 14.

Orselli, Cesare. 1988. "La nostre attività." *L'Opera* (January): 41.

Ortona, Egidio. 1991. "La comunicativa inesauribile di Menotti." In *Spoleto Festival 1991*. Spoleto: Associazione Festival.

Ottolenghi, Silvana, ed. 1989. *Opera '88: Annuario EDT dell'opera lirica in Italia*. Turin: EDT Edizioni di Torino.

———, ed. 1990. *Opera '89: Annuario EDT dell'opera lirica in Italia*. Turin: EDT Edizioni di Torino.

———, ed. 1991. *Opera '90: Annuario EDT dell'opera lirica in Italia*. Turin: EDT Edizioni di Torino.

———, ed. 1992. *Opera '91: Annuario EDT dell'opera lirica in Italia*. Turin: EDT Edizioni di Torino.

Pastonesi, Marco. 1989. "Quei calci? Legittima difesa." *La Repubblica* (5 May): 29.

Pedemonte, Valeria. 1987. "Teatro alla Scala di Milano." *L'Opera* (December): 40–49.

Pellegrini, Luca. 1991. "L'estate porta consiglio? [Did the summer bring a change?]" *L'Opera* (September): 19–21 (English trans.: 114).

Pestelli, Giorgio. 1980. "Turin." In *New Grove Dictionary of Music and Musicians*. London: Macmillan Press Ltd.

Pinzauti, Leonardo. 1967. *Il Maggio Musicale Fiorentino: Dalla prima all trentesima edizione*. Florence: Vallecchi Editore Firenze.

Pirrone, Gianni. 1984. *Il Teatro Massimo di G. B. Filippo Basile a Palermo*. Rome: Officinia Edizioni.

Pougin, Arthur. 1881. *Verdi*. Milan: Ricordi.

Rebeggiani, Luca. 1987. "Un festival di atmosfere." *L'Opera* (July/August): 20–21.

———. 1987. "Un' istituzione ricca di fermenti e novità." *L'Opera* (July/August).

Romanelli, Marco. 1991. *Domus*. Pisa: Domus.

Roselli, Piero, Giuseppina Carla Romby, and Osanna Fantozzi Micali. 1978. *I Teatri di Firenze*. Florence: Casa Editrice Bonechi, s.r.l.

Rossano, Antonio. 1991. "Musical Miracles: The Valle d'Itria Festival." *Follow Me* (Edizione Pugliese) (June): 42–43.

Rossi, Michele. 1916. *Cento anni di storia del Teatro di Lugo: La patria di Rossini*. Lugo: Ferretti e C. editori.

Rossi, Nick. 1990. "Puccini at Home." *Opera Now* (August/September): 34–39.

———. 1991. Interview. *New York Opera Newsletter*: 10.

Rostirolla, Giancarlo, ed. 1982. *Wagner in Italia*. Turin: ERI/Edizioni.

Rothenstein, Sir John, ed. 1968. *New International Illustrated Encyclopedia of Art*. New York: Greystone Press.

Rubboli, Daniele. 1990. "Il Teatro Carlo Felice di Genova." *L'Opera* (April): 46–55.

Rubino, Maria Adele. 1988. *Teatro Massimo di Palermo*. Milan: SL Edizioni.

———. 1990. "Repertorio, ma non routine." *L'Opera* (December): 18–19.

Russell, John. 1990. "Operatic Memorabilia at La Scala." *New York Times* (2 December): 15, 31.

Sacchiero, V., ed. 1972. *Il Museo Donizettiano di Bergamo*. Bergamo: Il Museo Donizettiano di Bergamo.

Sachs, Harvey. 1987. *Music in Fascist Italy*. New York: W. W. Norton & Company, Inc.

Schrade, Leo. 1950. *Monteverdi: Creator of Modern Music*. New York: W. W. Norton & Company, Inc.

Sheafer, M. E. 1956. *Marvels of Ancient Rome*. New York: Phaidon Press.

"Spettacolo indimenticable in una cornice unica al mondo." 1937. *Giornale d'Italia* (8 August): 1.

Stanghellini, Enzo, ed. 1991. *Passport Verona*. Verona: Espro s.a.s.

Stendhal [Henri Beyle]. 1970. *Life of Rossini*. Trans. Richard N. Coe. Seattle: University of Washington Press.

Strunk, Oliver. 1950. *Source Readings in Music History*. New York: W. W. Norton & Company, Inc.

Taglioni, Tonino. 1988. "L'attività teatrale." In *Il Rossini di Lugo: Sul restauro di un celebre teatro*. Cittadella (Padua): Nuova Alfa Editoriale.

Teatri italiani, I. 1970. Milan: Istituto Editoriale Italiano.

"Teatro Comunale." 1932. *Firenze: Rassegna mensile del Comune* (May): 1–2.

Teatro Illustrato. 1988.

Terme di Caracalla—Teatro dell'Opera Roma: 1° Festival di Caracalla. 1991. Rome: L'Ufficio Stampa, Teatro dell'Opera di Roma.

Tosi, Bruno. 1988. "La storia sconosciuta del Teatro 'Pergolesi' di Jesi." In *Stagione Lirica e Concertistica 1988*. Jesi: Teatro di tradizione "G. B. Pergolesi."

Trezzini, Lamberto. 1987. *Due secoli di vita musicale: Storia del Teatro Comunale di Bologna*. Vol. 1. Bologna: Nuova Alfa Editoriale.

"Un'idea di Mussolini." 1937. *La Tribuna* (28 July): 1.

Weaver, William. 1991. "Festival or Not, Spoleto Shines." *New York Times* (19 May): section XX; 29, 39.

Wise, Ann. 1988. "To Subsidize or Not to Subsidize?" *Time* (14 November): 30–32.

Worsthorne, Simon T. 1954. *Venetian Opera in the Seventeenth Century*. Oxford: Clarendon Press.

Zavadini, Guido. 1948. *Donizetti: Vita—Musiche—Epistolario*. Bergamo: Casa Editrice.

GLOSSARY

This glossary includes Italian expressions found in the text as well as miscellaneous and theatrical terms and expressions that might prove useful in visiting opera houses and theaters in Italy.

all'aperto   Literally "in the open," generally refers to outdoor performances in arenas and piazzas.

anfiteatro   The first section of balcony seats in a theater.

aria   With reference to a stage, the cloth border that delineates the height of the stage area.

arlecchino   The velvet drape (the "grand drape" in American terminology) immediately behind the *piano fisso di boccascena*, or *mantovana* (the valance in American theaters); controlled by cables, it may be raised or lowered to change the height of the proscenium opening.

assegno   A bank check; an *assegno non trasferibile* is one that cannot be endorsed or cashed by a second party.

assessore   An alderman or councilman; the *assessore della cultura* (every Italian village, town, and city has one) is the city councilman responsible for cultural affairs.

astrolamp   Literally a "star lamp," generally refers to the massive brass chandeliers (at first oil lamps, later adapted for illuminating gas and electricity) that were suspended from the center of the dome-shaped ceilings of traditional baroque-style opera houses.

baldacchino   The dramatically festooned canopy that hangs over the royal box.

barcaccia   A stage box that is part of the proscenium arch itself.

basso buffo   Literally a "comic bass," generally refers to a bass with an agile voice suitable for comic roles.

basso continuo   A "continuous bass," generally refers to the 17th- and 18th-century practice of writing a single bass line (the basso continuo) that is realized by a keyboard instrument (generally a harpsichord or, later, a fortepiano) and a cello or string bass or bassoon or a combination of these. In early baroque music other instruments were added for variety such as a portable organ, a theoboro, and/or an archlute.

biblioteca   A library.

biglietteria   A box office.

biglietto   A ticket (plural, *biglietti*).

bis   Encore.

cabina elettrica   The lighting control booth of a theater.

camerata   A name used in the 16th century for small academies and that in opera generally refers to that group of literary men, musicians, and amateurs who met at the palace of Count Bardi in Florence to discuss the possibilities of a new style, one that came to be called *stile rappresentativo* and that led to the birth of the generic form known as opera.

camerini   Literally "little rooms," refers in a theater to the dressing rooms.

canzonette   A short piece of secular vocal music.

carlino   A coin worth about $1 today.

cartellone   A list of the season's bill of fare, including the titles of the operas, the names of their composers, the cast list, and the names of the conductors, choral directors (if there is a chorus involved), and stage directors (plural, *cartelloni*).

commedia dell'arte   A form of comedy that developed in Italy between the 16th and 18th centuries using improvised dialogue and masked characters (e.g., *Harlequin, Columbine, Scaramouche, Pantaloon, Il capitano, Il dottore*).

comunale   Literally "communal" or "municipal"; with reference to opera, a shortened form of the name of certain opera houses ("Teatro Comunale di . . ."); though technically an adjective, it is frequently employed as a noun: theater personnel as well as patrons refer to either a building in which operas are presented or to a company that produces them as a *comunale*.

condominiale   A condominium.

consiglio di amministrazione   A governing board of directors.

cortile   A courtyard.

ducat   A coin worth about $3 today.

ente   A corporation (plural, *enti*).

ente autonomo   An autonomous corporation.

ente autonomo lirici   The 12 state-sponsored and controlled opera houses (plural, *enti autonomi*).

ente morale   A nonprofit corporation.

favola pastorale   A 17th-century expression for a pastoral tale set to music or accompanied by incidental music.

ferragosto   The Feast of the Assumption (15 August), a day on which everything in Italy—restaurants and every imaginable sort of shop and store—closes.

fondale   The large drape or curtain on a stage that delineates the back of the stage area.

fossa orchestra   The orchestra pit, or (to use Wagner's expression) the "mystic gulf" (*golfo mistico*).

galleria   Literally a "gallery," refers to what is called a balcony in an American or English theater.

"Giovinezza"   The Fascist hymn.

golfo mistico   Wagner's expression ("mystic gulf"); refers to a sunken orchestra pit.

gradinata   Literally a "tier of seats," generally refers to the section of seats most remote from the main stage floor and the stage itself.

graticcia   The grid from which sets hang.

impresario   The independent person engaged to organize and manage the season for an opera house.

intermezzo   A short, light musical entertainment—with two characters (a soprano and a *basso buffo* plus two mimes)—interpolated between the acts of a serious opera (*opera seria*), an 18th-century custom (plural, *intermezzi*).

Liberty style (*stile Liberty*)   The Italian adaptation of the international turn-of-the-century art movement known as art nouveau; the Italian term is derived from the Liberty shop on the Strand, London, which specialized in oriental fabrics, a principal influence on the style.

libretto   Literally "little booklet"; the printed text of an opera.

lira   The Italian unit of currency, indicated either as *Lit.*, which stands for *lira italiana*, or by the same symbol the British use for pounds, £ (plural, lire).

loggione   A gallery or top balcony, usually with general as opposed to reserved seats.

maestro concertatore   A concertmaster.

maestro di cappella   The music director of a chapel, usually one belonging to a king, prince, bishop, doge, or nobleman.

Maggio Musicale Fiorentino   The Florence May Music Festival.

manifestazioni straordinarie   Literally "extraordinary shows."

mantovana   The velvet drape that stretches across the top of the proscenium opening; permanently anchored, it delineates the maximum height of the opening; known in American theater as the valance.

March on Rome   Historic event of 29 October 1922, when Mussolini and his Fascist cohorts marched on Rome, beginning Il Duce's (Mussolini's own term for his position) 21-year absolute dictatorship of Italy.

"**Marcia reale**"   Literally "Royal March," the Italian national anthem.

omaggio   An homage.

opera buffa   A comic opera of the 18th century with characters generally drawn from everyday life.

opera seria   A "serious" opera of the 17th and 18th centuries, frequently concerning mythological or heroic subjects and made up of conventional arias loosely connected by recitatives.

ordine   A row.

palco   A box.

palco centrale   A box in the center section.

palco laterale   A side box.

palcoscenico   The stage.

pallone   An extremely popular sport of the Marche region played with a round leather ball called a *sfero* (sphere).

panorama   On a stage, *panorama* refers to a cyclorama, a cloth curtain that completely encircles the back of the stage.

parti di sorbetto   An idiomatic expression meaning "time for the start of the show."

piano fisso di boccascena   The velvet drape that is permanently attached to the top of the proscenium arch and that delineates the maximum height of the proscenium opening; sometimes called a *mantovana*.

piccionaia   Literally a "pigeon loft," the slang expression in Italian for the *loggione* or gallery.

platea   The main floor of an opera house (parterre/stalls/orchestra).

podestà   Literally a "governor"; an expression used during the Fascist regime for the mayor (*sindaco*) of a city.

poltrona platea   A seat on the main floor.

premio   A prize.

prima   The first performance of a work.

prima assoluta   The "absolute" first performance, hence the world premiere of a work.

prima donna   Literally the "first lady" of an opera company; she is supported by a *seconda donna* and *terza donna*.

prima in italiana   The first performance of a work in Italy.

principale   An adjustable drape that controls the size of the proscenium opening with respect to height and width.

proscenico   The apron of the stage.

pubbliche relazioni   Public relations.

quinta   Commonly called a "leg" on the American stage; a drape (or flat) that delineates the left or right limits of the stage and masks the offstage area from the view of the audience.

recitativo   "Recitative" in English; a style of singing more closely related in rhythm to normal speech than song, though a melodic line can be discerned.

regista   A stage director; the masculine is *il regista*, the feminine, *la regista* (plural, *i registi*).

ridotto   The foyer of an opera house, frequently located on the first floor (the second floor in the American system of counting floors).

risorgimento   Literally a "revival"; commonly used to refer to the 19th-century movement for Italian unification that culminated in the establishment of the kingdom of Italy in 1861.

sala   Literally a "room," refers in an opera house to the main auditorium.

sartoria   A tailor shop.

seconda donna   Literally the "second lady," refers to a role or permanent position in an 18th-century company in which the singer is of secondary importance to the prima donna.

sipario   The house curtain.

sipario metallico   The fire curtain.

spettacolo   A spectacle; generally refers to any entertainment, show, or display, including opera.

soffito   The cloth border that delineates the height of the stage area.

sovrintendente   A general administrator.

stabile   "Established," as in an established (as opposed to a pick-up) orchestra.

stagione   Literally a "season," refers to the system under which an Italian house produces one opera at a time in multiple performances, which closes before another opera opens.

stile rappresentativo   The style of dramatic recitative practiced in the earliest operas, in which the rhythm was governed by the speech-pattern of the words.

teatrino   A small theater.

teatro   A theater.

teatro di tradizione   Literally a "traditional theater," but in contemporary Italian usage refers specifically to a group of 24 state-authorized and recognized regional opera companies, each self-governing but receiving a portion of its financial support from the state (plural, *teatri di tradizione*).

teatro stabile   An established theater.

telette   The velvet drapes (sometimes called *quinte mobili di boccascena*, and on the American stage, "legs") that hang immediately behind the proscenium arch and that determine the maximum width of the proscenium opening.

tempio della lirica   A "temple of opera," an opera house.

toise (French)   An ancient French unit of length roughly equivalent to 2 meters (6.5 feet).

trulli   The round, white-washed houses found in the Puglia region of Italy with 50-cm (18-inch) walls and ruddy or gray stone, cone-shaped roofs.

ufficio   An office.

ufficio stampa   A press office.

uscita di sicurezza   A fire or emergency exit.

vaglia postale   A postal money order.

INDEX

Numbers in italic refer to pages with black-and-white illustrations; numbers in bold refer to color plates.